International Law and Development in the Global South

Emeka Duruigbo · Remigius Chibueze ·
Sunday Gozie Ogbodo
Editors

International Law and Development in the Global South

Foreword by Chima Centus Nweze

palgrave
macmillan

Editors
Emeka Duruigbo
Rosenberg, TX, USA

Remigius Chibueze
San Francisco, CA, USA

Sunday Gozie Ogbodo
Enugu, Enugu State, Nigeria

ISBN 978-3-031-13740-2   ISBN 978-3-031-13741-9 (eBook)
https://doi.org/10.1007/978-3-031-13741-9

This Palgrave Macmillan imprint is published by the registered company Springer Nature Switzerland AG
The registered company address is: Gewerbestrasse 11, 6330 Cham, Switzerland

This book is dedicated to Professor Christian N. Okeke. The contributors of this work have been impacted in one way or the other by Prof. Okeke.

Foreword

Professor Dr. Christian Nwachukwu Okeke commenced his teaching career at the Faculty of Law, University of Nigeria, Enugu Campus. Subsequently, he became the pioneer Dean, Faculty of Law, Anambra State University of Science and Technology, Awka. He was, also, the pioneer Dean, Faculty of Law, Enugu State University of Science and Technology. He was, equally, the Deputy Vice Chancellor, Enugu State University of Science and Technology, Enugu.

In addition to the above first positions, he is the pioneer Pro-Chancellor and Chairman of The Governing Council, Godfrey Okoye University, Ugwuomu, Nike, Enugu. He is, currently, the Director of LL. M and SJD Programs and Director, Sompong Sucharitkul Center for Advanced International Legal Studies, Golden Gate University School of Law, San Francisco, California, United States of America.

A multi-juridical scholar, Prof. Christian Nwachukwu Okeke has taught International and Comparative Law in, almost, all the Continents of the world. He is an academic who is at home with the dynamics of Contemporary International and Comparative Law.

He is a polemicist and polyglot whose works on public international law; comparative law and international economic law are compulsory reading for undergraduate and graduate students across the globe. He has, as such, carved a niche for himself on that great pantheon where world-renown publicists and polemicists trade law.

Against the above background, this new book, a collection of essays titled *International Law and Development in the Global South* is a great tribute to Professor Christian Okeke's perseverance; versatility; diligence and nonpareil accomplishments in the academe. Edited by Professors Remigius Chibueze; Emeka Duruigbo and Gozie Ogbodo, the book boasts a vast collection of contributors on, almost, every conceivable aspect of International and Comparative Law.

This Book of Essays is, therefore, in honour of Professor Dr. Christian Nwachukwu Okeke as part of the celebration of his eightieth birthday and over five decades of teaching and legal scholarship works. The contributors to this book are friends and colleagues of Professor Okeke. Most of them are some of his former students, who are making their own marks in the judiciary, universities, legal practice, government institutions and other areas of the legal profession across the world.

The essays are as diverse as Professor Christian Nwachukwu Okeke's illustrious academic career. They provide the reader with informative and reasoned arguments on the topics covered. True, indeed, they are remarkable for their breadth; the lucidity of prose; the disarmingly felicitous style; their range and diversity. As a former student of Professor Okeke, I am delighted to have been invited to write this 'Foreword' for this book.

The honoree, Professor Okeke, is a tireless advocate of the teaching, promotion and application of law for the advancement of the society. He believes in the grooming of future leaders and educators of the law, which he considers a *sine qua non* for a better world. He is a champion of the teaching and promotion of international law generally, but specifically in Africa. He exemplifies the selfless and dedicated teacher who derives immense satisfaction from the success of his students and colleagues. He has maintained close relationship with his former students and colleagues, including myself. It is therefore not a surprise that they have deemed it worthy to commemorate his eightieth birthday with a work of scholarship, which is a staple of his distinguished career having authored numerous scholarly writings over the years.

For this same reason, in 2009, I pioneered a *Liber Amicorum* titled *Contemporary Issues on Public International and Comparative Law—Essays in Honour of Professor Dr. Christian Nwachukwu Okeke*. This new book is, therefore, a sequel to that initial work honouring this distinguished scholar. It attests to the earlier conviction that informed the first work that Professor Okeke is, exceptionally, unique. He, therefore, deserves this honour as his contributions to legal scholarship continue to grow in appreciation and circulation. He continues to exemplify his unique set of skills and humanity that led me to describe him as an intellectual troubadour.

Upon my intimate perusal of this breathtaking work, I, strongly and unreservedly, commend it to one and all—in particular, to all superior court Justices and Judges all over the world; Professors of Law; other law teachers and their students; Queen's Counsel and Learned Senior Advocates of Nigeria; Prosecutors; Law and Policy Makers and to anyone interested in International Law and Development in the global South.

Chima Centus Nweze, Ph.D.
Life Bencher; FCIArb, Justice
Nigeria Supreme Court
Abuja, Nigeria

Reflections

The Continuing Relevance and Importance of Pacta Sunt Servanda in Contemporary International Law: A Re-Appraisal

International law has expanded to cover new subjects[1] and new fields, such as the present dangerous global pandemic of the coronavirus that the world is experiencing. With a view to combating this pandemic and protecting the world's citizens, the World Health Organisation (WHO), the European Commission and France designed COVAX-19, bringing together governments, global health organisations, manufacturers, scientists, private sector, civil society and philanthropy, with the aim of providing innovative and equitable access to COVID-19 diagnostics, treatments and vaccines, particularly the latter. Furthermore, COVAX is aimed at ensuring that every state and people will get access to the COVID-19 vaccines, once they are available, regardless of their wealth. COVAX is coordinated by the (WHO), Gavi, the Vaccine Alliance, the Coalition for Epidemic Preparedness Innovations (CEPI), guaranteeing that every state secure doses of the vaccines. Higher-income countries could join as 'self-financing participants.' To do so, they could sign a standard legal agreement with Gavi, the legal administrator of COVAX

[1] C.N. Okeke, Controversial subjects of international law: An examination of new subjects of international law and their treaty-making capacity, 1974.

with the intention that, in the first phase of distribution, all countries participating in COVAX will receive doses for up to 20% of their population, with the option for self-financing parties to secure more afterwards. For lower-income funded nations, COVAX quite literally provides a lifeline and in some cases the only viable way in which their citizens will get access to COVID-19 vaccines to protect their citizens.

As Gavi signs only a single agreement with each pharmaceutical company, this would prevent states from outbidding each other to get better deals, guaranteeing a standard price for everyone as well as faster deliveries. Accordingly, COVAX is designed to serve the interest of both the high-income as well as lower-income funded nations. The role of international law can be seen in this global, multilateral approach in combating the pandemic.

International law has also extended its competence to include the important issue of climate change or global warming, which has been wreaking havoc in terms of natural disasters—floods, wildfires, etc. in the various regions of the globe—a type of climate pandemic.

This issue was negotiated and concluded within the United Nations Framework Convention on Climate Change (UNFCC), according to which the 197 Parties that adopted the Agreement and the 191 that have signed it and the 74 states and the European Union (as of 7 October 2016) that have ratified, accepted or undertook the obligation to mitigate climate change, and to limit the emission of greenhouse gas into the atmosphere.

As stated earlier, the rule of *pacta sunt servanda* is about the fulfilment of legal obligations by states: it is a fundamental, some would say, a foundational principle, of international law. Many of the principles of the Charter of the United Nations—the sovereign equality of states, the non-use of force by states in their international relations, the peaceful settlement of international disputes, are predicated on the principle, as indeed the Charter itself. The rule applies when these principles are embodied in an international treaty and the parties to such treaty are required to comply with or carry out their legal obligations in good faith.

The rule is recognised as part of customary international law. It is also present in the different legal systems of the world recognised as general principles of international law in terms of the Statute of the International Court of Justice. Articles 26 and 27 of the Vienna Convention on the Law of Treaties (VCLT) proceeded to codify it. According to Article 26: 'Every treaty in force is binding upon the parties to it and must be performed in good faith.' This is not to suggest that every provision in a treaty creates a legal obligation. Whether an obligation is legally binding depends on whether the parties intended it to be so, and according to the language in which the provision of the treaty is expressed. Where the verb 'shall' is used in a provision, it will be interpreted as creating a legal obligation; where 'should' or 'encourage' is used, the provision will be treated as a recommendation. The use of 'may,' may be considered a licence or permission and where 'should' is used as in 'support should be provided for developing countries,' it cannot be interpreted as creating a binding legal obligation, perhaps as a political commitment.

The conclusion to be drawn from the above is that *pacta sunt servanda* remains the rule. Legal obligations, compared to political or moral obligations, are legally binding on parties to the treaty and must be observed or implemented. This is irrespective of the character of the treaty whether bilateral or multilateral. The purpose of the rule is to guarantee the stability of the international legal order and to prevent behaviour not in conformity with the treaty obligations or with international law. This is important when it is realised that relations between states can only be conducted on the basis of good faith with the expectation that legal obligations undertaken will be fulfilled or observed.

In spite of the clarity of the rule, some states have occasionally rolled back from their legal obligations under a treaty, including the Charter of the United Nations. For example, the 2003 war in Iraq. Furthermore, and recently, a minister speaking on behalf of the British government in its effort to withdraw its membership from the European Union stated the United Kingdom was prepared to break its treaty obligations 'in a very specific and limited way.' Similar declarations or measures have been taken by other states, which are considered in breach of their legal obligations. Such declarations, actions or measures not only put into question the validity and effectiveness of the rule but undermines the stability of the international legal order and relations between states.

The intention of this contribution is not to censure but to underscore that to breach a legal obligation whether in a 'limited and specific way' cannot serve as a justification for a party not to carry out its legal commitments entered into in good faith and is a breach of international law. Questions regarding derogation, impossibility of performance, necessity, fundamental change of circumstance (*rebus sic stantibus*) or force majeure are to be considered in the context of the Vienna Convention on the Law of Treaties and in conformity with the treaty. In other words, *pacta sunt servanda* remains the rule as reflected in Articles 26 and 27 of the Law of Treaties. Article 27 stipulates that a party to a treaty is to ensure that its domestic obligations do not override its international legal obligations.

In the light of the foregoing, the following conclusions can be drawn: the principle of *pacta sunt servanda* remains a fundamental principle of international law today as in the past. It serves a useful purpose in establishing and regulating the legal relationship between states. It contributes immensely to the strengthening of the existing legal order, thereby precluding arbitrary behaviour in the international system. Finally, it must be noted that a breach of an international legal obligation constitutes a ground for invoking state responsibility.

No other individual epitomises the rule at a personal level than the scholar whose 80th birthday this *Liber Amicorum* is honouring.

The Hague, The Netherlands

A. G. Koroma
Former Judge, International
Court of Justice

Acknowledgements

The editors express their appreciation to Justice C.C. Nweze for accepting to write the foreword to this book and to Judge Koroma for his reflections on the continued relevance of the *pacta sunt servanda* principle. Additionally, the editors thank the contributors for taking time to respond to the invitation to contribute a chapter to this book. To the publishers, we thank you for your patience, understanding and cooperation throughout the process of working with us to make this a reality.

Contents

1 **Introduction** 1
Remigius Chibueze, Emeka Duruigbo, and Sunday Gozie Ogbodo

2 **The Case for Domestic Workers' Bill of Rights in Bangladesh: Preliminary Observations** 5
Zakia Afrin

3 **Causes and Implications of Worsening Insecurity in Nigeria: Developing a Cure Through the Law** 13
Nicholas O. Agbo

4 **Restorative Justice and Non-Custodial Measures as Panacea for Prison Decongestion in a Covid-19 Era: Nigeria in Perspective** 33
Chinyere Comfort Ani

5 **Principle of Responsibility to Protect: Implications for Sovereignty** 55
Eustace C. Azubuike

6 **International Law and Frozen Conflicts in Eastern Europe and the Caucasus** 79
Oleksandr Biryukov

7 **How U.S. Courts Handle GDPR in Discovery Process: An Examination of a U.S. Patent Infringement Case** 99
Azam Zare Chahoki

8 **International Criminal Jurisdiction of the African Court of Justice and Human and Peoples' Rights: Promoting or Obstructing Accountability?** 115
Remigius Chibueze

9 **The Supremacy of Might Over Right in the International Legal Order** 139
Larry O. C. Chukwu and Patience N. Tochukwu

10 **State Succession in International Law** 155
Andrew Conteh

11 **Local Regulation of Multinational Corporations** 177
Emeka Duruigbo

12 **Judicial Misconduct: Analyzing the Code of Conduct for Judicial Officers in Nigeria** 197
Ndubuisi J. Madubuike-Ekwe

13 **Development of International Commercial Arbitration in Virtual Reality During the COVID-19 Pandemic** 215
Aileen Huang

14 **Recovery from International Trade Crisis** 233
Ramesh Bikram Karky

15 **Surrogacy, Religious Culture, and the Imperatives of the Law: Any Caveats for Law Makers?** 251
Obiajulu Nnamuchi

16 **A Case for the Application of Strict Liability in Oil and Gas Pollution Cases in Nigeria** 273
Sunday Gozie Ogbodo and A. Chinwe Umadia

17 ***Nganjiwa V Federal Republic of Nigeria*—Judicial Contrivance of Immunity for Judges?** 301
Osita Nnamani Ogbu

18 A Critique of the Nigeria National Security Strategy 2019 321
M. Ozonnia Ojielo

19 The American Judiciary and Judicial Institutions on Trial 337
Ifeanyi Innocent Onwuazombe

20 The Unconformity of California's Gender Quota Law with the Contractual Theory of Corporate Law 355
Murat Can Pehlivanoğlu

21 The Role of the Judiciary in Development of an ISDS Mechanism in Vietnam 373
Chau Huy Quang

22 In-Country Processing as a Solution to the International Refugee Crisis: The Example of the CAM Program 393
Giulia Rettagliati

Index 409

Notes on Contributors

Afrin Zakia Golden Gate University School of Law, San Francisco, CA, USA

Agbo Nicholas O. Faculty of Law, University of Nigeria, Nsukka, Nigeria

Ani Chinyere Comfort Enugu State High Court, Enugu State Judiciary, Independence Layout, Nigeria

Azubuike Eustace C. Golden Gate University School of Law, San Francisco, CA, USA

Biryukov Oleksandr Institute of International Relations of Taras Shevchenko National University of Kyiv, Kyiv, Ukraine;
Fulbright Scholar, New York University School of Law, New York City, USA

Chahoki Azam Zare Golden Gate University School of Law, San Francisco, CA, USA

Chibueze Remigius Golden Gate University School of Law, San Francisco, CA, USA

Chukwu Larry O. C. Faculty of Law, University of Abuja, Abuja, Nigeria

Conteh Andrew California State University Stanislaus, Stanislaus, CA, USA

Duruigbo Emeka Thurgood Marshall School of Law, Texas Southern University, Houston, Rosenberg, TX, USA

Huang Aileen Golden Gate University School of Law, San Francisco, CA, USA

Gozie Ogbodo Sunday Enugu, Enugu State, Nigeria

Karky Ramesh Bikram School of Business, Conestoga College Institute of Technology and Advanced Learning, Kitchener, ON, Canada;
School of Accounting and Finance, Adjunct Faculty at the University of Waterloo, Waterloo, ON, Canada;
School of Law, Vrije Universiteit Brussel, Brussels, Belgium

Madubuike-Ekwe Ndubuisi J. Faculty of Law, Benson Idahosa University, Benin-City, Nigeria

Nnamuchi Obiajulu Faculty of Law, University of Nigeria, Enugu Campus, Enugu, Nigeria

Ogbu Osita Nnamani Faculty of Law, Enugu State University of Science and Technology (EUST), Agbani, Enugu State, Nigeria

Ojielo M. Ozonnia United Nations System, Bishkek, Kyrgyz Republic

Onwuazombe Ifeanyi Innocent Golden Gate University School of Law, San Francisco, CA, USA

Pehlivanoğlu Murat Can İstanbul Kent University, Istanbul, Turkey

Quang Chau Huy Saigon Centre, Ho Chi Minh City, Vietnam

Rettagliati Giulia Law Offices of Marco Ambron, San Francisco, CA, USA

Tochukwu Patience N. Faculty of Law, University of Abuja, Abuja, Nigeria

Umadia A. Chinwe Faculty of Law, Godfrey Okoye University, Enugu, Nigeria

Abbreviations

AAA-ICDR	American Arbitration Association-International Centre for Dispute Resolution
ACHPR	African Court on Human and Peoples' Rights
ACICA	Australian Center for International Commercial Arbitration
ACJ	Court of Justice of the African Union
ACJA	Administration of Criminal Justice Act
ACJHR	African Court of Justice and Human and Peoples' Rights
ACJL	Administration of Criminal Justice Law
ADR	Alternative Disputes Resolution
AI	Artificial Insemination
APC	All Progressives Congress
ART	Artificial Reproductive Technology
AU	African Union
BNWLA	Bangladesh National Women Lawyers' Association
CAM	Central American Minors
CAP	Corporate Accountability Project
CBRNE	Chemical, Biological, Radiological, Nuclear and Explosive
CIETAC	China International Economic and Trade Arbitration Commission
CIS	Commonwealth of Independent States
CJN	Chief Justice of Nigeria
CNN	Cable News Network
CPC	Civil Procedure Code
CPV	Communist Party of Vietnam
CSFR	Czech and Slovak Federative Republic
DHS	Department of Homeland Security

DOJ	Department of Justice
DPR	Department of Petroleum Resources
ECOWAS	Economic Community of West African States
EFCC	Economic and Financial Crimes Commission
EU	European Union
FDI	Foreign Direct Investment
FRY	Federal Republic of Yugoslavia
GATS	General Agreement on Trade in Services
GATT	General Agreement on Tariffs and Trade
GCL	General Corporation Law
GDPR	General Data Protection Regulation
GDR	German Democratic Republic
GPI	Global Peace Index
HCDT	Host Community Development Trust
HKIAC	Hong Kong International Arbitration Centre
ICA	India Council of Arbitration
ICC	International Chamber of Commerce
ICC	International Criminal Court
ICISS	International Commission on Intervention and State Sovereignty
ICPC	Independent Corrupt Practices & Other Related Offences Commission
ICSID	International Centre for Settlement of Investment Disputes
ICTR	International Criminal Tribunal for Rwanda
ICTY	International Criminal Tribunal for Yugoslavia
ILO	International Labour Organization
IMT	International Military Tribunal
IPOB	Indigenous People of Biafra
ISDS	Investor-State Dispute Settlement
ISTAC	Istanbul Arbitration Centre
IUI	Intrauterine Insemination
IVF	In Vitro Fertilization
JCA	Judge of the Court of Appeal
JSC	Justice of the Supreme Court
LCIA	London Court of International Arbitration
LNG	Liquefied Natural Gas
MACBAN	Miyetti Allah Cattle Breeders Association of Nigeria
MASSOB	Movement for the Actualization of the Sovereign State of Biafra
MDG	Millennium Development Goals
MFN	Most-Favored-Nation Treatment
MNC	Multinational Corporation
MOSOP	Movement for the Survival of Ogoni People
NAF	Nigerian Air force
NCSA	Nigerian Correctional Services Act

NDPVF	Niger Delta People's Volunteer Force
NDV	Niger Delta Vigilante
NESREA	National Environmental Standards and Regulations Enforcement Agency Act
NGO	Non-Governmental Organization
NJC	National Judicial Council
NNPC	Nigerian National Petroleum Company
NOSDRA	National Oil Spill Detection and Response Agency
NT	National Treatment
OECD	Organization for Economic Cooperation and Development
OSCE	Organization for Security and Cooperation in Europe
PIA	Petroleum Industry Act
SB	Senate Bill
SCC	Stockholm Chamber of Commerce
SDG	Sustainable Development Goal
SFRY	Socialist Federal Republic of Yugoslavia
SIAC	Singapore International Arbitration Centre
SPC	Supreme People's Court
SRSG	Special Representative of the Secretary General
SWG	Secure Web Gateway
UGM	Unknown Gun Men
UNCITRAL	United Nations Commission on International Trade Law
UNCRC	United Nations Convention on the Rights of the Child
UNDP	United Nations Development Programme
UNFCC	United Nations Framework Convention on Climate Change
UNHCR	United Nations Refugee Agency
UNSC	United Nations Security Council
USCIS	United States Citizenship and Immigration Services
USSR	Union of Soviet Socialist Republics
UWO	Unexplained Wealth Order
VCLT	Vienna Convention on the Law of Treaties
WHO	World Health Organization
WTO	World Trade Organization

CHAPTER 1

Introduction

Remigius Chibueze, Emeka Duruigbo,
and Sunday Gozie Ogbodo

This book deals with real problems that our world faces today. Some of these problems may be peculiar to the Global South or assume a different dimension in the area. Yet, some of the issues cut across geographical and ideological boundaries. In all these cases, this work presents a refreshing platform for tough conversations from the unique perspectives of voices from the Global South.

As our manuscript was being edited, the conflict between Russia and Ukraine entered into a more dangerous phase. Russia announced its

R. Chibueze
San Francisco, CA, USA
e-mail: rchibueze@ggu.edu

E. Duruigbo (✉)
Rosenberg, TX, USA
e-mail: emeka.duruigbo@tmslaw.tsu.edu

S. Gozie Ogbodo
Enugu, Enugu State, Nigeria
e-mail: gozieogbodo@yahoo.com

E. Duruigbo et al. (eds.), *International Law and Development in the Global South*, https://doi.org/10.1007/978-3-031-13741-9_1

recognition of some separatist provinces in Ukraine and followed it with the physical entry of Russian soldiers into Ukrainian territory. Two chapters in the book dealing with state succession and frozen conflicts had anticipated these developments and offered a resolution of the problems through the intervention and application of the principles of international law.

Various chapters involve incisive analysis that yields solutions or offers pathways to resolution of intractable issues that demand answers if the more peaceful and prosperous world of our dreams is to become a reality. Contributors have engaged in the painstaking task of bringing to the forefront past and recurring challenges and desirable changes for the future. Whether we are looking at prosecution of international crimes, management of natural resources, prosecution of environmental pollution in the oil and gas industry or protection of intellectual property, there is an abundant display of penetrating insights and practical pointers for greater societal benefit.

Contributors have not shied away from numerous other topics that careful observers of global affairs expect to be handled in a book that showcases viewpoints from the Global South. There are chapters on the effect of the COVID-19 pandemic on global trade and international commercial arbitration. The pandemic, undoubtedly, has reshaped trade, investment, and dispute resolution in ways that may outlive the presence of the disease and its health impact. Systems of administration, judicial ethics, and disciplinary control over erring judicial officers receive attention. A strong case is made that non-custodial sentencing options that have become the staple of penal systems outside Africa need to become more familiar in jurisdictions within Africa.

Questions continue to arise as to the relationship between power and law in international relations. More powerful nations tend to resort to might when it is expedient, to the detriment of established rights and legal obligations and moral principles of right and wrong. Some contributors tackle these knotty issues in light of recent events in the Middle East and elsewhere. A related issue is the inability or unwillingness of some states to protect their citizens that gave birth to the concept of The Responsibility to Protect, as closely discussed in the book.

Surrogacy is thoroughly examined within the contexts of law, ethics, and religion, among others. The position of major religions, including Christianity, Judaism, Islam, Hinduism, and Buddhism are discussed, taking note of the fact effective regulatory action in this area will not materialize if it ignores the role that religion plays in shaping the beliefs and behavior of people toward a particular practice.

There are chapters devoted to an examination of the security challenges bedeviling various parts of Nigeria and posing serious risk to overall peace and development of the country. Forging a realistic path forward requires dedicated efforts from the government and the governed. Ultimately, it will be in the greater national interest to anchor a national security strategy on a framework of human security.

Recent developments in American democracy and jurisprudence are sharply contrasted in one chapter with the acclaimed history and reputation of the United States as a champion and promoter of democracy, rule of law, good governance, human rights, and judicial independence across the globe. Deftly managing the current crisis in public affairs is essential to maintaining the image of the United States in these areas and restoring the hopes of people in other countries that have been shaken as they observed these attacks on venerable institutions and principles that have stood the test of time.

Corporate governance is also incorporated in the exchange of ideas through an x-ray and critical examination of California's mandatory gender quota statute. The role of the judiciary in developing mechanisms for resolution of investor-state disputes in Vietnam is examined. The idea is that the maintenance of a viable legal order is critical to attracting and retaining foreign direct investment for greater economic development.

The limits of current refugee policy have not gone without notice, prompting a proposal for a global solution to an international refugee problem that will cater to the needs of vulnerable individuals who are in life-threatening situations of immediate danger but are not able to leave their countries due to such constraining factors as age or disability. Modeled after the Central American Minors Program ("CAM") of the United States government for in-country refugees processing of minors in Honduras, El Salvador, and Guatemala, this proposal will close a gap in international refugee law that requires refugees to leave their countries in order to be considered for immigration into a new country.

In the end, this book presents a rich compilation that assures of a great intellectual feast to the reader. This is a deliberate effort for a project that was inspired by a desire to honor a deserving international legal scholar of great repute, Professor Christian Nwachukwu Okeke on the celebration of his 80th birthday. A small sample of proteges, mentees, former students, friends, and colleagues of this giant of international law, who have drawn inspiration or otherwise benefited over the years from his remarkable intellect, boundless energy, and generous spirit have gathered here to commemorate his life and achievements in the field he loves dearly.

It is our expectation that this collection of essays will meet present needs in international law while promoting avenues for future intellectual engagement by scholars, advocates, practitioners, policy makers, and students on these burning issues.

CHAPTER 2

The Case for Domestic Workers' Bill of Rights in Bangladesh: Preliminary Observations

Zakia Afrin

Happy was found with bruises all over her body crying inconsolably roaming the streets of Dhaka after fleeing her abusive employers. Discussing her ordeal, Salma Ali, a lawyer and president of the Bangladesh National Women Lawyers' Association (BNWLA), brought in comparisons with slavery, bonded labor and forced labor. In addition to merciless beatings, Happy was locked inside the house at all times, forced to sleep in the bathroom and was offered little leftovers from everyday meals. The reason her case reached international news was the high profile of her abusers. A rising cricket star and his wife was arrested in the following days.[1] While Happy's incident is one of the most severe ones, lack of legal and social frameworks to regulate informal labor in Bangladesh has

[1] https://www.cnn.com/2015/12/10/asia/bangladesh-maid-abuse-child-labor.

Z. Afrin (✉)
Golden Gate University School of Law, San Francisco, CA, USA
e-mail: zafrin@ggu.edu

E. Duruigbo et al. (eds.), *International Law and Development in the Global South*, https://doi.org/10.1007/978-3-031-13741-9_2

created loopholes that perpetuate domestic workers living undignified and abuse-ridden lives.

In Bangladesh there are estimated 10.5 million domestic workers, out of them 420,000 are children and 90% of all are females.[2] They are the most marginalized segment of society many ousted from homes by climate change, economic hardship and travel to urban areas from rural environment. During the COVID-19 pandemic, many of them have lost jobs, have returned home only to fall victims to poverty and familial violence. A study based on surveys from 500 domestic workers found 97% of both live in and live out workers to be women, one-fourth children and one-tenth reporting kin relationship with employers.[3] The survey reveals alarming trend in relation to the components of decent work, overwhelmingly workers reported underpay, overwork without pay, lack of rest and privacy at work.[4]

It is high time to legislate and execute a "Domestic Workers' Bill of Rights in Bangladesh"; a legislation that would offer prevention of exploitation, protection of workers' rights and prosecution for wrongdoings. The Bangladeshi migrants traveling to other parts of the world for domestic work share the grim reality as at home. That is another mammoth area of legal study. For the purposes of this writing, I will restrict my commentary to domestic workers serving within Bangladesh.

I will glance at existing framework supporting a comprehensive rights regime for the largely marginalized informal workforce and put forth humble recommendations to move toward steps to solving this.

Constitutional guarantees: The Constitution of Bangladesh came into force on November 4, 1972, little less than a year of the country's independence. It had been a thematic departure from the Constitution of the Islamic Republic of Pakistan from which Bangladesh earned her independence.[5] The newly liberated Constitution instilled ideological frameworks as preambles that fueled the demands for an independent

[2] https://www.ilo.org/wcmsp5/groups/public/---asia/---ro-bangkok/---ilo-jakarta/documents/presentation/wcms_617648.pdf.

[3] Report by RMMRU submitted to ILO Bangladesh Country Office, February 2019 Accessed Online at https://www.ilo.org/wcmsp5/groups/public/---asia/---ro-bangkok/---ilo-dhaka/documents/publication/wcms_674540.pdf.

[4] Id.

[5] https://www.liberationwarmuseumbd.org/

state.[6] Socialism, one of the fundamental principles of the Constitution interpreted as social justice for the disadvantaged is exactly what the domestic workers' rights would fulfil if and when it comes to fruition. It lays down the expectations in no uncertain terms, "it shall be a fundamental aim of the State to realize through the democratic process a socialist society, free from exploitation a society in which the rule of law, fundamental human rights and freedom, equality and justice, political, economic and social, will be secured for all citizens[7]". The present Constitution has been amended 15 times by democratic governments.

Moving on from the fundamental principles, support for domestic workers' rights can be found within fundamental policies of the government and specific rights guaranteed for all citizens in Bangladesh.

Right to choose employment,[8] equality before law[9] and equal protection before law and prohibition on forced labor[10] are the most relevant ones worth mentioning in this relation.

International obligations: "Respect for international law and principles enunciated in the United Nations Charter"[11] finds its place in the constitutions. Bangladesh is a signatory of the Universal Declaration of Human Rights[12] and many of this persuasive document's provisions support comprehensive rights for domestic workers. "All human beings are born free and equal in dignity in rights",[13] "Right to protection against interference with privacy, family, home, correspondence, or attack

[6] https://www.liberationwarmuseumbd.org/evolution-of-fundamental-principles-of-1972/

[7] The Constitution of Bangladesh, available at http://bdlaws.minlaw.gov.bd/act-367.html.

[8] Article 20 of the constitution of Bangladesh, accessed at http://bdlaws.minlaw.gov.bd/act-367/section-24568.html.

[9] Article 27 of the constitution of Bangladesh, accessed at http://bdlaws.minlaw.gov.bd/act-367/section-24575.html.

[10] Article 34 of the constitution of Bangladesh, accessed at http://bdlaws.minlaw.gov.bd/act-367/section-24582.html.

[11] Preamble of the Constitution of Bangladesh, id at 7.

[12] The Universal Declaration of Human Rights was proclaimed by the UN General Assembly on December 10, 1948 and seen as the most persuasive international statement in advocating for human rights around the world. Bangladesh.

[13] Article 1 of UDHR, accessed at https://www.un.org/en/about-us/universal-declaration-of-human-rights.

against honor and reputation",[14] "right to work, free choice of employment, just and favorable conditions of work, right to just and favorable remuneration to ensure dignified livelihood, right to join trade unions",[15] "right to rest and leisure including reasonable limitation of working hours and holidays with pay",[16] right to a standard of living adequate for the health and wellbeing of himself and of his family, special rights related to motherhood[17] and right to a social and international order conducive to full realization of the rights become possible[18]—these rights themselves can offer a comprehensive framework to support a legislation offering opportunities for domestic workers.

The international labor law has taken the most important step toward securing domestic workers' rights. The ILO Convention 189[19] could ease the Govt efforts in reinventing the wheel. Signing the Convention has led to significant improvement for many of the 32 countries; one such example is Argentine, where domestic workers are entitled to the same rights as all other employees including paid vacation days, sick leave and maternity protections, etc.[20]

The Convention addresses the urgent issues mentioned in the 2015 national policy; definition of domestic work and worker, age of workers, working hours, decent work conditioning and leave policy. The point of departure is clear as well. Contrary to the national policy, the Convention mandates a minimum age of workers or minimum wage that can be offered to workers. It also requires signatories to work with organizations representing workers in implementing the provisions and create framework for monitoring of compliance with the rights, complaint procedures and respect privacy of employers in situations of conflict.[21] The government perhaps realized the shortcomings of the current legal structure

[14] Article 12 of UDHR, id at 13.

[15] Article 23 of UDHR, Id at 13.

[16] Article 24 of UDHR, id at 13.

[17] Article 25 of UDHR, id at 13.

[18] Article 28 of UDHR, id at 13.

[19] https://www.ilo.org/dyn/normlex/en/f?p=NORMLEXPUB:12100:0::NO::P12100_ILO_CODE:C189.

[20] https://www.hrw.org/news/2021/06/16/celebrating-10-years-global-domestic-workers-rights#.

[21] Id at 18.

to allow such definitive measures to protect rights of domestic workers. The national policy has mentioned step toward supporting ILO 189 regarding domestic work.[22] Bangladesh must ratify this Convention and move forward with the promise.

National Law: The Labor Code of 2006 (amended in 2013) consolidates definitions, rights, duties, accountabilities and social security among other things in relation to the workforce in Bangladesh.[23] Unfortunately, informal sector workers including domestic workers are not within the purview of this legislation other than the age requirements.

The national effort to legislate is no small success. In 2015, Govt promulgated the Domestic Workers' Protection and Welfare Policy that offers answers to certain structural concerns around this informal workforce.[24]

Acknowledging that the child laboreres travel from distant villages to the cities to provide for the need of housework help for the city dwellers, it claims that numbers have gone down due to free education and available scholarship for girls without any references. Women travel from poverty pockets for financial gains. The policy tries to find justification on Preference given to women and girls for this type of employment without getting into the socio-economic reasons, it lists expectation of obedience toward the head of household and other members as primary motivators and ignores the exploitation cycle of cheap and free labor that women provide.

Few salient points mentioned in the policy are below[25]:

Domestic work is defined broadly and includes cooking, cleaning, taking care of the household, shopping, caring for children, elderly and others and prohibits business-related tasks.

Domestic worker is defined as person who is employed verbally or by written arrangement within a household, Mess, dormitory, etc. to

22 https://www.ilo.org/wcmsp5/groups/public/---ed_protect/---protrav/---travail/documents/publication/wcms_161104.pdf.

23 Bangladesh Labor Code 2006, accessed at https://www.dpp.gov.bd/upload_file/gazettes/14212_75510.pdf.

24 The policy is only available is Bangla, the national language of Bangladesh and translated unofficially by the author. Policy accessed at: https://idwfed.org/en/updates/bangladesh-cabinet-clears-draft-policy-to-protect-domestic-workers-rights/bangladesh_dw_policy2015_adopteddoc.pdf.

25 Id.

perform housework, full-time or part-time. Allowing for a verbal agreement, the arrangement could be difficult to enforce in case of any dispute. The minimum age of a worker is set at 14 and light work is allowed for 12 yrs and above consistent with the Labor Code, 2006.

Bangladesh is a participant in ILO's Decent Work initiative and thus adheres to the definition prescribed by ILO, namely employment opportunity, rights at work, living wage that fosters wellbeing and social protection.

The Policy promises decent workplace and honorable wages to live comfortably with family, overall welfare, decent relationship between employer and employee and also prescribes mechanism to resolve conflict.

The policy deals with fixing wages for labor provided in consultation with both parties. Wages must be consistent with the living standard and social status of the worker with his/her family. Food, lodging, clothing, etc. will be regarded as extra wage.

For workers between the ages of 14 and 18 in heavy work and 12 yrs old for light work must be done with consultation with guardians. Contracts can be oral if both parties agree to it in the presence of a mutually agreed upon third party.

The contract will include: Type of appointment/Date of appointment/wages/time for breaks and vacation; Type of work/living arrangement of the worker/grooming of worker and obedience of the worker. Both parties must adhere to the contract if they do not violate existing laws and policies of the country. To employ a worker who is 12, consideration must be provided to the facts of his physical wellbeing and barriers to education.

Domestic workers' work schedule will be distributed as such to allow adequate sleep, rest, entertainment and necessary time off. Safe and healthy space must be provided for domestic workers' rest and sleep. With permission of employer, the domestic worker will be eligible to take paid vacation.

Pregnant workers must be provided with 16 weeks of paid maternity leave (4 weeks prior giving birth and 12 weeks after the childbirth or as needed by the worker). The employer must ensure break from heavy work and medical consultation with Govt hospital during the pregnancy. Sick workers must be taken off work and the employer will bear the cost of medical expenses. Workers must be provided the opportunity to practice his or her religion. And if a worker gets injured, the employer needs to bear all expenses related to medical treatment, accident and other damages resulting from the event.

The policy expressly prohibits verbal, mental and physical abuse of any domestic worker by the employee. It provides for the remedy within existing legal framework. Similar rights are provided to the employer and family.

The domestic worker is under obligation to not abuse any household members and adhere to requirements to provide notice before leaving jobs.

This policy puts the Ministry of Labor and welfare in the driving seat to implement this policy together with Ministry of Home Affairs, Ministry of Women and Children, Ministry of Social Welfare and many layers of local government bodies throughout districts, upazillas and cities. The implementation strategy is meant to include monitoring cell as well as outreach through media outlets, in-person convenings, etc. for creating awareness among the public and to facilitate helpline number for complaints. Unfortunately, as of March 2021, there has been no movement in the direction of time-bound implementation.

Together with full implementation of the policy, introducing legislation defining domestic work in the broadest of terms, mandating minimum wage and leave policy in no uncertain terms and requiring yearly review of contractual obligations will go a long way. The task seems difficult yet possible, and it may not solve all the problems but project a step towards the right direction.

Will a comprehensive legislation prevent a child worker's trauma like Happy, the 11-year-old domestic worker suffered[26]? With implementation of all the promises, yes. The existing resources are not negligible, and it would only take political will to make the Bill of Rights for Domestic Workers a reality. Together with legislation massive effort in educating both the workers and the employers as well as public is a must. Bangladesh has created an enviable economy almost from scratch and made strides in women's rights in general. A domestic workers' bill of rights seems to be an extension to that journey. I would argue that realizing the dream of an ideologically unparallel socialist society manifested by such legislation, free from exploitation is the worthy commemoration of the 50th anniversary of Bangladeshi Independence.

[26] *Id.*, 1.

CHAPTER 3

Causes and Implications of Worsening Insecurity in Nigeria: Developing a Cure Through the Law

Nicholas O. Agbo

1 Introduction

The primary purpose of government is to ensure the security and welfare of the governed. The Nigerian 1999 Constitution expressly stated in Section 14(2)(b) thus: "the security and welfare of the people shall be the primary purpose of government..."[1] In the wake of various incidences of insecurity across the nation, ranging from kidnapping of hundreds of school children, kidnapping and killing of the kidnapped, even after the ransom has been paid, in some case, to the recent killing of two soldiers and abduction of one soldier from the safety of their barracks portends an ominous sign that the state has failed in the discharge of its primary duty. Events of recent years have shown that insecurity is a regional item in the

[1] CFR1999, Section 14(2)(b).

N. O. Agbo (✉)
Faculty of Law, University of Nigeria, Nsukka, Nigeria
e-mail: nicholas.agbo@unn.edu.ng

E. Duruigbo et al. (eds.), *International Law and Development in the Global South*, https://doi.org/10.1007/978-3-031-13741-9_3

menus of Nigerian national life. There is the Niger Delta crisis that began in the 1990s reaching its crescendo with the extrajudicial killing of the founder and leader of the Movement for the Survival of Ogoni People (MOSOP) in the South-South geopolitical zone of Nigeria. In the North East, North West and North Central geopolitical zones of the nation the Boko Haram, Armed Bandits and Fulani Herdsmen are unleashing havoc on the local populace, kidnapping, maiming and killing innocent citizens. In the South East you have the Kidnappers and Unknown Gun Men (UGM), while in the South West activities of the Bandits and Fulani Herdsmen are very noticeable. The insecurity situation in the nation is taking a bizarre status with an Islamic Scholar Ahmad Gummi maintaining that Bandits should be allowed to carry AK47 and should not be declared a terrorist organization. He gave as his reason the following:

> NE is already and is still devastated by this madness for over 12 years. If we allow, terror, to set in into these raw naïve unexposed bandits, NW will be in ruins sooner than later. Already IPOB are destroying SE, and Igboho has set the ball of confusion rolling in SW. For those who want to destroy the NW, it's a good recipe. Turn bandits into religious zealots. Tell me, what then remains of Nigeria?"[2]

The Global terror index 2020 ranked Nigeria 3 out of the top 10 Terrorist nations citing Boko Haram as the terrorist organization responsible for most of deaths.[3]

The 2021 Global Peace Index (GPI) has ranked Nigeria 146 among 163 independent nations and territories, according to its level of peacefulness. Nigeria moved one step from 147 in 2020, though it still ranked eighth among the least peaceful countries in Africa after South Sudan, Somalia, the Democratic Republic of the Congo, Libya, Central African Republic, Sudan and Mali.[4] On several occasion Nigerians living abroad

[2] Mohamed Babangida, 'Gumi Warns Buhari against declaring Bandits Terrorist' Premium Time: https://www.premiumtimesng.com/news/headlines/491666-gumi-warns-buhari-against-declaring-bandits-as-terrorists.html. Accessed November 6, 2021.

[3] Top Ten Terrorist Countries, Terrorism index 2020 https://www.visionofhumanity.org/global-terrorism-index-2020-the-ten-countries-most-impacted-by-terrorism/. Accessed November 5, 2021.

[4] Tope Templer Olaiya, Nigeria ranks 146th on Global Peace Index, 8th least peaceful in Africa. https://guardian.ng/news/nigeria/nigeria-ranks-146th-on-global-peace-index-8th-least-peaceful-in-africa/.

have been kidnapped, raped and sometime killed to the extent that some of them have sworn never to return back to Nigeria, choosing even to be buried in their respective countries of domicile, all to the nation's shame.

The implication of these classifications is that Nigeria, being an unsafe place, has the natural consequences that both nationals and foreigners will be scared to invest in the economy of the nation. Corollary to the foregoing is that Nigerian living in Diaspora who account for $34 billion[5] remitted into the country annually, may lose faith in the future of the nation and as a result decide to keep their money in the country of their domiciles with its very negative effect on an already crumbling economy.

With the inflow of such a huge sum stopped, some unemployed youth, restrained by the inflow from joining the deviant groups, may be pushed into criminal activities, including violent crimes to make a living and to take out their anger on a passive society, giving credence to the statement of Onyegbula that "the standard of living and the deteriorating social infrastructure like roads, refineries, hospitals and educational system have all contributed to a nation of desperate people."[6]

Every facet of Nigerian life has been adversely affected by the rising insecurity in the nation, educationally, socially, politically and economically. Businessmen and women, both citizens and residents, are moving their businesses out of Nigeria to a clime with better enabling environment for investment of selling military equipment to the insurgents who destabilize the country. The goal of this paper is to examine the causes and implications of rising insecurity of Nigeria, which reared its head in the 90s but appears to be worsening in a frightening proportion, and to critically look at how a solution could be achieved either through a law in existence or through new legislations.

[5] Kunle Aderinokun, 'Diaspora Remittances Hit $34bn as Nigerian Migrant Workers Top List'.
https://www.thisdaylive.com/index.php/2021/08/29/diaspora-remittances-hit-34bn-as-nigerian-migrant-workers-top-list/. Accessed November 6, 2021.

[6] Onyebgula, S. Democracy in Nigeria: A critical overview of the Journey sofa. CDD News Quarterly Journal of the Center for Democracy and Development.

2 Conceptual Analysis

A true definition of insecurity must be preceded by the knowledge of what is security. Security is the state of being free from danger or threat. Conversely insecurity is a state of being beset by danger and threat. Insecurity can be defined as a state of being insecure where insecure is defined as: "not safe, liable to collapse, give way."[7]

In the Nigerian context, the definitions offered by William appear very apt as will be seen in the discussion of implications of rising insecurity in the country. According to him, security is widely associated with mitigating the threat to cherished values which, particularly if left unchecked in the near future, threatens the existence of a specific referent object.

Security of life and property is the essence of government as undergirded by the social contract theory where the people to whom sovereignty belong surrender some of their rights to the government in exchange for protection as espoused by various theorist, especially Hobbes, Locke and Montesquieu[8].

Several scholars have described insecurity in one way or the other but Achumba, Ighomereho & Akpor-Robaro define insecurity in a way that captures the reality of the current situation of Nigeria. According to them, insecurity is a state of not knowing, a lack of control, and the inability to take defensive action against forces that portend harm or danger to an individual or group, or that make them vulnerable.

Insecurity has also been defined as "a state of fear, anxiety, restlessness, uncertainty."[9] In order words a person will be in a state of insecurity when he or she is in a "state of fear or anxiety stemming from a concrete or alleged lack of protection."[10] Insecurity is lack of safety or existence of

[7] New Webster's Dictionary and Thesaurus of the English Language, lexicon publications Inc., Revised and updated 1992. Danbury, Ct.

[8] Muyiwa, F. et al., 'Social Contract Theories And Governance In Contemporary Nigeria' (2016). https://www.researchgate.net/publication/308477261_SOCIAL_CONTRACT_THEORIES_AND_GOVERNANCE_IN_CONTEMPORARY_N.

[9] Ndubuisi-Okolo P, 'Insecurity in Nigeria: the implication for industrialization and Sustainable Development' (2019)5(6)7.

[10] Beland, D. (2005). The Political Construction of Collective Insecurity: From Moral Panic to Blame Avoidance and Organized Irresponsibility. Center for European Studies Working Paper Series 126.

danger; hazard; uncertainty; lack of trust; doubtful; inadequately guarded or protected; lack of stability; disturbed; lack of protection and unsafe.[11]

3 Causes of Insecurity in Nigeria

Insecurity in Nigeria is a result of years of systemic failure in Nigeria driven by distended corruption. Contributing factors to the insecurity challenges in Nigeria include but are not limited to failed government, corruption, Kleptocracy, absence of state police, un-remedied wrongs and porous borders.

a. Failed Government:

The central responsibility of every government is the protection of the governed. The Nigerian 1999 constitution, as amended, recognized this prime duty and codified it in Section 14(b)[12] but the trend of events shows, very "point blankly" that the nation have failed in the delivery of this responsibility which is the essence of government in the first place. Right on the heels of the failure of government to protect the governed is the fact that the nation is fast sliding into the status of a failed state. The Governor of Benue State Mr. Samuel Orton lamented that the nation is fast becoming a failed state.[13] In the same vein, the Governor of Taraba State, Mr. Darius Ishaku stated that even a blind man can see that the nation is sliding into anarchy and state failure while recounting the killings and reprisal killings between Tivs and Fulanis and calling for immediate amendment of the 1999 constitution to provide for state police as the federal police cannot be everywhere at all time to offer the much needed security.[14]

[11] I.C. Achumba et al., 'Security challenges in Nigeria and the implications for Business Activities and Sustainable Development', Journal of Economics and Sustainable Development, Vo. 4. No. 2.

[12] CFRN 1999 Section 14(b).

[13] Peter Duru, 'Nigerian is fast becoming a failed state' Vanguard News: https://www.vanguardngr.com/2021/07/nigeria-fast-becoming-a-failed-state-under-apc-ortom/. Accessed November 6, 2021.

[14] Sylvanus Viashima, 'Nigeria is fast becoming a failed state'Sun Newspapers: https://www.sunnewsonline.com/nigeria-fast-becoming-a-failed-state-governor-ishaku/. Accessed November 6, 2021.

It is becoming very obvious that the poorly trained ill-equipped security officers are often overwhelmed by the superior firepower of Bandits, Herdsmen, unknown Gunmen kidnappers, etc. Not too long ago, on April 26, 2021, to be precise, more than 30 Nigerian soldiers were killed in militant attack in Sokoto state.[15] As if this was not shameful enough, on July 18, 2021, bandits shot down a Nigerian Air Force (NAF) fighter Jet in northern Nigeria on the border between Zamfara and Katsina states confirming the superior firepower of the bandits over that of the state defense unit.[16]

b. Corruption:

Corruption can be defined as dishonest or fraudulent conduct by those in power, typically involving bribery. Transparency International defines corruption simply as abuse of entrusted power for private gain[17] but continues to state as follows: "Corruption erodes trust, weakens democracy, hampers economic development and further exacerbates inequality, poverty, social division and the environmental crisis."[18] Flowing naturally from the above is the fact that diversion of public funds for private interests, recruitment on mediocrity instead of excellence, manipulation of the electoral system to elect people against the will of the electorates are all products of corruption. As rightly stated by Onifade Comfort et al.,

> A peek into the spectrum of national life reveals the incidence of distended corruption and avarice as expressed by Nigerians in high and low places, conflict and confusion in various communities and region, selfishness and pervasive lawlessness in the conduct of daily life as the guiding principles of human social interaction.[19]

[15] More than 30 Nigerian Soldiers Killed in Militant Attack: https://www.voanews.com/a/africa_sources-more-30-nigerian-soldiers-killed-militant-attack/6205065.html. Accessed November 7, 2021.

[16] Chris Ewokor, 'Nigerian military jet shot down by Bandits-Military' (2021) BBC News https://www.bbc.com/news/world-africa-57893662. Accessed November 7, 2021.

[17] Transparency International, 'What is Corruption? https://www.transparency.org/en/what-is-corruption#.

[18] Ibid.

[19] Confort O. et al., 'Addressing the Insecurity Challenge in Nigeria: The imperative of Moral Values and Virtue Ethics'(2013) 2(13) Global Journal of Human Social Science

It is not uncommon to see a person who has never held any job who has no means of livelihood but few months after being elected or appointed into office he becomes a multimillionaire owning properties worth hundreds of millions all over the state and the nations in general. The fact that such overnight wealth is never questioned shows how distended and reeking the corruption in Nigeria is, so much that aberration has now been elevated to the norm. This is as further corroborated by the fact that Nigeria ranked 149 out of 180 countries in the Corruption perception index of Transparency International.[20]

Section 14(3) of the Nigerian Constitution Expressly provides,

> The composition of the Government of the Federation or any of its agencies and the conduct of its affairs shall be carried out in such a manner as to reflect the federal character of Nigeria and the need to promote national unity, and also to command national loyalty, thereby ensuring that there shall be no predominance of persons from a few State or from a few ethnic or other sectional groups in that Government or in any of its agencies.[21]

But this is just in theory as in practice the reverse is the case. In essence where the federal government makes appointment in such a way that the heads of all the security agencies are drawn from one ethnic group that act is actually corruption and a corruption from the top means a reeking corruption in the entire fabric of the country.

c. Kleptocracy:

The best form of government the world over is democracy described as government of the people, by the people and for the people and that is what Nigeria is supposed to be practicing. Key element of democracy includes but are not limited to:

Political Science. https://core.ac.uk/download/pdf/16701001.pdf. Accessed November 7, 2021.

[20] Council on Foreign Relations, 'Perception of Corruption in Nigeria remain high according to NGO' (2020). https://www.cfr.org/blog/perceptions-corruption-nigeria-remain-high-according-ngo. Accessed November 6, 2021.

[21] CFRN, 1999.

- free and fair elections: regularly scheduled elections in which all voters have an equal opportunity to participate and where final results reflect honest vote totals.
- checks and balances: a system of separate branches of government that ensures political power is not concentrated in the hands of a single branch.
- minimal corruption: public trust that most elected leaders and civil servants (e.g., police officers and judges) perform their jobs without bribery or criminality.
- rule of law: no one is above the law, including government leaders; transparency: information on how officials conduct the public business and spend tax payers money is available and easily understood.
- independent judiciary: judges have freedom to decide cases impartially, based on their interpretation of the law and the facts.[22]

The above essential elements of democracy are lacking in Nigeria's experiment with democracy. Elections are massively rigged so much that the electorates have lost faith in the ballot box. The only free fair and credible election Nigeria ever had was the June 12 1993 and those immediately before that. Prof. Humphrey Nwosu who supervised that historic election has this to say:

> the conventional methods of direct closed/open primaries had proved to be unsuitable for Nigeria given its present level of economic, social and political development. On the other hand, we viewed the nonconventional methods of selection as those indirect methods of selection that were more appropriate to Nigeria's level of political development.....Above all the generality of the Nigerian public as well as international observers had confidence in the process and the electoral outcome, until the shattering news of annulment on June 23, 1993[23]

The June 12 election and the election of governors, and state and national assemblies before it, was a strong foundation laid for what would

[22] Identifying essential elements of Democracy: https://int.nyt.com/data/documenthelper/476-identifying-essential-elements/fdb7620f42a7c76af5f2/optimized/full.pdf. Accessed November 6, 2021.

[23] Humphrey Nwosu, '*Laying the foundation for Nigeria's Democracy: My Account of the June 12, 1993 Presidential Election and its Annulment*' (2017) New York: Page Publishing Inc. 240.

have been a strong democratic nation but with its annulment, the country has tethered on the precipice of a very weak foundation at the danger of total collapse. "Undoubtedly, the June 12, 1993, presidential election was adjudged by both national and international observers as the freest, fairest and most peaceful election in Nigeria History."[24]

It remains a question to be answered why Nigeria will jettison a system that produced the only free fair and credible election in her history. Because of absence of credible election people get to power through various corrupt and manipulated ways and as such are not interested in serving the people but rather in serving their masters who got them there, in the first place. The result is that what we have, in practice, is a form of government known as Geriatric Kleptocracy. The same group of people who have been in government since Independence is being recycled over the years till date.

d. Absence of State Police:

In any true federalism there is always a state police that will be under the command of the state Executive Governor who is the chief security officer of the state. If all the 36 states have their own state police in addition to the federal police under the command of the federal government, security breaches will be foiled as soon they arose preventing their several repeat occurrence. Several well-meaning Nigerians, including the state chief executives under the aegis of Nigerian Governors Forum (NGF) have been calling for the state police as a means of containing the insecurity challenges in the country as it is obvious that the entire police force is so overwhelmed that, now and then, a huge number of military personnel have to be deployed to perform police duties with its serious implications on professionalism. In the words of the chairperson of Nigeria Governors' Forum, Dr. Kayode Fayemi:

> the call for state police is an extension of true federalism as each federating unit is supposed to have control of its security apparatus. Each of the federating units (which are the states) should have control over their own security apparatus. That is not to say that we still won't have a federal police which responds to federal issues but I terms of wider knowledge of what obtains in my locality, the best person to use is somebody from the

[24] Id n8 at p. 23.

locality who has a better much richer understanding and will be faster in response to immediate needs of that environment.[25]

It is high time that Section 214 (1) of the 1999 Constitution[26], which provides that "There shall be a police force for Nigeria, which shall be known as the Nigeria Police Force, and subject to the provisions of this section, no other police force shall be established for the Federation or any part thereof", was amended to give way for state police.

e. Un-Remedied Past Wrongs:

Section 15(2) of the Nigerian 1999 constitution provides that "national integration shall be actively encouraged, whilst discrimination on the grounds of place of origin, sex, religion, status, ethnic or linguistic association or ties shall be prohibited"[27]. Unfortunately, the above section has been observed more in breach than in performance. It is obvious that there is manifest discrimination against certain people because of their race or ethnic group. For instance, the fact that not one single person from the South East geopolitical zone is heading any of the security agencies of the nation cannot be a coincidence. It must be a deliberate act of discrimination, most likely in deference to President Buhari's 5%/95% principle. The sense of belonging and loyalty among all the people of the Federation as is envisaged under Section 14(4) of the 1999 constitution is definitely lacking.

When the Nigeria Biafran war ended in 1970 and no victor no vanquished was declared it was supposed to be followed up with Reintegration, Reconstruction and Reconciliation (3Rs). If the 3Rs had been strictly implemented there may not have been MASSOB, or IPOB and the rest of agitation groups within its progeny.

If the resource sharing formula had been equitably resolved there would not have been Movement for the Emancipation of the Niger Delta (Mend), Movement for the Survival of Ogoni People (MOSOP), Niger Delta People's Volunteer Force (NDPVF), Niger Delta Vigilante (NDV),

[25] The case for State Police, Thisdayliveonline: https://www.thisdaylive.com/index.php/2020/12/24/the-case-for-state-police/. Accessed November 7, 2021.

[26] CFRN 1999.

[27] CFRN 1999.

etc. Even with the extension and implementation of the Amnesty Program the restiveness of the Niger Delta is still very much alive showing that only the symptoms were treated while the main cause of the ailment remains unaddressed. It is high time government sat down with all the discriminated, injured and dissatisfied people and assuaged their grievances as way of stemming future agitation before they snowball into irredeemable centrifugal explosion.

f. Porous border:

One of the indispensable conditions of statehood is that the state must have a well-defined border. Nigeria's borders with its neighboring states appear very porous and it should be a thing of concern. Writing under the caption "Porous borders: Nigeria's endless security dilemma", Mr. Tunde Ajala wrote:

> The government's inaction is even more disturbing because it's been proven that the porous borders have aided illegal arms proliferation, especially through the northern borders, while criminals from different parts of the world stroll into the country, contributing immeasurably to the frightening level of insecurity Nigeria is grappling with today.
>
> The President, Major General Muhammadu Buhari (retd.), has repeatedly, since the inception of his regime in 2015, blamed the festering insecurity in the country on the influx of illegal arms from Libya and close associates of the country's former leader, Muammar Gaddafi, who was killed since 2011.[28]

The state of Nigerian borders cannot be better painted than the foregoing. It explained vividly that the security challenges in Nigeria are multidimensional, domestic and international. One bewildering phenomenon of the Nigeria porous border is the seeming likelihood that it was not actually by accident but by design. Not quite long ago, the governor of Bauchi State was seen on National TV advocating that Nigerian borders should be left open for Fulanis from any other part of the world to come in:

[28] Tunde Ajala, 'Nigerian Endless Security Challenges' Punch Newspaper: https://punchng.com/porous-borders-nigerias-endless-security-dilemma/. Accessed November 7, 2021.

> Fulani man is a global or African person. He moves from The Gambia to Senegal and his nationality is Fulani….So, we cannot just close our borders and say the Fulani man is not a Nigerian. In most cases, the crisis is precipitated by those outside Nigeria. When there is a reprisal, it is not the Fulani man within Nigeria that causes it. It is that culture of getting revenge which is embedded in the traditional Fulani man that attracts reprisal.[29]

The foregoing is very scary. It means that most of the mass killings in the country may have been done by foreigner who took advantage of Nigeria's open border police to stroll in and leave carnage in their track. The sooner our borders are fully secured to forestall the infiltration of armed bandits from other countries, the easier it will be for the country to tackle its domestic security challenges that are fast consuming her.

4 Implication of the Rising Insecurity

The implication of the rising insecurity in Nigeria is legion but may be analyzed under 3 major headings, namely Economic implications, emergence of more destabilizing multiple agitations and degeneration into failed state.

a. Economic implication:

In northern Nigeria, the Boko Haram group, founded in 2002 by Utaz Mohammed Yusuf, has made major cities in the northern region of Nigeria cities of fear. Surprisingly, despite all the calls for the organization to be proscribed as a terrorist organization nothing has been done to that effect even when many countries and non-governmental organizations have unequivocally declared it a terrorist organization. The executive summary of United States Country Report of Human Rights practices on Nigeria painted a vivid eerie picture of the activities of Boko Haram in Nigeria.

> The insurgency in the Northeast by the militant terrorist groups Boko Haram and the Islamic State in West Africa continued. The groups

[29] Citizenship Rights in Africa Initiative, 'Nigeria: Bauchi State Governor on Stateless Fulani: https://citizenshiprightsafrica.org/nigeria-bauchi-governor-on-the-stateless-fulani/. Accessed November 7, 2021.

conducted numerous attacks on government and civilian targets, resulting in thousands of deaths and injuries, widespread destruction, the internal displacement of more than two million persons, and the external displacement of somewhat more than an estimated 300,000 Nigerian refugees to neighboring countries as of December 14.[30]

According to Nwagboso, between 2007 and 2011 the Boko Haram group had carried out the following attacks in Nigeria:

i. The Boko Haram stormed Police station at Maiduguri in 2009 and this resulted in deaths of hundreds of Nigerians.
ii. The group freed hundreds of prisoners in Maiduguri jail in September 2010.
iii. In December 2010, the Boko Haram bombed the city of Jos and this led to death of 80 Nigerians.
iv. Dozens of Nigerians have been killed from 2007 to 2011 largely due to sporadic shootings in Maiduguri, the Borno State Capital by Boko Haram group.
v. Bombed several states in the north after the May 2011 inauguration of President Goodluck Jonathan.
vi. Bombed Police Headquarters, Abuja in June 2011.
vii. Bombing of churches in Kano, Kaduna, Niger, Bauchi, Adamawa, Abuja in 2011.[31]

As aptly noted by Nwagboso, the natural consequences of the criminal and unwholesome acts of the Boko Haram group "has not only made Maiduguri, Abuja, Suleja, Damaturu, Minna, among others, cities of fear but also made Nigeria unsafe for investors and tourists." For instance, between 2005 and 2008 Foreign Direct Investment (FDI) inflow to Nigeria averaged $5:3 billion annually but from 2015–2019 the FDI flow into Nigeria diminished to $3.3 billion annually owing to the heightened

[30] Country Report on Human Rights Practices: Nigeria: https://www.state.gov/reports/2020-country-reports-on-human-rights-practices/nigeria/. Accessed November 7, 2021.

[31] Chris I. Nwagboso, 'Security Challenges and Economy of the Nigerian State (2007–2011)', American Journal of Contemporary Research, Vol. 2 No.6 2012.

insecurity that marked the said period.[32] It is obvious that there is remarkable drop in the Foreign Direct Investment inflow into Nigeria as a result of these insecurity challenges. It is noteworthy that in 2012 a group of investors from Germany that had wanted to build a cement factory in Maiduguri had to withdraw from the project due to the activities of Boko Haram. With the drop in FDI, economic stagnation, unemployment, poverty, etc. will naturally follow.

As the continuous clashes between Fulani herders and local indigenous farmers persist, production plummets. There will not be enough for local consumption to talk less of exportation to earn foreign currency. In the same vein, resources that would have come into the country to boast the economy, both from citizens living in the diaspora and foreigners in tourism, may cease as many countries warn their nationals to desist from travelling to Nigeria. In desperate measure to contain the insecurity challenges, the government will be forced to spend disproportionate amount of the already scarce resources on security votes. Regrettably even such disproportionate security spending fuels the vehicle that drives Nigeria's hyper corruption.[33] As the threatening insecurity challenges continue to distort the economy of the nation whose official legal tender is almost worthless, having lost more than 80%[34] of its value, economic hardship will bite even harder and trigger brain drain resulting in the country losing most of its best brains.

With investors, both local and international, being scared away, the economy will take a hard knock resulting in stiff competition for the limited supply of very scarce goods.

b. Rising of multiple agitations:

We now have Miyetti Allah Cattle Breeders Association of Nigeria (MACBAN) in the north, Odua People's Congress and Amotekun in

[32] Financial Africa, 'Ten economic consequences of growing insecurity in Nigeria': Ten economic consequences of growing insecurity in Nigeria: http://www.financialnigeria.com/ten-economic-consequences-of-growing-insecurity-in-nigeria-blog-512.html. Accessed November 7, 2021.

[33] EFCC eventually uncovered how the said $2.1b was shared out as bribes to matters unrelated to security. The then National Security Adviser, Colonel Sambo Dasuki, who had custody of the money was eventually arrested along with many other suspects.

[34] It is sad to recall that in 1973 the Naira was exchanging at N1-$62 but today it the naira exchanges for N579-$1. See the Decline and fall of the Naira in Vanguard news of August 9, 2021.

the southwest, Eastern Security Network (ESN) in the southeast, Movement for the Emancipation of the Niger Delta in the south/south and the list goes on. These are created solely for the defense of its members or regions. These organizations sprang up as a result of agitation of marginalization or to fill the lacuna created by the failure of government to defend them and, now and then, they clash with each other and with government, thereby exacerbating the pervading complex insecurity in the nation. According to Onifade et al.:

> "the state of insecurity in the country has been sustained by a regressing economy…., unemployment and a growing sense of disenchantment that government and its representatives have not been fair to the people, thus pushing some citizens into criminal activities including violent crimes to make a living and to take out their anger on a passive society. Consequently, the state of increased lawlessness, violence and criminality that has become characteristic of life in Nigeria has further increase the dismalness of insecurity facing the country.[35]

It has become a cyclical issue for, as insecurity challenges fail to be addressed systematically, it triggers the practical demonstration of the disorganization theory where the physical environment breeds deviants who follow the crime-saturated atmosphere to propagate deviancy as a normal way of life.

c. Failed state status:

It is a well-established fact that the essence of government is to ensure the security and welfare of the people. It follows therefore that a state that refuses or fails to discharge this critical duty ought to cease from being a state. A state is said to have failed when it is consumed by micro or internal violence and ceases, or becomes unable, to deliver positive political goods to their inhabitants.[36] Commonly cited examples of failed states are Somalia, Liberia and Sierra Leone, Bosnia-Herzegovina, Rwanda,

[35] Comfort et al., 'Addressing the Insecurity Challenge in Nigeria: The imperative of Moral Values and Virtue Ethics'(2013) 2(13)Global Journal of Human Social Science Political Science https://core.ac.uk/download/pdf/16701001.pdf. Accessed November 8, 2021.

[36] Robert Bates, 'When Things Fell Apart: State Failure in Late Century Africa'(2008) (Cambridge: Cambridge University Press).

Sudan, etc. The present situation in Nigeria may not strictly qualify as a failed state but to the extent that the nation, acutely plagued by micro insecurity, is unable to deliver the political goods to the people, is overwhelmed by internal violence, so much so that even the military barracks are not safe, it is well on its way to junkyard of failed state as already pointed by some sitting governors of some states in the federation.[37]

5 Solution Through Law

The rising insecurity and its disastrous consequences in our nation are the direct product of state failure as identified above due, in large part, to violations of relevant constitutional and legislative provision created for that purpose. It follows, naturally, that the cure will be to double back on those provisions and legislation, in strict performance, underpinned by unequivocal political will to drive a vigorous implementation thereof.

Extant literature on the causes of worsening insecurity in Nigeria point at corruption as the chief culprit of the menace. To that end, the first port of call in finding solution will be to vigorously implement the laws targeted at corruption such as the Economic and Financial Crimes Commission (EFCC) Act and the Independent Corrupt Practices & Other Related Offences Commission (ICPC) Act,[38] enact Unexplained Wealth Order, and restore the dignity of the ballot through a credible electoral system.

a. Economic and Financial Crimes Commission (EFCC):

The EFCC was established in 2003 to tackle the advance fee fraud crimes popularly called 419 with Nuhu Ribadu as its premier chairman. It has powers to investigate all financial Crimes including the advance free fraud[39] and to examine and investigate all reported cases of economic and financial crimes with a view to identifying individuals, corporate bodies or groups involved. EFCC has handled many corruption cases but it has also been dogged by corruption itself culminating in the arrest of the immediate past Acting Chairman of the Commission Mr. Ibrahim Magu who

[37] Id Bauchi and Benue.

[38] Independ Corrupt Practices & Other Related Offences Commission Act, 2000.

[39] EFCC Section 6(c).

has been replaced by Mohammed Umar Abba. It is high time the government ensured that the leadership and staff of such a strategic commission are men and women of high moral standard that will be above board as far as corruption is concerned to be able to discharge their sacred duty.

b. Independent Corrupt Practices & Other Related Offences Commission (ICPC):

The ICPC has full powers to investigate and prosecute a person on whom allegation of corruption or any other financial crime has been made.[40] It has a provision for allegation against even the President or Governor of a state to be investigated by an independent counsel appointed by the Attorney General.[41] The problem is that due to long years of endemic corruption and the culture elevating the aberration as the norm, the political will is lacking for the highly placed individual to even have allegation of corruption against them talk less of prosecuting them and getting a conviction which would then serve as deterrent to others. That political will is needed now if the country is to heal.

c. Unexplained Wealth Orders:

Much of the socio-political tension that fuels the insecurity challenges in Nigeria comes from the politicians who get to power through illegitimate means and have formed what Onifade et al. called "a thieving and amoral minority whose only qualification is access to governance and the national till."[42] Once ensconced in their office, they recruit unemployed, vulnerable and impoverished youths "arming them with dangerous weapons to pursue and track down their political foes and to sustain a climate of repression, fear and cowardice so they can continue in

[40] ICPC ss 27–42; s54, 61.

[41] ICPC s54.

[42] Onifade C. et al., 'Addressing the Insecurity Challenge in Nigeria: The imperative of Moral Values and Virtues Ethics (2013) 2(13). https://core.ac.uk/download/pdf/16701001.pdf.

their political offices ad infinitum."[43] It is obvious that the wealth used to sustain the atmosphere of insecurity was acquired illegally and once the source of such illegal wealth is sealed its effect will equally cease. The fastest way to achieve this will be to put up a very stiff fight against corruption by the enactment of a new law akin to unexplained wealth orders (UWOs) of Great Britain.

UWOs are part of law introduced in the United Kingdom by Section 1–7 of Financial Crimes Act of 2017 and became effective in 2018.[44] The new law enables the court to grant orders that give new civil powers to UK law enforcement agencies to help them identify, investigate and seize property suspected to represent the proceeds of criminal activity. The high point of this new law is that it reverses the burden of proof and places it on the suspect to explain the source of his or her wealth where there is a probable cause to believe that his or her legitimate source of income cannot afford such property. With this kind of law in Nigeria the EFCC and ICPC will have more powers to proceed against corrupt politicians and their family members.

d. Restore The Dignity of The Ballot Through Credible Electoral System:

In the history of democratic experience of Nigeria there is one fact that all Nigerians and international community are agreed upon and that is the only free, fair, credible election Nigeria ever had was that of June 12, 1993, using option A4. Surprisingly after that election was annulled the system was jettisoned giving rise to rigged and manipulated electoral result that throws up unqualified and mediocre people into position of trust with its consequences that has brought the nation to her knees. This is more like killing the geese that lay the golden eggs. Option A4 has been said to be unconventional but so is the problem with Nigeria. It makes sense that an unconventional problem should be attacked and decimated with an unconventional weapon especially when every conventional weapon has failed over the span of almost 3 decades. It is time

[43] Onifade C. et al., 'Addressing the Insecurity Challenge in Nigeria: The imperative of Moral Values and Virtues Ethics (2013) 2(13). https://core.ac.uk/download/pdf/16701001.pdf.

[44] Transparency International Uk, 'Unexplained Wealth Orders-a brief guide'. https://www.transparency.org.uk/unexplained-wealth-orders-brief-guide.

to amend the electoral laws of Nigeria to reintroduce the only electoral system that had ever produced untainted results as well as stipulate more serious penalties for electoral fraudsters.

6 Recommendations

Of all the contributing factors to the rising insecurity in our nation, corruption is the substructure that sustains the malaise. This is because what was supposed to be a democracy is, in practice, a kleptocracy where the frail electoral system is manipulated to put an amoral thieving horde into office. The journey to national healing ought to start with Moral Re-armament because, "Providing moral leadership that eschews evil, corruption, vices, inequity, injustice and wickedness will compel the people to model the character of their leaders and vice versa."[45]

Against the backdrop of the foregoing this paper will make the following recommendations:

a. Restore the dignity of the ballot through credible electoral system by vigorous prosecution of electoral Crimes.
b. Return to true federalism where federating unit control their own economic resource while paying tax to the federal government.
c. Establishment of state police in keeping with the terms of true federalism obtainable in civilized countries, especially the United States of America, whose presidential system of government we are copying.
d. Pursue vigorous national integration as provided for in the Nigerian constitution by giving all states, races, and tribes a sense of belonging in the appointment of top selective offices of the federation.
e. Avoiding discrimination by choosing excellence over mediocrity.
f. Immediate proscription of Boko Haram as a terrorist organization.
g. Effective policing of all Nigerian borders to stop the infiltration of non-nationals especially the criminals.

[45] Onifade C. et al., 'Addressing the Insecurity Challenge in Nigeria: The imperative of Moral Values and Virtues Ethics(2013) 2(13). https://core.ac.uk/download/pdf/16701001.pdf.

7 Conclusion

The magnitude of spate of insecurity in the country today has never been witnessed in the history of the nation. Driving the conflagration is the distended corruption within the government itself. The most intractable obstacle to tackling corruption in Nigeria is that it has the blessing of the ruling APC (All Progressives Congress) government. This is well borne out by the confession of the then Chairman of the party and former Governor of Edo state Adam Oshiomhole, at the Edo state APC Presidential rally on Thursday January 17, 2019, that "once you join the APC, your sins are forgiven." It leaves no one in doubt that APC is a sanctuary of treasury looters and that President Buhari's fight against corruption is a window dresser and a witch hunt.[46]

But this is a time to stand up for the country. The nation had survived the Nigerian/Biafran war, it survived the Adaka Boro break-away attempt on February 23rd 1966,[47] but with more than half of the geopolitical zone spoiling for war of exit, it is very imperative that the genuine dialogue should be pursued, based on the above recommendations, if the saying that Nigeria must remain one will have any meaning.

[46] Sunday N, 'Once you join APC your sins are forgiven'(2019). Vanguard. https://www.vanguardngr.com/2019/01/once-you-join-apc-your-sins-are-forgiven-oshiomhole-says-as-ph-lambasts-him/. Accessed November 8, 2021.

[47] Eromo Egbejule,'The West African Nation that lasted 12 days'. https://www.ozy.com/true-and-stories/the-west-african-nation-that-lasted-only-12-days/282688/. Accessed November 8, 2021.

CHAPTER 4

Restorative Justice and Non-Custodial Measures as Panacea for Prison Decongestion in a Covid-19 Era: Nigeria in Perspective

Chinyere Comfort Ani

1 Introduction

The advent of the COVID-19 pandemic, in early 2020, took the entire world by storm and has affected the entire sphere of human endeavour. The pandemic poses severe threat to human life and has challenged governments and institutions to think out of the box on how to exist in the "new normal" way of life, which basically advocates social distancing amongst other universally approved measures.[1]

[1] Physical distancing, use of masks, and frequent hand washing with proper technique or use of alcohol-based sanitizers are recognized as measures that can help reduce the risk of transmission. See *COVID-19 and the US Criminal Justice System: Evidence for Public Health Measures to Reduce Risk October 2020 John Hopkings Bloomberg School of Public Health*, p. 2.

C. C. Ani (✉)
Enugu State High Court, Enugu State Judiciary, Independence Layout, Nigeria
e-mail: anicomfort@gmail.com

E. Duruigbo et al. (eds.), *International Law and Development in the Global South*, https://doi.org/10.1007/978-3-031-13741-9_4

Universally, imprisonment is still the cornerstone of penal systems. Despite its wide use, its drawbacks both to the offender and to society have become increasingly recognized and a search for alternative/non-custodial sanctions has been conducted for more than one century.[2] Overcrowding or congestion in Nigerian Correctional Centres has been a constant feature and problem of the Nigerian criminal justice system. This problem is largely as a result of over reliance by the courts on imprisonment and fine as disposition measures and the attitude that every case must go through the whole hug of the criminal trial process, thereby causing congestion and delay.

Detention facilities, no doubt, are exceptionally susceptible to outbreak of the pandemic if strict measures are not taken. This informed the directive by the Nigerian Comptroller General of Correctional Service at the wake of the outbreak in Nigeria to all Comptrollers of Corrections in the various States in Nigeria to temporarily suspend admission of inmates in the various prisons and also the production of inmates in courts. In the face of the still ravaging pandemic, it becomes very compelling for the stakeholders in the criminal justice sector to consider much more than before the application of restorative and non-custodial disposition measures in our laws as against the prevailing preference for imprisonment.

Nigeria has ratified a plethora of international instruments on restorative and non-custodial measures and has enacted laws with non-custodial and restorative justice content, yet these measures are usually disregarded in sentencing. The Nigerian Criminal justice system recently received a boost in legislative intervention as regards restorative and non-custodial measures with the passage of two major laws: The Administration of Criminal Justice Act (ACJA) 2015 (Federal)[3] and the Nigerian Correctional Services Act (NCSA) 2019. Various States have adopted the ACJA and passed it as the State Law.[4] These laws amongst other things have made provisions for non-custodial disposition measures or alternatives to imprisonment more than ever. The provisions are geared towards

[2] Available at: http://www.unicri.it/probation/prb_aboutus.htm. Accessed on 23/4/2021.

[3] Various states in Nigeria has also adapted and passed the Administration of Criminal Justice Laws.

[4] For instance, The Enugu State Administration of Criminal Justice Law, (ACJL) 2017, adopted the ACJA with minor differences.

compliance with international human rights standards with the aim of reducing prison overcrowding and increasing application of rehabilitation and reintegration programmes. The laws place more emphasis on restorative justice rather than retributive justice.

The objectives of sentencing as set out in the Administration of Criminal Justice Act, (ACJA), 2015[5] include: prevention, restraint, rehabilitation, deterrence, education, retribution and restitution. Deterrence, rehabilitation, education and restitution are all objectives that can be achieved by applying restorative and non-custodial sentencing measures. The fact that these objectives are mentioned by the Act shows the ultimate intent of the lawmakers to enthrone restorative justice as well as non-institutional measures, while not obliterating the retributive penal sentences.

2 Prison Congestion and Covid-19 Pandemic

Prison congestion with its attendant negative aspects is a problem in most nations of the world including Nigeria. However, developed countries realize the great danger this situation portends and they do all within their means to curtail the situation. Our judiciary has over the years, relied very heavily on imprisonment and fine as sentencing measures almost as if no other disposition measure is available for their application. While some jurists blame this on the absence of any clear sentencing policy in the criminal legislation others believe that there is a sentencing policy embodied in the law, which although may appear to be deficient in detail needs to be made more comprehensive and definite in terms of imprisonment to be imposed in any given circumstance.

[5] Section 401(2) of the ACJA provides that in determining a sentence, the court shall have the objectives in mind, and may decide in each case the objectives that are more appropriate or possible.

2.1 *Table showing Total prison population in Nigeria*[6]

Year	*Total prison population*
2000	44,450
2002	40,048
2004	38,999
2006	40,953
2008	41,143
2010	46,586
2012	51,560
2014	56,785
2018	71,522
2020	72,627
2021	67, 631

Nigeria has an estimated national population of 210.08 million persons. The official capacity of the prison system in Nigeria is 50,153. As at 30th of March, 2021, total Nigerian prison population stood at 67,631, including pre-trial detainees/remand prisoners. Pre-trial or remand detainees account for 72.7% of the population.[7] Nigerian prisons are overpopulated by extra 17,478 inmates.

The COVID-19 pandemic also known as the coronavirus was first identified in December 2019 in Wuhan, China. It is an ongoing pandemic caused by severe acute respiratory syndrome coronavirus 2 (SARS-CoV-2). In March 2020, the World Health Organization (WHO) declared the COVID-19 outbreak a pandemic.[8] Viral Transmission SARS-CoV-2 is transmitted through direct or indirect contact with people already infected with the virus. Respiratory droplets from the nose and mouth are thought to be the primary mode of transmission of SARS-CoV-2. These droplets spread the virus from person to person through talking, coughing and sneezing. Those in close contact with infected people can be directly infected when secretions enter the mouth, nose or eyes, or

[6] Source: World Prison Brief, available at: https://prisonstudies.org/country/nigeria.

[7] World Prison Brief-Nigeria. Available at: https://prisonstudies.org/country/nigeria.

[8] Corona Virus Disease 2019 (COVID 19), available at: https://www.mayoclinic.org/diseases-conditions/coronavirus/symptoms-causes/syc-20479963. Accessed on 24/4/2021.

they can be indirectly infected by touching objects or surfaces that the droplets may have landed on, then touching their mouth, nose or eyes. Respiratory droplets fall quickly to the ground after they are expelled, typically within 3 feet (1 m). Physical distancing guidance is based on this mode of transmission.[9]

As at 26th of April, 2021, Nigeria has recorded a total of 164,756 cases of infected persons and a total number of 2,062 deaths. Statistics from some other countries are: USA—Total cases—32, 875, 045, Total deaths—586, 611); India—Total Cases 17, 636, 307, Total deaths—197, 894; France—Total Cases—5, 503, 996, Total Deaths—103, 256; UK—Total Cases—4, 406, 946, Total Deaths—127, 434; Argentina—Total Cases—287, 677, Total deaths—62, 087; South Africa-Total Cases—1, 576,320, Total Deaths—54, 186; Canada—Total Cases—1, 187,918, Total deaths—24, 024.[10]

The number of coronavirus cases in Nigeria appears low when compared with some other countries. Nevertheless, it is important to prevent the wider spread of the virus by taking proactive measures including actions geared at decongesting the correctional centres. The risk of transmission is higher in indoor environments, particularly for those who are enclosed in a space with little opportunity for physical distancing. WHO recommends avoiding indoor gatherings when possible or using spaces with good ventilation.[11] In crowded living conditions, incarcerated individuals are in close contact with others, and physical distancing amongst infected or exposed people is nearly impossible.

Overcrowding is a known risk factor for infection and high-density prisons can more than double the risk of major infections, such as tuberculosis and COVID-19.[12] The Nigerian Correctional Centres like all other detention facilities worldwide are highly susceptible to the spread of COVID-19 because of the overcrowding in the facilities, which propagates the spread of respiratory infections and the comorbidities of many incarcerated individuals.

[9] *COVID-19 and the US Criminal Justice System: Evidence for Public Health Measures to Reduce Risk.* Op. cit. note 1, p. 1.

[10] COVID-19 Coronavirus- Update. Last updated: 2021-04-27 13:20:06 UTC. Available at: https://virusncov.com/. Accessed on 27/4/2021.

[11] *COVID-19 and the US Criminal Justice System: Evidence for Public Health Measures to Reduce Risk.* Op. cit. note 9, p. 2.

[12] Ibid., p. 3.

3 Elucidation of Notions

3.1 Restorative Justice

Restorative Justice refers to a process for resolving crime that focuses on redressing the harm done to the victims, holding offenders accountable for their actions and, often also, engaging the community in the resolution of that conflict. It reacts to crime by restoration rather than retribution.[13] According to Tom Cavanagh, restorative justice is a value-based approach to responding to wrongdoing and conflict, with a balanced focus on the person harmed, the person causing the harm and the affected community.[14] It focuses on transforming wrongdoing by healing the harm, particularly to relationships, that is created by harmful behaviour. Walgrave sees restorative justice as "an option for doing justice after the occurrence of an offence that is primarily oriented towards repairing the individual, relational and social harm caused by that offence".[15] Eva Achjani Zulfa considers restorative justice as a model approach which emerged in the 1960s in an effort to solve criminal cases. Unlike the approach used in conventional criminal justice system, this approach focuses on the direct participation of perpetrators, victims and society in the settlement process.[16]

Restorative justice is generally applicable to people of all ages but it is mostly used in relation to juvenile and young offenders as it can stop the process of a young offender turning into an adult offender and provides the option of having a lasting positive impact on their emotional and moral development.[17] A restorative justice system holds the offender accountable by facilitating and enforcing reparative agreements, including

[13] Ani C. C., "Using Mediation as an Instrument of Peace", in Peter Fogam (Ed.) *Essays on Mediation as an ADR Tool: Lagos State Experience (Lagos State Citizens' Mediation Centre)*, 2017, pp. 270–271.

[14] Available at: http://www.evangelizationstation.com/htm_html/moral%20theology/Death%20Penalty/restorative_justice_and_the_comm.htm. Accessed on 23/4/2021.

[15] Walgrave, Lode, *Restorative Justice, Self-interest and Responsible Citizenship*, (Cullompton: Willan Publishing, 2008), p. 21.

[16] Eva Achjani Zulfa *Restorative Justice* in Indonesia: Traditional Value No. 1 - Volume 2, May –

August 2011 *Indonesia Law Review*, p. 33.

[17] Melia, Manuel Cancio, "Victim Behaviour and Offender Liability: A European Perspective", *7 Buff.*

Crim. L.. Rev. 513 (2003–2004) pp. 513–514.

restitution. Restorative justice recognizes that we must give offenders the opportunity to right their wrongs and redeem themselves, in their own eyes and in the eyes of the community. Restorative justice programmes emphasize more on addressing the problems caused by a criminal conduct than trial and punishment of the offender.

With restorative justice, the victim, the offender and the community all participate in the crime disposal process. Basically, the victim is compensated as much as can be reasonably achieved; the offender is effectively reintegrated back into the community of responsible citizens; and the community is restored to normalcy.[18]

Retributive justice, on the other hand, is more concerned about who committed the offence, what laws were broken and what punishment is due to the offender. In contrast, restorative justice focuses on the type of harm ensuing from the crime; actions to be taken to repair the harm done or restore the victim as nearly as possible to the status quo before the harm and makes the offender responsible for the repair or restoration.[19]

3.2 Non-Custodial Measures

A custodial sentence is a judicial sentence, imposing a punishment consisting of mandatory custody of the convict, either in prison or in some other closed therapeutic and/or (re)educational institution, such as a reformatory, maximum security psychiatry or drug detoxification facility.[20] A non-custodial sentence or measure on the other hand is the opposite of custodial sentence. They are those sentences a court can impose on an offender which does not involve keeping him in prison or any other penal facility. They include compensation, damages, costs, restitution, restoration, plea bargain, community service, suspended sentence, probation and parole.

[18] Odoh Ben, "Creative Approaches to Crime: The Case for Alternative Dispute Resolution (ADR) in the Magistracy in Nigeria" *Uruchi Journal of Law, Policy and Globalization, Vol.36*, 2015 (Online), p.
5.

[19] Edit Törzs, "Restorative justice models and their relevance to conflicts in intercultural settings" Deliverable 3.1: Report on restorative justice models, p. 6.

[20] Available at: http://en.wikipedia.org/wiki/Custodial_sentence. Cited in Ani C. C, "Forging New Trends in Sentencing: Overview of UN Standard Minimum Rules for Non-Custodial Measures and the Lagos State Administration of Criminal Justice (ACJ) Law 2007" *The Justice Journal, FMOJ,* 2nd ed. 201, p. 120.

Non-custodial alternatives to imprisonment have been recognized as an effective means of treating offenders within the community to the best advantage of both the offenders and society.[21] If appropriately applied they facilitate the social reintegration of offenders within the community rather than subjecting them to the unnecessary de-socializing and harmful effects of prison.[22]

Non-custodial measures address all the aims of traditional incarceration including retribution, reparations, deterrence and incapacitation in addition to rehabilitation.[23] Some of the measures imposed may include a condition to undergo treatment for an addiction, while others may include referral to an educational or personal development centre, or oblige offenders to undertake unpaid work beneficial to the community, on the understanding that, as well as being penalized, they are acknowledging and repaying the damage they have caused to the community by committing an offence.[24] They may also be required to pay compensation or make restitution.[25] Research has shown that most victims of crime in Nigeria prefer restitution and compensation of their victimizers to imprisonment or fine.[26]

Section 454 ACJ Act, 2015 provides a great impetus for the use of non-custodial sentences by the courts. It provides that where the court thinks that the charge is proved but is of the opinion that having regard to: (a) the character, antecedents, age, health or mental condition, of the defendant charged; (b) the trivial nature of the offence; or (c) the extenuating circumstances under which the offence was committed, it is

[21] See the Preamble to the *UN Standard Minimum Rules for Non-Custodial Measures (The Tokyo Rules)*.

[22] *Custodial and Non-Custodial Measures Social Reintegration Criminal Justice Assessment Tool kit* (New York: United Nations, 2006), p. 2.

[23] Klein A. R., *Alternative Sentencing. A Practitioner's Guide,* (Anderson Publishing Co., 1988), p. 1.

[24] Ibid.

[25] Ani C. C, "Forging New Trends in Sentencing: Overview of UN Standard Minimum Rules for Non-Custodial Measures and the Lagos State Administration of Criminal Justice (ACJ) Law 2007 *op. cit. note 20,* p.118.

[26] Odekunle F., "Restitution, Compensation and Victims Remedies: Background and Justifications" in Adetiba S., (Ed.) *Compensation and Remedies for Crime Victims in Nigeria*, (Lagos: Federal Ministry of Justice, 1990), p. 157.

inexpedient to inflict a punishment or any order than a nominal punishment or that it is expedient to release the defendant on probation, the court may, without proceeding to conviction, make an order specified in subsection (2) of this section, such as (a) dismissing the charge; or (b) discharging the defendant conditionally on his entering into a recognizance, with or without sureties, to be of good behaviour or order; (c) the defendant to pay such damages for injury or compensation for any loss suffered by a person by reason of the conduct or omission of the defendant, and to pay such costs of the proceedings as the court thinks reasonable.

4 Restorative and Non-Custodial Sentences

4.1 Fine

Fine is the most commonly specified non-custodial sentence in our penal system. It is used either by itself or in conjunction with other sentence. The penal policies pursued in imposing fines are those of retribution, deterrence, revenue collection, victim compensation and prevention. Fine is commonly specified as the exclusive penalty for a wide range of petty offences against local regulations, traffic offences, postal offences, food and drugs offences, shipping offences, tax invasion, etc.

The court is empowered to use its discretion to impose a fine in lieu of imprisonment where it has authority under any written law to impose imprisonment for any offence but has no specific authority to impose a fine for that offence.[27] A court in fixing the amount of a fine to be imposed on a convict shall take into consideration, amongst other things, the means of the convict.[28]

The amount of the fine to be imposed is also at the discretion of the Magistrate, but it is not to exceed the maximum fine authorized to be imposed by the Magistrate under the law.[29] For the Magistrates no term of imprisonment imposed in default of payment is to exceed the maximum fixed in relation to the amount by the scale in the Fourth Schedule of the ACJ Act, 2015 or Section 422 of the Administration of Criminal Justice

[27] Section 420 (1) ACJA 2015, Section 415 ACJL, 2017, Enugu.

[28] S 427 (1) ACJA, 2015.

[29] Section 420 (3), ACJA, 2015 and S. 415 (3) of the ACJL Enugu.

Law, 2017 (ACJL) Enugu.[30] For the High Court, imprisonment for non-payment of a fine shall be at the discretion of the court and is not to exceed 2 years.[31]

Fines can deter the offender if he is poor enough and to some extent make restitution but it certainly cannot reform an offender.[32] W. A. McEwen articulated the advantages of using fines as a means of treating offenders as follows:

1. It provides an alternative in some cases to imprisonment, and saves the offender from the embarrassment and stigma of being a prisoner.
2. It saves the offender from the contamination, degeneration and callousness of which he is exposed, if he has to serve a prison sentence.
3. It is a less expensive means of correction to the state.[33]

4.2 Community Service Order

Community service order is a novel sentence in the Nigerian criminal justice system. It first appeared in Nigeria in the Lagos State Administration of Criminal Justice Law, 2007. It was later in 2015 added in the Federal law, the ACJ Act, which has also been adopted and passed into law by many states in Nigeria.[34]

A community service order is a restorative justice measure as it is an order from the court whereby an offender is offered the opportunity of compensating society for the wrong she/he has done by performing work for the benefit of the community, instead of going to prison. Sections 460(2) ACJ Act and 469 ACJL Enugu resoundingly state that where a court suspends the sentence it imposed on a convict, the

[30] Section 420 (3) (b) ACJA and Section 415 (3) (b), ACJL, Enugu.

[31] Section 420(2) ACJA 2015 and Section 415 (2) ACJL Enugu.

[32] McEwen W. A. "Non-Institutional Treatment of Offenders" in *The Nigerian Magistrate and the Offender*, p. 99.

[33] Ibid.

[34] See Sections 460–466 ACJ Act and Section 469–475 ACJL Enugu.

court may with or without conditions sentence the convict to perform community service. Community service may be in lieu of sentence or fine.

The nature of the community services available include:

(a) environmental sanitation, including cutting grasses, washing drainages, cleaning the environment and washing public places;
(b) assisting in the production of agricultural produce, construction, or mining; and
(c) any other type of service which in the opinion of the court would have a beneficial and reformative effect on the character of the convict.[35]

Before making a community service order, the court is enjoined to consider the circumstances, character, antecedents of the convict and other factors.[36] The community service sentence shall be performed as close as possible to the place where the convict ordinarily resides to ensure that the community can monitor his movement.[37] A convict sentenced to community service is not to be sentenced to a term of imprisonment for the same offence, but may in default of performing his community service diligently and to the satisfaction of the court, be sentenced to a term of imprisonment for the remaining part of his community service to which he is in default or neglect.[38]

The community service order shall be performed for a period of not more than six months and the convict shall not work for more than five hours a day.[39] The Chief Judge is to establish a Community Service Centre in every Judicial Division to be headed by a Registrar to oversee execution of community service orders.[40]

The imposition of a community service order can be justified for the following reasons: Prisoners are expensive to maintain considering the enormous taxpayers fund spent on feeding, housing and caring for prisoners. Many of the people in the various prisons are not violent or

[35] Section 461 (4) and Sect. 470 (4) ACJL, Enugu.

[36] Section 461 (6) ACJA and Sect. 470 (6) ACJL Enugu.

[37] Section 461 (5) ACJA and Sect. 470 (5) ACJL Enugu.

[38] Section 461 (7) ACJA and Sect. 470 (7) ACJL Enugu.

[39] Section 462 (1) ACJA and Sect. 471 (1) ACJL Enugu.

[40] Section 461 (1) ACJA and Sect. 470 (1) ACJL Enugu.

dangerous criminals that would require the protection of the society from them. Many of the prison population are people of poor background who committed simple offences like environmental offences, traffic offences, affray, assault, etc. By sending such offenders to community service, the community benefits positively and the population of the already congested prison is not increased, thereby reducing the possibility of the spread of deadly diseases such as COVID-19.

4.3 Restoration and Restitution

Restoration involves giving back; to make something look as it looked originally by repairing, etc. to put back into place.[41] Restoration strictly so called in the criminal process arises when a person is made to disgorge a benefit, which he has unjustly acquired. Such an order can be made where the defendant has acquired a benefit through his own wrongful or criminal act, such as may occur in the case of stealing or obtaining property by false pretence.[42]

Section 336 (1) ACJ Act provides that whenever a person is convicted of an offence attended by criminal force and it appears to the court that by such force, any person has been dispossessed of any immovable property, the court, if it deems fit, is to order the possession of the property to be restored to such person.[43] The court is to order property taken during arrest or suspected to have been stolen, etc., except one used in the Commission of the offence to be delivered to the person entitled to its possession.[44]

The idea of restitution and restoration is that the victim of a property offence should as far as possible be put back into the position he enjoyed before the offence.[45] Restitution refers to the return of movable property dishonestly acquired or taken without authority.

[41] Ani C. C, "Forging New Trends in Sentencing: Overview of UN Standard Minimum Rules for Non-Custodial Measures and the Lagos State Administration of Criminal Justice (ACJ) Law 2007, *op. cit. note 20*, p.141.

[42] F. O. Babafemi., "Restitution and Compensation of Criminal Justice" in Adeyemi, A. A. (Ed.), *The Nigerian Criminal Process*, (University of Lagos Press, 1977), p. 251.

[43] See also Section 489 ACJL Enugu.

[44] Section 337 ACJA and Section 491 ACJL Enugu.

[45] A. Milner, *The Nigerian Penal System*, (London: Sweet and Maxwell, 1972), p. 127.

Section 321 ACJ Act and Section 442 ACJL Enugu provide that in addition to or in lieu of any other penalty authorized by law, a court may order the convict to make restitution or pay compensation to any victim of the crime for which the offender was convicted, or to the victim's estate. The court may order for the restitution or compensation for the loss or destruction of the victim's property and in so doing may direct the convict: to return the property to the owner or to a person designated by the owner; if the return of the property is impossible or impracticable, to pay an amount equal to the value of the property, or if the property to be returned is inadequate or insufficient, to pay an amount equal to the property calculated on the basis of what is fair and just.

Section 341 of the ACJ Act deals with restoration and disposition of property found on person arrested. It also deals with the restoration of stolen property. By that provision, the court convicting an offender is to order that such property or a part thereof be restored to the person who appears to it to be the owner thereof, either on payment or without payment by the owner to the person in whose possession such property or a part thereof then is, of any sum named in such order. This provision does not apply to:

(a) a valuable security which has been paid or discharged in good faith by a person liable to pay or discharge the instrument; or
(b) a negotiable instrument which has been received in good faith by transfer or delivery by a person for a just and valuable consideration without notice or without any reasonable cause to suspect that it had been stolen.

4.4 Compensation Order

Compensation is a form of personal reparation disbursed to the victim of crime by the offender upon the order of a court after a conviction of the offender with a view to preventing the unjust enrichment of the offender as well as effectively ensuring that the victim is restored as far as possible to the *status quo ante criminem*. It is usually resorted to where restitution or restoration is impracticable and it is applied to relieve the victim of any loss which he may have suffered, physically or financially.

Compensation is usually resorted to mainly in cases of personal injury such as assaults and sexual offences and offences relating to property, especially where the property is either damaged or destroyed or cannot be found.

The *Declaration of Basic Principles of Justice for Victims of Crime and Abuse of Power* calls on states to endeavour to provide compensation when it is not fully available from the offender.

Section 440 ACJL Enugu states that a court may, within the proceedings or while passing judgement, order that the defendant or convicted person shall pay a sum of money as compensation to any person injured by the offence, irrespective of any other fine or other punishment that may be imposed or that is imposed on the defendant or convict, where substantial compensation is in the opinion of the court recoverable by civil suit.

Compensation may also be ordered to compensate a bona fide purchaser for value without notice of the defect of the title in any property in respect of which the offence was committed and has been compelled to give it up; or in defraying expenses incurred in medical treatment of a person injured by the defendant in connection with the offence. In default of payment of compensation, the court may award a term of imprisonment or community service. A person to whom compensation is awarded may refuse to accept the compensation.[46]

By Sects. 325 ACJA and Section 447 ACJL Enugu, any compensation ordered to be paid under this Act or any other Act, relating to any criminal proceedings, may be enforced as if it were a fine.

4.5 *Whipping or Corporal Punishment*[47]

Whipping or corporal punishment is the physical chastisement of a convicted offender. Though rarely used by our courts, it is one of the non-custodial disposition methods in our statute books. Under the Penal Code applicable in the northern part of Nigeria, it is called "Haddi lashing" and applies only to offenders of the Muslim faith. Men and women over 45 years cannot be caned.

The ACJ Act did not make provisions for corporal punishment but the ACJL Enugu retained whipping as a sentencing measure for juvenile offenders under Chapter 36. No juvenile offender shall be sentenced to be

[46] Section 324 ACJA.

[47] Sections 478–483 ACJL Enugu.

whipped more than once for the same offence and no sentence of whipping shall be passed on any female or on any male other than a juvenile offender. Whipping shall be with a light cane or birch or whip, and the number of strokes shall be specified in the sentence and shall not exceed twelve. Where a juvenile offender is convicted of one or more offences at one trial the total number of strokes awarded shall not exceed twelve.[48]

Some criminologists have recommended the abolition of caning as a form of punishment as it is considered more retributive than deterrent or reformative. There are also some human rights concerns about whipping. Whereas countries like the UK and America have stopped its use, it is still applicable in Singapore, Malaysia, Pakistan, etc. Nevertheless, it is posited that whipping is still a relevant and desirable sentencing measure for juveniles especially in Nigeria where there are very few penal facilities for juvenile reformation and the prison conditions are still far below recommended human rights and international standards.

4.6 *Binding Over*

The essence of binding over is to enhance peace and orderliness in the community. The court may bind over the complainant or defendant, or both or any of them, with or without a surety or sureties, to be of good behaviour, and may order any person so bound, in default or compliance with the order, to be imprisoned for any term not exceeding three months or one year for indictable offences, in addition to any other punishment to which such person is liable.[49]

Binding over can be applied in minor offences such as environmental sanitation offences, street fighting, street trading, etc. as it saves the prison of the possibility of more congestion and at the same time, does not add to the state financial burden of prisoner maintenance.

4.7 *Parole*

Parole is the conditional release of a person convicted of a crime prior to the expiration of that person's term of imprisonment, subject to continued supervision and monitoring as well as compliance with certain

[48] Sections 478–480 ACJL, Enugu.

[49] S. 369 ACJA and S 212 ACJL Enugu.

terms and conditions for a specified period. Parole may be granted on medical or compassionate grounds. Section 468 of the ACJ Act 2015 introduced parole.

The Comptroller General of Prisons is authorized by Section 268 ACJ Act to make a report to the court recommending that a person sentenced and serving his sentence in prison is of good behaviour, and has served at least one-third of his prison term if he is sentenced to a term of imprisonment, or at least 15 years if he is sentenced to life imprisonment, the court may order after hearing the prosecution and the prisoner or his legal representative, order that the remaining term of his imprisonment be suspended, with or without conditions.

4.8 Confiscation and Forfeiture

Forfeiture is a type of punishment and criminal disposition measure. It is the loss or confiscation of one's property in consequence of a crime or breach of obligation. Asset forfeiture laws allow for the seizure and eventual forfeiture of property connected with criminal activity.[50] Confiscation and forfeiture are designed to weaken the economic foundations of the illicit activity.

Confiscation and forfeiture are essential law enforcement tools. Provisions on forfeiture or on confiscation and forfeiture of proceeds of crime are embedded in various legislation enacted to fight corruption.

Adedeji Adekunle has identified three forms of penal forfeiture or confiscation.[51] They include:

1. Forfeiture of proceeds or assets acquired through proceeds derived from the offence for which the offender is convicted.
2. Forfeiture calculated by reference to the benefit derived by the convict from the offence.
3. Forfeiture of all traceable assets of the convicted person.

[50] Ani C. C. "Criminological Foundations of Forfeiture-Including Types of Forfeiture Regimes". Paper presented at the Nigerian Institute of Advanced Legal Studies (NIALS) Training Workshop on Seizure and Forfeiture of the Proceeds of Crime, 26–29 October, 2015.

[51] A. Adekunle, "Seizure of Proceeds of Criminal Activity: in Recent Financial Crimes Legislation in Nigeria", in *Modern Practice Journal of Financial and Investment Law*, Vol. 3 No.2, 1999, pp. 253–254.

Besides the deterrent effect of this form of punishment, it is also targeted at making the crime unattractive by ripping the offender of the benefits of the crime, thereby incapacitating the offender financially.[52]

Section 27 of the Economic and Financial Crimes Commission (EFCC) Act[53] requires a person arrested for committing an offence under the Act to make a full disclosure of all his assets and properties by completing an Assets Declaration Form. Section 28 further provides that where a person is arrested for an offence under the Act, the Commission shall immediately trace and attach all the assets and properties of the person acquired as a result of such economic or financial crime and shall thereafter cause to be obtained an interim attachment order from the court.[54]

From the wordings of this provision, it is clear that the Commission is empowered to trace, and attach the assets of a person who is alleged to have committed an offence, once the person has been placed under arrest. The section also adopts the use of the word *immediately,* implying that it is instant.[55] Sections 37 (1), 45 and 46 of the ICPC Act also deal on non-conviction-based confiscation, while Section 47 of the ICPC Act is on prosecution/conviction-based confiscation and forfeiture.[56] Section 333 ACJA and Section 484 ACJL Enugu are on confiscation and forfeiture of property.

4.9 Suspended Sentence

Suspended sentence involves the imposition of a definite sentence, usually, that of imprisonment, which is suspended for a specified period, invariably on the condition that the offender will be of good behaviour and will

[52] Ibid., p. 252.

[53] *Cap El,* Laws *of the Federation of Nigeria 2004.*

[54] See *Ani C. C.* Ani Comfort Chinyere, *Tools for Effective Prosecution of Corruption and Related Cases, in B. Owasanoye, S. Akinrinade and E. O. Okebukola (Eds.) ICPC and the War Against Corruption in Nigeria, (Anti Corruption Academy of Nigeria, 2020)* pp. 337–338.

[55] Ani C. C, "Emerging Trends on the Presumption of Innocence and the Right to Silence in Nigeria", *University of Benin Journal of Private and Property Law,* 2010, Vol. 1, No. 1, pp. 1–26.

[56] See *Ani C. C.* Ani Comfort Chinyere, *Tools for Effective Prosecution of Corruption and Related Cases,* op. cit. note 54, p. 341.

not commit any crime during the period of suspension. The Administration of Criminal Justice (ACJ) Act 2015 introduced suspended sentence. Where the court sees reason, it may order that the sentence it imposed on the convict be with or without conditions, suspended, in which case the convict shall not be required to serve the sentence in accordance with the conditions of such suspension if any.[57]

The court may, with or without conditions, sentence the convict to perform specified service in his community or such community or place as the court may direct.[58] Suspended sentence order is not to be made for an offence involving the use of arms or offensive weapon, or for an offence in which the punishment exceeds imprisonment for a term of three years. In making the order, the court shall have regard to the need to reduce congestion in prisons; need to rehabilitate prisoners by making them to undertake productive work; and need to prevent convicts who commit simple offences from mixing with hardened criminals.

4.10 Recognizance

When a person is convicted of any offence the court may, instead of passing sentence, release the offender upon his entering into his own recognizance, with or without sureties, in such sum as the court may think fit, on the condition that he shall appear and receive sentence at some future sitting of the court or when called upon.[59]

4.11 Probation

Probation is a widely used non-custodial sentencing option all over the world. It has a long and deeply rooted tradition in Common Law countries where the sanction is commonly applied, mostly upon a discretionary decision by a prosecutor or a judge.[60] Probation is a non-custodial court

[57] Section 460 ACJ Act and Sect. 469 ACJL Enugu.

[58] Section 469 (2) ACJL.

[59] Section 454 ACJ Act and Section 393 of ACJ Law Enugu.

[60] M. Day, Alternatives *to Custodial Sentencing A Manual for the Implementation of Community Service Orders in the O.E.C.S.* Available at: http://74.6.238.254/search/srpcache?ei=UTF-8&p=non+custodial+sentencing+options&xa=Nk9uAakW.xjA.qE0qN.TAw--%2C1290905265&fr=yfp-t-701

sanction by which a juvenile or adult defendant, who has been adjudicated or found guilty of an offence, is diverted from commitment to a juvenile or adult correctional institution and released, subject to certain conditions imposed by the court and under the supervision of a probation officer.[61]

Offenders who are placed on probation are set at liberty conditional upon their being of good behaviour. They are usually required to enter into a "bond" or "recognizance", which incorporates certain conditions for their release. If they breach a condition of their bond, they may be called up by the court for re-sentencing. Supervised probation requires an offender to be placed under the supervision of a probation officer. Probation includes restrictions on their personal freedom, with opportunities and assistance for them to address problems and issues associated with their offending behaviour. It can incorporate reparation by requiring the offender to make financial amends to the victim and/or undertake work or service of benefit to the victim or community.[62]

Probation as a punishment offers the opportunity of rehabilitation and reintegration into the community without the social and family disruption caused by imprisonment. This is particularly true of juvenile supervision. Statutory provisions for probationary sentences have always existed in our statutes, but regrettably, except for juveniles, our Judges and Magistrates hardly make use of it.

4.12 Deportation

Where a defendant is convicted of an offence punishable by imprisonment without the option of a fine, the court may, in addition to, or instead of any other punishment make a recommendation to the Minister of Interior that the convict be deported, where it appears to the court to be in the interest of peace, order and good governance.[63]

[61] Ibid.

[62] Available at: http://www.scotborders.gov.uk/criminaljustice/nationalobjectives/cj/standards/htm/typesofprobationorder.html Accessed on 2/12/2020.

[63] Sections 439 and 440 ACJ Act. By Section 439, "deported" means the deportation from Nigeria of a person not being a citizen, to his country.

4.13 Rehabilitation and Correctional Orders

This stems from rehabilitation as one of the objectives of sentencing as stated in Section 401 of the ACJ Act. Under the provisions of Section 467 (1) ACJ Act and Section 476 ACJL Enugu, a defendant convicted of an offence triable summarily may be sentenced and ordered to serve the sentence at a Rehabilitation and Correctional Centre in lieu of imprisonment. A court in making an order of confinement at a Rehabilitation and Correctional Centre shall have regard to the age of the convict; the fact that the convict is a first offender; and any other relevant circumstances necessitating an order of confinement at a Rehabilitation and Correctional Centre.[64] The order may be used for children.[65]

4.14 Plea Bargain

Plea bargain is one of Nigeria's attempts at extending the concept of restorative justice within the criminal justice system. Plea bargaining is a concept that originated in the US and has evolved to become a prominent feature of American criminal justice.[66] It has also spread to the UK, Canada and many other jurisdictions. It is a process whereby a person accused of a crime pleads guilty to a specified charge in return for an agreed sentence, recommended to the judge, or the dismissal or reduction of other charges. Typically, defence counsel and the prosecutor negotiate the charges to be brought. If the bargain pertains to the sentence to be meted out, a judge may also participate unless barred from doing so.[67]

Under the provision guiding plea bargain in Section 270 (4) (a), of the ACJ Act, the prosecutor and the defendant or his legal practitioner may only enter into an agreement in respect of the term of the plea bargain, amongst other things, only after consultation with the police responsible for the investigation of the case and the victim or his representative.

[64] Section 476 (2) ACJL Enugu.

[65] Section 467 (3) and Section 476 (3) ACJL Enugu.

[66] Rosie A. Joseph, "Plea Bargaining a Means to an End" Available at: www.manupatra.com/roundup/326/Articles/Plea%20bargaining.pdf.

[67] Oxford Companion to the Supreme Court, available at: http://www.answers.com/topic/plea-bargain. See generally, Ani C. C, ''Plea Bargain: Immunity from Punishment?'', in Epiphany Azinge and Laura Ani (Eds.) *Plea Bargaining*, (NIALS, 2012), p. 271.

The prosecutor is also mandated in determining whether it is in the public interest to enter into a plea bargain, to weigh all relevant factors, including *inter alia,* the defendant's willingness to make restitution or pay compensation to the victim where appropriate.[68]

The prosecution is to afford the victim or his representative the opportunity to make representations to the prosecutor regarding:

1. the content of the agreement; and
2. The inclusion in the agreement of a compensation or restitution order.[69]

The presiding Judge or Magistrate is mandated to make an order that any money, asset or property agreed to be forfeited under the plea bargain is transferred to the victim or his representative or any other person as may be appropriate or reasonably feasible.[70] The prosecutor on his part is enjoined to take reasonable steps to ensure that any money, asset or property agreed to be forfeited or returned by the offender under a plea bargain is transferred to or vested in the victim, his representative or other person lawfully entitled to it.[71]

5 Conclusion

There are abundant legal provisions both internationally and domestically mandating criminal justice practitioners to adopt restorative justice processes and non-custodial sentences as viable alternatives to the wholly retributive model of justice. Restorative sentences when applied along with other non-institutional disposition measures meet the purposes of sentencing. They can no longer be disregarded as they hold the offender accountable to the harm done, while assuaging the victim of crime in a more meaningful way.

Courts are to ensure that pre-trial detention is considered only under rare circumstances, such as when an individual has made credible, serious

[68] Section 270 (4) (b) (ix) of the ACJ Act 2015.

[69] Section 270 (5) ibid.

[70] Section 270 (11) ibid.

[71] Section 270 (12) ACJ Act.

threats of violence or flight from prosecution. The use of imprisonment as a substitute for non-payment of fines should be stopped.

Imprisonment should be used only in respect of those who are really dangerous, and from which the society needs to be protected. The Correctional Services has established the non-custodial departments but the courts are yet to take cognizance of that in their sentencing. This has kept the newly established department in the various prisons redundant.

The Chief Judges in the various States in Nigeria are to establish Community Service Centres in the various jurisdictions in the States without further delay and also encourage the Judges and Magistrates to apply community service and other restorative and non-custodial sentencing measures.

It is important to train Judges, Magistrates and Prosecutors on restorative justice and non-custodial measures. The victims, offenders and lawyers are to be encouraged to embrace restorative justice as it is beneficial to the victim, offender and society. They are also viable tools for prison decongestion particularly in this COVID-19 era.

There is need for synergy and collaboration between the Correctional Service, the courts and the police/law enforcement agencies/prosecutors for effective implementation of the restorative and non-custodial measures.

CHAPTER 5

Principle of Responsibility to Protect: Implications for Sovereignty

Eustace C. Azubuike

1 Introduction

Perhaps the most evident changing dimension of international law is in its principles, one of which is sovereignty. Here, there are two opposing views: the one contends that, as a corollary to the principle of sovereignty, the principle of non-interference should be maintained, which requires that practices within the sphere of a state should not be the concern of the international community. The other proposes that, with the increase in gross violations of the human rights of citizens by their states, the idea of absolute sovereignty should be jettisoned, thus allowing the international community, in appropriate cases, to interfere in the domestic affairs of a state, for example, on humanitarian grounds. This second position has led to the development of the principle of Responsibility to Protect (R2P), a principle that is seen as a growing norm in international law. This chapter examines the implications, of the Responsibility to Protect, for sovereignty.

E. C. Azubuike (✉)
Golden Gate University School of Law, San Francisco, CA, USA

E. Duruigbo et al. (eds.), *International Law and Development in the Global South*, https://doi.org/10.1007/978-3-031-13741-9_5

The chapter is divided into five sections. Section 1 offers a general introduction to the work. Section 2 discusses sovereignty as the pivot of international law. It examines the Peace of Westphalia as it affects sovereignty in international law. Equally explored in this section are the principles of equality of states and non-interference, which are constituents of sovereignty. Section 3 touches upon the early tensions that existed between the principle of non-interference and human rights. It examines the status of human rights during medieval and pre-World War era, and under the regime of the United Nations (UN). It also traces the evolution of the principle of Responsibility to Protect. Section 4 is devoted to the implications of the Responsibility to Protect on sovereignty. A conclusion follows in Sect. 5. The chapter concludes that the principle of responsibility to protect is a qualification of sovereignty, and not an abrogation of it. It also canvasses the view that, although it is considered a new norm, the responsibility to protect appears to have been in existence since the coming into effect of the UN Charter. This is because it would seem to be covered in the wide interpretation given to the powers of the Security Council under Chapter VII of the UN Charter.

2 Sovereignty as a Bedrock Principle of International Law

2.1 *Treaties of Westphalia*

It has been remarked that: "[i]n spite of the abhorrence one might have for the concept of sovereignty, it is still with us. State sovereignty remains basically the cornerstone of international law, in spite of certain important limitations which have come to restrict its scope…"[1] Sovereignty is not a new concept in international law, yet its real meaning has so much been debated.[2] The meaning attributed to the concept has largely depended

[1] See Donat Pharand, *Perspectives on Sovereignty in the Current Context: A Canadian Viewpoint*, 20 Can.-U.S. L. J. 19, 19 (1994).

[2] See Kalmo & Skinner, Eds., SOVEREIGNTY IN FRAGMENTS: THE PAST, PRESENT, AND FUTURE OF A CONTESTED CONCEPT, 1 (2010). Sovereignty has variously been defined as: (1) a personalized monarch (real or ritualized), (2) absolute, unlimited control or power, (3) political legitimacy, (4) political authority, (5) self-determined, national independence, (6) governance and constitutional order, (7) criterion of jurisprudential validation of all law, (8) juridical personality of sovereign equality, (9) international recognition, (10) formal unit of a legal system, (11) legal immunities,

on its user and the intended objectives of the user.[3] The formal origins of sovereignty, and, in fact, international law, are traced to the period of the Peace of Westphalia, which was achieved by the conclusion of the Treaties of Westphalia.[4] Prior to this period, that is, during the Middle Ages, sovereignty resided with the Catholic Church, which was headed by the Pope as a representative of God.[5] Every other power, including feudal and monarchical authority, was derived from the Church, which was seen as the repository of the ultimate and unchallengeable sovereignty of God.[6] This concept of sovereignty is believed to have been devoid of any connection to territory, but rather it was concerned with relationships involving individuals.[7] However, with time, European monarchs and feudal lords started to assume and exercise powers that were parallel to, and independent of, the authority of the Church. Besides, there was the Protestant movement, which had challenged the authority of the Pope. The result was a power struggle, both religious and secular in nature[8] that culminated in a thirty-year war[9] with devastating effects on many

and (12) the jurisdictional competence to make and/ or apply law. See Winston P. Nagan, FRSA & Craig Hammer, *The Changing Character of Sovereignty in International Law and International Relations*, 43 Colum. J. Transnat'l L. 141, 143–145 (2004).

[3] See W. Michael Reisman, *Sovereignty and Human Rights in Contemporary International Law*, 84 Am. J. Int'l L. 866, 866 (1990).

[4] See Tom Ginsburg, *Eastphalia As the Perfection of Westphalia*, 17 Ind. J. Global Legal Stud. 27, 29 (2010); Victoria Tin-bor Hui, *Toward a Confucian Multicultural Approach to a Liberal World Order: Insights from Historical East Asia*, 99 Am. Soc'y Int'l L. Proc. 413, 413 (2005) This view has been described as Eurocentric considering the fact that other civilizations, in their works, have articulated the concept of sovereignty. See Sophie Clavier, *Contrasting Franco-American Perspectives on Sovereignty*, 14 Ann. Surv. Int'l & Comp. L 1, 4 (2008).

[5] See Clavier, *supra*, note 4, at 4–5.

[6] Ibid; & at 6.

[7] See Ronald A. Brand, *Sovereignty: The State, the Individual, and the International Legal System in the Twenty First Century*, 25 Hastings Int'l & Comp. L. Rev. 279, 281, 285 (2002).

[8] See Stephen Carley, *Limping Toward Elysium: Impediments Created by the Myth of Westphalia on Humanitarian Intervention in the International Legal System*, 41 Conn. L. Rev. 1741, 1745 (2009).

[9] The War was fought between 1618 and 1648. See Daniel Albahary, *International Human Rights and Global Governance: The End of National Sovereignty and the Emergence of a Suzerain World Polity?*, 18 Mich. St. J. Int'l L. 511, 521 (2010).

European countries.[10] The cessation of the war was achieved with the conclusion of the two treaties which constitute the Peace of Westphalia.[11]

The Peace of Westphalia gave sovereignty a new meaning, and stripped it of its divine connotation. In fact, it secularized sovereignty, a position reflected in the writings of Thomas Hobbes.[12] Sovereignty thus moved from the Church to the state, thereby vesting the state with some basic rights expressed in principles such as sovereign immunity, equality of states, non-interference and territorial integrity.[13] The treaties laid down the framework for the practice of sovereignty without necessarily mentioning the words sovereign state.[14] With this new order, the European world was able to fashion out its first European Constitution,[15] and the "verticality of the political-religious relations of the Middle Ages gives way, in the international scene, to the formal horizontality between

[10] Franca Filho has this to say of the war: "The Thirty Years' War represented a titanic conflict between the rival dynasties of Bourbon (France) and Hapsburg (lords of Spain and of the Holy Roman Empire, with territories in Austria, Bohemia, the Netherlands, Bavaria, north of Italy, Belgium and Hungary) for the domain of continental Europe. Few military conflicts in History have caused such devastation to the civilian population. It is estimated that at least half of the German and Bohemian people lost their lives... It was the greatest catastrophe of the German people: the country came out of it extremely poor, undeveloped and politically divided into small princedoms, ruled in the north by mean Lutheran rulers and in the south by neglectful Catholic prelates, while in the few larger States absolutism was established in the French way." See Marcilio Toscano Franca Filho, *Westphalia: A Paradigm? A Dialogue between Law, Art and Philosophy of Science*, 8 German L. J. 955, 958 (2007).

[11] The Treaty of Osnabruck ("between the Holy Roman Emperor and German Princes with the Protestant Queen of Sweden") and "the Treaty of Munster with the Catholic King of France". See Carley, *supra*, note 8, at 1745–1746; Franca Filho, supra, note 10, at 965. Osnabruck and Munster are located in modern day Germany.

[12] See Michael J. Kelly, *Pulling at the Threads of Westphalia: "Involuntary Sovereignty Waiver"- Revolutionary International Legal Theory or Return to Rule by the Great Powers?*, 10 UCLA J. Int'l L. & Foreign Aff. 361, 374–375 (2005), citing THOMAS HOBBES, LEVIATHAN (Richard Tuck, ed, 1991) (1651). The author argues that with the emergence of the Peace of Westphalia, both the Pope and the European monarchs could no longer lay claim to the supernatural as the source of their authority.

[13] See Kelly, *supra*, note 12, at 376; Ginsburg, *supra*, note 4, at 29.

[14] See Anthony Sammons, *The "Under-Theorization" of Universal Jurisdiction: Implications for Legitimacy on Trials of War Criminals by National Courts*, 21 Berkeley J. Int'l L. 111, 116 (2003).

[15] See Franca Filho, *supra*, note 10, at 966.

the States, with intense individual character."[16] This new sovereignty, as reflected in the treaties, became known as the Westphalian sovereignty,[17] and set the boundaries of the authority of the Emperor and the kings.[18]

In the words of Janis:

> The Peace of Westphalia legitimated the right of sovereigns to govern their peoples free of outside interference... The two 1648 peace treaties elaborated in great detail which sovereign ruled what. The Peace... most significantly inaugurated... the organizing principle of the state, particularly the sovereign state. Sovereignty as a concept formed the cornerstone of the edifice of international relations that 1648 raised up... The treaties of Westphalia enthroned and sanctified sovereigns, gave them powers domestically and independence externally.[19]

The form of sovereignty ushered in by the Peace of Westphalia was virtually absolute. However, as would be revealed later, in recent times, the idea of absolute sovereignty is becoming unpopular in view of human rights and humanitarian concerns. An examination of some of the tenets of sovereignty follows.

2.2 *Equality of States in International Law*

The principle of equality of states is at the center of international law and international relations. In its political, as well as legal, sense, the principle originated from the works of ancient writers and philosophers such as Cicero, who predicated the existence of liberty on its availability to everyone,[20] and Rousseau, who had identified two forms of inequality: (1) natural inequality, which, according to him is brought by nature and manifests in differences in age, health, bodily strength, and the qualities of the mind or of the soul, and (2) political inequality, which is

[16] See Franca Filho, *supra*, note 10, at 969.

[17] See John H. Jackson, *Sovereignty- Modern: A New Approach to an Outdated Concept*, 97 Am. J. Int'l L. 782, 786 (2003).

[18] See Viet D. Dinh, *Nationalism in the Age of Terror*, 56 Fla. L. Rev. 867, 871 (2004).

[19] See Mark W. Janis, AN INTRODUCTION TO INTERNATIONAL LAW, 162, 4th ed. (2003), quoted in John Hilla, *The Literary Effect of Sovereignty in International Law*, 14 Widener L. Rev. 77, 112 (2008).

[20] See Cicero, DE REPUBLICA LIBER, I, 47.

the artifact of men.[21] Equality of states also derives from the natural equality of individuals,[22] as has been captured by Vattel, who believed that men are by nature equal and have the same individual rights and obligations. He further believed that states, as the composition of men, are by nature equal and are given the same rights and obligations.[23] In another sense, the principle of equality of states is an offspring of sovereignty since implicit in sovereignty is the idea that every state possesses the legal capacity to operate on the international plane on the same level as other states.[24] To this extent, the principle developed from the Peace of Westphalia, and has been in operation since that period. Thus, Pharand notes that following the Berlin Conference of 1885 and the two Hague Peace Conferences of 1899 and 1907, equality of states was manifested in the practice of one state one vote to adopt the unanimity rule when making decisions on substantive matters, and also under the League of Nations Covenant.[25] By implication, the notion of equality of states requires that states be treated similarly under international law irrespective of the degree of their political power or influence, although legal equality does not necessarily imply political equality.[26] As a foundation of international law, the principle of equality of states is reflected in the United Nations Charter. Precisely, Article 2(1) provides that "the Organization is based

[21] See, generally Rousseau, A DISSERTATION ON THE ORIGIN AND FOUNDATION OF THE INEQUALITY OF MANKIND, Ch. 1 (1754).

[22] The equality of individuals is littered all over international instruments, particularly those dealing with human rights. For examples, see Articles 1 and 7 of the Universal Declaration of Human Rights (Universal Declaration of Human Rights, G.A. Res. 217A (III), U.N. Doc A/810 at 71 (1948); Article 26 of the International Covenant on Civil and Political Rights (ICCPR) (International Covenant on Civil and Political Rights, 999 U.N.S.T. 171, December 16, 1966).

[23] See Ulrich K. PreuB, *Equality of States- Its Meaning in a Constitutionalized Global Order*, 9 Chi. J. Int'l L. 17 (2008), citing Emmerich De Vattel, THE LAW OF NATIONS OR THE PRINCIPLES OF NATURAL LAW: APPLIED TO THE CONDUCT AND TO THE AFFAIRS OF NATIONS AND OF SOVEREIGNS, 7, vol. 3 (James Brown Scott, ed.) (1916).

[24] See RH Steinberg, *Who Is Sovereign?*, 40 Stanford J. Int'l L. 329, 329 (2004). There is a close relationship between the degree of sovereignty a state has and the degree of equality it enjoys in international relations. See Kelly, *supra*, note 12, at 377, citing HENRY WHEATON, ELEMENTS OF INTERNATIONAL LAW, 33, 3rd ed. (1866).

[25] See Pharand, *supra* note 1, at 22.

[26] Pharand, ibid.

on the principle of the sovereign equality of all its Members." In compliance with this principle, each member of the General Assembly is entitled to one vote. Similarly, the Declaration on Principles of International Law Concerning Friendly Relations and Cooperation among States in Accordance with the Charter of the United Nations has a provision on equality of states.[27]

In reality, there are doubts that all states are equal, and that they have the same duties and the same rights. Thus, Kelsen has noted that such an assertion is not correct, and must be restricted to general international customary law.[28] He suggests a modification of the position that states are equal, and comes up with a new proposition.[29] Various labels have been used to categorize states in international law, which many times tend to underscore the fact that states are not truly equal. Such labels include: "failed states," "outlaw states," "great powers" ("superpowers, "hegemonic powers"), "weak states," "civilized states," "uncivilized states," "decent states," and "rogue states."[30] But it should be noted that these terms, in many situations, do not have a universal acceptance; rather they are adopted by those employing them to serve their own purpose.[31] There is an argument suggesting that a state may be denied equality with other states if that state fails in its international law obligation.[32] The validity of such view is challenged when one recalls that a breach by a state of its international obligation engages the responsibility of that

[27] See G.A. Res. 2625, UN GAOR, 25th Sess., Supp. No. 28. at 121, U.N. Doc. A/8028 (1970) (hereinafter Friendly Relations).

[28] He however notes that even under general international law, states do not have the same rights and duties. See Hans Kelsen, *The Principle of Sovereign Equality of States as a Basis for International Organization*, 53 Yale L. J. 207, 208–209 (1944).

[29] "According to general international law all the States have the same capacity of being charged with duties and of acquiring rights; equality does not mean equality of duties and rights, but rather equality of capacity for duties and rights. Equality is the principle that under the same conditions States have the same duties and the same rights." See ibid.

[30] See PreuB, *supra*, note 23, at 17–19; Mortimer Sellers, *Great Powers and Outlaw States: Unequal Sovereigns in the International Legal Order. By Gerry Simpson. Cambridge, New York: Cambridge University Press, 2004*, 99 Am. J. Int'l L. 949, 950 (2005).

[31] PreuB, ibid.

[32] Sellers, ibid.

state;[33] such responsibility is mainly satisfied through the making of reparation by the defaulting state for the injury caused by the breach, and not by a loss or abuse of its equality with other states. Perhaps, it is when such a state fails to make reparation that its equality with other states may be threatened.

The grant of a special favor or consideration by one state to another may be an illustration of the "inequality" among states as it amounts to discrimination which is inconsistent with the principle of equality. But it is said that mere differences of treatment do not amount to discrimination where the differentiation is based on reasonable and objective criteria, and the purpose is legitimate and the means employed are not disproportionate.[34] In other words, "discrimination occurs" where those who are, in all material respects, the same are treated differently, or where those who are in material respects different are treated in the same way.[35] The articulation of the principle of equality of states in the UN Charter is contradicted by the composition and operation of the Security Council.[36] This depicts the UN as giving substance to great power hegemony, while at the same time showing a mere rhetorical commitment to the equality of states.[37] On the whole, the principle of equality of states is only a legal construct, not a political reality.

2.3 Principle of NonIntervention in the Internal Affairs of States

The nonintervention principle holds that practices within the sphere of a state should not be the concern of international law. It therefore obligates

[33] See *Corfu Channel (United Kingdom v Albania)* 1949 I.C.J. 4, 43; *Factory at Chorzow (Germany v Poland)* 1927 P.C.I.J. (Ser. A) No. 9, 21.

[34] See Torkel Opasahl, *Equality in Human Rights Law with Particular Reference to Article 26 of the International Covenant on Civil and Political Rights*, in MANFRED NOWAK, ED FORTSHRITT IM BEWUBTSEIN DER GRUND- UND MENSCHENRECHTE: FUR FELIX ERMACORA, 55, 62 (1988).

[35] See Richard Plender, *Equality and Non-Discrimination in the Law of the European Union*, 7 Pace Int'l L. Rev. 57, 63 (1995).

[36] See generally Article 27 of the UN Charter, especially sub (3) on the veto power of the Permanent Members of the Security Council.

[37] See Sellers, *supra*, note 30, at 951.

states to refrain from interfering in the domestic affairs of other states.[38] The principle, which is a consequence of sovereignty, has been in existence since the seventeenth century, and has been embodied in many international instruments,[39] including the United Nations Charter,[40] where it is given a pride of place. The principle is equally present in resolutions of the General Assembly.[41] The International Court of Justice has also given it judicial recognition.[42] All this shows that nonintervention is considered a part of customary international law.[43] Though an important principle, it has not enjoyed an inviolability or non-qualification, and it may not be out of place to say that its exact boundaries are not settled. The UN Charter is seen to contain seeming contradiction and ambiguities that affect the connotation of the principle of nonintervention.[44] Article

[38] See Ravi Mahalingam, *The Compatibility of the Principle of Non Intervention with the Right of Humanitarian Intervention*, 1 UCLA J. Int'l L. & Foreign Aff. 221, 221 (1996).

[39] See e.g., Article 4 of the Constitutive Act of the African Union (Constitutive Act of the African Union, available at http://www.au2002.gov.za/docs/key_oau/au_act.htm); Article 21 of The Charter of Organization of American States (Charter of the Organization of American States, available at http://www.cidh.org/basicos/english/Basic22.Charter%20OAS.htm); Article 8 of the Charter of League of Arab States (Charter of the League of Arab States, available at http://www.docstoc.com/docs/83051528/The-Charter-of-the-Arab-League).

[40] See Article 2(4), (7) UN Charter. However, there is a proviso in 2 (7), namely that the principle of non intervention "shall not prejudice the application of enforcement measures under Chapter VII" of the Charter.

[41] See Friendly Relations, *supra*; note 27; Declaration on the Inadmissibility of Intervention in the Domestic Affairs of States and the Protection of Their Independence and Sovereignty, G.A. Res. 2131, UN GAOR, 20th Sess., Supp. No. 14, at 11, U.N. Doc. A/6014 (1965); Definition of Aggression, G.A. Res. 3314, U.N. GAOR, 29th Sess., Supp. No. 31, at 142, U.N. Doc. A/9631 (1974); Declaration on the Inadmissibility of Intervention and Interference in the Internal Affairs of States, G.A. Res. 36/103, U.N.GAOR, 36th Sess., 91 Plen. mtg., U.N. Doc. A/RES/36/103 (1981).

[42] See *Military and Paramilitary Activities in and Against Nicaragua (Nicaragua v. United States)* 1986 I.C.J. 14, 108 (hereinafter Nicaragua case); *Case Concerning Armed Activities on the Territory of the Congo (Congo v Uganda)* 2005 I.C.J. 116, 164–165.

[43] In the Nicaragua case, the I.C.J. observed that: "The principle of non intervention involves the right of every sovereign State to conduct its affairs without outside interference; though examples of trespass against this principle are not infrequent, the Court considers that it is part and parcel of customary international law. ..." See Nicaragua case, *supra*, note 42, paras. 202–204.

[44] See Eric S. O'Malley, *Destabilization Policy: Lessons from Reagan on International Law, Revolutions and Dealing with Pariah Nations*, 43 Va. J. Int'l L. 319, 329 (2003).

2(4), which prohibits the threat of or use of force by states "against the territorial integrity or political independence of any state..." has suffered some polysemy.[45] This has led states to proffer arguments to justify their unilateral interventions in other states, even where those arguments are clearly inconsistent with the purposes of the United Nations.[46] Article 2(4) is also considered to be incompatible with Article 1(2), which identifies the purposes of the United Nations to be, inter alia: "... to develop friendly relations among nations based on respect for the principle of equal rights and self-determination of peoples..."[47] Similarly, Article 2(7) has also been prone to controversy with a claim from some quarters that the wording of that provision suggests that it bars every form of intervention, whether on human rights ground or for any other purpose.[48] While this assertion may be defended if it were to apply under Article 2(4), it is objectionable, considering the caveat at the end of Article 2(7), that "this principle shall not prejudice the application of enforcement measures under Chapter VII," which in essence reinforces the Security Council's power to maintain or restore international peace and security.

It would thus appear that the only ground on which the UN, as a body, can derogate from the principle of nonintervention is when it is acting through the Security Council in the exercise of its enforcement powers, which must be tied to the maintenance or restoration of international peace and security. This position leaves the Security Council with too much, and, perhaps, unlimited, power to determine when there is a threat to international peace and security, and what amounts to a measure aimed at international peace and security.[49] The exercise of this Security

[45] See Eustace C. Azubuike, *Probing the Scope of Self Defense In International Law*, 17 Ann. Surv. Int'l & Comp. L. 129, 139–143 (2011) (providing some of the interpretations given to Article 2(4) of the UN Charter).

[46] Ibid.

[47] O'Malley, ibid.

[48] See Mahalingam, *supra*, note 38, at 244- 245.

[49] The wide powers of the Security Council under Chapter VII came to the fore in Prosecutor v Tadic. See *Prosecutor v Tadic*, Appeals Chamber, International Criminal Tribunal for the former Yugoslavia, 1992, Case No. IT-94-1-AR72, 35 I.L.M. 32 (1996). See also *Case Concerning Questions of Interpretation and Application of the 1971 Montreal Convention Arising from the Aerial Incident at Lockerbie (Libya v USA)*, 1992 WL 190214; 1992 I.C.J., 423, where Libya argued that the resolution passed by the Security Council following the Lockerbie bombing orchestrated by Libyan nationals, was ultra vires the Security Council under Chapter VII because there was no threat to the

Council's broad power may lead to serious abuses on the right to nonintervention. With respect to the relations of states, the only exception to the principle of nonintervention seems to be when a state is exercising its right to self-defense under Article 51, UN Charter. Any other form of intervention is unjustifiable.

Despite the foregoing, states have intervened in the affairs of other states when such intervention is consented to. This takes the form of assistance on request, particularly during internal armed conflicts. For example, an incumbent government of a state which is at war with rebel forces can seek the assistance of a foreign state so long as the requesting state remains in effective control of the state.[50] Such right of assistance does not accrue to rebel forces,[51] and if the assisted government loses its hold on power, thereby becoming ineffective, or if the rebel forces achieve a significant success in the armed conflicts, the rebel forces may be treated as belligerents. This would dis-entitle either party from seeking assistance from outside states.[52]

A more recent excuse making waves, for the breach of the principle of nonintervention, is the protection of human rights, or what is often called humanitarian intervention—a conception that has not been easy to articulate.[53] The legality of this trend is highly contested. On the one hand, the argument in support of humanitarian intervention holds that

peace warranting the passing of the resolution. Unfortunately, the ICJ did not have the opportunity to rule on the merits of the case.

[50] See David Wippman, *Change and Continuity in Legal Justifications for Military Intervention in Internal Conflict*, 27 Colum. Hum. Rts L. Rev. 435, 446 (1996).

[51] *See the Nicaragua case, supra*, note 42, at 126.

[52] See Wippman, *supra*, note 50, at 446, 447; Michael J. Mattler, *The Distinction Between Civil Wars and International Wars and Its Legal Implications*, 26 N.Y.U. J. Int'l L. & Pol. 655, 657 (1994).

[53] See Steve G. Simon, *The Contemporary Legality of Unilateral Humanitarian Intervention*, 24 Cal. W. Int'l L.J. 117, 119–120 (1993) (acknowledging the problem of defining humanitarian intervention, and also providing some of the definitions offered by writers). Humanitarian intervention has been limited to "those instances in which a nation unilaterally uses military force to intervene in the territory of another state for the purpose of protecting a sizable group of indigenous people from life-threatening or otherwise unconscionable infractions of their human rights that the national government inflicts or in which it acquiesces." See David J. Scheffer, *Toward a Modern Doctrine of Humanitarian Intervention*, 23 U. Tol. L. Rev. 253, 264 (1992) (citing Verwey, *Humanitarian Intervention Under International Law*, 32 Neth. Int'l L. Rev., 357, 367–375 (1985). It is "the use of force by a State or group of States against a target State in order to protect

the principle of nonintervention does not prohibit the use of force to stop the violation of human rights since the concept of state jurisdiction is not a license for states to breach the human rights of their citizens.[54] This argument is countered by an opposing view, which canvasses firmly the argument that the right to humanitarian intervention does not exist under international law. Besides, such right is not specifically granted by the UN Charter.[55] There is yet a middle position that legitimizes humanitarian intervention only to the extent that it is employed to achieve a positive result.[56] Humanitarian intervention, if it did exist before the Cold War, was minimally used. Major discussions of humanitarian intervention in the international arena started with the end of the Cold War.[57] Thus, in the recent period, there have been instances where states intervened in the affairs of other states and sought to justify their actions on the need to protect the human rights of people. In 1991, there was an allied intervention in Iraq[58]; the North Atlantic Treaty Organization's (NATO's) elaborate intervention in Yugoslavia in 1999 was purportedly premised on human rights concerns even when NATO did not receive the prior endorsement of the Security Council.[59] There is evidence that the only form of humanitarian intervention that has legitimacy is collective intervention authorized by the Security Council, and

the citizens of the target State from inhumane or cruel treatment at the hands of the sovereign." See Mahalingam, *supra*, note 38, at 226.

[54] See Mattler, *supra*, note 52, at 682 (citing Fernando R. Teson, HUMANITARIAN INTERVENTION, 205–221 (1988); Sellers, *supra*, note 30, at 73.

[55] Mattler, *supra*, note 52, at 681- 683. Objections to humanitarian intervention have been metaphorically premised on the fact that it would be abused if allowed, since its proponents would fail to "device a means that is both conceptually and instrumentally credible to separate the few sheep of legitimate humanitarian intervention from the herds of goats which can too easily slip through." See Thomas M. Franck & Nigel S. Rodley, *After Bangladesh: The Law of Humanitarian Intervention by Military Force*, 67 Am. J. Int'l L. 275, 284 (1973), quoted in Dino Kritsiotis, *Reappraising Policy Objections to Humanitarian Intervention*, 19 Mich. J. Int'l L. 1005, 1020 (1998).

[56] See Henry Hodges, THE DOCTRINE OF INTERVENTION, 87–96 (1915), cited in Mahalingam, *supra*, note 38, at 227.

[57] See Kelly, *supra*, 12, at 395–397 (stating that humanitarian intervention is a product of post Cold War).

[58] See Scheffer, *supra*, note 53, at 268.

[59] See Kelly, *supra*, note 12, at 397.

that unilateral humanitarian intervention by states cannot be justified.[60] Therefore, any state that forces itself into the territory of another constitutes itself into a meddlesome interloper, and such is against the principle of nonintervention.

3 Early Tensions Between Principle of NonIntervention and Human Rights

3.1 *Status of Human Rights in Medieval and Pre-World War Era*

The idea of human rights in the medieval period was a carryover of the writings of the earlier centuries, when human rights were discussed under natural rights by natural law thinkers. Even though these rights had been identified as inherent in people as a result of their birth, there seemed to have been more concern for orderly government than for human rights.[61] The situation did not change much during the period preceding the end of the first half of the twentieth century. Consequently, the issue of human rights was not on the front burner.[62] This was due to the Westphalian sovereignty, which had come to be viewed in absolute terms. States could not allow any interference with their sovereignty on any ground at all. Thus, the principle of non-interference overshadowed human rights protection such that "[a]s long as states persecuted only their own citizens, there was little that other states could do legally to stop the violence."[63] In this period, in the face of human rights violations by governments, the citizens knew they could not look to the outside

[60] See Jianming Shen, *The Non-Intervention Principle and Humanitarian Interventions under International Law*, 7 Int'l Legal Theory 1, 19–20 (2001).

[61] See Brian Tierney, *The Idea of Natural Rights: Origins and Persistence*, 2 Nw. U. J. Int'l Hum. Rts 2 (2004), available at http://www.law.northwestern.edu/journals/jihr/v2/2/2.pdf.

[62] Perhaps it is this observation that is reflected in the words of Baxi, when he notes that: "Much of the Twentieth Century, especially its later half, will be recalled as an "Age of Human Rights." No preceding century of human history has been privileged to witness a profusion of human rights enunciations on a global scale. Never before have the languages of human rights sought to supplant all other ethical languages." See Upendra Baxi, *Voices of Suffering and the Future of Human Rights*, 8 Transnat'l L. & Contemp. Probs. 125, 125 (1998).

[63] See William Magnuson, *The Responsibility to Protect and the Decline of Sovereignty: Free Speech Protection Under International Law*, 43 Vand. J. Transnat'l L. 225, 258 (2010).

world for help.[64] They only hoped that their governments would be touched by the appeal to universal morality.[65] No wonder that those who perpetrated the killings of the Armenians, and the massacre in Czarist Russia and Romania did so with impunity.[66] Human rights were relegated to the background during the pre-World War period because of the deference given to state sovereignty. However, this was to change by the Nuremberg trials,[67] and under the United Nations regime.

3.2 *Status of Human Rights Under the UN Era*

With the end of the Second World War, the principle of nonintervention and the inviolability of sovereignty suffered much relaxation in the midst of a shift in emphasis to the protection of human rights.[68] The international community had to universalize the idea of human rights in order to avoid a repeat of the atrocities of the Holocaust. This was to mark the beginning of a new world order, and when the UN Charter was signed in 1945, it recognized the importance of human rights in Article 1(3), which states that one of the purposes of the United Nations is to achieve "international cooperation in… promoting and encouraging respect for human rights and for fundamental freedoms for all without distinction as to race, sex, language, or religion."[69] In addition, Articles 55 and 56 commit the UN member states (and indeed all other states), and the organization to the achievement of the purpose of the UN Charter with respect to human rights.[70] It is however not settled whether or not these UN Charter provisions confer rights on individuals and whether they are legally binding or not.[71] The inability of states to agree to the inclusion of

[64] See Thomas C. Buergenthal, *The Human Rights Revolution*, 23 St. Mary's L.J. 3, 5 (1991).

[65] *Id.*

[66] *Id.*

[67] See Ronald A. Christaldi, *International Human Rights by Jack Donnelly, Westview Press, Boulder: 1993 PG. 206*, 6 J. Transnat'l L. & Pol'y 571, 573–574 (1997).

[68] See Magnuson, *supra* note 63, at 259; Albahary, *supra* note 9, at 514–515.

[69] Article 1(3), UN Charter.

[70] See Lori F. Damrosch, et al., INTERNATIONAL LAW: CASES AND MATERIALS, 957–958 (2009).

[71] Two schools of thought have emerged in this respect. The one argues that the provisions do not create an obligation on states, and that what the provisions confer

an international bill of rights in the UN Charter during the negotiations leading to its adoption resulted in the drafting of the Universal Declaration of Human Rights.[72] Although the Declaration was not intended to be a binding law, in recent times, some of its provisions have been given some measure of legal character.[73] Since the Declaration, the seeds of human rights have sprouted and have blossomed, as evidenced by the numerous human rights treaties on the international plane,[74] laced with UN declarations on various aspects of human rights.[75] It is evident from the foregoing that, unlike in the past, human rights have gained primacy in the twenty-first century.

3.3 *Principle of Responsibility to Protect: Evolution*

The doctrine of responsibility to protect can be viewed as a culmination of the efforts of international law to not allow sovereignty impede the realization of human rights. It is seen as the answer to the incongruity of reconciling respect for sovereignty with the necessity of protecting municipal populations from violations of their human rights by their own government.[76] As far back as the period following the end of World War II, concerns became rife for states to defend humanity from the absoluteness of sovereignty. For instance, the Appellate Chamber of the International Criminal Tribunal for the former Yugoslavia had noted that: "[i]t would be a travesty of law and a betrayal of the universal need for justice, should the concept of State sovereignty be allowed to be raised

on individuals are benefits, not rights. See H. Kelsen, THE LAW OF THE UNITED NATIONS, 29 (1950); J. G. Starke, INTERNATIONAL LAW, 350 (1984). The other maintains that the provisions are legally binding on states. See Philip Jessup, A MODERN LAW OF NATIONS, 91 (1949); EZEJIOFOR, PROTECTION OF HUMAN RIGHTS, 113 (1962); Schwelb, *The International Court of Justice and the Human Rights Clause of the Charter*, 66 A.J.I.L. 337 (1972).

[72] See Buergenthal, *supra*, note 64, at 7.

[73] See Albahary, *supra*, note 9, at 528.

[74] See, for example, ICCPR, supra, note 22; International Covenant on Economic, Social and Cultural Rights, 993 U.N.T.S. 3, December 16, 1966. (ICESCR). For some of the human rights instruments operating on regional level, see Lori F. Damrosch, et al., *supra*, note 70, Ch. 13.

[75] See Buergenthal, *supra*, note 64, at 8–9.

[76] See Christopher C. Joyner, *"The Responsibility to Protect": Humanitarian Concern and the Lawfulness of Armed Intervention*, 47 Va. J. Int'l L. 693, 708 (2007).

successfully against human rights. Borders should not be considered as a shield against the reach of the law and as a protection for those who trample underfoot the most elementary rights of humanity."[77] However, it was not until the 1990s and early 2000s that these concerns started to coalesce into a seeming norm.[78]

Moved by the events of Rwanda and Kosovo, the then UN Secretary-General, Kofi Anan had framed the big poser: "[I]f humanitarian intervention is, indeed, an unacceptable assault on sovereignty, how should we respond to a Rwanda, to a Sebrenica– to gross and systematic violations of human rights that offend every precept of our common humanity?"[79] In reaction to this poser which brings out the conflict between human rights and sovereignty, the Canadian government, in September 2000 established the International Commission on Intervention and State Sovereignty (ICISS) to "promote a comprehensive debate on the relationship between intervention and sovereignty, with a view to fostering global political consensus on how to move from polemics towards action within the international system."[80] ICISS, in 2001, issued a report, entitled "The Responsibility to Protect," which gave birth to the principle.[81] The message in the report is that due to the globalization of the world and the growing concern for human rights, the notion of sovereignty as control must change to sovereignty as responsibility.[82] "Sovereign states have a responsibility to protect their own citizens from avoidable catastrophe– from mass murder and rape, from starvation– but... when they are unwilling or unable to do so, that responsibility must be borne by

[77] See *Prosecutor v Tadic*, Decision on the Defense Motion for Interlocutory Appeal on Jurisdiction, 58 (October 2, 1995).

[78] Magnuson, *supra*, note 63, at 267.

[79] The Secretary-General, Millennium Report of the Secretary-General, We the People: The Role of the United Nations in the 21st Century, 48, U.N. Doc. A/54/2 (2000).

[80] See Emma McClean, *The Responsibility to Protect: The Role of International Human Rights Law*, 13 J. Conflict & Security L. 123, 127 (2008).

[81] See Mehrdad Payandeh, *With Great Power Comes Great Responsibility? The Concept of the Responsibility to Protect within the Process of International Lawmaking*, 35 Yale J. Int'l L. 469, 472 (2010); Lori F. Damrosch, et al., *supra*, note 70, at 1212.

[82] See Carlo Focarelli, *The Responsibility to Protect Doctrine and Humanitarian Intervention: Too Many Ambiguities for a Working Paper*, 13 J. Conflict & Security L. 191, 194 (2008).

the broader community of states."[83] With regard to humanitarian intervention, the report called for a shift from the "right to intervene" to the "responsibility to protect."[84] The report is made up of three propositions. The first is that the international community has a responsibility to prevent conflicts by addressing them before they escalate to full-fledged crisis; a responsibility to respond to crisis by taking appropriate measures, even if coercive; and a responsibility to rebuild after the occurrence of a crisis.[85] The report also recommends military intervention only when there is a just cause,[86] and such intervention must be in accordance with certain precautionary principles.[87] The report fails to take a clear position on the initiation of intervention without the authorization of the Security Council, noting, on the one hand, that the international order would be affected if the Security Council is bypassed, and on the other hand, that there would be damage to the international order if human beings are killed while the Security Council takes no action.[88]

The report of the ICISS was adopted by the Secretary-General's High-Level Panel on Threats, Challenges, and Change, *A More Secure World: Our Shared Responsibility*,[89] in 2004. The High-Level Panel is in agreement with the ICISS report that the state has a responsibility to cater to the needs of the people, and that where the state fails to do so, the international community has a responsibility to protect.[90] It identifies this

[83] See Int'l Comm'n on Intervention and State Sovereignty, The Responsibility to Protect, at VIII (2001) (hereinafter ICISS).

[84] See Payandeh, *supra*, note 81, at 472.

[85] Jonah Eaton, *Student Note an Emerging Norm? Determining the Meaning and Legal Status of the Responsibility to Protect*, 32 Mich. J. Int'l L. 765, 775 (2011).

[86] "Just cause" consists in interventions to prevent "large scale loss of life" or "large scale ethnic cleansing." See ICISS, supra, note 83, at XII.

[87] The elements that make up the precautionary principles which would regulate humanitarian intervention are (1) right intention, i.e., for the purpose of stopping human suffering; (2) last resort, i.e., all non military options have to be exhausted; (3) proportional means, ie, the scale, duration, and intensity of the response should be the minimum necessary; and (4) reasonable prospects, i.e., there must be a reasonable probability that the intervention would succeed. Ibid.

[88] See Payandeh, *supra*, note 81, at 474.

[89] High-Level Panel on Threats, Challenges, and Change, a More Secure World: Our Shared Responsibility, U.N. Doc. A/59/565 (December 2, 2004) (hereinafter High-Level Panel Report).

[90] See, generally, High-Level Panel Report, *supra*, note 89, pp. 29, 36, 202–203.

responsibility as an "emerging norm…," which includes both the right to intervene and the responsibility to protect when there is avoidable catastrophe.[91] In the Report, the UN is urged to adopt the emerging norm of the responsibility to protect in situations of "genocide and other large-scale killing, ethnic cleansing or serious violations of international law."[92] While reiterating the powers of the Security Council, under Chapter VII of the UN Charter, to act, when there is gross abuse of human rights, it calls on the permanent members to not veto any resolution that is intended to tackle genocide and gross human rights violations.[93] The report of the High-Level Panel is said to contain slight variations from the report of the ICISS.[94] However, both identify the Security Council as the most appropriate body to exercise the responsibility to protect.[95]

The responsibility to protect as articulated in the report of the ICISS also received attention in the report of the UN Secretary-General, titled, *In Larger Freedom: Towards Development, Security and Human Rights for All*,[96] in which it is observed that the idea of responsibility to protect should be embraced, and, when necessary, acted upon.[97] However, the emphasis is to apply the responsibility to protect through peaceful means, and not necessarily through military intervention, so that the ultimate purpose of promoting states' commitment to the rule of law and human security may be achieved.[98]

In 2005, the responsibility to protect was discussed at the World Summit, attended by heads of states and governments. The deliberation resulted in the *World Summit Outcome Document*,[99] which contains two

[91] See Carsten Stahn, *Responsibility to Protect: Political Rhetoric or Emerging Norm*, 101 Am. J. Int'l L. 99, 100 (2007).

[92] See Nicholas J. Wheeler, *A Victory for Common Humanity? The Responsibility to Protect After the 2005 World Summit*, 2 J. Int'l L. & Int'l Rel. 95, 98 (2005).

[93] See High-Level Panel Report, *supra*, note 89, pp 200, 202, 256.

[94] See McClean, *supra*, note 80, at 132.

[95] Ibid.

[96] U.N. Secretary-General, In Larger Freedom: Towards Development, Security and Human Rights for All, U.N. Doc. A/59/2005 (March 21, 2005) (hereinafter In Larger Freedom).

[97] In Larger Freedom, *supra*, note 96, p. 135.

[98] See Stahn, *supra*, note 91, at 107.

[99] 2005 World Summit Outcome, G.A. Res. 60/1, U.N. Doc. A/RES/60/1 (October 24, 2005) (hereinafter Outcome Document).

important provisions as guidelines for the application of the responsibility to protect. Paragraph 138, in part, states that "[e]ach individual State has the responsibility to protect its populations from genocide, war crimes, ethnic cleansing and crimes against humanity."[100] Under paragraph 139, the international community, represented by the United Nations, has the responsibility to help protect populations, through "diplomatic, humanitarian and other peaceful means in accordance with Chapters VI and VIII..." of the UN Charter.[101] There exist some differences between the responsibility to protect as espoused in the ICISS report and in the Outcome Document. For instance, while, under the former, what is needed to trigger the action of the international community is the failure or inability of a state to protect its citizens; under the latter, there has to be a manifest failure on the part of a state to protect its citizens in order to warrant outside intervention.[102] The responsibility to protect under the ICISS applies when there is "large scale loss of life," or "large scale ethnic cleansing," while its application under the Outcome Document is in respect of specific crimes.[103]

The adoption of the Outcome Document was greeted with some expression of relief, as is evident in the comment that "no longer is it necessary to finesse the tensions between sovereignty and human rights in the Charter; they can now be confronted. Sovereignty no longer implies the license to kill."[104] Since then, the responsibility to protect has received articulation in the Security Council,[105] and states, as well as regional organizations, have referenced it before international fora. However, it is doubtful if the principle has received a universal endorsement.[106]

[100] Outcome Document, *supra*, note 99, p. 138.

[101] Ibid., p. 139.

[102] See Alison McCormick, *From Sovereignty to Responsibility: An Emerging International Norm and Its Call to Action in Burma*, 18(1) Indiana Journal of Global Legal Studies 563, 571 (2011).

[103] See Payandeh, *supra*, note 81, at 476. For other differences between the two reports, see McCormick, ibid.

[104] See Eaton, *supra*, note 85, at 781 (citing Ramesh Thakur & Thomas G. Weiss, *R2P: From Idea to Norm– and Action*, 1 Global Res. To Protect 22, 23 (2009).

[105] See S.C. Res. 1674, P 4, U.N. Doc. S/RES/1674 (April 28, 2006).

[106] See Payandeh, *supra*, note 81, at 476, 477.

4 Implication of the Principle of Responsibility to Protect on Sovereignty

4.1 Is It a Qualification of Sovereignty?

In the context of the period of Westphalia, sovereignty empowered a state to exercise absolute control over its territory and citizens, and other states are restrained from interfering in a state's internal affairs.[107] Under this model of sovereignty, states are seen as the only subjects of international law. The implication of this is that, individuals, as objects of international law, can only derive their rights from the sovereignty of states.[108] However, this idea of sovereignty, if it has not lost popularity yet, is constantly losing popularity. The new thinking in international law is that states, as constituents of the international community, should observe the universal values upon which that community is founded, and any failure on their part to do so, would be a justification for interference with their sovereignty.[109] From the foregoing, it would mean that the responsibility to protect principle, which seeks to give the international community a mandate to interfere in the domestic affairs of a state, is a reflection of this new thinking, and is, therefore, a qualification of sovereignty. It is thus a shift from the traditional conception of sovereignty. However, it is argued that, there has never been a time sovereignty existed in absolute terms. Rather, sovereignty has always come with certain responsibilities.[110] But, a statement to the effect that states can no longer "hide behind the shield of sovereignty…"[111] goes to show that there was a time sovereignty was absolute. The responsibility to protect principle has reshaped state sovereignty, a confirmation of the fact that the period of

[107] See Joyner, *supra*, note 76, at 703.

[108] See Albahary, *supra*, note 9, at 522 (observing that traditional classical international law gave more emphasis on the inviolability of state borders than on the freedom of individuals).

[109] See Kelly, *supra*, note 12, at 399.

[110] See Payandeh, *supra*, note 81, at 486.

[111] See Payandeh, *supra*, note 81, at 485 (citing Ved P. Nanda, *The Protection of Human Rights Under International Law: Will the U.N. Human Rights Council and the Emerging New Norm Responsibility to Protect Make a Difference?*, 35 Denv. J. Int'l L. & Pol'y 353, 373 (2007).

absolute sovereignty in international law has come and gone.[112] It is thus not incorrect to say that the responsibility to protect is a qualification of sovereignty.

4.2 *Is It an Abrogation of Sovereignty?*

If the responsibility to protect can be viewed as a modification of sovereignty, then it cannot also be an abrogation of sovereignty. What the principle has done is to balance the sovereign power of a state with the protection of the human rights of its citizens. This is the reason the documents, espousing the responsibility to protect, not only have set parameters for its application, but also have identified the situations in which the principle can apply.[113] Any intervention in the internal affairs of a state by the international community that is outside the purview of the responsibility to protect would therefore be illegal under international law. Sovereignty is still the bedrock of international law, even though the question has been asked if sovereign state is withering away.[114] It has also been thought that if national sovereignty no longer holds supreme in international discourse that could mean the death of sovereignty.[115] An important concept such as sovereignty cannot be abrogated. Its qualification does not amount to its demise.

4.3 *Can It Be Construed as an Exercise of Sovereignty?*

From another angle, the responsibility to protect is considered a consequence, and not a demise of, sovereignty.[116] This is because as far back as the time of Grotius, sovereignty has always been associated with the

[112] See Lillich, *Sovereignty and Humanity: Can They Converge?*, in Grahl-Madsen & Toman, Eds, THE SPIRIT OF UPPSALA, 406, 406–407 (1984).

[113] For instance, under the ICISS report, responsibility to protect can be invoked when there is "large scale loss of life," or "large scale ethnic cleansing," while its application under the Outcome Document is limited to "genocide, war crimes, ethnic cleansing and crimes against humanity."

[114] See Lori F. Damrosch, et al., *supra*, note 70, at 27–28 (citing Schachter, *The Decline of the Nation-State and Its Implications for International Law*, 36 Colum. J. Transnat'l L. 7 (1997).

[115] See Albahary, *supra*, note 9, at 552.

[116] See McCormick, *supra*, note 102, at 573.

protection of the life and safety of the citizens.[117] The duty of a sovereign state is two-fold: internal and external. A state discharges its internal duty by guaranteeing and protecting the human rights of its citizens, while the external duty consists in respect for the sovereignty of other states.[118] Thus, the responsibility to protect would appear to be only reiterating this position. If the foregoing were correct, then there may be no basis to see national sovereignty and human rights as two opposing concepts, or to, as has been done elsewhere, give primacy to human rights over sovereignty.[119] Shen has therefore cautioned that the two concepts should not be seen as "enemies" struggling for superiority; rather their interaction should be complementary.[120] To this extent, the responsibility to protect can be viewed as an exercise of sovereignty.

5 Conclusion

If the responsibility to protect were to be considered an emerging norm in international law as has been articulated,[121] what would be the future of sovereignty in international law? But it is doubtful if the principle is actually a norm of customary law as it is yet to meet the preconditions for attaining the status of customary law norm. As expressed in the documents espousing it, the principle gives room for some objections. For example, there seems to be no agreement as to its contents. This was demonstrated in the 2009 debates of the Summit Outcome, where there was controversy over coercive military intervention. Besides, it is not clear whether the responsibility to protect is coterminous with, or different from, humanitarian intervention even though some academic discussions seem to conflate the two. The use of the word "responsibility" would suggest that the principle does not impose an obligation on states. The word may have been deliberately chosen since humanitarian intervention, the guise under which the principle is invoked, cannot be

[117] See Eaton, *supra*, note 85, at 775 (citing Hugo Grotius, DE JURE BELLI AC PACIS, Bk. II, Ch. XXV (1625)).

[118] See Anne Peters, *Humanity as the A[lfa] and [Omega] of Sovereignty*, 20 Eur. J. Int'l L. 513, 524–525 (2009).

[119] See William B. Wood, *Geography: A Lesson for Diplomats*, 23 Fletcher F. World Aff. 5, 14 (1999), cited in Shen, *supra*, note 60.

[120] See Shen, ibid.

[121] See, generally, McCormick, *supra*, note 102.

said to amount to jus cogens, in contrast to the principle of nonintervention—a corollary to sovereignty, which can be considered jus cogens. Even though the responsibility to protect has impacted on sovereignty, in the sense that it is a qualification of sovereignty, the influence may not have drastically changed the concept of sovereignty from what it was at the inception of the United Nations. This is because, although it is seen as a new norm, the responsibility to protect appears to have been imbedded in the UN Charter by virtue of the wide powers of the Security Council under Chapter VII. If the perception of the responsibility to protect as an emerging norm that allows for domestic interference were to be espoused, then the international community may be on the path to creating a new vista in international law. With the proliferation of internal armed conflicts in some states and the attendant human rights violations, there is the danger that other states will have the tendency to interfere in those states to address those violations, even without the approval of the Security Council. While in some instances such interference or intervention may be borne out of a genuine concern over the plight of the citizens whose rights are violated, in other instances the intervention may be for some other motive, for instance, it may provide an opportunity for states which are sympathetic to one of the factions of the conflict to register their solidarity. The danger in the continued, or arbitrary, application of the responsibility to protect is that it may be abused by the international community, and such will occasion unjustifiable interference with state sovereignty. As observed earlier, it is not incorrect to say that the principle has not received full endorsement by the international community.

While this paper does not downplay states' violations of their citizens' human rights which sometimes are in large scale, states acting under the doctrine of responsibility to protect, should be precluded from unilaterally or arbitrarily interfering in the domestic affairs of other states. A guarded application of the principle of responsibility to protect that is done only within the parameters used by the Security Council is therefore advocated, otherwise the principle may become an unruly horse and sovereignty—the cornerstone of international law, as important as it is, may be on the path of withering away.

Acknowledgements I acknowledge, in a special way, the assistance of my brothers—Paschal Azubuike and Dr. Lawrence Azubuike who funded my Master's and Doctoral programs.

CHAPTER 6

International Law and Frozen Conflicts in Eastern Europe and the Caucasus

Oleksandr Biryukov

1 Introduction

Globalization is the foremost feature of the modern world. The global integration process makes nations move in the opposite directions toward dissolution. People seek identity in order to preserve their national values, culture, etc., although these processes may occasionally cause ethnic tensions and even clashes.

The author wishes to thank Jeffrey Aaron, a Fulbright Scholar (Ukraine, 2016), Public Defender of Mendocino County, California, U.S.A., for reviewing the first draft of the chapter and providing important comments and valuable suggestions.

O. Biryukov (✉)
Institute of International Relations of Taras Shevchenko National University of Kyiv, Kyiv, Ukraine
e-mail: alexbir@ukr.net

Fulbright Scholar, New York University School of Law, New York City, USA

E. Duruigbo et al. (eds.), *International Law and Development in the Global South*, https://doi.org/10.1007/978-3-031-13741-9_6

Since the collapse of the Soviet Union in 1991, a large part of the European continent has been dragged into the conflicts in Georgia, Armenia, Azerbaijan, Moldova, and Ukraine. The international community was outraged by secession developments in Eastern Europe and the Caucasus as international law appeared unable to halt the escalation of long-lasting conflicts.

In the contemporary history of Eastern Europe and the Caucasus, ethnic clashes have turned into separatist movements. These, in turn, resulted in self-proclaimed new entities that constituted independent states—the Nagorno-Karabakh Republic, the Republic of Abkhazia, the Republic of South Ossetia, the Republic of Transnistria, the Republic of Crimea, the Donetsk People's Republic, and the Luhansk People's Republic—that were not recognized by the international community.

Currently, while these conflicts, with the exception of Eastern Ukraine, are frozen, they remain on the international radar of security issues. Taking into consideration that long-lasting regional contradictions threaten the security of Europe and potentially the whole world, a study of the international law norms application may help us rethink the current situation in the region. We should give special attention to the legal aspects of perspective developments of unrecognized self-proclaimed states in the context of international law principles, including such principles as territorial integrity, inviolability of borders, and the non-use of force in international relations.

In this context the current situation in Ukraine is of paramount importance. The military occupation of Crimea and its further annexation by the Russian Federation has changed the geo-political situation in Europe. The main international law principle of non-use of force was violated by the latent use of armed troops. The precedent of a state annexing a part of a neighboring country undermines the basic principles of international law regarding peace and security. The current armed conflict in Eastern Ukraine, the deadliest in the region, has been ongoing for seven years now—much longer than the World War II.

In this quite severe situation in Eastern Europe and the Caucasus one may assume that international law cannot address these new challenges. The key question remains: has international law exhausted all its remedies to provide a solution? The answer is that international law does have sufficient remedies to resolve these conflicts and restore international peace and security on the continent.

2 Ethnic Conflicts: Heritage of the Soviet Union

The end of the Cold War, followed by the fall of the Berlin Wall in 1989 and the dissolution of the Union of Soviet Socialist Republics (USSR) in 1991 resulted in a major transformation of the political landscape in Europe.[1] This was the single most noteworthy turning point in the modern history of Post-World War II Europe. This drastic reaction to decades of socialist dictatorships, starting from the disintegrations of Yugoslavia and Czechoslovakia, redrew the map of Europe.[2] It gave impetus to the so-called parade of sovereignties—a movement stemming from the various declarations of independence by the former Soviet republics and the formation of new states.

The parade of sovereignties gave birth to fifteen new states on the territory of the former Soviet Union. Technically the USSR was broken up into four regions where each had their own history, culture, traditions, languages, and religions.[3] The nations among which are the founders of the USSR—Russia, Belarus, Ukraine, and Moldova—announced their secession from the Soviet Union and founded their own states in the European part of the former USSR. The Russian Federation stayed within the administrative borders of the former Russian Soviet Federative Socialist Republic. Three nations in the South Caucasus founded the Georgian, Armenian, and Azerbaijanian Republics. The Baltic states—Latvia, Lithuania, and Estonia—which historically were a part of Europe,[4] returned back to the European family of nations. On the Asian continent

[1] See Ara Ghazarians, *From Frozen Conflicts to Unrecognized Republics: The de facto States in the Emergent Region of the Post-Soviet States of the South Caucasus*. A Thesis Presented to the Faculty of the Fletcher School of Law and Diplomacy as a Paper for the Degree of Doctor of Philosophy (December, 2007). An electronic copy of the paper is available at: https://sites.tufts.edu/fletcherrussia/files/2018/09/2007-Ara-Ghazarians-From-Frozen-Conflicts-to-Unrecognized-Republics.-The-de-facto-States-in-the-Emergent-Region-of-the-Post-Soviet-States-of-the-South-Caucasus.pdf.

[2] See Benjamin Smith, *Separatist Conflict in the Former Soviet Union and Beyond: How Different Was Communism?* 65 World Politics 350 (2013).

[3] Later, in December 1991, the newly established states that were the former Soviet Union republics were assembled in the Commonwealth of Independent States (CIS), but only five states ratified this decision.

[4] The Baltic republics were the last territories that were forcibly incorporated into the Soviet Union in 1944. *Peter Van Elsuwege assumes* that the Soviet Union obtained this region under a protectorate in the course of Molotov-Ribbentrop secret pact. See Peter

five new states came into existence—Kazakhstan, Kyrgyzstan, Tajikistan, Turkmenistan, and Uzbekistan.

The most extraordinary feature of that process was that this tremendous multinational state that comprised of many large and small nations and nationalities ceased its existence peacefully. The international community considered the dissolution of the USSR as a good example of the civilized "amicable divorce" of many nations with the creation of new states.[5]

There were two decisions made during that process that have a crucial importance for understanding the current situation in the region. First, it was agreed to allow establishing new states within the administrative borders of the respective Soviet republics. Second, as a result of negotiations among Russia, Belarus, Ukraine, and Kazakhstan, a portion of every former republic of the USSR's property was verified and calculated as a percentage of the USSR's total assets.[6] So these states divided the assets of the USSR with the condition that they bear responsibility for the debts of the dissolved state.

Later, another important event occurred that has a direct impact on the understanding of today's situation in Ukraine. In exchange for Ukraine's refusal to keep nuclear weapons, four leading nations, namely the United States, Germany, France, and the Russian Federation, signed the Budapest Memorandum on Security Assurances on December 5, 1994, providing guarantees to Ukraine of territorial integrity and inviolability of the borders. Ironically, despite this international agreement, a neighboring country, and one of the guarantors of Ukraine's sovereignty, committed an act of aggression against Ukraine and annexed a part of its territory:

Van Elsuwege, *From Soviet Republics to EU Member States: A Legal and Political Assessment of the Baltic States' Accession to the EU*, 1 STUDIES IN EU EXTERNAL RELATIONS XXII (2008). Annexation of Baltic states got a powerful national resistance; so-called Guerilla war lasted from the end of the World War II till 1956.

[5] See Galina Starovoitova, *Sovereignty After Empire: Self-Determination Movements in the Former Soviet Union*, Vol. 31, No. 19 UNITED STATES INSTITUTE OF PEACE (1997).

[6] According to the calculation that was based on the contribution in the joint property of the Soviet Union that became a part of the Treaty between Russia, Belarus, Ukraine, and Kazakhstan dated December 4, 1991 the Russian Federation's share was 61.3%, Ukrainian—16.4%, Belarussian—4.1%, and Kazakhstan's share was 3.9%. See Efim Khesin (ed), MEZHDUNARODNYE VALYUTNO-KREDITNYE I FINANSOVYE OTNOSHENIA, LITRES (2018).

according to the Kremlin, Crimea became a new federative unit of the Russian Federation.

The dissolution of the USSR unleashed a number of serious ethnic problems in the region. Being unresolved during the Soviet ruling, they constituted a heritage of the Soviet regime. The collapse of this multinational state by itself did not halt the ethnic collisions, but instead produced a ground for new tensions and confrontations. It very likely stoked potential conflicts that pushed the process of self-declaration of states within the former Soviet republics: some ethnic hostilities in the region grew into military conflicts or even wars.

In the post-Soviet era, those conflicts, even when frozen, influence the stability in the region, and the states in Eastern Europe and the Caucasus continue to suffer from ongoing tensions and even military clashes.

3 Frozen Conflicts: Origins and Development

The conflicts in Eastern Europe and the Caucasus in the late 1980s and early 1990s are mostly described as ethnic or nationalist conflicts.[7] This situation arose from the collapsing power of communism and echoed the earliest struggles within the Soviet Union.[8] Such conflicts are not surprising since previous termination of any empire led to quite similar conflicts.[9]

Under the communist regime any ethnic tension did not have a prospect to be resolved since, by fiat, it literally could not exist: during the whole Soviet period the ruling regime demonstrated that no conflicts could exist in the USSR[10] under leadership of the Communist Party.

[7] See James Hughes & Gwendolyn Sasse, *Comparing Regional and Ethnic Conflicts in Post-Soviet Transition States: An Institutional Approach*. Report at ECPR Joint Sessions, London School of Economics and Political Science, Grenoble 7–11 April 2001. Report is available at: https://ecpr.eu/Filestore/PaperProposal/ec9fdf8c-c39a-4c11-97c3-869bd4f489ac.pdf.

[8] Ibid.

[9] Mark Bessinger names the USSR the Soviet Empire. See Mark R. Beissinger, *Nationalism and the Collapse of Soviet Communism*, Vol. 18, No. 3 Contemporary European 331 (August 2009).

[10] In some scholar articles such regimes are called controlled. Ian Lustick notes that it is an effective mean of conflict regulation in deeply divided societies. See Ian Lustick, *Stability in Divided Societies: Consociationalism v. Control*, 31 World Politics (April 1979).

Shortly before the breakdown of the Soviet Union, a separatist movement arose in the South Caucasus and the European part of the former Soviet Union. This process then resulted in the creation of new independent entities within the existing states. Those new states are the Nagorno-Karabakh Republic, the Republic of Abkhazia, the Republic of South Ossetia, the Republic of Transnistria, the Republic of Crimea, the Donetsk People's Republic, and the Luhansk People's Republic.

Practically all self-declared states went through three phases: separatism, secessionism, and accessionism.[11] It is important to note that there is no multinational treaty on secession.[12] This process[13] for many of the above-mentioned states was quite similar: self-declaration of independence, declaration of a new state, and, as usual, a request to unite with a neighboring state. Nagorno-Karabakh, Abkhazia, South Ossetia, Transnistria, and Crimea followed this pattern. However, only in the case of Crimea its petition to join the Russian Federation has been satisfied.

It is important to note that each of the previously mentioned regional conflict had its own specific features, although there are many similarities in their development and transformation into frozen conflicts.

One example of the long-lasting ethnic tension is the conflict between Armenia and Azerbaijan around *Nagorno-Karabakh* (also known as Republic of Artsakh). This conflict is the longest ethnic conflict that originated in the Soviet era.[14]

Shortly before the collapse of the Soviet Union in 1988, the Armenians of Nagorno-Karabakh declared their independence, announced

[11] This formulation is used here in order to reveal a willingness of a self-declared state to be incorporated into another state as a territorial unit—to accede another state. This process assumes an initiative on the part of the entity that is willing to join another state. It is opposite to annexation where initiative comes from the state which incorporates the new entity into its state structure.

[12] William R. Slomanson, *supra* note 12.

[13] William R. Slomanson says that there are normally three paths to statehood: succession, secession, and self-determination. See William R. Slomanson, *Legitimacy of the Kosovo, South Ossetia, and Abkhazia Secessions: Violations in Search of the Rule*, 9 MISKOLC JOURNAL OF INTERNATIONAL LAW (Hungary, 2009). Reprinted in 3 UKRAINIAN YEARBOOK OF INTERNATIONAL LAW (Kiev, 2010).

[14] In order to resolve the tension between Armenians and Azerbaijani at the early stages of the Soviet Union state-building, Nagorno-Karabakh Autonomous Oblast was established in 1923 within the territory of the Azerbaijan Soviet Socialist Republic. Armenians living in Nagorno-Karabakh region constantly continued their demands for reunification with the Soviet Armenia.

the creation of the Republic of Mountainous Karabakh, and expressed their desire to unite with Armenia. Azerbaijan's refusal to recognize the independence of this region turned the unrest into the war between Armenia and Azerbaijan (Republic of Armenia and Azerbaijan Democratic Republic). Only in 1994 was a ceasefire reached as a result of generous efforts of the international community.

The year 2020 became another turning point in this conflict. After six weeks of fighting between Azerbaijan and ethnic Armenians a new peace deal was signed by the presidents of the Russian Federation, Azerbaijan, and Armenia's prime minister in September 2020.[15]

According to international law, this territory is a part of the Republic of Azerbaijan. The region of Nagorno-Karabakh is an enclave within the Republic of Azerbaijan. This is the starting point in analyzing the applicable international law norms.

In the relations between Armenia and Azerbaijan regarding this conflict, international law requires both states to respect the right of the people in Nagorno-Karabakh (in this case both—Armenian and Azerbaijani) to determine its destiny, including its sovereign right to determine its status, but within the territory of Azerbaijan.[16] Another principle crucial in this case is the principle of territorial integrity, which holds that no actions of one state against the territorial integrity of another are permissible. As Nagorno-Karabakh is a part of Azerbaijan it has a right to determine its internal political status. No external interference is lawful. The basic international rule here is to adhere to the principle of equality of peoples, having the right to determine their own fate but within the territory of their own national state. Respecting these international law standards contributes to the development of friendly relations between these nations, which is of course necessary to finding a solution to this conflict.

The secessionist movement in Georgia began with declarations of independence by two out of the four ethnic groups residing in this state—in Abkhazia and South Ossetia.

[15] See *Armenia, Azerbaijan and Russia Sign Nagorno-Karabakh peace deal*, BBC News (10 November 2020). https://www.bbc.com/news/world-europe-54882564.

[16] See O. Merezhko, The Problem of Nagorno-Karabakh and International Law, Publishing House of Dmitry Burago (Kyiv, 2014).

Abkhazia had a status of a Soviet Socialist Republic from the time the USSR was founded in 1922. In 1931 this former Soviet Union Republic became a part of Georgia with a status of an Autonomous Republic.

In 1988 Abkhazia's government initiated the process of reacquiring the legal status of a Republic, but that appeal to the Soviet central government received no response. In 1990 Georgia reaffirmed Abkhazia's status as an Autonomous Oblast of the Republic of Georgia. In the course of political disagreements about the status of Abkhazia, this tension evolved into a military conflict between Abkhazia and Georgia. Later, this ethnic confrontation escalated into sporadic military clashes and then into a war (1992–1993).

Before open clashes between Abkhaz people and Georgians began in 1992, the process of issuing Russian passports[17] to Abkhazians took place. This tactic has also been used in the South Ossetia, Transnistria, Crimea, and then in the Eastern part of Ukraine—Donetsk and Luhansk oblasts (regions).[18]

Toru Nagashima argues that the Russian policy of ongoing distribution of Russian citizenship in the post-Soviet states applied in unrecognized republics should be regarded as "expansionist" policy.[19] This policy exacerbates existing confrontations in the post-Soviet countries.

Recently there were proposals in the European Union to develop a plan for the coordinated policy of non-recognition of Russian passports issued to the citizens of Eastern Ukraine, which is not controlled by Ukraine.[20] The Lithuanian Foreign Policy representative said that they were "actively

[17] More about the policy of passportization in the Russian Federation, see Irina Molodikova, *The Transformation of Russian Citizenship Policy in the Context of European or Eurasian Choice: Regional Prospects,* Vol. 6, No. 1 CENTRAL AND EASTERN EUROPEAN MIGRATION REVIEW 98 (2017).

[18] Later the idea to "rescue nationals abroad" aiming at protecting ethnic Russians was modified to a doctrine of protection the Russian-speaking citizens and now it aims at not only ethnic group members, nationals, or Russian passports holders inhabiting in a foreign country but any person speaking Russian and supporting the ideas of the Russian World.

[19] See Toru Nagashima, *Russia's Passportization Policy Toward Unrecognized Republics A Bkhazia, South Ossetia, and Transnistria,* Vol. 66, No. 3 PROBLEMS OF POST-COMMUNISM 186 (2019).

[20] See Halya Coynash, *EU Is Reporting to Refuse Recognition of Russian Passports Illegally Issued to Donbas Residents*, KHARKIV HUMAN RIGHTS PROTECTIONS GROUP (12 August 2019) http://khpg.org/en/1565361379.

working on a coordinated response at EU level to the continuing violations of Ukraine's sovereignty and territorial integrity, including the illegal issue by the Russian Federation of documents to residents of Ukraine living in the Donetsk and Luhansk oblasts which are temporarily occupied by Russia."[21] Estonia's Foreign Minister Urmas Reinsalu commented on this situation:

> [G]ranting expedited Russian citizenship to the residents of eastern Ukraine is another attempt to undermine the independence of Ukraine and perpetuate the current unstable security situation in eastern Ukraine. It goes completely against the spirit of the Minsk agreements.[22]

The Ministry of Foreign Affairs of the Republic of Latvia has adopted a decision on the non-recognition of such passports.[23] Similar decisions were taken earlier concerning passports issued by the diplomatic missions of the Russian Federation in Sukhumi and Tskhinvali (Abkhazia) as well as by the illegitimately established institutions of the Russian migration authorities.

South Ossetia enjoined from the status of Autonomous Oblast (region) since it had been incorporated into the USSR in 1992 within the Transcaucasian Soviet Federative Socialist Republic.[24]

In 1989 the South Ossetian Council (the governing body of the Autonomous Oblast) requested the Government of Georgia to recognize it as an autonomous republic, which has a higher status. The very next year, not having received a response to the petition, South Ossetia proclaimed itself the South Ossetia Democratic Republic. In response

[21] See *Litva Trebuet Nepriznania Rossiiskikh Pasportov Zhitelej Donbassa v EC*. DELFI (6 August 2019) https://ru.delfi.lt/news/politics/litva-trebuet-nepriznaniya-rossijskih-pasportov-zhitelej-donbassa-v-es.d?id=81917161.

[22] Estonia applies an additional measure in response to Russia's aggression in Ukraine. Statement of Republic of Estonia Ministry of Foreign Affairs, 5 August 2019. https://vm.ee/en/news/estonia-applies-additional-measure-response-russias-aggression-ukraine.

[23] Latvia welcomes EU Guidance on non-recognition of passports issued by Russia to residents of Donetsk and Luhansk regions. Statement of Ministry of Foreign Affairs of the Republic of Latvia, dated October 3, 2019 https://www.mfa.gov.lv/en/news/latest-news/64470-latvia-welcomes-eu-guidance-on-non-recognition-of-passports-issued-by-russia-to-residents-of-donetsk-and-luhansk-regions.

[24] This republic comprised of Georgia, Armenia, and Azerbaijan and existed from 1922 till 1936.

to this, the President of Georgia deprived South Ossetia of the status of an Autonomous Oblast. The disagreement between these two parties sparked a war in which both sides disregarded the guiding principle of international humanitarian law and committed attacks against civilians.

The ceasefire agreement concluded in 1992 between Georgia and South Ossetia was guaranteed by the Joint Peacekeeping Force which was comprised of Georgian, Russian, and Ossetian troops. Since then, the Organization for Security and Cooperation in Europe (OSCE) has monitored the situation in South Ossetia.

The second war in South Ossetia unfolded in 2008 when the new President Mikheil Saakashvili came to power through the "Rose Revolution." In response to the establishment of the pro-Georgian government in South Ossetia, Russia invaded Georgia. This act of aggression was justified, according to Russian policy, to protect Russian citizens in South Ossetia. The policy, according to which Russia obtained the right to military intervention into all parts of the former Soviet Union wherever ethnic Russians' human rights were allegedly violated, was formally announced in October 2003.[25]

The peace plan for Abkhazia and South Ossetia negotiated by former French President Nicolas Sarkozy, and developed with the participation of the European Union, resulted in the end of this war in August 2008. However, Russian troops were not withdrawn from Georgia. As rationalized by Russia, they continue to act as peace-keeping forces in the region.

One of the key factors that significantly supported the secessionist movement of the self-declared republics in Georgia and Moldova was the presence of the Russian 58th Army on the territory of South Ossetia[26] and the Russian 14th Army in Moldavian Transnistria.[27] As previously explained, they fulfilled the tasks of peace-keeping mission in these

[25] William R. Slomanson, *supra* note 12.

[26] See Giorgi Menabde, *Russian Army Again Threatening Georgia from the Occupied Territories*, Vol. 14, No. 84 Eurasia Daily Monitor (22 June 2017). https://jamestown.org/program/russian-army-threatening-georgia-occupied-territories/.

[27] See *Moldova Insists on Withdrawal of Russian Troops from Transnistria,* UAWire (12 September 2019) https://uawire.org/moldova-insists-on-withdrawal-of-russian-troops-from-transnistria.

regions, but technically they became a powerful instrument for exerting pressure on the leadership in these states in their internal disagreements.[28]

Transnistria is another unrecognized Russian-backed region like Abkhazia, South Ossetia and Nagorno-Karabakh, which is located on the territory of the Republic of Moldova.[29] This small self-declared republic, like some other former Soviet Union regions, expressed a desire to become a part of the Russian Federation as a federative unit.

Before the World War II, Transnistria was a part of the Ukrainian Soviet Socialist Republic with the status of an autonomous republic called the Moldovan Autonomous Republic (1924–1940). After the World War II, according to the Molotov-Ribbentrop Pact between the Soviet Union and Nazi Germany, modern Moldova (a part of Romania, Bessarabia, and North Bukovina) became a part of the Moldavian Soviet Socialist Republic.[30]

A conflict between the Moldovan government and the de facto authorities of Transnistria began during the Soviet rule. In 1989, the opposition of the Russian-speaking ethnic minorities living in the Republic grew into a confrontation when a political movement to unite with Romania emerged in Moldova. This movement progressed under the slogan "one language—one nation." The activists initiated transliteration of the Moldavian language into the Latin alphabet.

On August 31, 1989, the Supreme Soviet of the Moldavian Soviet Socialist Republic (the Parliament) enacted two laws: one that made Moldovan an official language and the other that stipulated a return to the Latin alphabet. On September 2, 1990, the Pridnestovian Moldovan Soviet Socialist Republic proclaimed itself Transnistria ("Pridnestrovie").

[28] See Sabine Fischer (ed.), NOT FROZEN! THE UNRESOLVED CONFLICTS OVER TRANSNISTRIA, ABKHAZIA, SOUTH OSSETIA AND NAGORNO-KARABAKH IN LIGHT OF THE CRISIS OVER UKRAINE, SWP RESEARCH PAPER STIFTUNG WISSENSCHAFT UND POLITIK GERMAN INSTITUTE FOR INTERNATIONAL AND SECURITY AFFAIRS, 9 September 2016, Berlin.

[29] Transnistria is a strip of land nestled between the Dniestr River and the border of Ukraine (less than 30 kilometers wide, approximately 400 kilometers long), slightly more than one tenth of Moldova's territory. See Christopher Borgen, *Thawing a Frozen Conflict: Legal Aspects of the Separatist Crisis in Moldova*, LEGAL STUDIES RESEARCH PAPER SERIES, Paper #06-0045 (July 2006).

[30] See Imogen Gladman, *Eastern Europe, Russian and Central Asia*, EUROPE PUBLICATIONS, TAYLOR & FRANCIS 722 (3rd Edition, 2002).

The President of the USSR, Mikhail Gorbachev, signed a decree declaring this decision void on December 22, 1990.

Military clashes occurred between Transnistrian forces—including the Transnistrian Republican Guard, militia, and volunteers who came from the Russian Federation (the members of the Cossacks' paramilitary organization from the Don, Kuban, Orenburg, Siberia and Black Sea branches)—and Moldovan troops and police. Prior to these clashes, about 9,000 volunteer militiamen were trained and armed by the officers of the Russian 14th Army.[31] From the early 1990s to 1992, violent clashes that broke out between the Moldovan government and the de facto authorities of Transnistria resulted in several hundred deaths. The relatively short war ended with a ceasefire in July 1992.

Since then the Republic of Moldova and Transnistria have been involved in negotiations searching for a solution. Despite considerable mediation efforts by regional and international actors (Russia, Ukraine, OSCE, and observers from the EU and the United States), little progress for settling the dispute has been made. The association agreement of Moldova with the European Union gives hope that the parties to the conflict will continue, and eventually successfully conclude, the negotiations.

4 Self-Declaration and State-Building: Legal Dimension

The regional movements of separatism, secessionism, and accessionism raise the issue of the legality of those republics' self-declarations, state-building projects, and ongoing statehood development. One may notice that international law norms were breached, among which are the self-determination of peoples and nations, territorial integrity, inviolability of borders, sovereign equality of the states, and the non-use of force in international relations.

While under the Soviet rule, various ethnic groups sought to have more autonomy after the dissolution of the USSR in 1991, they later claimed independence mostly in order to be incorporated into another

[31] Moldova continues stating that stationing of the Russian 14th Army contingent in Transnistria is illegal.

state, such as the Russian Federation or Armenia. However, Nagorno-Karabakh was not incorporated into Armenia, nor did Abkhazia, South Ossetia, Transnistria, or the Donetsk and Luhansk People's Republics unite with the Russian Federation. Only Crimea became a new federal unit in the structure of the Russian Federation according to the Russian Federation.

Now all self-declared states, such as Nagorno-Karabakh, Abkhazia, South Ossetia, and Transnistria, are de facto independent, but *de jure* internationally unrecognized.[32] It was rather anticipated that the self-declared states, which were created in violation of international law rules would not be recognized by the international community.[33] Even the Russian Federation which favored the establishment of the newly independent states within existing states of the former Soviet Union did not recognize Donetsk and Luhansk People's Republics as independent states.

Shahen Avakian notes that:

> [A]ccording to the principles of international law, an entity can be considered an independent state if it possesses the following attributes: a defined territory, permanent population, a permanent administration, organized under common political institutions, exercising exclusive jurisdiction on a defined territory and people, a government engaged in discussions with foreign states.[34]

[32] Usually along with the Russian Federation only its international partners and affiliates do recognize the self-proclaimed states. For instance, a newly declared state—the Republic of Crimea—besides the Russian Federation was recognized by few countries among which were: North Korea, Venezuela, Afghanistan, Syria, Cuba, Bolivia, Nicaragua, Sudan, Uganda, and Zimbabwe. Certainly, among those states are Russian affiliates Belarus, Kazakhstan, Kyrgyzstan, and Armenia. A group of unrecognized nations that are under influence of Russia—Abkhazia, South Ossetia, and Nagorno-Karabakh also recognized the referendum and independence of Crimea.

[33] William R. Slomanson agrees that none of those secessions were entitled to recognition under the international law. See, *supra* note 12.

[34] Shahen Avakian, professor of law at the French University of Armenia and Yerevan State University, in his work "Nagorno-Karabakh: Legal Aspects" explains the use of self-determination of people principle. See SHAHEN AVAKIAN, NAGORNO-KARABAKH: LEGAL ASPECTS 39 (2005).

Undoubtedly, all the states mentioned above lack those attributes.

In academic literature these kinds of entities (unrecognized) are sometimes called quasi-states.[35] Marcin Kosienkowski states that "[Q]uasi-states resemble normal states except for one difference: they lack international recognition or enjoy it only at a minimal level. This means that their territories formally belong to universally recognized states."[36] He says that quasi-states may also seek to join another country, raise their status within the parent state (gaining autonomy, etc.), seize power over the whole parent state, or maintain the status quo.[37]

So-called quasi-states founded in violation of international law norms and principles do not have a chance to be recognized, but activating the process of creating such entities may give a tactical advantage for the party seeking to heat up the situation in the region. In fact, these so-called quasi-states can be used to destabilize the parent state and notably influence foreign policy of neighboring countries. As a political tool, the conflict may make the Euro integration plan of a nation practically impossible—the state with a conflict cannot apply for membership in the European Union.[38] This is what happened in the case of Ukraine.

The process of accession of self-declared states to a neighboring sovereign state has been accomplished only once: Ukrainian Crimea was incorporated into the Russian Federation with the status of a federal unit. The newly established states (Nagorno-Karabakh Republic, Republic of Abkhazia, and Republic of South Ossetia) were not internationally recognized, which deprived their statehood from further development. Non-recognition of the new entities turned the process of the statehood building into the form of a frozen conflict.

The current situation around unrecognized states remains unclear, which creates uncertainty, and that requires an appropriate solution. Potentially, any separatist conflict may remain frozen, morph into a violent

[35] See Marcin Kosienkowski, *Is Internationally Recognised Independence the Goal of Quasi-States? The Case of Transnistria* (4 August 2013). Marcin Kosienkowski says that "[E]xamples of quasi-states are as follows: Northern Cyprus located in the territory of the Republic of Cyprus, … and Somaliland in Somalia."

[36] *Id.*

[37] *Id.*

[38] *See* Diana Dascalu, *Frozen Conflicts and Federalization: Russian Policy in Transnistria and Donbass*, JOURNAL OF INTERNATIONAL RELATIONS (Columbia, May 22, 2019).

form, or even descend into military clashes. As Paul Taylor says, the frozen conflicts could heat up again.[39] This is a case of Nagorno-Karabakh.

As previously discussed, self-declared states did not receive a promise to join another state. In case of Moldova, it is worthwhile to note that the accession of Transnistria to the Russian Federation was quite unusual: they do not have common land borders. The case of Crimea shows how difficult it would be to implement this idea. Marcin Kosienkowski explains that when Transnistrian authorities understood that receiving full recognition could be impossible, "they started to pursue the goal of creating a confederation with the parent state, although a federation could also be accepted."[40]

The Russian Federation as a successor of the Soviet Union firmly pursues the idea that self-declared institutions should remain within the parent state, but with the status of a federal unit. If the separatist movement in Eastern Europe is used by the Russian Federation to prevent it from building closer ties with the West, federalization can achieve practically the same objective—it will allow to some extent keeping control over the self-proclaimed entity and influence the parent state's internal and foreign policy. This is the case of Moldova and Ukraine.

Federalization should require a creation of a new constitutional framework with reasonable levels of autonomy. Ultimately, this would mean reintegrating pro-Russian territories in a way that gives them a disproportionate level of influence.[41] This is how the Russian Federation will benefit from federalization, and it is an important reason why Russia has always publicly insisted that Transnistria and Donbas (the eastern part of Ukraine) are parts of their respective countries.

5 Ukraine: Current Situation

In modern regional developments, Ukraine appeared to be in the center of the international political scene. Military occupation of the Crimean Peninsula in 2014 and further annexation by the Russian Federation have greatly changed the geo-political situation in Europe.

[39] See Paul Taylor, *Dusting Off Cold War Thinking*, The New-York Times (17 March 2014) https://www.nytimes.com/2014/03/18/business/international/ukraine-crisis-revives-cold-war-thinking.html.

[40] Marcin Kosienkowski, *supra* note 35.

[41] Diana Dascalu, *supra* note 38.

Several months before the annexation, a political crisis occurred in Ukraine. The crisis was triggered by the refusal of President Yanukovych to sign the Association Agreement between the European Union and Ukraine that was being prepared over the previous several years.[42] Victor Yanukovych fled the country as mass protests occurred in Kyiv.[43]

Military intervention by the Russian Federation in Ukraine started with gunmen without identification (called in the media "green men") entering the Crimean territory and pro-Russian local self-defense forces laying siege to all Ukrainian military and navy installations in Crimea.[44] Ostensibly, the invasion commenced with the motive to protect Russian-speaking citizens residing in Crimea. Everything indicates that the occupation and then the annexation of Crimea were triggered by the Russian leadership's attempt to prevent Ukraine, a strategic former Soviet republic, from building close ties with the West.

Russian military troops seized the Verkhovna Rada of the Ukrainian Autonomous Republic of Crimea (Crimean Parliament).[45] In doing so, Russia violated Ukraine's territorial integrity.[46] The Crimean Parliament in a closed session on March 11, 2014 under control of military forces adopted a Declaration of Independence and arranged a referendum for March 16, 2014 on the legal status of Crimea. The Foundation of the Republic of Crimea was announced and an appeal to join the Russian Federation was adopted.

[42] Paul Taylor, *supra* note 39.

[43] After the former President of Ukraine Victor Yanukovych refused to sign the Agreement of Association with European Union on 29 November 2013 thousands of Ukrainians from every region of the country gathered in Kyiv on Independence Square—Maidan Nezalezhnosti on continuing Euromaidan. Very soon the peaceful protests became violent: police took several attacks to suppress protesters. This event received a name the Revolution of Dignity.

[44] See Tim Sullivan & Vladimir Isachenkov, *Russian Troops Take Over Ukraine's Crimea Region*, AP News (1 March 2014). https://apnews.com/article/94305e58d1574ec0bde5aa8d42538f1e.

[45] According to the Constitution of Ukraine Crimea had a status of Autonomous Republic with comprehensive autonomy: the Autonomy had its Constitution, Parliament (Verkhovna Rada of Autonomous Republic of Crimea), and the Cabinet of Ministers. The City of Sevastopol had a special status—it directly subordinated to Kyiv.

[46] See Christian Marxsen, *The Crimea Crisis—An International Perspective. Zeitschrift fur auslandisches offentliches Recht und Volkerrecht,* 74/2 Heidelberg Journal of International Law 367 (2014).

The day after the approval of the results of the referendum, on March 18, 2014, the Russian Federation and the self-declared Republic of Crimea signed a treaty of accession of the Republic of Crimea and Sevastopol City into the Russian Federation in the form of the new territorial units. The Republic of Crimea existed for only one day.

The annexation of Crimea affected a number of international law norms and principles, including the self-determination of peoples and nations, territorial integrity, inviolability of borders, sovereign equality of the states, and non-use of force in international relations.

Reviewing international documents gives grounds to conclude that the way the annexation of Crimea occurred meets the UN definition of aggression. The UN General Assembly Resolution 3314 elaborates on the concept of aggression. It provides that:

> [N]o consideration of whatever nature, whether political, economic, military or otherwise, may serve as a justification for aggression; 2) a war of aggression is a crime against international peace. Aggression gives rise to international responsibility; 3) no territorial acquisition or special advantage resulting from aggression is or shall be recognized as lawful.[47]

In case of the Russian aggression against Ukraine there were no legal grounds for using force on the Crimean Peninsula. The fact of the illegal annexation of Crimea by the Russian Federation in the course of the forceful occupation has been recognized by the international community. Professor Oleksandr Merezhko notes that, according to Article 42 of The Hague Convention on the laws and customs of land war of October 18, 1907: "[T]he territory is considered occupied when it is actually placed under the authority of the hostile army. The occupation extends only to the territory where such authority has been established and can be exercised."[48] In addition, Oleksandr Merezhko claims that, from the perspective of international law, the conflict in Eastern Ukraine should

[47] Definition of Aggression, United Nations General Assembly Resolution 3314 (XXIX), adopted 14 December 1974. An electronic copy of the paper is available at: http://hrlibrary.umn.edu/instree/GAres3314.html.

[48] O. Merezhko, *supra* note 15.

be considered as not only Russian aggression but also as a war against Ukraine.[49]

On March 27, 2014, the UN General Assembly adopted Resolution 68/262 on the "Territorial Integrity of Ukraine" regarding the annexation of Crimea.[50] A majority of the UN member states affirmed that the announcement of Crimea as an independent state with further secession from Ukraine and incorporation into the Russian Federation within three days violated international law. The member states declared Crimea's referendum invalid and called on all states, international organizations, and specialized institutions not to recognize any alteration of the status of the Autonomous Republic of Crimea and the City of Sevastopol.

Marc Weller acknowledged that Russia, by annexing a part of Ukraine, violated several international agreements and treaties[51]: the Alma Ata Declaration of December 1991 on dissolution of the Soviet Union (regarding the inviolability of borders of the former Soviet Union republics); the Budapest memorandum of 1994 (regarding guarantees of Ukraine's sovereignty within existing borders provided by France, Germany, the USA, and Russia); and the Bilateral International Treaty on Friendship, Cooperation, and Partnership between Russia and Ukraine (regarding stationing of the Russian Black Sea fleet in Crimea). Eric Engle emphasized that by occupying a part of Ukraine's territory, besides declarations and international treaties obligations, Russia has violated the universally recognized principle of the territorial integrity of states.[52]

One must note that the principle of non-use of force in international relations, as set forth in the UN Charter, Article 2 (4), is the key principle for the entire system of contemporary international law and international

[49] See O. Merezhko, *International Legal Aspects of Russia's War Against Ukraine in Eastern Ukraine*. In S. Sayapin & E. Tsybulenko (eds), The Use of Force against Ukraine and International Law, T.M.C. Asser Press, The Hague (2018).

[50] Resolution 68/262 "Territorial integrity of Ukraine" adopted on 27 March 2014 by the General Assembly at Sixty-eighth Session Agenda, A/RES/68/262. An electronic copy of the paper is available at: https://www.securitycouncilreport.org/atf/cf/%7B65BFCF9B-6D27-4E9C-8CD3-CF6E4FF96FF9%7D/a_res_68_262.pdf.

[51] See Marc Weller, *Analysis: Why Russia's Crimea move fails legal test,* DDC News (10 VII 2014). http://www.bbc.com/news/world-europe-26481423.

[52] See Eric Engle. *A New Cold War? Cold Peace. Russia, Ukraine, and NATO,* 59 St.L.U.L.J. 97 (2015). Electronic copy of the article available at: http://ssrn.com/abstract=2419414.

security. The definitive statement is found in the Declaration on Principles of International Law concerning Friendly Relations and Cooperation among States in accordance with the Charter of the United Nations (1970): "Every State has the duty to refrain in its international relations from the threat or use of force against the territorial integrity or political independence of any State, or in any other manner inconsistent with the purposes of the United Nations."

The occupation of Crimea and its subsequent annexation by the Russian Federation in violation of the primary principles of international law resulted in changing the borders on the European continent. This extraordinary incident practically divided the development of modern Europe into two periods—before and after Crimea. Annexation of a part of the territory by a neighboring state sends a worrying message and undermines the basic principles of international law regarding global security.

Following the intervention of a neighboring state in Donbas, Russia appeared likely to follow the same pattern as in Transnistria. As with the 1992 Transnistrian ceasefire, in 2015 Minsk II Agreement ended the Ukrainian conflict's active phase on conditions favorable to Russia. Yet the military phase of the conflict in Ukraine has still not ended due to the ceasefire never being properly implemented.

6 Conclusion

The conflicts in Eastern Europe and the Caucasus that were discussed in this paper remain a serious concern on the international agenda. Because of these unresolved conflicts, thousands of persons have died or suffered, millions more have been internally displaced, and still the conflicts remain alarmingly dangerous. The neighboring countries suffer from instability. Moreover, these long-lasting conflicts threaten European security, and potentially the security of the entire world, since a frozen conflict can turn into an active one at virtually any moment.

Separatist movements in Georgia, Armenia, Azerbaijan, and Moldova, and ongoing military conflict in Eastern Ukraine have different political, legal, economic, social, and cultural backgrounds and are, of course, different by their nature. Nevertheless, all of these conflicts share some distinguishing features, such as, in particular, issuing Russian passports before the conflicts escalated, orchestrating referendums, self-declarations of independent states, secessions from the state, and expressions of desire to join another state. These features quite evidently indicate that a third party stands behind the conflicts.

International law has not yet exhausted all of its remedies to deal with severe situations around the world. Yet there are high expectations and hopes for modern international law. There is a hope that a response to the challenges in the region of Eastern Europe and the Caucasus will be effective and that solutions will be developed on the basis of international law.

An appropriate response of the international community to the challenges the region is facing could be implementing existing legal mechanisms in order to eliminate or at least decrease the risk of ruining the international order in Europe and assure regional security.

Proposals to effectively deal with the problems in Eastern Europe and the Caucasus should be based on the shared values in the sphere of international security presumptions. Therefore, the secession of a part of one country and then joining another state should be done in accordance with the existing legal procedures, and then an international treaty must be concluded based on the recognition of mutual obligations.

CHAPTER 7

How U.S. Courts Handle GDPR in Discovery Process: An Examination of a U.S. Patent Infringement Case

Azam Zare Chahoki

1 Introduction

The protection of personal data from unwanted and unknown sharing is a fundamental right in the European Union (EU) and the General Data Protection Regulation[1] (GDPR) is the cornerstone of the EU data protection laws. But what happens when a United States (U.S.) company with offices in Europe is sued in the U.S. and the personal data of European citizens is slated to be produced as evidence in that lawsuit? Does U.S. discovery laws overrule the GDPR protections?

[1] Council Regulation 2016/679, of the European Parliament and of the Council of 27 April 2016 on the Protection of Natural Persons with regard to the Processing of Personal Data and on the Free Movement of Such Data, and Repealing Directive 95/46/EC (General Data Protection Regulation).

A. Z. Chahoki (✉)
Golden Gate University School of Law, San Francisco, CA, USA
e-mail: azare@my.ggu.edu

E. Duruigbo et al. (eds.), *International Law and Development in the Global South*, https://doi.org/10.1007/978-3-031-13741-9_7

The focus of this paper is on how U.S. courts approach the enforcement of GDPR, especially in the discovery process. Herein, this paper would analyze two different approaches through two different cases; namely ***Finjan, Inc. v. Zscaler, Inc.***[2] and ***United States v. Microsoft Corp.***[3] In both cases, the defendant cited GDPR protections and objected to the disclosure of personal information in the discovery process.

Understanding the GDPR protection is key to analyzing how the U.S. courts handled the GDPR issues raised. The GDPR made many key changes to the EU's previous laws and is devoted to "protect[ing] fundamental rights and freedoms of natural persons and in particular their right to the protection of personal data."[4] The GDPR, through the function of specific rights such as right to rectification, right to erasure (right to be forgotten), right to restriction of processing, right to data portability, and right to object has improved individual's personal data control in online services.[5]

According to GDPR article 4(2), data processing includes a wide range of personal data operations such as disclosure by transmission, dissemination, or otherwise making the data available.[6] Companies processing personal data of individuals residing in the EU countries might be subject to the GDPR.[7] Under GDPR article 3 conditions, it does not matter that the company's location is not in the EU as long as the company processing data subjects' personal data in the EU.[8] In addition, the regulation applies to the processing of personal data by controllers and processors in the EU even if the processing itself is not in the EU.[9] The GDPR defines six bases for the lawfulness of processing and companies shall have one of the bases to process the data.[10] These bases

2 *Finjan, Inc. v. Zscaler, Inc.*, No. 17-cv-06946-JST (KAW) at 1 (N. D. Cal. Feb. 14, 2019).

3 *United States v. Microsoft Corp.*, 138 S. Ct. 1186, 1187 (2018).

4 GDPR, art 1.2.

5 GDPR, art 15–21.

6 GDPR, art 4. 2.

7 GDPR, art 3.

8 GDPR, art 3. 2.

9 *Id.*

10 GDPR, art 6.

are consent, contract, legal obligation, vital interest, public task, and legitimate interests.[11]

Foreign discovery, namely; when requests within the discovery process affecting foreign interests, in the U.S. courts is limited to the information which is directly relevant and material to the issues before the court.[12] Under the U.S. courts' standard, courts would not ordinarily grant the requests for information that could lead to admissible evidence, but a court might in some instances order disclosure of the identity and location of persons who may have knowledge of such information, or production of documents that may lead to such information.[13]

There are two relevant discovery situations under which a party may be placed into a conflict where complying with the U.S. discovery demands to disclose personal data would result in violation of the GDPR. The first is where one party to the litigation in the United States is located in the EU and is subject to the general discovery obligations of the U.S. courts. The second situation occurs when a party to the litigation in the United States has requested the disclosure of some information from a non-party that is located in the EU.

The U.S. courts have treated the GDPR in different ways depending on the facts of the lawsuit. In the Zscaler case, the court did not make inquiry about the GDPR and mentioned that Zscaler Inc. as defendant has the burden of proof that the GDPR bars the production of information to the plaintiff, Finjan Inc.[14] However, in the Microsoft case, the Supreme Court of the United States asked the EU to submit an amicus brief about the GDPR issue in the discovery process.[15] These two examples show that the U.S. legal system needs to develop a harmonic approach to handle discovery requests affecting foreign interests including GDPR.

[11] *Id.*

[12] Restatement (Third) of the Foreign Relations Law of the United States § 442 (1987).

[13] *Id.*

[14] *Finjan, Inc. v. Zscaler, Inc.*, No. 17-cv-06946-JST (KAW) at 1 (N. D. Cal. Feb. 14, 2019).

[15] *United States v. Microsoft Corp.*, 138 S. Ct. 1186 (2018).

In determining whether the foreign statute excuses noncompliance with the discovery order, the U.S. courts consider the balancing test.[16] This paper concludes that the U.S. courts should include GDPR considerations while considering the balancing test and specifically when analyzing whether the discovery is unnecessary, or unduly burdensome.[17] The importance of consideration is to mitigate the risk of conflict of law with GDPR and advance international comity between the U.S. and the EU's countries.

2 U.S. Procedural Approach: Requests in Discovery Process Affecting Foreign Interests

In civil litigation, requests to produce documents or information affecting foreign interests are not merely in the form of a demand by a private party, but the U.S. courts issue an order.[18] In fact, issuing the discovery order by the court would ensure that the court would scrutinize a discovery request concerning the production of documents, objects, or information located abroad, more closely than it would scrutinize comparable requests for information located in the United States.[19]

Under rule 26(b)(1) of the Federal Rules of Civil Procedure, "discovery may extend to any matter not privileged which is relevant to the subject matter of the action, even if the information sought would be inadmissible at trial, if it appears reasonably calculated to lead to the discovery of admissible evidence."[20] However, foreign discovery in the U.S. courts is limited to information necessary to the action which is directly relevant and material. Thus, requests for information that could lead to admissible evidence would ordinarily not be granted under this standard, but a court might in some instances order disclosure of the identity and location of persons who may have knowledge of

[16] Restatement (Third) of the Foreign Relations Law of the United States § 442 (1987).

[17] *Id.*

[18] *Id.*

[19] *Id.* at §§ 403, 421(1).

[20] Fed. R. Civ. P. 26(b)(1).

such information, or production of documents that may lead to such information.[21]

3 U.S. Substantive Approach: Requests in Discovery Process Affecting Foreign Interests

In general, a foreign country's statute precluding disclosure of evidence "do not deprive an American court of the power to order a party subject to its jurisdiction to produce evidence even though the act of production may violate that statute."[22] In determining whether the foreign statute excuses noncompliance with the discovery order, the U.S. courts consider the balancing test.[23] However, the balancing test permits courts to easily prioritize U.S. interests over foreign interests, because the U.S. Supreme Court did not provide an explicit procedure for weighing the interests.[24] In fact, in a majority of cases where the balancing test was applied, the U.S. courts decided that the U.S. interests outweighed foreign interests and ordered conducting discovery requests under the U.S. rules.[25] This part of the paper would discuss two different U.S. courts' approaches related to the GDPR issues in the discovery process.

3.1 Finjan, Inc. v. Zscaler, Inc.

Finjan, Inc. v. Zscaler, Inc.[26] is a patent infringement case. Plaintiff, Finjan Inc., headquartered in East Palo Alto, California, owns the patented technology used in cybersecurity.[27] A Secure Web Gateway (SWG) is one of its patented products.[28] Mr. Warner directed Finjan Inc.' sales within the

[21] *Id.*

[22] *Societe Nationale Industrielle Aerospatiale v. U.S. Dist. Court for S. Dist. of Iowa*, 482 U.S. 522 (1987).

[23] *Id.*

[24] Samantha Cutler, *The Face-Off Between Data Privacy and Discovery: Why U.S. Courts Should Respect EU Data Privacy Law When Considering the Production of Protected Information*, 59 B.C.L. Rev. 1513 (2018).

[25] *Id.*

[26] *Finjan, Inc. v. Zscaler, Inc.*, No. 17-cv-06946-JST (KAW) at 1 (N. D. Cal. Feb. 14, 2019).

[27] *Id.*

[28] *Id.*

United Kingdom (UK) from 2002 to 2014.[29] At the time of considering this case at the United States District Court for the Northern District of California, Mr. Warner is Zscaler Inc.'s director of all sales to any business or government entity in the UK. According to Finjan Inc., "Mr. Warner has intimate knowledge of Plaintiff's patented technology and was familiar with all of the SWG's technical aspects and could explain them inside out."[30] Here, Finjan Inc. sought the production of Mr. Warner's emails and the question for the court was if Finjan Inc. can have access to Mr. Warner's emails? or the GDPR excuses Zscaler Inc. to disclose Mr. Warner's emails?[31]

The United States District Court for the Northern District of California in deciding whether or not the GDPR excuses noncompliance with the discovery order examines the balancing test's factors mentioned in the Restatement Third of Foreign Relations Law which are:

1. The importance of the documents or other information requested to the litigation;
2. The degree of specificity of the request;
3. Whether the information originated in the United States;
4. The availability of alternative means of securing the information;
5. The extent to which noncompliance would undermine important interests of the United States; and
6. The extent and the nature of the hardship that inconsistent enforcement would impose upon the person.[32]

First, the court considers the importance of Mr. Warner's emails at the infringement claim.[33] Generally, the U.S. courts have been unwilling to violate foreign law where the outcome of litigation does not rely on discovery order, or where the evidence sought is cumulative of existing evidence.[34] However, where the evidence is directly relevant, courts have

[29] *Id.*

[30] *Id.* at 3.

[31] *Id.*

[32] *Id.*

[33] *Id.* at 5.

[34] *Richmark Corp. v. Timber Falling Consultants*, 959 F.2d 1468, 1471 (9th Cir. 1992).

found that this factor weighs in favor of disclosure.[35] In the Zscaler case, Finjan Inc. contends that Mr. Warner's emails may prove the fact and timing of Zscaler Inc.'s infringement and willfulness.[36] Moreover, the court considers Mr. Warner's overlapping roles and his personal knowledge of the technical aspects of the patented technology.[37] Thus, the court found that Mr. Warner's emails are directly relevant to the infringement claim.[38]

Second, the court reviews the specificity of Finjan Inc.'s discovery request.[39] When the disclosure of information is prohibited under foreign law, parties should request specific discovery searches.[40] Finjan Inc. proposed five search terms which are "Finjan," "zero*day or zeroday or 0*day," "malicious," "obfuscat*," and "sandbox*."[41] These selected words are because patents concern "Malicious Mobile Code Runtime Monitoring System and Methods" and Zscaler Inc, allegedly infringing Cloud Sandbox technology which is designed to prevent zero-day exploits.[42] Zscaler Inc., argues that the search request is overbroad and the search terms should be limited to "Finjan" and the asserted patent numbers, rather than the technical terms requested by Finjan Inc.[43] However, the court found that Finjan Inc. has limited its request to itself, Finjan, and terms related to the patents at issue.[44] Limiting the e-mail search to patents by number would eliminate emails discussing the patents.[45] Therefore, the court finds that this factor also weighs in favor of disclosure.[46]

35 *Id.*

36 *Finjan, Inc. v. Zscaler, Inc.*, No. 17-cv-06946-JST (KAW) at 3 (N. D. Cal. Feb. 14, 2019).

37 *Id.*

38 *Id.*

39 *Id.* at 6.

40 *Richmark Corp. v. Timber Falling Consultants*, 959 F.2d 1468, 1471 (9th Cir. 1992).

41 *Id.*

42 *Finjan, Inc. v. Zscaler, Inc.*, No. 17-cv-06946-JST (KAW) at 5 (N. D. Cal. Feb. 14, 2019).

43 *Id.*

44 *Id.*

45 *Id.*

46 *Id.*

Third, the court considers the location of information and parties.[47] In the ordinary course of business, people and documents are subject to the law of the country that they are located.[48] In the Zscaler case, Mr. Warner is located in the UK, but Zscaler Inc., is an American company, subject to American discovery law.[49] Thus, the court found that this factor fairly weighs in favor of disclosure.

Fourth, the court considers the availability of alternative means of obtaining the information.[50] There is no reason to require a party to violate foreign law, if the information can easily be obtained by alternative means.[51] However, the alternative means of obtaining the information must be substantially equivalent to the requested discovery.[52] In the Zscaler case, the court did not find substantially equivalent alternative means of obtaining the information.[53]

Fifth, the court considers the balance of national interests. The court found that there is a strong American interest in protecting American patents and further recognized that the UK's interest in protecting privacy is diminished where the court has entered a protective order preventing disclosure of the secret information.[54]

Finally, the court considers the extent and the nature of the hardship that a discovery order would impose upon Zscaler Inc.[55] The court found that the party relying on foreign law has the burden of showing that such law bars disclosure.[56] The court requires Zscaler Inc. to present evidence regarding the manner and extent to which the UK enforces

47 *Id.* at 7.

48 *Richmark Corp. v. Timber Falling Consultants*, 959 F.2d 1468, 1471 (9th Cir. 1992).

49 *Id.*

50 *Id.* at 8.

51 Richmark Corp. v. Timber Falling Consultants, 959 F.2d 1468, 1471 (9th Cir. 1992).

52 *Id.*

53 *Finjan, Inc. v. Zscaler, Inc.*, No. 17-cv-06946-JST (KAW) at 8 (N. D. Cal. Feb. 14, 2019).

54 *Id.* at 9.

55 *Id.* at 11.

56 *Id.*

GDPR.[57] However, "Defendant provides no information on the likelihood of enforcement."[58] Thus, the court finds that "the burden on Defendant does not weigh against disclosure."[59]

In conclusion, by considering all the factors together, "the court concludes that the GDPR does not preclude the court from ordering Defendant to produce the requested e-mails in an unredacted form, subject to the existing protective order."[60]

3.2 *United States v. Microsoft Corp.*

In United States v. Microsoft Corp.,[61] the Supreme Court of the United States in the matter of a warrant to search a certain e-mail account controlled and maintained by Microsoft Corp. asked the European Commission (EC) to submit an amicus brief.[62] The question that EC answered in the brief is about "whether 18 U.S. C. § 2703 authorizes a court in the United States to issue a warrant that compels a U.S.-based provider of email services to disclose data stored outside of the United States."[63]

Microsoft Corp. case concerns personal data stored in a data center in the EU that is operated by an EU-based subsidiary of Microsoft Corp.[64] Storing such data and transferring it from the EU to the U.S. constitutes data processing to which the EU data protection rules apply.[65] According to the brief, the EC recognizes significant EU interests in the case.[66] The EC mentioned that "the European Union has an interest in ensuring that

[57] *Id.*

[58] *Id.*

[59] *Id.*

[60] *Id.*

[61] *United States v. Microsoft Corp.*, 138 S. Ct. 1186 (2018).

[62] Brief of the European Commission on Behalf of the European Union as Amicus Curiae in Support of Neither Party at 1, *United States v. Microsoft Corp.*, No. 17–2 (2d Cir. Dec. 13, 2017).

[63] *Id.*

[64] *United States v. Microsoft Corp.*, 138 S. Ct. 1186 (2018).

[65] GDPR, art 4. 2.

[66] Brief of the European Commission on Behalf of the European Union as Amicus Curiae in Support of Neither Party at 48, *United States v. Microsoft Corp.*, No. 17–2 (2d Cir. Dec. 13, 2017).

the Court proceeds based on a correct understanding of EU law."[67] The EC by discussing GDPR article 6 recognized that "the transfer could potentially qualify as necessary for the purpose of the legitimate interests pursued by the controller- namely, the interest in not being subject to legal action in a non-EU state."[68] At the end, EC takes no position on the ultimate question and offers an explanation concerning EU data protection rules in order to facilitate the U.S. Court's inquiry under U.S. law.[69]

4 Are the U.S. Courts Limited to the Materials Presented by the Parties to Determine Foreign Law?

Generally, a U.S. court is under no obligation to apply foreign law when parties do not raise the issue of the applicability of foreign law.[70] However, the court may apply foreign law, even if a party does not request the court to apply foreign law.[71] In addition, court ruling in determining foreign law is a question of law. To determine a question of law, "court can conduct its own research on the subject, the court is free to insist on a complete presentation by counsel."[72] Therefore, the U.S. courts are not limited to the materials presented by the parties to determine foreign law.[73]

[67] *Id.*

[68] *Id.* at 10.

[69] *Id.*

[70] *Oparaugo v. Watts*, 884 A.2d 63, 67 (D.C. 2005).

[71] *Id.*

[72] *Id.*

[73] D.C. Super. Ct. R. Civ. P. 44.1 (2004).

5 What if the United States District Court in the Zscaler Case Had Made Inquiry About GDPR?

In the Zscaler case, although Zscaler Inc. raised the issue of GDPR limitations on disclosing Mr. Warner's emails, the United States District Court for the Northern District of California found that the party relying on foreign law has the burden of showing that such law bars production.[74]

If the United States District Court for the Northern District of California had inquired about the GDPR, the first question would be whether disclosing Mr. Warner's emails is within the GDPR's territorial scope. The importance of this question is because it determines if processing Mr. Warner's emails falls under the scope of the GDPR and therefore, Zscaler Inc. must comply with the GDPR requirements to disclose emails.

According to GDPR article 4(2), data processing includes a wide range of personal data operations such as disclosure by transmission, dissemination, or otherwise making the data available.[75] GDPR article 3 determines whether particular processing by a controller or a processor falls within the scope of the GDPR. As a general principle, the European Data Protection Board (EDPB) asserts that where the processing of personal data falls within the territorial scope of the GDPR, all provisions of the regulation apply to such processing.[76]

GDPR article 3(1) ensures that the regulation applies to the processing by a controller or processor carried out in the context of the activities of an establishment of that controller or processor in the EU, regardless of the actual place of the processing.[77] While the notion of main establishment is defined in GDPR recital 36, the GDPR does not provide a definition of establishment for the purpose of article 3. However, recital 22 clarifies that an "[e]stablishment implies the effective and real exercise of activities through stable arrangements. The legal form of such arrangements, whether through a branch or a subsidiary with a legal

[74] *Finjan, Inc. v. Zscaler, Inc.*, No. 17-cv-06946-JST (KAW) at 1 (N. D. Cal. Feb. 14, 2019).

[75] GDPR, art 4. 2.

[76] Andrea Jelinek, *Guidelines 3/2018 on the territorial scope of the GDPR (Article 3)-Version for public Consultation,* European Data Protection Board (2018).

[77] GDPR, art 3. 1.

personality, is not the determining factor in that respect."[78] Indeed, the Court of Justice of the European Union (CJEU) ruled that the notion of establishment extends to any real and effective activity even a minimal one exercised through stable arrangements.[79] Therefore, in some circumstances, the presence of one single employee or agent of the non-EU entity may be sufficient to constitute a stable arrangement if that employee or agent acts with a sufficient degree of stability.[80]

In the Zscaler case, Mr. Warner is in the UK and directs Zscaler Inc.'s UK sales. The UK branch can be considered to be a stable arrangement, which exercises real and effective activities. Therefore, the UK branch could be considered as an establishment in the Union, within the meaning of the GDPR.

Next step to determine whether GDPR article 3(1) applies to a specific data processing is to determine whether the processing is carried out in the context of the activities of that establishment. According to the EDPB, the inextricable link between the activities of a local establishment in an EU country and the data processing activities of a data controller or processor established outside the EU may trigger the applicability of EU law, even if that local establishment is not actually taking any role in the data processing itself.[81]

The EDPB also mentioned that revenue-raising in the EU by a local establishment, to the extent that such activities can be linked to the processing of personal data taking place outside the EU may be indicative of processing by a non-EU controller or processor being carried out "in the context of the activities of the EU establishment," and may be sufficient to result in the application of EU law to such processing.[82]

In the Zscaler case, the fact that Mr. Warner is Zscaler Inc.'s director of all sales to any business or government entity in the UK and he previously directed Finjan Inc.'s UK sales from 2002 to 2014 are the main reasons that Plaintiff, Finjan Inc., would like to process Mr. Warner's emails. Thus, there is a link between processing Mr. Warner's emails and

[78] GDPR, recital 22.

[79] Andrea Jelinek, *Guidelines 3/2018 on the Territorial Scope of the GDPR (Article 3)-Version for Public Consultation*, European Data Protection Board (2018).

[80] *Id.*

[81] *Id.*

[82] *Id.*

the activities of Zscaler Inc.'s branch in the UK to determine patent infringement. In addition, Zscaler Inc.'s raising revenue in the EU by a UK establishment could be indicative of processing being carried out in the context of the activities of the EU establishment. Therefore, processing Mr. Warner's personal data specifically disclosing his emails for the purpose of the discovery request could be considered as carried out in the context of the activities of the UK office, as an establishment in the EU, and therefore be subject to the GDPR article 3(1).

Article 3(2) of the GDPR provides that "this regulation applies to the processing of personal data of data subjects who are in the Union by a controller or processor not established in the Union, where the processing activities are related to: (a) the offering of goods or services, irrespective of whether a payment of the data subject is required, to such data subjects in the Union; or (b) the monitoring of their behavior as far as their behavior takes place within the Union."[83] However, GDPR article 3(2) does not apply to the Zscaler case because Zscaler Inc. has an establishment in the UK.

Under GDPR article 6(1), every processing of personal data must meet one of the six bases to be lawful.[84] According to EC's amicus brief in the Microsoft case, processing data could potentially qualify as "necessary for the purposes of the legitimate interests pursued by Microsoft Corp., namely, the interest is not being subject to legal action in the U.S."[85] Similarly, Zscaler Inc. could disclose Mr. Warner's emails because disclosure is necessary for the purpose of the legitimate interest of the defendant, Zscaler Inc., which is not being subject to the legal action in the U.S. court. As a result, making inquiry about the GDPR would make clear that Zscaler Inc. has a legitimate interest in disclosing Mr. Warner's emails to Finjan Inc. and the United States District Court for the Northern District of California still can require Zsclaer Inc., to comply with the Finjan Inc.'s discovery request.

[83] GDPR, art 3.2.

[84] GDPR, art 6.

[85] Brief for the EC as Amicus Curiae at 1, *United States v. Microsoft Corp.*, No. 17-2 (2d Cir. Dec. 13, 2017).

6 Why Making Inquiry of Foreign Law Is Important?

The importance of making inquiry into the foreign law especially when it is raised by one of the parties is advancing international comity and mitigating the risk of conflict with foreign law. International comity is an international judicial principle for respecting the sovereign power of other countries and facilitating harmony in the global legal system.[86] This concept has been acknowledged in U.S. jurisprudence since the 1800s.[87] International comity involves the balancing of international and domestic interests.[88] One country will allow the law of another country to apply within its jurisdiction. In other words, even if a court has jurisdiction over a case and its parties, the doctrine of international comity obligates judges to contemplate how the outcome will affect the concerned foreign nations.[89]

The purpose of the international comity analysis is to determine whether, and to what extent, foreign interests outweigh those of the United States.[90] The EU and its member countries are parties to numerous treaties and international agreements providing for law enforcement cooperation with the United States, including the EU–U.S. Privacy Shield and Safe Harbor Agreement. These agreements reflect the value that the EU and the U.S. attach to international law enforcement cooperation.[91]

[86] Samantha Cutler, *The Face-Off Between Data Privacy and Discovery: Why U.S. Courts Should Respect EU Data Privacy Law When Considering the Production of Protected Information*, 59 B.C.L. Rev. 1513 (2018).

[87] *Id.*

[88] *Id.*

[89] *Id.*

[90] *Id.*

[91] Brief of the European Commission on Behalf of the European Union as Amicus Curiae in Support of Neither Party at 48, *United States v. Microsoft Corp.*, No. 17–2 (2d Cir. Dec. 13, 2017).

7 How to Balance the Interests of Two Different Jurisdictions?

In balancing respective national interests in ruling on requests for discovery of documents affecting foreign interest, courts should scrutinize more carefully requests by private parties than requests initiated by the U.S. government. When the United States brings a lawsuit, a decision has already been made that the matter is important to the national interest, whether it concerns an antitrust violation, patent infringement, securities fraud, or tax evasion.[92] Private litigants cannot be expected to have comparable concerns for the national interest or for abiding by international undertakings.[93]

In making the necessary determination of the interests of the United States, the court or authorized agency should take into account not merely the interest of the prosecuting or investigating agency in the particular case, but the long-term interests of the United States. generally in international law enforcement cooperation in giving effect to formal or informal international agreements, and international relations.[94]

In making the necessary determination of foreign interests, a court or agency in the United States should consider not merely a foreign country's general policy to resist intrusion upon its sovereign interests, or to prefer its own system of litigation, but whether producing the requested information would affect important substantive policies or interests of the foreign country.[95]In fact, the court or agency will look to the expressions of interest by the foreign country, the significance of disclosure in the regulation by the foreign country, and to indications of the foreign country's concern for confidentiality prior to the controversy.[96]

[92] Restatement (Third) of the Foreign Relations Law of the United States § 442 (1987).

[93] *Id.*

[94] *Id.*

[95] *Id.*

[96] *Id.*

8 Conclusion

International comity that prohibits unreasonable interference with the sovereign authority of other countries is recognized by the EU and the United States Supreme Court's precedents.[97] In fact, the standard of review that U.S. courts choose toward foreign law would affirm their commitment to international cooperation to enforce law.[98] In general, a foreign country's statute precluding disclosure of evidence "do not deprive an American court of the power to order a party subject to its jurisdiction to produce evidence even though the act of production may violate that statute."[99] However, making inquiry into the content of foreign law including GDPR would mitigate the risk of conflict and advance international comity between countries.

[97] *Id.*

[98] *Id.*

[99] *Societe Nationale Industrielle Aerospatiale v. U.S. Dist. Court for S. Dist. of Iowa*, 482 U.S. 522, 524 (1987).

CHAPTER 8

International Criminal Jurisdiction of the African Court of Justice and Human and Peoples' Rights: Promoting or Obstructing Accountability?

Remigius Chibueze

1 Introduction

The International Criminal Court (ICC) was a creation of persistent agitation of more than 80 years sustained by constant atrocities and egregious acts of criminality devoid of any criminal accountability.[1] On July 18, 1998, the perseverance resulted in the establishment of the ICC.[2] Africa

[1] See Cherif Bassiouni, THE STATUTE OF THE INTERNATIONAL CRIMINAL COURT: A DOCUMENTARY HISTORY 3 (1998) [hereinafter Bassiouni, Documentary History], where he notes that "since the end of World War 1 (1919), the world community has sought to establish a permanent international criminal court."

[2] See The Rome Statute of the International Criminal Court, U.N. Doc. A/CONF. 183/9 (July 17, 1998), *reprinted* in 37 I.L.M. 999 (1998) [hereinafter Rome Statute].

R. Chibueze (✉)
Sompong Sucharitkul Centre for Advanced International Legal Studies, Golden Gate University School of Law, San Francisco, CA, USA
e-mail: rchibueze@ggu.edu

E. Duruigbo et al. (eds.), *International Law and Development in the Global South*, https://doi.org/10.1007/978-3-031-13741-9_8

and Africans, just like the rest of the world, through their governments and Non-governmental Organizations, participated fully and supported the creation of the ICC.[3] The overriding purpose of the ICC was and remains, to end the era of impunity and usher the regime of individual criminal accountability, both nationally and internationally.[4] Toward this objective, the ICC was conferred with jurisdiction to prosecute individuals with greatest responsibility for committing egregious crimes such as genocide, war crimes, crimes against humanity, and war of aggression.

After the creation of the ICC, the African continent, expressed full support for the ICC, which was reflected in the continent's ratification rate of the Rome Statute. As of the year 2021, about 123 countries have ratified the Rome Statute. Out of them, 33 are African States, 19 are Asia–Pacific States, 18 are from Eastern Europe, 28 are from Latin American and Caribbean States, and 25 are from Western European and other States.[5]

With the same enthusiasm or perhaps, ulterior motives, African political/governmental leaders were the first to refer situations in their countries to the ICC for investigation and possible prosecution. As such, the first sets of the ICC's cases have all been situations from Africa.[6] Curiously, just as the ICC accepted these referrals and began to look at all possible perpetrators, including the possibility of prosecution of political office holders, some African political leaders became uncomfortable with the ICC. These political leaders accused the ICC of undue focus on Africa and alleges a Western agenda against the African continent through the

[3] For a complete list of states and organizations represented at the Conference, see Final Act of the United Nations Diplomatic Conference of Plenipotentiaries on the Establishment of an International Criminal Court, July 17, 1998, U.N. Doc. A/CONF.183/10, Annex II, III (1998) [hereinafter Diplomatic Conference].

[4] Rome Statute, *supra* note 2, preamble, paras. 4 & 5.

[5] See ICC, The States Parties to the Rome Statute, available at https://asp.icc-cpi.int/en_menus/asp/states%20parties/Pages/the%20states%20parties%20to%20the%20rome%20statute.aspx (visited January 31, 2022); Multilateral Treaties Deposited with the Secretary-General, available at https://treaties.un.org/Pages/ViewDetails.aspx?src=TREATY&mtdsg_no=XVIII-10&chapter=18&clang=_en (visited January 31, 2022) [hereinafter Multilateral Treaties].

[6] Web page, ICC, *Situations and Cases*, available online (last visited on June 4, 2021). African case docket since all 8 of its active investigations (situations) and all 18 prosecutions (cases) are against Africans.

activities of the ICC.[7] However, in essence, the concern with the ICC is, in part, based on ICC's refusal to inoculate Heads of State from prosecution on the basis of customary immunity protection. As such, the African governments have gone as far as to demand a collective withdrawal of all African countries from the ICC[8] and noncooperation with the ICC.[9] Additionally, AU has created a criminal jurisdiction for the African Court of Justice and Human and Peoples' Rights ("ACJHR") ostensibly as an alternative to the ICC.

This chapter examines the so-called Africa's opposition to the ICC. The chapter focuses on the creation of an international criminal jurisdiction for the ACJHR. The chapter argues that as a measure of regional integration, ordinarily, the extended criminal jurisdiction is a step in the right direction. However, the chapter questions the rationale for the extended criminal jurisdiction taking into consideration the motive behind the creation manifested mainly in the immunity provision inoculating Heads of State and certain office holders from immediate prosecution and the lack of formal relationship with the ICC. Mindful of these concerns, the chapter argues that the legitimacy of the court has been placed in doubt. Also, the chapter argues that structurally, the international criminal jurisdiction of the ACJHR will be ineffective.

[7] See e.g., Richard Lough, *African Union Accuses ICC Prosecutor of Bias*, REUTERS (January 30, 2011), available online at: https://www.reuters.com/article/ozatp-africa-icc-20110130-idAFJOE70T01R20110130.

[8] On February 1, 2017, the African Union called for the mass withdrawal of member states from the International Criminal Court (ICC), see BBC News, African Union backs mass withdrawal from ICC, available online at: https://www.bbc.com/news/world-africa-38826073 (visited February 15, 2022).

[9] See, Decision on the Meeting of African States Parties to the Rome Statute of the International Criminal Court (ICC)," Assembly/AU/Dec.245(XIII) Rev.1 [July 2009 Non-Cooperation Decision]. As a sign of non-cooperation, in 2010, the AU rejected a proposal by the ICC to open a liaison office in Addis Ababa, Ethiopia, see, Decision on the Progress Report of the Commission on the Implementation of Decision Assembly/AU/Dec.270 (XIV) on the Second Ministerial Meeting on the Rome Statute of the International Criminal Court (ICC), Assembly/AU/Dec.296 (XV), para. 8).

2 Criticisms of ICC's "African Only" Docket Are Inapposite

Until 2017, situations in African countries were the basis of the ICC's activities as of the Court's 18 prosecutions (cases) are against Africans.[10] This fact has given rise to the argument that the ICC's focus on Africa, almost exclusively, in the face of widespread commission of ICC covered crimes in other parts of the world shows a deliberate attempt by the Western countries to use ICC to prosecute Africans only. Thus, ICC is accused of serving as an instrument of Western imperialism and neo-colonialism used to target African leaders.[11] Unfortunately, this claim appears to ignore the scope of application of ICC jurisdiction and the circumstances under which the ICC came to be seized of "African Only" docket. In this section, we discuss this matter, albeit briefly to explain the jurisdictional limitation and trigger of the ICC. It is important to note that this author disagrees with the claim that Africa or Africans oppose the ICC. The majority of Africans and African countries do not oppose the ICC.

2.1 *The Basis of the ICC's Exercise of Jurisdiction*

ICC does not have universal jurisdiction. Rather, the Court will exercise complementary jurisdiction with national courts over a limited number of individuals who bear the greatest responsibility for committing any of the four crimes of genocide, crimes against humanity, war crimes, or aggression.[12] As such, the Court's jurisdiction only extends to a natural persons "who commits a crime within the jurisdiction of the Court [who] shall be

[10] ICC, Situations and Cases, available online at: https://www.icc-cpi.int/pages/situation.aspx (ICC has since opened formal investigations in Afghanistan, Colombia, Georgia, Guinea, Honduras, Ivory Coast, Nigeria and the Palestinian territories) (last visited on February 15, 2022).

[11] Chile Eboe-Osuji, Administering International Criminal Justice Through the African Court—Opportunities and Challenges in International Law, 838 at 844 in THE AFRICAN COURT OF JUSTICE AND HUMAN AND PEOPLES' RIGHTS IN CONTEXT—Developments and Challenges (Charles C. Jalloh, Kamari M. Clarke and Vincente O. Nmehielle, eds Cambridge, 2021) Judge Eboe-Osuji was formerly a judge of the ICC.

[12] Rome Statute, *supra* note 2, Preamble para.10, arts. 1, 17(1), & 19(2)(b).

held individually responsible and liable for punishment ...".[13] Thus, the Court's jurisdiction does not extend to states or organizations.[14] Additionally, the Court's jurisdiction will not apply retroactively because the Rome Statute limits the Court's jurisdiction to crimes committed after July 1, 2002, being the date the Rome Statute entered into force.[15] With respect to States that become parties to the Rome Statute after its entry into force, the Court will exercise its jurisdiction only for crimes committed after the State becomes a party to the Rome Statute, unless the State has made a declaration accepting the Court's jurisdiction at an earlier time.[16] The ICC has jurisdiction if the crimes have been committed in the territory of a State which has ratified the ICC Statute or on its vessel and aircraft; or when the crimes have been committed by a national of a State which has ratified the ICC Statute.[17]

Also, the Court may exercise jurisdiction against nationals of a non-state party or for a crime committed in the territory of a non-state party in one of two ways. First, the Court may exercise jurisdiction over crimes committed in the territory of a non-party State or crimes committed by a national of a non-party State if the State which has not ratified the ICC's Statute makes a declaration accepting the Court's jurisdiction over the crime.[18] Second, where a situation is referred to the Court by the Security Council pursuant to Article VII of the UN Charter, the Court's territorial jurisdiction literally extends to the whole world.[19] In other words, the Court has jurisdiction over such situation whether or not the crime occurred in the territory of a State Party and/or whether or not the accused is a national of a State Party. It is also immaterial that the non-party State in whose territory the crime occurred or whose national is accused of the crime did not consent to the Court's jurisdiction.

With respect to subject matter jurisdiction, the Court can only exercise jurisdiction for acts that qualify as war crimes, crimes against humanity,

[13] *Id.*, Arts. 1, 25.

[14] *Id.*, Art. 25(4) (stating that "no provisions of this Statute relating to individual criminal responsibility shall affect the responsibility of States under international law").

[15] *Id.*, Art. 11(1).

[16] *Id.*, Arts. 11, 12(3).

[17] *Id.*, Arts. 12; 13(a)(c).

[18] Rome Statute, *supra* note 2, Arts. 12(3).

[19] *Id.*, Arts. 13(b).

and genocide occurring from July 2002 when the ICC's Statute went into force for those 60 states that ratified the Rome Statute on that date. For other State Parties, the date of the Court's exercise of jurisdiction over those three crimes will be based on the date those countries ratified the ICC statute after the July 2002 date. The Court's jurisdiction also covers the crime of aggression following the amendment of the Rome Statute in 2012. Since the amendment, only 68 states have ratified the amendment to allow the Court to exercise jurisdiction for the crime of aggression occurring in their territory. Based on the amendment, the earliest date the Court may exercise jurisdiction over the crime of aggression would be July 2022.

2.2 *The Emergence of "Africa Only Docket" in the ICC*

Article 13 of the Rome Statute provides three mechanisms to trigger the Court's exercise of jurisdiction. As such, for a case to be brought before the Court, it must be initiated by 1) a State Party to the Rome Statute as detailed under Articles 12 and 14. Second, a case can be initiated by a referral to the Prosecutor by the Security Council acting under Chapter VII of the Charter of the United Nations. Third, the ICC Prosecutor may initiate an investigation in respect of such a crime within the jurisdiction of the Rome Statute in a manner detailed under Article 15. Further, under Article 12(3), a non-state party to the Rome Statute may by a declaration refer a situation to the ICC's Prosecutor. In essence, the only time the ICC may begin a case is only when the ICC Prosecutor *proprio motu* commence an investigation in accordance with Article 15. Such investigation may be truncated by the ICC Pre-Trial Chamber[20] or suspended by the UNSC under Article 16.[21] Other than that, all other investigations are commenced through a referral by a State or the UNSC.

From the time the ICC went into operation in 2003, it investigated situations and prosecuted cases in six African countries. Four of these situations were referred to the Court by the states in question—the situations in Uganda, Democratic Republic of Congo, Central African Republic, and Côte D'Ivoire. The situations in Sudan and Libya, non-party States,

[20] Rome Statute, *Supra* note 2, Arts. 15 and 17.

[21] *Id.*, Art. 16 allows the UNSC to defer an investigation or prosecution periodically for 12 months at a time.

were referred to the ICC by the UN Security Council acting under its Chapter VII powers. Within the relevant time, the ICC Prosecutor "triggered" the Court's jurisdiction one time relating to situations concerning post-election violence in Kenya, and initially, with the approval of the government of Kenya.

As can be seen above, there is no grounds for the claim that the ICC is deliberately targeting the African continent. However, there is reason to feel that the UNSC's referrals have not been consistent. For instance, a legitimate argument can be made that the Court should be investigating and prosecuting the situations in Syria, Argentina, Myanmar, Iraq, etc. However, some of these countries including Syria are not State Parties to the ICC statute. As such, absent self-referral by the States, which is implausible, the other option is a referral by the UNSC. A UNSC referral requires the concurrence of all five permanent members of the UNSC. It is unlikely that this will happen because Russia, and possibly China, are likely going to use their veto powers to prevent any UNSC resolution to refer the situations especially, in Syria to the Court. Therefore, the validity of the claim that ICC is biased toward Africa can only be justified when viewed from situations in other non-African States that should have been brought before the ICC. However, these situations can only have been brought before the ICC by the States or through the UNSC referral. The inconsistency in UNSC's exercise of its referral authority cannot and should not be attributable to the Court. Historically, UNSC has not had a uniformity of actions. Its activities have been dictated more by geopolitics than by objectivity or uniformity.

Concerned about the effect the UNSC's actions may have on the ICC, this writer had previously warned that:

> While the Security Council's cooperation with the Court [ICC] will enhance its effectiveness, ... States, particularly developing and "third" world countries, may view the Court as another vestige of western domination.[22]

But that does not mean that the perception is a reality especially in the context of how the ICC acquired "African only" docket. In response

[22] Remigius Chibueze, Bottlenecks to the Rome Statute, 12 ANN. SURV. INT'L & COMP. L. 185, 202 (2006).

to the criticism that ICC is biased toward Africa, Fatou Bensouda, Chief Prosecutor for the ICC, an African, opined as follows:

> With due respect, what offends me most when I hear criticisms about the so-called African bias is how quick we are to focus on the words and propaganda of a few powerful, influential individuals and to forget about the millions of anonymous people that suffer from these crimes ... because all the victims are African victims.[23]

There is no African bias by the ICC as an institution. The so-called African opposition to the Court is an attempt to discredit the ICC by a few African political and military leaders to avoid international criminal accountability. The genocidaires, war criminals, and perpetrators of crimes against African nationals should not hide under the guise of advocating for their victims to avoid international accountability for their crimes.

3 The Creation of the African Court of Justice and Human and Peoples' Rights (ACJHR)

One of the forms of opposition to the ICC that has been advocated by some African Head of States is the creation of the International Criminal Jurisdiction of the African Court of Justice and Human and Peoples' Rights (ACJHR). The section of this chapter is concerned with the extension of the jurisdiction of the ACJHR to include competence to prosecute crimes which are under the jurisdiction of the ICC. The ACJHR was not an original conception. Rather, the court resulted first from a merger of two independent courts. Subsequently, the merged court was renamed, and its jurisdiction expanded remarkably as discussed below.

[23] David Smith, *New Chief Prosecutor Defends International Criminal Court*, The Guardian, May 23, 2012, available online (last visited on February 27, 2013); and Fatou Bensouda, *Law as a Tool for World Peace and Security*, Open Society Initiative for Southern Africa, June 4, 2012, available online (last visited on February 27, 2013).

3.1 *The Establishment and Mandate of the African Court on Human and Peoples' Rights (ACHPR)*

The first court created by the African Union is the African Court on Human and Peoples' Rights ("ACHPR") which was established on June 10, 1998, in Ouagadougou, Burkina Faso.[24] The ACHPR was modeled after the other regional human rights courts such as the European Court of Human Rights and the Inter-American Court of Human rights. It came into force on January 25, 2004, after it was ratified by more than 15 countries. The ACHPR has its permanent seat in Arusha, the United Republic of Tanzania. The Court applies the provisions of the African Charter on Human and Peoples' Rights and other human rights instruments ratified by the States concerned.

The mandate of the Court is to complement and reinforce the functions of the African Commission on Human and Peoples' Rights (the "African Commission" or "the Banjul Commission"), which is a quasi-judicial body charged with monitoring the implementation of the African Charter on Human and Peoples' Rights ("Charter").[25] As such, the ACHPR has authority to hear all cases and disputes submitted to it regarding the interpretation and application of the Charter, the Protocol, and any other relevant human rights instrument ratified by the concerned States.[26] Also, the ACHPR can hear complaints of human rights violations brought by individuals against their home states.[27]

[24] The Protocol to the African Charter on Human and Peoples' Rights on the Establishment of an African Court on Human and Peoples' Rights adopted June 10, 1998, in Ouagadougou, Burkina Faso and entered into force on January 25, 2004 ("ACHPR Protocol").

[25] The African Court on Human and Peoples' Rights, Basic Information, available at: https://www.african-court.org/wpafc/basic-information/

[26] ACHPR Protocol, *supra* note 24, Art. 3.

[27] *Id.*, Art. 5(3); 34(6) requiring that a State at the time of ratifying the Protocol to make a declaration accepting the competence of the Court to receive cases under Article 5(3).

3.2 *The Establishment and Mandate of the Court of Justice of the African Union (ACJ)*

The Court of Justice of the African Union ("ACJ")was created on July 11, 2003, in Maputo, Mozambique.[28] The ACJ was originally created to act as the principal judicial organ of the African Union.[29] ACJ's primary competence was to decide disputes between AU countries over the interpretation of AU treaties.[30] The ACJ entered into force on February 11, 2009, after the Protocol was ratified by 15 states. However, the ACJ never went into operation because the AU decided to merge it with the ACHPR to form the African Court of Justice and Human Rights (ACJHR).[31]

3.3 *Establishment and Mandate of the African Court of Justice and Human Rights (ACJHR)*

As noted above, the Merger Protocol merged the ACHPR and the ACJ to create a single court to be known as the African Court of Justice and Human Rights ("ACJHR").[32] The ACJHR will have the combined jurisdictional competence of the ACHPR and ACJ.[33] The decision to merge the two courts was the concern at the growing number of AU institutions, which the AU could not afford to support.[34] Therefore, a merger

[28] The Protocol of the Court of Justice of the African Union adopted July 11, 2003, in Maputo, Mozambique, available at https://au.int/en/treaties/protocol-court-justice-african-union ("ACJ Protocol").

[29] ACJ Protocol, *supra note* 28, Art. 2.2.

[30] *Id.*, Art. 19.

[31] African Union, Protocol on the Statute of the African Court of Justice and Human Rights, 1 July 2008 ("Merger Protocol"), available online at: https://au.int/sites/default/files/treaties/36396-treaty-0035_-_protocol_on_the_statute_of_the_african_court_of_justice_and_human_rights_e.pdf.

[32] *Id.*

[33] *Id.*, Art. 28.

[34] Kamari M. Clarke, Charles C. Jalloh and Vincent O. Nmehielle, Origins and Issues of the African Court of Justice and Human and Peoples' Rights in THE AFRICAN COURT OF JUSTICE AND HUMAN AND PEOPLES' RIGHTS IN CONTEXT DEVELOPMENT AND CHALLENGES, Kamari M. Clarke, Charles C. Jalloh and Vincent O. Nmehielle, eds. (Cambridge University Press, 2018) 1 at 6.

of the ACHPR and ACJ was justified as part of the rationalization and cost-cutting measures undertaken by the AU.[35]

3.4 Establishment and Mandate of the African Court of Justice and Human and Peoples' Right

In June 2014, the Assembly of Heads of State and Government of the AU ("Assembly") adopted the Protocol on the Amendment of the Protocol on the Statute of the African Court of Justice and Human Rights (the "Malabo Protocol").[36] The Statute of the Court annexed to the Malabo Protocol among others, changed the name of the African Court of Justice and Human Rights to the African Court of Justice and Human and Peoples' Rights.[37] At the time of the amendment, the merged court has not entered into force as the Protocol; has not been ratified by the required number of states.

Unlike the merged court that did not have criminal jurisdiction, the new ACJHR, once the Malabo Protocol enters into force, will in addition to the original jurisdiction of the ACJHR, possess the competence to investigate and try 14 international/transnational/regional crimes. Ultimately, the new ACJHR now has three separate chambers and jurisdictions[38]: (1) the General Affairs Section ("GA Section"),[39] (2) the

[35] *Id.*

[36] African Union, Protocol on Amendments to the Protocol on the Statute of the African Court of Justice and Human Rights, 27 June 2014, available online at: https://au.int/en/treaties/protocol-amendments-protocol-statute-african-court-justice-and-human-rights ("Malabo Protocol").

[37] *Id.*, Art. 1.

[38] Art. 16(1) as amended by Art. 6 of the Annexed Statute to the Malabo Protocol.

[39] The GA Section is sized with the jurisdictional competence of the ACJ with jurisdiction to examine all cases and disputes of a legal nature, with the exception of those involving the interpretation and the application of the African Charter, the Charter on the Rights and Welfare of the Child, the Protocol to the African Charter on Human and Peoples' Rights on the Rights of Women in Africa, or any other legal instrument relating to human rights, ratified by the States Parties concerned, or those relating to international criminal law. See Malabo Protocol, Art. 17(1) and Merger Protocol Arts. 17; 28(a-b; d-g).

Human and Peoples' Rights Section ("HPR Section"),[40] and (3) the International Criminal Law Section ("ILC Section").[41]

3.5 Innovations of the Malabo Protocol

The creation of the new ACJHR with a combined three Section addressing "inter-state disputes, human rights and penal aspects into a single court with a common set of judges represents a significant development in Africa and in wider regional institution building and law making."[42] Some of these innovative aspects of the Malabo Protocol are discussed below.

Codification and Expansion of International Crimes

The Malabo Protocol created an expansive international criminal jurisdiction. Under the ICL Section, the Protocol confers the ACJHR with subject matter criminal jurisdiction to prosecute legal and natural persons for (1) genocide; (2) crimes against humanity; (3) war crimes; (4) the crime of unconstitutional change of government; (5) piracy; (6) terrorism; (7) mercenarism; (8) corruption; (9) money laundering; (10) trafficking in persons; (11) trafficking in drugs; (12) trafficking in hazardous wastes; (13) illicit exploitation of natural resources; and (14) the crime of aggression.[43] Other than genocide, crimes against humanity, war crimes, and aggression that are included in the Rome Statute, the Malabo Protocol effectively created twelve new international/regional crimes.

Hitherto their inclusion in the Malabo Protocol, most of these twelve new crimes were merely prohibited by treaties that created obligations for State Parties mandating the States to take necessary domestic steps

[40] The HPR Section is sized with the jurisdictional competence of the ACPHR, described very broadly in Article 28 of the Merger Protocol as relating to "the interpretation and the application of the African Charter, the Charter on the Rights and Welfare of the Child, the Protocol to the African Charter on Human and Peoples' Rights on the Rights of Women in Africa; or any other legal instrument relating to human rights, ratified by the States Parties concerned" Malabo Protocol, *supra* note 36, Art. 17(2); Merger Protocol, *supra* note 31, Arts. 17(2); 28(c).

[41] Article 17(3) the Malabo Protocol provides that the ICL Section is seized with the jurisdiction to investigate and try 14 international/transnational/regional crimes which are fully listed Malabo Protocol Art. 28A and defined in subsequent articles.

[42] Clarke, Jalloh, and Nmehielle, *supra* note 34, at 1.

[43] Malabo Protocol, *supra* note 36, at Art. 28A.

to prohibit and prosecute those crimes at national level.[44] However, now that the Malabo Protocol has listed and defined these crimes and conferred the ACJHR with jurisdiction over these crimes as well as provides for individual criminal responsibility for perpetrators of these acts,[45] the Malabo Protocol has created an explicit international and/or regional international crime in this regard.[46]

Some of these crimes are peculiar to and of more importance to Africa. F.K. Tiba observes that "Africa has been watching itself helplessly as numerous governments were unconstitutionally overthrown, its human and material resources looted, became a dumping ground for hazardous wastes and its waters infested by pirates."[47] Similarly, Matiangai Sirleaf notes that African borders are notoriously non-natural and porous, rendering them even more susceptible to transnational crimes such as drug and arms trades, armed insurgents, and terrorist attacks.[48] The ACJHR will now have jurisdiction to investigate and prosecute these crimes, and perhaps help usher an era of accountability for the perpetrators of these crimes.

There is no doubt that if the ACJHR takes off successfully, the AU would have contributed immensely to the expansion and development of international criminal law, even if some of these laws may be regional in context and in application. Equally commendable is the inclusion of Article 28(A)(2) which authorizes the AU Assembly to, upon consensus of the State Parties, extend the jurisdiction of the Court to incorporate additional crimes to reflect the developments of international law. This gives the AU the authority to continue to "create" more regional and/or transnational international crimes to address emerging issues.

[44] For example, African Charter on Democracy Election and Governance (ACDEG), 7 adopted in 2013, obliges AU member states to "take legislative and regulatory measures to ensure that those who attempt to remove an elected government through unconstitutional means are dealt with in accordance with the law."

[45] Malabo Protocol, *supra* note 36, at Art. 46B(1).

[46] Ademola Abass, Prosecuting International Crimes in Africa: Rationale, Prospects and Challenges, 24 EURO J.INT'L L. (2013) 933, at 939.

[47] Firew Kebede Tiba, Regional International Criminal Courts: An Idea Whose Time Has Come?, 17 CARD J.CONF RES. (2016) 521, at 544.

[48] Matiangai V.S. Sirleaf, Regionalism, Regime Complexes and International Criminal Justice in Africa, COL. J.TRANS.L. 699, at 732–733 (2016).

Establishment of Corporate Criminal Responsibility
Another innovative aspect of the Malabo Protocol is in Article 46C which confers jurisdiction on the ACJHR over legal persons, with the exception of States. It goes further to state that "Corporate intention to commit an offense may be established by proof that it was the policy of the corporation to do the act which constituted the offence"[49] where the policy provides "the most reasonable explanation of the conduct of that corporation."[50] Also, "[c]orporate knowledge of the commission of an offence may be established by proof that the actual or constructive knowledge of the relevant information was possessed within the corporation"[51] even if the relevant information is divided between "corporate personnel."[52] Importantly, "criminal responsibility of legal persons does not exclude the criminal responsibility of natural persons who are perpetrators or accomplices of the same crimes."[53]

It has been suggested that one of the most ground-breaking aspects of the Malabo Protocol is the inclusion of corporate criminal liability under Article 46C.[54] There is no doubt that the inclusion of corporate criminal responsibility is significant in that corporate entities have sponsored many of the conflicts that have plagued African States.[55] On the other hand, they have managed to avoid accountability both domestically and in the new international criminal accountability which has focused more on natural persons.[56] The attention to corporations for possible international criminal law violations originated in the Nuremberg trials when the

[49] Malabo Protocol, *supra* note 36, at Art. 46C(2).

[50] *Id.*, at Art. 46C(3).

[51] *Id.*, at Art. 46C(4).

[52] *Id.*, at Art. 46C(5).

[53] *Id.*, at Art. 46C(6).

[54] See W. Scholtz, The Proposed International Criminal Chamber Section of the African Court of Justice and Human Rights: A Legal Analysis, 37 SOUTH AFRICAN YR. INT'L. L. (2012), 248 at 258; Matiangai V.S. Sirleaf, *supra* note 48 at 736; Firew K. Tiba, *supra* note 47 at 544.

[55] Vincent O. Nmehielle, "Saddling" the New African Regional Human Rights Court with International Criminal Jurisdiction: Innovative, Obstructive, Expedient?, 7 AFRICAN J.L.STUD. (2014) 30.

[56] See Rome Statute, *supra* note 2, Art. 25(1) stating that the Court only has jurisdiction over natural persons.

Allied Control Council passed laws aimed at punishing the corporations that were complicit with the Nazi regime.[57]

Africa's unsatisfactory experience of the implication of corporate entities in certain exploitative crimes that impact negatively in Africa is clearly at the heart of the expansion. Corporate criminal accountability will play a significant role to reduce corporate involvement in the promotion of unconstitutional change of government in Africa, corruption, money laundering, and illicit exploitation of natural resources. To remove impunity from corporations operating in Africa that engage in criminal conduct, criminal accountability is a necessary tool.

3.6 *The Malabo Protocol is Conceptionally Inadequate and Obstructive to International Criminal Law*

The above laudable innovations notwithstanding, the creation of the ACJHR is conceptionally inadequate and raises concerns as to the Court's viability and role in the promotion of international criminal accountability. We discuss some of these concerns here.

ACJHR's [Lack of] Relationship with the ICC

While it is true that the AU has long considered the creation of a regional court with criminal jurisdiction, the past efforts usually died in the early stages. The last effort began in 2009 when the AU Assembly passed a resolution in Addis Ababa requesting the African Commission on Human and Peoples' Rights and the African Court on Human and Peoples' Rights (ACHPR) to investigate the possibility of vesting the [merged] Court with an international criminal law jurisdiction.[58] This time, the effort to create a regional criminal court gained momentum without doubt because of some African Head of States concerned with the ICC. The impact of AU's objections to the ICC to the adoption of the Malabo Protocol was noted by some commentators as follows:

> The process of negotiating and adopting the Malabo Protocol was influenced by political concerns and push back at the ICC by some African

[57] Vincent O. Nmehielle, *supra* note 55, at 34.

[58] AU Assembly, "Decision on the Implementation of the Assembly Decision on the Abuse of the Principle of Universal Jurisdiction" Twelfth Ordinary Session 1–3 February 2009 Addis Ababa, Ethiopia Doc. Assembly/AU/3(XII), para. 9.

> States under the scrutiny of The Hague, including most prominently Kenya. That context would lead to a key amendment to the clause concerning immunity of high-level officials and also fast tracked the eventual adoption of the draft regional treaty at Malabo towards the end of June 2014.[59]

Yet, with a view to distancing itself from the ICC, the Malabo Protocol made no mention of the ICC. Regardless, it has been noted that the creation of the ACJHR is consistent with international law and the United Nation's Charter which encourages regional arrangements and agencies in dealing with related matters.[60] Eboe-Osuji further notes that International law, and specifically, the Rome Statute does not forbid criminal jurisdiction for a regional court like the AC, but cautions that such regional arrangements should not be set up in bad faith to deliberately undermine existing arrangements [such as the ICC].[61]

Unfortunately, this is what the AU have done with its creation of the ACJHR ICL Section. Under the ICL Section, the ACJHR, when operational, will exercise the same subject matter jurisdiction with the ICC in its core four crimes—Genocide, Crimes against Humanity, War Crimes, and Aggression in States that are or would be parties to the Rome Statute and the Malabo Protocol. While the ICC and the ACJHR, respectively, provide for complementarity jurisdiction with the courts of State Parties, the Malabo Statute, as a later statute, failed to provide for complementarity and/or any other form of relationship between the ACJHR and the ICC. This intentional oversight is counterproductive and disappointing. The lack of reference creates a deliberate confusion on how these two courts would relate with each other.

With respect to the four crimes for which both courts may exercise jurisdiction, it is important to determine the basis of their exercise of overlapping jurisdiction over those crimes. This is necessary to clarify the basis of recognition of criminal prosecution before the ACJHR. It has been suggested that even if the ICC will defer to ACJHR's prosecutions, such deferment must be on the same basis as is constructed under the complementarity principle between the ICC and the court of State Parties to the Rome Statute. In other words, the ICC will defer to genuine ACJHR's

[59] Clarke, Jalloh, and Nmehielle, *supra* note 34, at 2.

[60] Chile Eboe-Osuji, *supra* note 11, at 838.

[61] *Id.*, at 839.

prosecutions and contingent on the "ACJHR's acceptance of the binding nature of ICC complementarity judgments on forum allocation."[62]

Further, the failure of the Malabo Protocol to clarify the relationship between the ICC and the ACJHR makes it difficult for States that are parties to the Rome Statute (with continuing obligations to the ICC), and that may become parties to the Malabo Protocol, to reconcile their obligations to the two Courts. Without a clarification of the relationship with the ICC, State Parties to the Rome Statute may be reluctant to ratify the Malabo Protocol because their obligations to the Protocol may interfere with and/or conflict with their existing obligations to the Rome Statute. It is possible that this may account in part for while there has not been any ratification of the Malabo Protocol. Also, a relationship with the ICC is unavoidably necessary for the promotion of international criminal justice and accountability and to avoid conflicts between the two courts.

With respect to cooperation, both the Rome Statute and the Malabo Protocol appreciate the need for such cooperation. The Rome Statute provides for cooperation between the ICC and "regional organizations.[63]" On the other hand, the Malabo Protocol provides that the ACJHR "shall be entitled to seek the co-operation or assistance of regional or international courts ... and may conclude Agreements for that purpose."[64] This cooperation is inevitable and is in the interest of the promotion of international criminal law. Both courts and their prosecutors may need the assistance and cooperation of each other in the investigation and prosecution of crimes within their various courts. Amnesty International ("AI") expressed the hope that the ACJHR will invoke this provision to establish a working relationship with the ICC. However, AI notes that "the feasibility of establishing such a relationship is likely to be dependent on the broader relationship between the AU and the ICC [which] at present is at its lowest."[65] For instance, AI notes that in 2010,

[62] See, Amnesty International, MALABO PROTOCOL: LEGAL AND INSTITUTIONAL IMPLICATIONS OF THE MERGED AND EXPANDED AFRICAN COURT (2016) fn. 113 referring to, The ICC at a Crossroads: The Challenges of Kenya, Darfur, Libya and Islamic State, available at: https://www.chathamhouse.org/sites/default/files/field/field_document/ICC%20at%20a%20Crossroads%20Meeting%20Summary%20FINAL%2014%20April%202014.pdf.

[63] Rome Statute, supra note 2, Arts. 54(3)(c) and 87(6).

[64] Malabo Protocol, *supra* note 36, at Art. 46L(3).

[65] Amnesty International, *supra* note 62, at 23.

the AU rejected a proposal by the ICC to open a liaison office in Addis Ababa, Ethiopia and has consistently called on its members not to cooperate with the ICC.[66] However, it is necessary to streamline a working relationship between the ICC and the ACJHR particularly as it relates to the exercise of jurisdiction between the two courts.

Immunity Provision in the Malabo Protocol

One of the most controversial provisions of the Malabo Protocol is the provision on immunity. Article 46Abis of the Statute of the ACJHR Statute provides as follows:

> No charges shall be commenced or continued before the Court against any serving African Union Head of State or Government, or anybody acting or entitled to act in such capacity, or other senior state officials based on their functions, during their tenure of office.[67]

Contrast with Article 27 of the Rome Statute which provides that:

> 1. This Statute shall apply equally to all persons without any distinction based on official capacity. In particular, official capacity as a Head of State or Government, a member of a Government or parliament, an elected representative or a government official shall in no case exempt a person from criminal responsibility under this Statute, nor shall it, in and of itself, constitute a ground for reduction of sentence.
>
> 2. immunities or special procedural rules which may attach to the official capacity of a person, whether under national or international law, shall not bar the Court from exercising its jurisdiction over such a person.[68]

There is no doubt that Article 46Abis directly conflicts with Article 27 of the Rome Statute and that Article 46Abis was intended to rectify the effects of Article 27 of the Rome Statute. Ostensibly, Article 46Abis is intended to drive home the objections of some AU Head of States to

[66] *Id.*, at 23; Decision on the Progress Report of the Commission on the Implementation of Decision Assembly/AU/Dec.270 (XIV) on the Second Ministerial Meeting on the Rome Statute of the International Criminal Court (ICC), Assembly/AU/Dec.296 (XV), para. 8.

[67] Malabo Protocol, *supra* note 36, at Art. 46A bis.

[68] Rome Statute, *supra* note 2, Art. 27(1)(2).

the prosecution of sitting Head of States such as Uhuru Kenyatta and Omar Bashir. Article 46Abis is clearly intended to proffer immunity from prosecution before the ACJHR to serving Head of States of the AU and other senior state officials ("Covered Persons") based on their functions while in office. There appears to be some confusion as to the category of persons covered by reference to the words "other senior state officials." To the extent that the immunity provision is intended to circumvent the non-immunity provision of the Rome Statute, the reference "other senior state officials" should be interpreted to refer to the same persons denied immunity under the Rome Statute Article 27 which, in addition to Head of State or Government, also includes "a member of a Government or parliament, an elected representative or a governmental official."[69]

It has been argued that the immunity provision is not inconsistent with customary international law, and that it is in conformity with Article 27 of the Rome Statute. This argument is inapposite. Article 27 recognizes that immunity provisions are procedural rules that shield *when* a person is brought to justice and, as such, clearly provides that such immunity provisions cannot preclude, delay, or serve as a basis to inoculate the accused person from prosecution.[70] On the contrary, the immunity provisions of the ACJHR, prevent the Covered Persons from being held accountable for their actions, until such a time they are no longer entitled to the immunity.

Suffice it to state that Article 46Abis is also in conflict with Article 46B(2). While Article 46B(2) states that the official position should not hinder prosecution, Article 46Abis provides that certain individuals because of their official positions, notably Head of States and senior government officials shall not be prosecuted while in office.

Also, contrary to the argument that immunity of Head of States is customary international law, Article 27 of the Rome Statute represents a codification of the Nuremberg Principles No. III and IV which repudiated such law as it pertains to the prosecution of any person before an international forum.[71] Shortly after the completion of the Nuremberg trials, the UN General Assembly on December 11, 1946, adopted

[69] *Id.*, Art. 27(1).

[70] Rome Statute, *supra* note 2, Art. 27(2).

[71] Chile Eboe-Osuji, *supra* note 11, at 844.

by unanimous vote Resolution 95(I), entitled "Affirmation of the Principles of International Law Recognized by the Charter of the Nuremberg Tribunal."[72] Principles III and IV provide that a person who acts in his capacity as Head of State or as a government official and one who acts on the orders of the government or of a superior are not thereby relieved of responsibility. Through Resolution 95(1), the UN affirmed the principles of international law recognized by both the IMT Charter[73] and espoused in the Judgment of the Nuremberg Tribunal.[74] This meant that in the General Assembly's view, the IMT had taken into account already existing principles of international law, which the tribunal had only to "recognize." Thus, by Resolution 95, the UN confirmed the principle of individual criminal responsibility under international criminal law and the customary law nature of the provisions contained in the London Agreement.[75] Article 27 as is the case with Principle III applies only to the prosecution of Head of States in international courts and not national courts.[76]

[72] Affirmation of the Principles of International Law Recognized by the Charter of the Nuremberg Tribunal, G.A. Res. 95, U.N. GAOR, U.N. Doc. A/64/Add Sess. 1, pt. 2, 55th Plen. Mtg. at 188 (1946) [hereinafter UN Resolution 95]. For a discussion of the legislative history of this resolution, see The Charter and Judgment of the Nuremberg Tribunal: History and Analysis, U.N. Doc. A/CN 4/5, at 11-33.

[73] Agreement for the Prosecution and Punishment of Major War Criminals of the European Axis, August 8, 1945, the Charter of the International Military Tribunal, 82 U.N.T.S. 279, 284, 59 Stat. 1544, 1546 [hereinafter the IMT Charter].

[74] The Nuremberg Tribunal noted that "crimes against international law are committed by men, not abstract entities and only by punishing individuals who commit such crimes can the provisions of international law be enforced." See Trial of Major War Criminals before the International Military Tribunal, Judgment, Nuremberg, 14.11.1945—1.10.1946, Official Documents, 1947, Vol. I, s. 223.

[75] "Article 6 of the Nuremberg Charter has since come to represent general international law." See Ian Brownlie, PRINCIPLES OF PUBLIC INTERNATIONAL LAW 562 (Oxford, 1991); M. Shaw, INT'L L. 471 (Cambridge, 1998).

[76] Head of States immunity applies under international law as a basis to inoculate Head of States from criminal prosecution before national courts of other States. The immunity provision is inapplicable as a basis to deny international courts of jurisdiction over Head of States. See, Arrest Warrant of 11 April 2000 (Democratic Republic of the Congo v. Belgium), ICJ Reports 2002, para. 59; *R v. Bow Street Metropolitan Stipendiary Magistrate, ex p Pinochet Ugarte* (No. 3) (2000) 1 AC 147; Court of Cassation, Criminal Chamber, Appeal No. 00–87215, Appeal judgment, Decision No. 64; ILDC 774 (FR 2001), 13 March 2001; Chile Eboe-Osuji, *supra* note 11, at 846 (observing that Head of States immunity will also apply to deny regional international courts of jurisdiction over

The existence of such customary international law must have been lost to AU State Parties to the Rome Statute or they must have repudiated such law by ratifying the Rome Statute without reservation to Article 27. As such, the AU countries that are State Parties to the ICC have already acquiesced to the fact that immunity provisions are no longer a legitimate basis to avoid immediate accountability for international crimes. It should be stressed that majority, if not all of these international crimes will not occur without the active participation or enabling of the Covered Persons.

Furthermore, it has been argued that the immunity provision merely postpones the culpability of the Covered Persons, and that the Malabo protocol provides that there is no statute of limitation.[77] Yet, it is also true that the longer it takes to hold these Covered Persons accountable, there is the risk that the evidence will disappear, witnesses will die off or suffer memory loss, interest in prosecution will wane, other issues will become more pressing, covered parties will age or die.[78] In the end, accountability will be less efficacious and meaningless, ultimately justifying the maxim that justice delayed is justice denied. The whole essence of international individual criminal accountability is that prosecution of such crimes will deter perpetrators from engaging in such crimes. Postponing the accountability time for Covered Persons is tantamount to rendering the deterrence factor irrelevant.

Additionally, the immunity provision may create unintended consequences in the sense that Covered Persons may hang on to power/office to avoid criminal prosecution. By so doing, this may result in instability and lead to corruption, aggression, or unconstitutional change of government in contravention to the new transnational crimes created by the Malabo Protocol.

Inadequate Human and Financial Resources

As earlier noted, the ACJHR was not a novel court but was an amalgamation of two prior courts—the ACJ and ACHPR. When the merger occurred, the merger court inherited all the jurisdictions of the two courts without an expanded personnel or resources. The same format

the prosecution of Head of States of States that are not within the region that created such regional courts).

[77] Malabo Protocol, *supra* note 36, Art. 28A(3).

[78] As was the case with the principal parties in the Khumer Rouge regime, etc.

was followed with the expanded ACJHR. The jurisdiction of the new ACJHR encompasses the original (expanded) jurisdiction of the merged court plus the additional new ICL jurisdictions of the ACJHR. The inclusion of these expanded, but different subject matter jurisdictions of the ACJHR are contained in three separate sections—a GA Section, a HPR Section, and an ICL Section.[79]

Like the ICC, the ICL Section is further divided into three Chambers comprised of a Pre-Trial Chamber, a Trial Chamber as well as a new Appellate Chamber. It is intended that appeals are allowed only for the ICL Section, not the Human Rights or General Sections, giving prosecutors and defendants a right to appeal from a decision of the Pre-Trial Chamber or the Trial Chamber.[80] The right to appeal was provided to ensure compliance with current international human rights standards, in particular, the right to a second level review pursuant to Article 14 of the International Covenant on Civil and Political Rights which is widely deemed to be customary international law.[81]

However, the Malabo Protocol did not provide the ACJHR with additional judges to handle the enhanced original and new appellate jurisdictions. Contextually, when the ACHPR and ACJ were created, each was supposed to have eleven judges.[82] After the merger of ACHPR and ACJ, the merged court was supposed to have 16 judges instead of 22.[83] The merged court was supposed to have only two chambers—the General Affairs Chamber and the Human and Peoples Right Chamber, each chamber with 8 judges, respectively.[84] The new ACHPR will be composed with the same number of 16 judges. Instead of the GA Section and HPR Section with 8 judges as was the case in the merger court, both Sections are now composed of 3 judges.[85] The new ICL Section would be composed of 1 judge for the Pre-trial Chamber, 3 judges for the Trial Chamber, and 5 judges for the Appellate Chamber.[86] On the

[79] Malabo Protocol, *supra* note 36, at Art. 17.

[80] Art. 18(2).

[81] Clarke, Jalloh, and Nmehiell, *supra* note 34, at 13.

[82] ACJ Statute, *supra* note 28, Art. 11; ACHPR Statute, *supra* note 24, Art. 11.

[83] Merger Protocol, *supra* note 31, Art. 16.

[84] *Id.*, Art. 19.

[85] Malabo Protocol, *supra* note 36, at Art. 21(1)(2).

[86] Malabo Protocol, *supra* note 36, at Art. 21(3)(4)(5).

other hand, the ICC with jurisdiction only over four crimes is composed of 18 judges.[87] This glaring inadequate judicial personnel has led some to questioned whether there will be enough judicial capacity to do anything close to the justice that the ACJHR with expansive civil, human rights, and criminal jurisdiction proposes.[88]

In addition, with the expanded jurisdiction, the Malabo Protocol also created the relevant Office of the Prosecutor, the Registry, and the Defense Office. These offices have to be staffed, equipped, and financed. Further, exercise of criminal jurisdiction involves a lot more funding than the Human and Peoples' Right Section and the GA Section. Funds are required for operational costs relating to investigations, obtaining evidence, prosecutions, and associated costs concerning the participation of victims and witnesses. Detention facilities will need to be procured and operated and if volunteered by State Parties to the Protocol, would need logistical supports. Yet, the AU has historically provided a comparatively low budget for the existing AU Courts which pales in comparison to the budgets of the ICC or the ad hoc tribunals such the International Criminal Tribunal for Yugoslavia (ICTY) and the International Criminal Tribunal for Rwanda (ICTR) that had narrower judicial mandates.[89]

4 Conclusion

The claim of ICC bias toward African countries is unsupported by the factual basis for the ICC's cases relating to African countries. Therefore, AU opposition to the ICC is unwarranted. The creation of new regional/transnational/international crimes, especially of particular concerns to Africa is commendable. However, the extension of the ACJHR to include fourteen crimes under its ICL jurisdiction without addition of human and financial resources to the ACJHR unduly overburdens and overextends the resources of the ACJHR. All these new additional operational costs, human resources, and infrastructural needs

[87] Rome Statute, *supra* note 2, Art. 36(1).

[88] Max du Plessis, Implications of the AU decision to give the African Court jurisdiction over international crimes, at 7, Institute for Security Studies (ISS), ISS Paper 235, June 2012, available at: https://www.files.ethz.ch/isn/145422/Paper235-AfricaCourt.pdf (last visited February 10, 2022).

[89] *Id.*, at 9; Clarke, Jalloh and Nmehielle, *supra* note 34, at 42–43.

seem overwhelming for the AU that has historical institutional funding challenges.[90]

Relatedly, the extension of international criminal jurisdiction to the ACJHR without any formal relationship with the ICC is inexplicable. A relationship with the ICC is unavoidably necessary for the promotion of international criminal justice and accountability and to avoid conflicts between the two courts. Further, the inclusion of immunity provision in the Malabo Protocol to shield Head of States and other government officials from prosecution while in office contravenes international law position on Head of States immunity. The immunity provision only applies to deny the ACJHR jurisdiction and the ICC will not consider such failure to investigate and/or prosecute as a basis to deprive the ICC of jurisdiction. Normalization of the relationship between the ACJHR and the ICC will require the removal of the immunity provisions.

[90] Clarke, Jalloh and Nmehielle, *supra* note 34, at 6 (noting that AU had merged the ACJ and ACHPR because of inability to fund the growing number of AU institutions).

CHAPTER 9

The Supremacy of Might Over Right in the International Legal Order

Larry O. C. Chukwu and Patience N. Tochukwu

1 Introduction

Perhaps, only a relatively small number of rules of public international law do not owe their existence to the consensus of members of the international community. These are either the logical precondition for the existence of any legal system, such as rules of interpretation and rules providing sanctions, or they are the logical precondition for the existence of a multiple-state system, such as the rules delimiting the jurisdiction of individual states. Rules of this kind are binding on all small states, regardless of their consent. They can be called the common or necessary international law, the *jus necessarium* of the modern state system. Their binding force does not affect the sovereignty of the individual nations. Indeed, it makes sovereignty as a legal concept possible. For, without the mutual respect for the territorial jurisdiction of the individual nation, and without the legal enforcement of that respect, international law and a

L. O. C. Chukwu (✉) · P. N. Tochukwu
Faculty of Law, University of Abuja, Abuja, Nigeria
e-mail: lariceejay@yahoo.co.uk

E. Duruigbo et al. (eds.), *International Law and Development in the Global South*, https://doi.org/10.1007/978-3-031-13741-9_9

state system based on it could not exist. Aside from these few common and necessary rules of international law, each individual nation survives as the highest law-giving authority, insofar as rules of international law binding on her are concerned.

The injustices of war and other predatory tendencies in international relations impelled the Dutchman, Hugo Grotius (1583–1645), to seek for more humane ways to conduct international politics. His efforts earned him the sobriquet "father of international law". Building upon the foundations laid by Hugo Grotius, especially his magnum opus, *On the Law of War and Peace* (published in 1625), other writers and publicists of his era developed and consolidated the core principles of international law governing the rights and responsibilities of states in relation to one another. However, it was left for multilateral agreements, beginning with the Treaty of Westphalia 1648[1] and culminating in a concatenation of treaties wrought in the eighteenth through the twentieth centuries, to accomplish a codification of that early system of international law.

Over the years, it has become apparent that international adjudication has by no means been effective in checkmating the powerful and ambitious nations. Thus, the superpowers holding the aces, not only call the shots, but determine what is right or wrong. Even when a dispute becomes a subject of international adjudication, indeed, they control the adjudicating organs and processes. By and large, it is the most powerful nations that are always right and the weaker nations often have to swallow the better pill.

2 The Theoretical Context

Judicial adjudication via a hierarchical court system serves as a restraint and exerts a profound pacifying influence on conflicts within the municipal order. What inhibits the extension of this ideal to the international scene remains a vexed question. An efficient judicial system necessarily will have three fundamentals of compulsory jurisdiction, hierarchy of judicial decisions, and the application of the rule of *stare decisis*. Unfortunately, international law is deficient in all these characteristics.

[1] This Treaty terminating the Thirty Years' War ended the power of the Holy Roman Empire, with France emerging as the dominant European power.

Professor John Chipman Gray[2] remarks that "on no subject of human interest, except theology, has there been so much loose writing and nebulous speculation as on international law". Another international law scholar[3] postulates that sovereign states are losing political and legal authority to alternative governmental structures, and the outstanding new fact of modern international politics is that "the grand simplicity of the sovereign state, on which the positivist paradigm is grounded, is in serious decline and the theory and reality of indivisible sovereignty will be weaker still in the coming century". On his part, Singh[4] holds the view that, although the creation of international tribunals during the twentieth century indicates progress, the concept of sovereignty remains a potent barrier to adjudication.

3 The Politics of International Law

It does appear that an increasing number of writers express the opinion that there is no such thing as international law. This scepticism, however, arises from the politics of international law. It is trite law that treaties are only valid if made between the subjects of international law, and these are basically state entities,[5] at least, in the classical sense or before the emergence of non-state actors in international relations that are also subjects of international law. However, it is in the nature of law that it is partly driven by political ideologies and class interests.[6] And, sure enough, international law is not immune to this contradiction in jurisprudence. Before the nineteenth-century growth of colonial and imperialist ambitions in Europe, European jurists had propagated the law of nations (international law) within the classical and fundamental principle of the natural law

[2] *Nature and Sources of the Law* (New York: The Macmillan Company, 1927), 127.

[3] Janis, M. W., "International Law?" (1991) *Harvard International Law Journal*, Vol. 32, No. 2, 363 at 369.

[4] Singh, N., *The Role and Record of the International Court of Justice* (Dordrecht, The Netherlands: Martinus Nijhoff, 1989), 39.

[5] See Bennion, T., "Treaty-making in the Pacific in the Nineteenth Century and the Treaty of Waitangi", (2004) *Victoria University of Wellington Law Review*, Vol. 35, No. 1, 165; see also Agwu, F. A., *Themes and Perspectives on Africa's International Relations*, (Ibadan: University Press, 2013), 16–17.

[6] See Uchegbu, A., *The Jurisprudence of the Nigerian Legal Order* (Lagos: Ecowatch Publications, 2004), 14–17.

ideology, which was the universality of the family of nations, irrespective of area, race, colour, or creed.[7]

However, with the emergence of colonialist and imperialist ambitions, some European jurists began to look for ways and means of using positivist thinking to justify or legitimize their governments' incursion into other parts of the world, thus prompting the designing by these jurists of a Euro-centric international law that draws a distinction between the "civilized" and "uncivilized" peoples.[8] Hence, from Grotius, Cornelius van Bynkershoek, Liebnitz, and Montesquieu to Wheaton, among others, early European writers espoused the Euro-centric view of the distinction between the "European law of nations" and "that of other races of mankind". Bynkershoek, for instance, wrote that "the law of nations is that which is observed in accordance with the light of reason, between nations, if not among all, at least certainly among the greater part, and those the most civilized".[9] Wheaton, on his part, opined that "there is then … no universal law of nations … binding upon the whole human race—which all mankind in all ages and countries, ancient and modern, savage and civilized, Christian and Pagan have recognized in theory or in practice, have professed to obey, or have in fact obeyed".[10]

Within this Euro-centric perspective, therefore, the existence of a state became necessarily a matter of fact, not of law; and "the idea of a state necessarily implies that of a habitual obedience of its members to those persons on whom the superiority is vested, and of a fixed abode, and definite territory belonging to the people by whom it is occupied".[11] The essence of the criterion of statehood is considered imperative because, in its absence, no body politic would exist with the capability of making the cession of sovereignty, and the requirement of a fixed abode is to prevent "an unsettled horde of wandering savages not yet formed into a civil society" from laying claim to statehood.[12]

[7] See Bennion, *supra* note 5.

[8] *Ibid.*

[9] Quoted *ibid.*

[10] Wheaton, H., *Elements of International Law*, 8th ed. (Boston: Little, Brown and Company, 1866), 17–18.

[11] *Ibid*, at 26, 30.

[12] *Ibid.*

More importantly, there is the requirement of a high standard of civilization, which is said to have been propounded by John Westlake and Lawrence Oppenheim.[13] This, according to Wheaton, translates to "a form of civilization which renders it [the state] able to apply the rules of that [international] law, and it must be in communications with the states already enjoying it".[14] This is, more or less, the same requirement in Article 1 of the Montevideo Convention (1933) that a state must have the capacity to enter into international relations. Thus, for Oppenheim's positivist and Euro-centric conception of statehood, "it must be a civilized state which is in constant intercourse with members of the Family of Nations".[15] The upshot of all these propositions, therefore, is that until a state became civilized to the "high standard" required for recognition or admission into the existing European community, the European nations owed it no duties in international law.[16] Thus, international law is essentially an instrument in the hands of the strong and privileged.

For this reason, a number of observers hold the view that international law, if duly codified and extended to even-handedly regulate the political relations of states, could become (through its own inner force, if not a substitute for) at least a restraining influence on the struggle for power on the international scene. However, as Brierly[17] perceptively observes:

> Too many people assume, generally without having given any serious thought to its character or its history, that international law is and always has been a sham. Others seem to think that it is a force with inherent strength of its own, and that if only we had the sense to set the lawyers to work to draft a comprehensive code for the nations, we might live together in peace and all would be well with the world. Whether the cynic or the apologist is the less helpful is hard to say, but both of them make the same mistake. They both assume that international law is a subject on which anyone can form his opinions intuitively, without taking the trouble, as one has to do with other subjects, to inquire into the relevant facts.

13 See Bennion, *supra* note 5.

14 Wheaton, H., *Elements of International Law*, 6th ed. (London: Stevens and Sons, 1929), Vol. 1, 30.

15 Quoted in Bennion, *supra* note 5.

16 *Ibid.*

17 Brierly, J. L., *The Outlook for International Law* (Oxford: The Clarendon Press, 1944), 2.

In view of a widespread misconception in this respect, it bears reward to note that during the centuries of its existence, international law has, in most instances, been substantially observed. When one of its rules was violated, it was, however, not always enforced. And when action to enforce it was actually taken, it was not always effective. Yet, to deny that international law exists at all as a system of binding legal rules flies in the face of all available evidence. All the same, to recognize that international law exists is not tantamount to asserting that it is as effective a legal system as the national legal systems are and that it is effective in regulating and restraining the struggle for power on the international scene.[18]

The sole source of the jurisdiction of international courts is the will of the states submitting disputes for adjudication. It is axiomatic in international law that no state can be compelled against its will to submit a dispute with another state to an international tribunal. In other words, no international court can assume jurisdiction over international disputes without the consent of the states concerned. In the *Eastern Carelia Case*,[19] the Permanent Court of International Justice (of the League of Nations) lent credence to this aphorism when it stated thus:

> It is well established in international law that no state can, without its consent, be compelled to submit its disputes with other states either to mediation or to arbitration, or to any other kind of pacific settlement.

However, it is instructive to note that no legal system can be effective in limiting the activities of its subjects without compulsory jurisdiction over their disputes. The care with which states generally guard the contractual character of the jurisdiction of international courts is illustrated by Sir Hersch Lauterpacht,[20] who observes that "this has been done, as a rule, not for the reason that another international agency was competent to decide the issue, but on the ground that the state in question was not bound by any commitment to have recourse to a judicial settlement". For instance, the declaration of the United States

[18] Morgenthau, H., *Politics Among Nations: The Struggle for Power and Peace*, 6th ed. (New York: Mcgraw-Hall, 1985), 226.

[19] P.C.I.J. Series B, No. 5, p. 27.

[20] *The Function of Law in the International Community* (Oxford: The Clarendon Press, 1933), 427.

on 14 August 1946 accepting the compulsory jurisdiction of the International Court of Justice is illustrative of an acceptance so weakened by far-reaching reservations as to reduce the strict legal obligation to the vanishing point.

4 International Adjudication

The establishment of the Permanent Court of International Justice and of its successor—the International Court of Justice (of the United Nations)—marked an important step towards the centralization of adjudicatory functions in the field of international law. Up until the establishment of the Permanent Court in 1920, judicial administration in the international sphere was completely decentralized. That is to say, whenever two states agreed upon the adjudication of a specific dispute, they also agreed on a particular person, such as the Pope, a leader, a famous international lawyer, or a group of persons to function as a tribunal for the determination of the particular case. With the settlement of such a dispute, that tribunal would become *functus officio*. The adjudication of another dispute would require the establishment of another ad hoc tribunal.

The Hague Conventions for the Pacific Settlement of International Disputes in 1899 and 1907 tried to overcome the decentralization of the adjudicatory machinery by creating the Permanent Court of Arbitration. That consisted of a panel of some 120 judges, appointed by the different signatories to the Convention. From this panel, the parties to a specific dispute could select the members of a tribunal to be constituted for the adjudication of the specific dispute. The name of the institution was rather misleading. It was neither permanent nor a court. The so-called court did not even exist as a body. As such, it did not fulfil judicial or any other functions. It was actually nothing more than a list of individuals "of recognized competence in questions of international law enjoying the highest moral reputation".[21] It facilitated the selection of judges for one of the special tribunals to be organized for the adjudication of a specific dispute. It is, however, interesting to note that the Permanent Court of Arbitration never decided a case. Only individual members of the panel did. By and large, it accentuated the decentralization of adjudicatory system

[21] Article 44 of the Convention.

in the global arena, while at the same time recognizing the need for a centralized judicial authority.

The International Court of Justice, whose members are elected for a period of nine years and may be re-elected, provides for continuity in the performance of its judicial task. This quality is necessarily absent in a tribunal convened for the settlement of a specific dispute, and terminating its existence with the rendering of judgement. A court whose membership is bound to remain approximately identical for many years—the judges being elected for nine-year terms—cannot fail to develop a tradition of its own, which it transmits to its successive members and on the continuance of which the prospective parties can rely. These elements of calculability and stability which are thus introduced into the operations of an international tribunal are in sharp contrast to the haphazard proceedings typical of the arbitral institutions established before the First World War.

It has to be pointed out, however, that stability and calculability are the psychological results of a permanent organization rather than the legal effect of the judicial decisions of the court. Indeed, concerning the legal effect of the judicial decisions of the court, the Statute pays tribute to the principle of decentralization by providing in Article 59 that "the decision of the court has no binding force except between the parties and in respect of that particular case". Although the social fact of the continuing operation of the same person within one organization is conducive to the development of uniformity and of a tradition in the jurisprudence of the Court, the Court is under no legal duty to follow the rule of *stare decisis* and to justify its decisions in the light of precedents. As Lord Denning[22] perceptively observes, two great objects are to be achieved in a good legal system: "One is to see that the laws are just: the other that they are justly administered. Both are important; but of the two, the more important is that the law should be justly administered". In primitive societies, individuals often settle their conflicting claims through fighting. They abstain from seeking a decision by violent means only when in the appeal to the authoritative decision of impartial judges they find a substitute for their appeal to arms. It, therefore, seems right to conclude that if only such impartial judges were available for the authoritative decision in international disputes, the main cause of war would be removed.

[22] Denning, A., *The Road to Justice* (London: Steven and Sons, 1955), 6–7.

However, the above statement, even though logical, misses the mark. The analogy between the pacifying influence of domestic courts and the anticipated similar effect of international courts is mistaken. Courts decide disputes on the basis of the law as it is. The law as it is provides the common ground on which the plaintiff and defendant meet and espouse their claims. Such is the fundamental issue with which courts—domestic and international—must deal. And such is the nature of virtually all cases with which international courts have actually dealt. However, those are not the issues which entail the risk of war, and which set nations against nations in deadly conflicts. Hedley Bull[23] opined that "war is organized violence carried out by political units against each other". And Hans Morgenthau[24] hit the point that what is at stake in those international conflicts which are rightly called "political" and which have caused all major wars is not what the law is, but what it ought to be. The issue here is not the interpretation of the existing law, recognized as legitimate by both sides, but the legitimacy of the existing law in the face of the demand for change. For example, in 1938, everybody knew what the legal situation was with regard to Czechoslovakia. What Germany was opposed to in regard to Czechoslovakia was not a particular interpretation of international law but the existing legal order. Germany was demanding a new legal order to replace the old, a demand that was resisted by Great Britain and France. The incompatibility between the demand for a new legal order and the defence of the old triggered the Second World War.

Any particular distribution of power, once it has attained some degree of stability, hardens into a legal order. Any system of existing law is of necessity an ally of the *status quo*, with the courts as its custodians. Therefore, since it is in its essence the *status quo* couched in legal terms, existing law favours the *status quo*, and the court can only apply the existing law to whatever case is in hand. It cannot grant *anti-status quo* or imperialistic demands without destroying the very foundations on which its authority rests. In our view, a dispute that has a direct bearing on the overall power relations of the disputants or concerned nations cannot be settled by adjudication. In such a situation, factors of power will rationally and inevitably determine those questions of power. Indeed, as Professor

23 "War and International Order" in Alan James (ed.), *The Bases of International Order* (London: Oxford University Press, 1973), 116.

24 See Morgenthau, H., *supra* note 18, 464.

Omotola[25] aptly remarks: "Revolutionary change is never achieved by mere enactment. Revolution is never a product of law. You do not enact revolution".

Of the twenty decisions rendered by the Permanent Court of Arbitration, there is none that can be called political. Of the thirty judgements and twenty-seven advisory opinions rendered by the Permanent Court of International Justice, there is only one that can be called political. This was the "advisory opinion" in the case of the Austro-German Customs Union. Even then, the request for an advisory opinion by the Council of the League of Nations only served to draw the court into a confusion that led to the greatest intellectual debacle in its history. The fact that there were four different opinions—and that, out of fifteen judges, seven felt the need to identify themselves with the two concurring opinions and seven signed a dissenting opinion—illustrates the extent of the confusion.

The point being made is that the inability of so highly competent a tribunal to cope adequately with the case of the Austro-German Customs Union was the inevitable result of the nature of the case. With the proposed Customs Union, Germany and Austria challenged the *status quo* of 1919. The Permanent Court of International Justice was intellectually prepared to deal with any case arising within the framework of the *status quo*. The legal order to that *status quo* furnished it with the intellectual instruments to perform that task. Confronted with a challenge to that *status quo*, the Court was thrown off-balance by its inability to find grounds above the contentions of the parties from which to determine the claims and counterclaims. Being an organ of the *status quo*, and performing functions that had to take the legitimacy of that *status quo* for granted, the Court found itself faced with a task no court of law was capable of performing—to pass judgement on the legitimacy of the *status quo* itself by finding upon the legality of the projected Austro-German Customs Union. Judge Anzilloti, in his brilliant concurring opinion, puts his finger on the essentially political problem that faced the Court, saying that it could not meet with the judicial means at its disposal. He said:

> Everything points to the fact that the answer depends upon considerations which are for the most part, if not entirely, of a political and economic kind. It may therefore be asked whether the Council really wished to obtain

[25] Omotola, J. A., *Law and Land Rights: Whither Nigeria?* (An Inaugural Lecture) (Lagos: University of Lagos Press, 1988), 33.

> the Court's opinion on this aspect of the question and whether the Court ought to deal with it.... I grant that the Court may refuse to give an opinion which would compel it to depart from the essential rules governing its activity as a tribunal.[26]

The Court did not refuse to give an opinion. However, by trying to decide a conflict between the *status quo* and the desire for a change, it departed "from the essential rules governing its activity as a tribunal". The International Court of Justice strives to avoid this pitfall in which its predecessor had fallen. From its establishment in 1946 through 1980, the court dealt with only 59 contentious cases and issued another 21 advisory opinions on issues submitted by organs of the United Nations.[27] When in 1951 Great Britain submitted to it the case of the Anglo-Iranian Oil Company, it declined jurisdiction. The Iranian Government had nationalized the property of the Anglo-Iranian Oil Company in obvious violation of the existing treaties. The dispute between Iran and Great Britain did not concern the applicability of existing law. It rather concerned the legitimacy of the *status quo*, codified in the existing law, opposed to the legitimacy of a new legal order. A court must assume the legitimacy of the existing legal order and defend it by its judgements.

It was perfectly logical that Britain, interested in the preservation of the *status quo*, would appeal to the International Court of Justice, while Iran, interested in the change of the *status quo*, raised an objection to the Court's jurisdiction. By assuming jurisdiction, the Court could only have sided with Britain without considering the real issue of the case. But by declining jurisdiction on technical grounds, it recognized implicitly the limitation of adjudication in international conflicts.

5 The Primacy of Realism

In December 1989, the United States invaded Panama in order, among other reasons, to topple the undemocratic regime of General Manuel Noriega. That armed attack successfully achieved the goal, but it touched

[26] P.C.I.J. Series A/B, No. 41, pp. 68–69.

[27] Rourke, J. T., *International Politics on the World Stage*, 4th ed. (Connecticut: Dushkin Publishing Group, 1993), 268.

off a serious debate as to whether or not it was a violation of international law and the United Nations' Charter provisions.[28] In the ultimate analysis, it attracted widespread condemnation by the United Nations, the Organization of American States, and the international community at large. Yet, the international condemnation did not deter the United States (in cahoots with her allies) from re-enacting similar unjustified acts of impunity and sheer display of power in Iraq in 2003 and in Libya in 2011, both culminating in the brutal murder of their rulers and institution of the United States-favoured governments in both countries.

A scenario of Might versus Right among nations conjures an imagery of Sovereign Power versus International Law. More than that, we can say that it mirrors the theoretical debate between Realism and Idealism. When Adolf Hitler[29] remarked that "power is the supreme law", indeed, he was simply echoing the realist thinking. Might may not make right, but might often determines the winner in international politics. This truism underscores the amoral slant of the global political arena.

As postulated by Professor Hans Morgenthau,[30] the history of modern political thought is the story of a contest between two schools of thought that differ fundamentally in their conceptions of the nature of man, society, and politics. One believes, assuming the essential goodness and infinite malleability of human nature, that a rational and moral political order, derived from universally valid abstract principles, can be achieved. The other school believes that the world—imperfect as it is, from the rational point of view—is the result of forces inherent in human nature. To improve the world, one must work with those forces, not against them. This being inherently a world of opposing interests, and of conflict among them, moral principles can never be fully realized, rather they can at best be approximated through the ever temporary balancing of interests, and the ever precarious settlement of conflicts. Morgenthau identifies the latter school of thought as the political realists. Of the two, political realism or the realist theory of international politics perfectly underpins the central theme of the present discourse.

[28] Farer, T. J., "Panama: Beyond the Charter Paradigm", (1990) *American Journal of International Law*, 84.

[29] *Mein Kampf* (Translated by Ralph Manheim), (Boston: Houghton Mifflin & Co., 1943), 175.

[30] See Morgenthau, H., *supra* note 18, chap. 1.

John Herz[31] succinctly illuminates the essence of political realism, which "takes into consideration the implications for political life of those security and power factors which are inherent in human society". Even though Herz does not precisely align himself with realists, he apparently believes that those factors grow out of the "security dilemma" which flows from the individual's consciousness that others are seeking his destruction, and that he must be ever ready to kill them before they kill him. Indeed, there can be no better demonstration of this phenomenon than the assassination of the Commander of the Quds Force of Iran's Islamic Revolutionary Guard Corps, General Qassem Soleimani (widely touted to be the second most powerful man in Iran), on 3 January 2020 at Baghdad Airport by the United States-deployed drone. This is one of the most topical issues of international discourse at the time of writing this paper. While justifying the dastardly act, President Donald Trump had this to say: "Soleimani was plotting imminent and sinister attacks on American diplomats and military personnel, but we caught him in the act and terminated him".[32] It is noteworthy that Trump made no mention of any specific attempt or overt act by the assassinated General to execute the alleged sinister plot. Whether the allegation be true or false, surely, the American approach is consistent with the "security dilemma" alluded to by Herz.

As Adesina Sambo[33] aptly observes, "conflict resolution is at the heart of politics". It is the ability to recognize and take into account the potentiality of conflicting interests among nations and individuals—a potentiality that is inevitable, that is derivative of the fundamental inner drives of individuals and nations—which basically stands realism apart from other theoretical paradigms. Sure enough, realities always differ from fantasies, in that the former takes into account the costs of reaching one's goal. As the Lord Jesus Christ once asked rhetorically,

[31] *Political Realism and Political Idealism* (Chicago: University of Chicago Press, 1951), 105.

[32] Available at https://www.aljazeera.com/news/2020/01/iran-tensions-latest-updates-200103022407743.html (accessed 5 January, 2020).

[33] "On the Relevance of Traditional Rulership Institution in Government and Administration," in Olugbemi, S. O. (ed.), *Alternative Political Futures for Nigeria* (Lagos: Nigerian Political Science Association, 1987), 402.

> what king, going to encounter another king in war, will not sit down first and take counsel whether he is able with ten thousand to meet him who comes against him with twenty thousand? And if not, while the other is yet a great way off, he sends an embassy and asks terms of peace.[34]

It is against this backdrop that the present threat of reprisal attacks by Iran in the aftermath of the assassination of General Soleimani by agents of the United States is viewed by many as analogous to the proverbial threat by the toad to avenge the death of its offspring that were trampled to death by an elephant. If the experience of the United States' invasion of the neighbouring Iraq is anything to go by, Iran should be guided by the age-old saw "discretion is the better part of valour"! All the same, there is no denying the fact that Iran has both the capability and propensity to create a nightmare scenario for not only the United States, but indeed the rest of the world if urgent steps are not taken to de-escalate the situation.

6 Conclusion

The saying "power tends to corrupt and absolute power corrupts absolutely"[35] has since become a universal maxim. Power itself is the best and only reliable antidote to power. Early in the twentieth century, one of the foremost modern teachers of international law, Oppenheim,[36] saw the concept of global power balancing as "an indispensable condition of the very existence of international law". In the same vein, Professor Hans Morgenthau observed as follows[37]:

> International peace and order are a function of the balance of power – that is, of an approximately equal distribution of power among several nations or a combination of nations, preventing any one of them from gaining the upper hand over the others. It is this approximate, tenuous equilibrium that provides whatever peace and order that exists in the world of nation states.

[34] *The Holy Bible* (RSV), Luke 14:31–32.

[35] The *fons et origo* is traceable to a letter written by Lord Acton to Bishop Creighton, see Korda, M., *Power! How to Get it, How to Use it*, (New York: Ballantyne Books, 1975), 10.

[36] Oppenheim, L., *International Law*, 2nd ed., Vol. 1 (London: Longmans, Green and Co., 1912), 80.

[37] See Morgenthau, H., *supra* note 18, 388.

Quite apart from conflicting national interests, this imperative of power balancing explains why the United States and Russia—two super powers from opposite sides of the Atlantic—are always in opposing camps in most conflicts all over the world, the most prominent example being the current conflict in Syria. By contrast, regrettably, the other European super powers, namely Britain and France, appear to be ever inclined to kowtow to the United States even when she clearly oversteps the bounds of decency in wielding her self-appropriated authority as the policeman or sheriff of the world.

In the *Rights of Man* (1791), Thomas Paine postulated that "Governments arise either out of the people or over the people". International law arose out of nations. Accordingly, its drive to "arise over" sovereign nations has met with formidable obstacles. It is our view that the causal nexus of this predicament is embedded in the very sovereignty of these nations. Because power is the pragmatic lever, which in the final analysis effectively determines the actions and reactions of sovereign nation-states, it accords with logical expectations that these nation-states primarily strive to attain an expedient power position. In the course of this striving for power, international legalities and niceties are often thrown overboard and the supremacy of might over right becomes a stark reality.

CHAPTER 10

State Succession in International Law

Andrew Conteh

For over a century, international lawyers have been paying special attention to the problems of "succession of nation-states."[1] The subject no doubt derives its "autonomy" from the importance and specificity of the events whose scope and effects fall within its framework. The difficulty of the exercise, however, resides precisely in the fact that its outcome appears to be largely dependent on making allowances for legal and other factors which transcend the limits traditionally assigned to the subject. And the assessment of these quite diverse elements sometimes proves particularly complex. Accordingly, any approach to the subject will have to be preceded by an analysis of the legal nature of the State: its definition and attributes, birth, continuity and extinction of its personality, determination of its constituent elements, effect of the changes which affect these elements, especially the territorial basis, etc.

[1] The first monographs on the subject were written by Gabba Questioni di diritto civile-X: Successione du Stato a Stato-Torino, 2nd ed. (1885) and Selosse(Traite de l'annexion au territiore francais et de son deinembrement, Paris, Larose, 1880).

A. Conteh (✉)
California State University Stanislaus, Stanislaus, CA, USA
e-mail: aconteh2@csustan.edu

E. Duruigbo et al. (eds.), *International Law and Development in the Global South*, https://doi.org/10.1007/978-3-031-13741-9_10

Similarly, beyond the subject, due regard will have to be had, if need be, for rules whose existence will have been established and which govern, from the point of view of their foundations, the peculiar legal relationships to be considered for purpose of the legal effects of succession.[2]

1 Definition of State Succession

There is a definite distinction to be made between state succession and state continuity. State Continuity means that a State continues to exist regardless of changes in government, until it is extinguished by absorption into another state or by dissolution.[3] Changes in government, as well as in types of government either by legal or by unconstitutional means, do not affect the continuity of the state in terms of its international legal personality. By the same token, a state is bound by any acts, or engagements that may have become extinct. It is immaterial that the latter had established itself in breach of the constitution, provided that it wielded the only effective power in the state.

State succession, on the other hand, concerns the legal consequences that follow when one state replaces another. Succession can occur in a variety of ways for example, total absorption of one state from another; merger of two existing states; or dismemberment of one state into distinct parts. In such a circumstance certain questions of international law must be considered. They can be summed up as follows: to what extent are the existing rights and obligations of the predecessor State extinguished and to what extent does the successor State take up those rights and obligations? An event of state succession affects a long list of subject matter. Ratione Material succession usually involves treaty rights and obligations, territorial rights, membership in international organizations, and contractual rights and obligations, including concessionary contracts, public debts, clams in tort, public funds and public property, nationality, private and municipal rights, and the like.

Ratione Personae succession includes rights and obligations: 1. Between the new State and the predecessor State; 2. Between the new

[2] See Professor Ian Brownlie, Principles of Public International Law, Oxford, 3rd ed., 1979, p. 658.

[3] J. Crawford, The Creation of States in International Law (197), p. 400.

State and third States; 3. Of the new State with respect to individuals (including legal persons).

2 Who Decides Whether State Succession Has Taken Place?

Obviously, the international community can influence this determination. Third State decisions are not, however determinative, creating a problem similar to that of recognition of State; as third States cannot recognize an entity as a sovereign State that does not want to be one, likewise third States cannot impose their view on cases of State succession.

3 Date of State Succession

The case of Yugoslavia illustrates most clearly the nature of State succession as a historical, political, and legal process of dissolution. Thus, the Badinter Commission stated in its first opinion on November 25, 1991, that the Socialist Federal Republic of Yugoslavia (SFRY) was in the process of dissolution. The Commission cited the referenda in Slovenia, Croatia, and Macedonia, the declaration of independence of Croatia and Slovenia, a sovereignty resolution adopted by the parliament of Bosina and Herzegovina, and the armed conflicts between the different elements of the Federation in support of its conclusion.[4] These facts evidenced the Federation's delinquency, falling apart, and the dysfunction of the Federation's organs.

The definition of State succession in the two Vienna Conventions is useful. State succession is the moment when a successor State appears on the international stage not the moment when the predecessor State disappears.[5] The latter moment is often impossible to establish. The international community cannot treat a State as identical with its predecessor if the new State wants recognition as a successor State. The international community can, however, keep a State bound to the obligations of a

[4] Michla Pomerance, The Badinter Commission: The Use and Misuse of the International Court of Justice's Jurisprudence, 20 MICH. J. INT'L L. 31 (1998). Available at: https://repository.law.umich.edu/mjil/vol20/iss1/2.

[5] Article 1(e): Vienna Convention on Succession of States in respect Treaties 1978 Done Vienna on 23rd August 1978. Entered into force on 6 November 1996. United Nations, Treaty Series, Vol1946, p.3.

predecessor State even if the State denies its status as a successor State, thus trying to sever burdensome relations.

4 Basic Doctrinal Positions

It is not possible to give, in the lines that follow, any detailed account of the various doctrinal positions taken by writers on the subject in the course of times. Highlighting the main features of the development of ideas in the matter will have to suffice in the awareness of the limitations inherent in any attempt to classify the various opposing theses.

5 "Civilian" Theory of Universal Succession

Hugo Grotius first introduced the idea of universal succession into international law, from the Roman law[6] doctrine, "Haeres, which applied to succession of an individual to property of a deceased person. Haeres." In Roman Law, Keir or universal succession in the event of death, the heir is he who actively or passively succeeds to the entire property of the estate-leaver. He is not only the successor to the rights and claims but also to the estate-leaver's debt and in relation to his estate to be regarded as the identical person of the estate-leaver, in as much as he represents him in all his active and passive relations to his estate.[7]

Accordingly, to Grotius, upon state succession, all rights and duties of the predecessor State automatically pass to the successor State because, in spite of the changes that have taken place, the legal personality of the state continues and thus there is no change of state identity.[8] The sovereign personality of the State is considered permanent and immortal and thus transmissible to the successor State. The territory of the State is considered as property "estate" and thus rights and duties are attached

[6] Hershey, "The Succession of States" pp. 296–297; A. B. Keith, The Theory of Sate Succession, with Special Reference to English and Colonial Law, p. C.G. Fenwick, International Law, P. 172, D. P. O'Connell, State Succession in Municipal Law and international Law, P. 9.

[7] M.C. Black, Black's Law Dictionary (4th ed.) St Paul, Minn. West Publishing Co., 1951) p.841.

[8] D.P. O'Connel, State Succession in Municipal Law and International law, p.9; see also Hersh Lanterpacht, Private Law Sources and analogies of International Law: with Special Reference to International Arbitration, London, 1927, P. 125.

to the inherited territory as well as to the State. Hugo Grotius did not make any distinction between State and government successions. As far as the transmission of the obligations of the predecessor to the successor is concerned, there was no limit. The successor, therefore, was liable for all the obligations which were undertaken by the prince as part of his princely office and those undertaken by the prince in his personal capacity; he was against the continuity of the latter.

Jurists like Hall, Hallock, Kent, Philmore, Wheaton, and Oppenheim later adopted the same view as Grotius and it has been asserted that Pufendorf, Vattel, Hefter, Bluntschli, Fiore, and Calvo did the same. But some of these jurists made some modifications to the theory of universal succession held by Grotius.

6 The Popular Continuity Theory

According to this theory, the social personality survives political changes because "the legal condition of people" remains unaffected and "territory and the men who occupy it are inseparably connected and form a permanent social personality despite the alteration of the political personality of the State."[9]

However, this theory recognized the distinction between government and state succession and accepts the non-continuity of obligations said to be of political character. State succession is considered as a fiction or metaphor affecting only the political organization of the State. The sovereign identity of the State to which rights and obligations are attached continues after state succession occurs. The State succession theory based on the popular continuity concept, similar to that of the theory of universal succession, relied on the operation of municipal law to govern the consequence of state succession and denied the rupture of state identity after state succession. The theory did not receive much support from the beginning.

The organic substitution theory of continuity makes much clearer the distinction between state and government succession. This theory may be considered as an improvement on the universal succession or the popular continuity theory. First, it recognizes the right of option of the successor State, in other words, the taking over of rights and obligations is not

[9] A.B. Keith, Theory of Succession of State with special reference to English and Colonial Law, London (Waterlow & Sons, 1907), p. 4.

compulsory. Second, Huber clearly stated the complete extinction of the personality of the predecessor State and thus rejected any continuity of the identity of the predecessor State. He asserted the fact that it is the "substitution" of the old personality by a new personality in the surviving organic elements of the State. This substitution of international personality entails the continuity of rights and obligations of the predecessor State to the successor State.

7 The Classical Clean-Slate Doctrine

The *tabula rasa* or clean-slate doctrine of state succession is a product of the nineteenth-century theories of international law. Gareis, Cavaglieri, Focherin, Strupp, Keith, Zorn, and Schonhorn, it has been asserted, developed the clean-slate doctrine in an attempt to discredit the old theories of state succession which advocated continuity of rights and obligations of the predecessor State to the successor State.

The theory of the clean-slate doctrine seems coherent and more consistent with the other theories of the State and general rules of contemporary international law. Although the clean-slate doctrine is more widely accepted today than before, there are very few cases of state succession where the doctrine was literally applied.

The clean-slate doctrine was most widely accepted and adhered to in state practice until the end of the Second World War when the process of decolonization of the Afro-Asian nations began. That means the events of the state succession changed not only their geographical association from Europe (and the Americas) to the continents of Asia, and Africa, but the roles of the European States were reversed to a large extent and they thus had to play the role of the nineteenth-century colonial period. Some Western jurists and the colonial officers began advocating the revival of the pre-nineteenth-century theories of universal succession or inheritance of rights and obligations of the predecessor State by the successor State. Such an attempt no doubt represents an effort to minimize the disruptive effects of the liquidation of the colonial empires on the vested economic interests of the colonial powers by binding the emerging state through some sort of legal gimmicks.

8 Codification of the Rule of State Succession

The Topic of "succession of States and government" was included in the provisional list of topics selected for codification by the International Law Commission at its first session in 1949. The topic was included in its program of work in 1962 following Resolution 1686(Xvi) adopted by the General Assembly of the United Nations on December 18, 1961. At its fourteenth session in 1963, the Commission endorsed the conclusions of the Sub-Committee set up from among its own members to submit suggestions on the scope of the topic and the method of approach for its study. It thus decided, among other things, that "the succession of governments" would, for the time being, be considered only to the extent necessary to supplement the study on State succession[10] and to divide the topic under three headings:

1. Succession in respect of treaties,
2. Succession in respect of rights and duties resulting from sources other than treaties, and
3. Succession in respect of membership in international organizations.

Similarly, the commission endorsed the Sub-Committee's view that the objectives should be a survey and evaluation of the law and practice in the matter of State succession and the preparation of draft articles on the topic in the light of new development in international law.[11]

Following the election to the International Court of Justice of Mr. Lachs, the first Rapporteur, the Commission divided the topic under three headings, in accordance with the Sub-Committee's recommendations, appointed Sir Humphrey Waldock Special Rapporteur for "succession in respect of treaties" and Mr. Mohammed Bedjaoui Special Rapporteur for "succession in respect to rights and duties resulting from sources other than treaties" and decided to leave aside the third heading for the time being. Five reports were submitted by Sir Humphrey Waldock from 1968 to 1972 and one in 1974 by Sir Francis Vallat, who was appointed to

[10] See the Yearbook of the International Law Commission, 1963, Vol., II, P. 261.

[11] Ibid., p. 261.

succeed him when Sir Humphrey was elected to Judge of the International Court of Justice. For his part, Mr. Mohammad Bedjaoui submitted thirteen reports to the Commission between 1968 and1981.

At its twenty-sixth session in 1974 the International Law Commission settled the find text of its "Draft articles on succession of States in respect of treaties." A Conference of Plenipotentiaries was convened thereon by the General Assembly; it met at Vienna from April 4 to May 6, 1977, and again from July 31 to August 23, 1978. The Vienna Conventions on Succession of States in Respect of Treaties was adopted at the conference on August 22, 1978, and remained open for signatures from August 23, 1978 to August 31, 1979.

As regards the succession of States in respect of State Property, Archives and Debts the International Law Commission adopted the final text of its draft articles at its thirty-third session in 1981. The Conference of plenipotentiaries was convened by the General Assembly to consider those draft articles that were held in Vienna from March 1 to April 8, 1983. It adopted the Vienna Convention on Succession of States in respect of States Property, Archives and Debts on April 7, 1983.

At its forty-fifth session (1993), the Commission decided to include in its agenda the topic entitled "State Succession and its impact on the nationality of natural and legal persons." The General Assembly endorse the commission's decision in Paragraph 7 of resolutions 48/31 or December 9, 1995, on the understanding that the final form to be given to the work on the topic was to be decided after the presentation of a preliminary study to the Assembly. At its forty-sixth session (1994), the Commission appointed Mr. Vadou Mikula as a special rapporteur for the topic.

At its forty-seventh (1995) and forty-eight (1997) sessions, the Commission considered the Special Rapporteur's first and second reports. The Commission established at its forty-seventh session a Working Group entrusted with the mandate to identify issues arising out of the topic, categorize those issues which are closely related thereto, give guidance to the Commission as to which issues could be most profitably pursued given contemporary concerns and present the Commission with a calendar of action. The Working Group completed its task as regards the preliminary study of the topic at the forty-eighth session.

At its forty-eighth session, the Commission recommended to the General Assembly that it take note of the completion of the preliminary study of the topic and request the Commission to undertake the substantive study of a topic entitled "Nationality in relation to the succession of States" in accordance with the proposed plan of action, which inter alia, envisaged: (a)that consideration of the question of the nationality of natural persons would be separated from that of the nationality of legal persons and that priority would be given to the former, and (b) that the decision on how to proceed with respect to the question of nationality of legal persons would be taken upon completion of the work on the nationality of natural persons and in the light of the comments that the General Assembly might invite States to submit to it on the practical problems raised by a succession of State in the field.

The General Assembly endorsed the Commission's recommendations in Paragraph 8 of its resolution 51/160 of December 16, 1996.

At its forty-ninth session (1997), the Commission considered the Special Rapporteur's third report, containing a set of draft articles with commentaries on the question of the nationality of natural person in relation to the succession of States. The General Assembly, in Paragraph 2 (a) of its resolution 52/156 of December 15, 1997, drew the attention of governments to the importance of having their views on the draft articles and urged them to submit their comments and observations in writing by October 1, 1998.

At its fiftieth session (1998), the Commission reiterated its request to Government for written comments and observations on the draft articles on nationality of natural person in relation to the succession of States adopted on first reading in 1997, so as to enable it to begin the second reading of the draft articles at its fifty-first session.

At the same session, the Commission had before it the Special Rapporteur's fourth report dealing with the question of the nationality of legal persons in relation to the succession of States.[12] It also established a Working Group to consider the question of the possible orientation to be given to the second part of the topic.[13] At that session, the Commission had before it the Memorandum by the Secretariat (A/CN.4/497) containing an overview of the comment and observations of governments made either orally in the sixth Committee or in writing.

[12] A/Cn. 4/489.

[13] For the consideration of this part of the topic see paras. 456 to 468 of the Report of the Commission of the work of it fiftieth session (A/53/10).

At its 2566th meeting, on May 4, the Commission decided to re-establish the Working Group on "Nationality in relation to the succession of States." The Working Group held five meetings, from May 4 to 11. The Commission considered the Report of the Chairman of the Working Group (A/CN.4/l/572) at its 2572 meeting, on May 14, and referred the draft preamble and a set of 26 draft articles (hereinafter "draft articles on nationality of natural persons in relation to the succession of States") to the Drafting Committee.

The Commission considered the report of the Drafting Committee 9A/CN.4/L/573, Corr. 1(English only) and Corr. 2 (French only) at its 2579th and 2580th meeting and adopted the final text of the draft articles on nationality of natural persons in relation to the succession of States. At its 2603rd to 2606th meeting, from July 15, 1999, the Commission adopted the commentaries to the abovementioned articles and decided to recommend to the General Assembly the adoption, in the form of a declaration, of the draft articles on nationality of natural person in relation to the succession of States.

Recalling the conclusion of the Working Group that "in the absence of positive comments from the States, the Commission would have to conclude that States ae not interested in the study of the second part of the topic," and taking into account that no such comments have been submitted by States, the commission decided to recommend to the General Assembly that, with the adoption of the draft articles on nationality of natural persons in relation to the succession of States, the working of the Commission on the topic "Nationality in relation to the succession of States" be considered concluded. The Convention, however, remains to be adopted, as part of the codification and progressive development of international law.

9 Common Features of the Conventions Already Codified

The two adopted Conventions, the text of which departs only slightly from the drafts in second reading by the Commission, have-like the draft on which they were based—comparable structures. Like those drafts, they contain common clauses and set forth common basic principles. Lastly, the features peculiar to each of the two topics have warranted a number of solutions particular to each of the two Conventions.

Each Convention begins with a preamble followed by a Part I entitled "General Provisions." In the 1978 Convention of succession of States in respect of Treaties, this is followed by a Part II (Succession in Respect of Part of Territory), a Part III (Newly independent state), and a Part IV (Uniting and Separating of States).

As for the Convention of 1983 on Succession of States in respect of States Property, Archives and Debts, its Parts II (State Property), III (State archives), and IV (States Debts) each contain a specific introductory section followed by a Sect. 2 entitled "Provisions Concerning Specific Categories of Succession of state." The 1978 Convention has a Part VI entitled "Settlement of Disputes" and a Part VII entitled "Final Provisions." In the 1983 Convention the corresponding parts, with identical titles, are Part V and Part VI. Lastly, an annex dealing with the settlement of disputes is attached to each of the two Conventions.

The preambles of the two Conventions already signed contain practically identical provisions. They refer in particular to the "profound transformation of the international community" brought about by the decolonization process, to codification "as a means of ensuring greater juridical security in international relations, to the universal recognition of the principles of free consent, good faith and *pacta sunt servanda,"* to the "principles of international law embodied in the charter of United nations, such as the principles of equal rights and self-determination of peoples, of the sovereign equality and independence of all States, of non-interference in the domestic affairs of States, of the prohibition of the threat of use of force, and of universal respect for, and observance of, human rights and fundamental freedoms for all" to the "respect for the territorial integrity and political independence of any State" which is required by the Charter of the United Nation, etc.

In addition to the preambles, the two Conventions have a set of "general provisions" in common. These are the provisions on the scope of each Conventions, the terms used in them, the cases of succession covered by them, and their temporal application. Lastly, the two Conventions contain, in addition, identical provisions for the settlement of disputes and in addition, similar "final provisions."

10 Convention of Succession of States in Respect of Treaties

The 1978 Vienna Convention on Succession of States in Respect of Treaties, constitutes, for the particular field of application which it is intended to govern, a sort of extension of 1969 Vienna Convention of the Law of Treaties, Article 73 of which specifies, expressly, that its provisions "shall not prejudge any question that may arise in regard to a treaty of succession of State." The 1978 Convention, by specifically referring twice in its preamble to the 1969 Vienna Convention, appears to endorse the conclusions of the International Law Commission expressed by it in the following terms:

> The task of Codifying the law relating to succession of States in respect of Treaties appears, in the light of State practice, to be rather one of determining Within the law of treaties, the impact of the occurrence of a "succession of States" than vice versa. It follows that, in approaching question of secession of States in respect of treaties, the implications of the general law of treaties have Constantly to be born in mind. As today the most authoritative statement of the General law of treaties is that contained in the Vienna Convention on the Law Of Treaties (1969), the Commission felt bound to take the provisions of that Convention as an essential framework of the law relating to succession of States in respect of treaties.[14]

In this respect, and within the material limits set by its purposes, the 1978 Vienna Convention on the Succession of States in Respect to Treaties reproduces, in some cases with adaptations, certain provisions and texts of the 1969 Vienna Convention on the Law of Treaties. Apart from making case-by-case borrowing of provisions, the 1978 Convention

[14] See the yearbook of the International law Commission 1974, Volume II (part One), p. 163.

repeats the general principles set forth in the 1969 Convention, albeit with a particular working where appropriate.

The 1978 Convention, however, is of interest purely because of the distinct legal effects which it attributes to the various cases of "succession in respect of part of territory," "newly independent States." If one were to outline in general terms the solutions endorse therein regarding the first and third cases, one can say that Convention opts for a "traditional" solution for the first and for a more "moderate" solution for the other. The Convention thus adopts, for the case of succession in respect to part of a territory, the traditional "moving treaty frontiers" principle and, in the case of "uniting or separation of State" the rule of continuity, in the case of the newly independent State however, it reasserts as the fundamental norm the "tabula rasa" principle. It must, however be stressed that, although this solution is aimed, in conformity with the principles of the Charter of the United Nations and in particular the right self-determination of peoples, to afford maximum protection of every newly independent States freedom to determine for itself its treaty relations, it does not at the same time endorse the idea of a "total break." According to this Convention, newly independent States remain bound to respect boundary settlements and certain other territorial regimes established by a treaty. Article 11 provides that a "succession of states" does not as much affect other territorial regimes established by treaty which it mentions; treaty obligations of a predecessor State providing for the establishment of foreign military bases are expressly excluded from the scope of application of this article.

The Convention enables, in addition, a newly independent State to establish, by means of a mere notification procedure, its status as a "party" or as a "contracting State" to the multilateral treaty which at the date of the succession was applied to its territory by the "predecessor State," this faculty is open to it regardless of the contents of the final causes of the treaty in question, so as to ensure the continuity of the treaty relations in question if so desired by the newly independent State. In the case of restricted multilateral treaty, however, the participation on grounds of bilateral treaties is, in the same perspective, subordinated to the consent of the newly independent State and of the other State party. Last but not the least, it must be noted that the 1978 Vienna Convention on Succession of State in Respect of Treaties contains an express provision to the effect that nothing in it "shall affect the principles of international law affirming the permanent sovereignty of every people and every State over its natural wealth and resources."

11 The Former Soviet Union

As an operating principle, agreements between the USA and USSR that were in force at the time of the dissolution of the Soviet Union have been presumed to continue in force with respect to the former republics.

Except for the Baltic States, which the USA never recognized as part of the Soviet Union, the USA regarded the emergence of Russia and other former republics to have stemmed from what was essentially the complete breakup of the Soviet Union. Thus, continuity of treaty relations is supported by state practice, and by the policy considerations underlying this rule. Perhaps most importantly, however, continuity has been supported by the republics themselves, who affirmed this approach in the *Alma Ata Declaration* when they guaranteed "the fulfilment of international obligations stemming from the treaties and agreements of the former USSR."[15]

This approach does not lead irrefutably to the continuation of all agreements with all republics. Indeed, there are exceptions even under a strict rule of continuity, such as where the agreement is relevant only to the territory of one republic or if it is simply not feasible to continue a particular agreement on its terms. Moreover, if an international accord creates indivisible and non-recreatable rights and obligations, as is the case with the Non-Proliferation Treaty, then it simply would be unworkable to apply the terms of such agreement to all the republics of the former Soviet Union. The parties may, in any event, terminate a treaty by consensual agreement or by unilateral action in accordance with the agreement's terms. Nevertheless, a presumption of continuity helps to preserve what is, by and large, a useful legal framework for the conduct of foreign relations.

[15] Text of Declaration: "Mutual Recognition" and "An Equal Basis, "New York Times, December 22, 1991, at A12.

12 State succession to Boundaries and Territorial Regimes

12.1 The principles of the inviolability of Boundaries

The principle of "recognizing and respecting each other's territorial integrity and the inviolability of existing boarders" is, together with the rule of *pacta sunt servanda*, probably the most important precept of international law. We find this principle in Article 2, Paragraph 4 of the U.N. Charter, in the Charter of the Organization of African Unity(OAU) of May 25, 1963, now African Union (AU),[16] in the Final Act of the Conference on Security and Cooperation in Europe at Helsinki of August 1, 1975, in Preamble of *Alma Ata* Declaration, in the Minsk charter of the Common Wealth of Independent States of January 22, 1993, in the "2 + 4 Treaty," in Paragraph 6 of the Preamble of the Unification Treaty, and finally in the Guidelines for the Recognition of New States in Eastern Europe and in the Soviet Union of December 16, 1991, of the European Political Cooperation.[17]

It is therefore generally accepted that State succession does not affect boundaries and territorial regimes, at least in so far as third States are concerned. Most authors even pretend that so-called "territorial connected treaties" always remain in force, even in decolonization cases. The ILC, however, rightly distinguishes between boundaries and territorial regimes and the treaties that had established them. It is the territorial situation that remains unaffected. Vienna I therefore states [a]succession does not as such affect:

4. A boundary established by a treaty; or
5. Obligation and rights established by a treaty and relating to the regime of a boundary. (art.11).

[16] The African Union (AU) was born during a meeting of African leaders in Durban, South Africa and thus became the successor of Organization of African Unity (OAU).

[17] U.N. CHARTER, art.2, para 4; Organization of African unity, Charter, May 25, 1963, art. II((1)(c), 49 U. N. T. S. 39, 72; Conference on Security and Cooperation in Europe: Final Act, Aug.1, 1975, art III, 14 I.L.M. 1292, 1294; Alma Ata Declaration, supra note 70,31 I.L. M. at 149; Minsk Charter of the Commonwealth of Independent States of January 22, 1993; "2 + 4 Treaty," supra note 147 at 1, 29 I. L M. at 1188; Unification Treaty, supra note 103, pmbl., para 6, 30, I.L.M. at 463; Guidelines for the Recognition of New States in Eastern Europe and in the Soviet Union, supra note 17, 31 I.L M.at 1487.

Vienna 1 Continues:
A succession of State does not as such affect:

1. obligation relating to the use of any territory, or to restrictions upon its use, established by a treaty for the benefit of any territory of a foreign State and considered attaching to the territories in question;
2. rights established by a treaty for the benefit of any territory and relating to the use, or to restrictions upon the use, of any territory of a foreign State and considered as attaching to the territories in question.
3. A succession of States does not as such affect:

    1. Obligation relating to the use of any territory, or to restrictions upon its use established by a treaty for the benefit of a group of States or all States and considered as attaching to that territory;
    2. Rights established by a treaty for the benefit of a group of States or of all States and relating to the use of any territory, or to restrictions upon its use, and considered as attaching to that territory. (Article 12)

The distinction is wise, all the more so since a great many boundaries were not fixed by treaties subject to international law, but instead were established either by colonial powers as administrative delimitations, by treaties otherwise completely obsolete, such as the Versailles Treaty or the Peace Treaties of Westphalia (1648), or go back to times immemorial. Hence the doctrine of *uti possidentis iuris.* There is no doubt that the boundary between Cameroon and Nigeria is the one fixed by the German and British Empires in a number of treaties and protocols, but are these new African States therefore to be considered as successor States to the colonial powers and bound by these treaties in all their details by virtue of State Succession?

Res transit cum onere suo is the principle underlying the stability of boundaries and territorial regimes in cases of State succession. And the Vienna Convention on the Law of Treaties expressly excludes the applicability of the *clausula rebus sic stantibus* of treaties establishing a boundary.

12.2 Boundaries with Third States and Between Successor States

There can be no doubt that States succession cannot affect boundaries and territorial regimes in the relationship between a successor State and a third State. However, disputes are frequent between successor States or between a predecessor State and a successor State having separated from it. Thus, the Federal Republic of Yugoslavia (Serbia and Montenegro) refused to recognize the other successor State of the SFRY, especially in regard to their boundaries. The Badinter Commission in its Opinion No. 3 of January 11, 1992, not only ruled that the external boundaries had to be respected, but that the boundaries between Croatia and Serbia, Bosnia and Herzegovina and Serbia, and other States could only be changed by a mutual consent. The former internal boundaries had become boundaries protected by international law. This followed, in the view of the Commission, from the principle of respect for the territorial status quo and from the doctrine of *uti possidetis,* all the more so since the constitution of the SFRY had established that the boundaries of the Republics could not be changed without their consent.

Boundary changes by force were without legal effect. *Uti pssidentis* doctrine makes it superfluous to rely upon boundary treaties as legal basis and only confirms the factual possession of a territory. The Badinter Commission consequently renounced any investigation into the genesis of the intra-Yugoslav boundaries. Of course, if there has been a treaty it can and should be used as proof of the exact delimitation of the boundary, as is being done in the border dispute between Cameroon and Nigeria.

The Commonwealth of Independent States (CIS) states have guaranteed each other the respect of their boundaries, that is, the last internal, administrative boundaries of the defunct USSR. And yet there are boundary conflicts, such as the Russian-Ukrainian dispute about the Crimea. Here the solution seems obvious, the last internal boundary is the basis which can only be changed by agreement.

The dispute between Russia and Estonia is quite different. In this circumstance, Russia wants to maintain the last internal boundary between the two Socialists Republics, whereas Estonia demands to return to the boundary of the Peace Treaty of February 2, 1920, between Estonia and Russian Socialist Federal Soviet Republic. Estonia can invoke its universally accepted thesis, contested only by Russia, that it had never legally been part of the Soviet Union but instead the victim of an occupation contrary to international law. Therefore, any subsequent intra-USSR changes are irrelevant with respect to Estonia.

13 State Succession and its Impact on the Nationality of Natural and Legal Persons

If one state replaces another "in the responsibility for the international relations of a territory," this very likely affects the inhabitants of this territory, be they natural or legal person. Nationality in this context means to be under personal sovereignty of a given State. In case of dual or multiple nationality of a person, it is usually the nationality of the State where the person is domiciled which prevails in practice. Not all States recognize the dual nationality—the claim of another State to intervene on behalf of a given person possessing that State's nationality. State succession does not result in an automatic change of nationality, as there is no rule of treaty or customary international law to that effect. Yet some successor States oblige the inhabitants of their new territories to choose the successor State's nationality or leave the territory. "Ethnic cleansing" is the most drastic method to deal with this issue, and it has a long tradition.

The successor State on whose territory the person in question actually stays has the main responsibility for solving problems that may arise in this context. However, other States, especially the predecessor States or another successor State, may be obliged to receive persons expelled or persecuted by that State or may claim a right to protect them. There are frequently real conflicts over nationality. Yet, the ILC's Rapporteur on this subject sees at present no prospect for international codification and instead recommends the drawing up of guidelines or minimum standards for the automatic attribution of nationality.

14 Dissolution of Federations: The Cases of the CSFR, the USSR, and the SFRY

In all three of these Federations, a natural person had the citizenship of the Federation and the citizenship of one of the federal Republics. Both were indicated in the passports. Nobody could have the citizenship of two or more Republics. Many people now live in a successor State other than the one to which they belonged according to their passport.

Currently, when renewing or prolonging their passports, people are obliged to choose between the Republic to which they once belonged or the Republic to which they are now domiciled. Recognizing dual nationality could be a solution to many problems for the individual in this context. Russia and Kazakhstan seem to have concluded an agreement on February 20, 1995, in which Kazakhstan allows its citizens to acquire Russian nationality without loss of the Kazakh nationality. On the other hand, dual nationality can be a burden for the relations between successor States because of the legal and political recognition of ethnic minorities which can claim the protection of their State of origin against the State of their domicile. But a negotiated agreement between the successor States concerned dully respecting the human rights of individuals and minorities is probably preferable to unilateral measures. The draft treaty of the International Conference on Yugoslavia, for example, expressly admits dual nationality.

14.1 The Reunification of Germany

No problems presented themselves in the case of Germany's Reunifications. The Unification Treaty does not even mention the question of dual nationality. According to the Fundamental law of the Federal Republic of Germany, the citizens of the German Democratic Republic (GDR) were "Germans in the sense of Article 116." On October 3, 1999, this Fundamental Law entered into force on the territory of the former GDR, and the other federal laws were extended to the new lander. Therewith the separate GDR citizenship disappeared and there is no lander citizenship in addition to the German citizenship.

Some conclusions:

1. Summing up State succession affects in different degrees:

   a. the States directly concerned including the predecessor State, if it survives, and the successor States;
   b. third States, as parties to bilateral treaties, creditors, debtors, States where assets are situated or where persons affected are domiciled, or States called upon to protect their citizens living in a successor State, etc.;
   c. the "community of international law" parties to multilateral treaties interested in maintaining the territorial coverage of the

treaty in spite of State succession events, but also natural and legal persons concerned by multilateral "law making" treaties.

aa. The States directly concerned have to settle their problems through direct negotiations leading to overall agreements in all fields. The Unification Treaty and the agreement between the Czechs and Slovaks show that this is possible. The CIS also seems to be on the right path to finding a network of multilateral and bilateral agreements covering a whole range of problems. International law can only offer guidelines for such agreements and interim solutions.

bb. Third States should not be affected; this principle seems to be generally accepted. If Vienna I and II grant "newly independent States," that is States born out of the decolonization process, the privilege of a "clean Slate" as to bilateral and multilateral treaties and debts of the predecessor State, the idea is that third States still can rely on the predecessor State. Yet this privilege was the main reason for the very low degree of acceptance of these two Conventions. And in cases of disintegration of a State such as the USSR, the Federal Republic of Yugoslavia (FRY), and the Czech and Slovak Federative Republic (CSFR), there is no predecessor State left. Here, Vienna I and II properly opt for continuity of treaties and State debt.

cc. If one takes seriously the admirable efforts spent on international lawmaking, be it in the fields of human rights, warfare and armed conflicts, trade, private international law, traffic, telecommunications, etc., one cannot but hope that events of State succession may neither exclude territories from the scope of such lawmaking treaties nor create periods of legal insecurity. Nor is it tolerable that boundaries or territorial regimes be questioned because of events of State succession.

2. The theory of continuity is just the starting point. If a successor State or its treaty partners think that a certain treaty is no more adequate to change circumstances they can renegotiate it, abrogate it, denounce it, invoke the *clausula rebus sic stantibus*, etc. The Vienna Convention on the Law of Treaties gives all the necessary remedies. Debts can be renegotiated, rescheduled, etc.

3. The four cases of State succession contemplated (and future cases imaginable) thus show that theory and practice on the international law of State succession should and could aim at the following goals: to assure a smooth transition toward the integration of the successor States into the international community; to minimize the effects of State succession on third States and on a natural and legal persons—both citizens of successor States and third States; and not to disturb the process of international law making. Clean-slate doctrines or legal agnosticism advocating worldwide consultation processes leading to case-by-case settlements lead to very long period of legal insecurity and frustrate the effort toward a worldwide rule of law.

CHAPTER 11

Local Regulation of Multinational Corporations

Emeka Duruigbo

> Poor people . . . understand that most problems faced by their communities are not legal problems, but political and economic ones. Even if the law is "on their side," unless poor people have political or economic power as well, they are not likely to prevail.[1]

1 Introduction

The incidences of human rights and environmental abuses linked to the activities of multinational corporations operating in developing countries have become the subject of increasing attention. While this problem is not the exclusive preserve of any type of industry, abuses connected to the extractive industries, especially oil and natural gas, seem to take the

[1] Luke W. Cole, Empowerment as the key to Environmental Protection: The Need for Environmental Poverty Law, 19 ECOLOGY L.Q. 619, 648 (1992).

E. Duruigbo (✉)
Thurgood Marshall School of Law, Texas Southern University, Houston, TX, USA
e-mail: emeka.Duruigbo@tmslaw.tsu.edu

E. Duruigbo et al. (eds.), *International Law and Development in the Global South*, https://doi.org/10.1007/978-3-031-13741-9_11

lion's share. A few years ago, a coalition of non-governmental organizations (NGOs) under the aegis of the California Global Corporate Accountability Project (CAP) examined the overseas activities of some California-headquartered oil and high-tech companies in four local areas: human rights, labor, environment, and community development. CAP concluded that while some companies are clear "leaders" in some of these areas, many companies are "laggards" operating in de facto unaccountability where they are not held accountable by home governments, host governments, and the international system.[2]

In recent years, there have been strident efforts and proposals to oversee corporate operations overseas through international mechanisms and national institutions. One commentator sets the background of the problem as follows:

> When MNCs are allowed to operate in weak regulatory environments, it is clear that little or no meaningful development can ever take place in the sense of the human development index and that human rights generally deteriorate. Under such circumstances, inward investment becomes injurious to the host state, because it culminates in the depletion of natural resources, assists corrupt regimes to consolidate their power, while exacerbating poverty and under-development. This is absurd, because investment is meant to augment growth and emulate solid democratic governance practices. Poor regulation further breeds poor corporate conduct, driven by the desire of corporate directors to please shareholders and of elite service providers to find loopholes in the system.[3]

International policymakers, grassroots activists, and academic commentators seeking solutions to these problems may be categorized into two groups: "Nationalists" (who argue for accountability through strengthened national institutions) and "Internationalists" (who favor international mechanisms).

Unfortunately, amid the inordinate focus on national and international solutions, little attention has been paid to what could be a very effective center of oversight—politically and economically. This chapter draws

[2] Michelle Leighton; Naomi Roht-Arriaza; Lyuba Zarsky, BEYOND GOOD DEEDS: CASE STUDIES AND A NEW POLICY AGENDA FOR CORPORATE ACCOUNTABILITY (2002).

[3] Ilias Bantekas, The Emerging UN Business and Human Rights Treaty and its Codification of International Norms, 12 George Mason Int'l L.J. 1, 9–10 (2021).

from the critical points of the divergent positions while diverging from them at another juncture. It shares agreement with the nationalists that a better guarantor of human rights is effective domestic institutions, but notes that these institutions need not be national only, but can include subnational efforts. It is also in accord with the internationalists that while we anticipate the emergence of strong national institutions, the international community needs to institute interim measures or arrangements to protect individuals and communities suffering from corporate human rights and environmental abuses. It departs from the internationalists by noting that interim measures could also consist of community-focused efforts that contribute to national institution building, community protection, and corporate accountability.

The examination of this issue is done in the context of Nigeria. Two areas in which community political and economic empowerment may be manifested are revenue management and resource ownership. Past and subsisting arrangements for managing oil revenues in Nigeria to improve the lot of oil-producing communities and promote development equity have been met with persistent failure. Two primary reasons accounting for this failure are the pervasiveness of corrosive corruption and the almost complete absence of public participation. It is imperative to design an arrangement that transcends these failings and assures revenue management in a transparent and accountable manner. In 2021, Nigeria enacted the Petroleum Industry Act ("PIA") which, among other things, provides for the establishment of community trusts, which can meet these requirements.[4] These trusts also hold the additional benefit of affording community members with the opportunity to practice democratic decision-making and engage the political process in a way that is transferable to other spheres. Such level of political awareness and astuteness will come in handy in demanding accountability not just from the local trustees but also from corporate and public leadership based outside their communities. Trusts are also likely to leave community members in a better economic shape than current arrangements. However, a more aggressive and ambitious way of improving the economic fortunes of community members and thereby more properly positioning them to police corporate activities in their community is by granting community

[4] See the Petroleum Industry Act 2021, at http://www.petroleumindustrybill.com/2021/09/01/the-official-gazette-of-the-petroleum-industry-act-2021/#.YfbA7erMJPZ (accessed January 30, 2022).

members a level of ownership over resources on their land. Thus, while the community trusts are a good starting point, it is not too early to start thinking beyond them.

This chapter proceeds as follows. Part I discusses the nationalist–internationalist debate in the context of corporate accountability for overseas human rights abuses. Part II hypothesizes that local economic and political empowerment holds a valuable key to unraveling the conundrum of retaining attractiveness to foreign investment while simultaneously promoting accountability of corporate actors to the communities and environment in which they operate. Part III examines the value, validity, and viability of community trusts as a tool for promoting local political and economic development. Part IV is the conclusion.

2 Nationalists Versus Internationalists

Embedded in the growing emphasis on corporate accountability is the raging debate between "nationalists" and "internationalists." Nationalists believe that the most effective way of deterring and redressing corporate human rights abuses or securing corporate compliance with the dictates of international human rights law is to strengthen national democratic institutions.[5]

The nationalist position is also premised on the point that international law lacks the capability to resolve the most difficult political, military, and economic issues that confront humanity and that "only the nation-state and its domestic legal system has been able to do so successfully."[6] Implicit in this contention is the recognition that at present, the nation-state is the only possible judicial entity with enough power to keep the activities of multinational corporations from prejudicing other human interests.[7]

[5] See e.g., John Ruggie, *Opening Statement to United Nations Humans Rights Council*, (Sept. 25, 2006) (expressing fears about turning multinational corporations into "benign twenty-first century versions of East India companies, undermining the capacity of developing countries to generate independent and democratically controlled institutions capable of acting in the public interest – which to my mind is by far the most effective guarantor of human rights.").

[6] Jonathan I. Charney, *Transnational Corporations and Developing Public International Law*, 1983 DUKE L.J. 748, 772.

[7] *Id*. There may be questions as to the continued validity of this observation in light of modern realities relating to the power of the State and policy options at its disposal.

This argument is further accentuated by the observation that the raison d'etre of regional and international human rights regimes is "to cause States internally to guarantee basic rights and not merely to allow access to the [regional or international] system."[8] It can hardly be gainsaid that we defeat that purpose, at least partially, when we place an overwhelming focus on international processes at the expense of, or with scant regard to the development of internal guarantees at national levels.[9] Besides, the experience with the International Criminal Court ("ICC"), marked by frustration and unfulfilled expectations as opposed to the euphoria that greeted its emergence, has shown the limitations of excessive focus on international channels.[10]Accordingly, there have been calls for a modification and emphasis on national prosecution with the ICC playing a proactive role in assisting the States in that regard.[11]

Internationalists differ from nationalists and counter the latter's position from two major angles. One angle argues that national solutions are inadequate and that certain contemporary problems that have a global dimension including climate change, HIV-AIDS, and human rights can only be addressed at a level beyond the nation-state, through supranational entities, mechanisms, and processes.[12]To this list may be added the COVID-19 pandemic that has had a huge global impact since 2020. The other angle is anchored on the argument that even if effectiveness of

See, e.g., Philip Alston, *The Myopia of the Handmaidens: International Lawyers and Globalization*, 8 EUR. J. INT'L L. 435, 435 (1997) (stating that "the policy options open to states in any real sense have, especially in recent years, become increasingly constrained, both in practice and as a matter of international law.").

[8] Bernard Robertson, *Exhaustion of Local Remedies in International Human Rights Litigation—The Burden of Proof Reconsidered*, 39 INT'L & COMP. L.Q. 191, 196 (1990).

[9] See Duruigbo (Fordham) 1290–91 (making a similar argument in the context of international litigation to address human rights).

[10] See William W. Burke-White, *Proactive Complementarity: The International Criminal Court and National Courts in the Rome System of International Justice*, 49 HARV. INT'L L.J. 53 (2008).

[11] *Id.*

[12] See e.g., Mark Malloch Brown, *Who Should Pick the World Bank Chief?* L.A. Times (May 18, 2007); Stephen J. Kobrin, *Multinational Corporations, the Protest Movement and the Future of Global Governance*, in LEVIATHANS: MULTINATIONAL CORPORATIONS AND THE NEW GLOBAL HISTORY 219, 229 (Alfred D. Chandler, Jr. and Bruce Mazlish eds. 2005).

national solutions is accepted, the process of creating and strengthening national institutions would be slow and laborious, necessitating the introduction of international measures in the interim until national institutions are ready to shoulder the burden.[13]

It is beyond controversy that many instances of corporate human rights and environmental abuses have gone without redress or remedy.[14]Some governments have not called corporations to account because they participate in human rights abuses themselves or work in concert with the corporations in the preparation of the wrongs against their citizens. The fact that developing countries are eager to attract foreign investment further weakens their position in terms of regulating or controlling MNCs. On the other hand, MNCs would unhesitatingly move their operations to more favorable environments, especially those with lax regulatory frameworks over business or industrial activities.[15]Citizens in many developing countries are also hamstrung in their quest to ensure accountability of corporate actors because of the absence in these countries of the technical expertise and legal experience that are essential for monitoring or regulating complex activities such as environmental pollution.[16]

[13] See INTERNATIONAL NETWORK FOR ECONOMIC, SOCIAL AND CULTURAL RIGHTS, CONSULTATION ON HUMAN RIGHTS AND THE EXTRACTIVE INDUSTRY 28 (Joint NGO Submission) (Dec. 9, 2005).

While building the capacity of national governments to provide protection by 'regulating and adjudicating' the role of transnational corporations and other business enterprises is important, the SRSG should recognize that in reality in conflict prone countries or in countries with a poor human rights record this is not something that is achievable in the short-term. In the interim there is an urgent need for the international community to offer some means to protect the rights of the victims of corporate malpractice.

[14] The notion that rights and remedies go together is a bedrock jurisprudential principle that should not be allowed to be frustrated with ease. For further discussion of the idea that where there is a right, there is also a remedy (*ubi ius ibi remedium*) see 3 WILLIAM BLACKSTONE, COMMENTARIES 109 (1765) *cited* in Marbury v. Madison, 5 U.S. 137, 163 (1803) ("For it is a settled and invariable principle… that every night, when withheld, must have a remedy, and every injury it's proper redress."); see also Richard A Epstein, *Standing and Spending—The role of Legal and Equitable Principles*, 4 CHAP. L. REV. 1, 13 (2001); Richard Zimmerman, *Roman-Dutch Jurisprudence And Its Contribution To European Private Law*, 66 TUL. L. REV. 1685, 1696 (1992).

[15] Matthew Lippman, *Transnational Corporations and Repressive Regimes: The Ethical Dilemma*, 15 CAL. W. INT'L L.J. 542, 545 (1985).

[16] *Id.*

Some political leaders, primarily interested in maintaining their privileged political positions are not eager to battle with the corporations, cognizant of the role that corporations can play in toppling their governments.[17]Therefore, they turn a blind eye to corporate misdeeds. This observation should not be construed as an excuse for some of these irresponsible rulers who are willing to work with the corporate sector to the detriment of their citizens.[18]

Even where national regulators are active, international regulation still appears to be the preferred choice because the ability of national officials to "actually control the behavior of corporations operating within their borders has been substantially diminished by the global dispersion of assets" thus making it virtually impossible for any single nation-state to be able to place some of these corporations under their control or exercise any meaningful influence over them.[19]

[17] The United Fruit Company (UFC) (now known as Chiquita Corporation), a United States multinational, seriously concerned that land reforms then going on in Guatemala would jeopardize its interests, orchestrated a coup in that country in 1954. See Ariadne K. Sacharoff, *Multinationals in Host Countries: Can They Be Held Liable Under the Alien Tort Claims Act For Humans Rights Violations?* 23 BROOK. J. INT'L L. 927 (1998). The same UFC also engineered an armed invasion of Honduras. See THOMAS DONALDSON, THE ETHICS OF INTERNATIONAL BUSINESS 9 (1989). Similarly, ITT played a prominent role in the overthrow of the Allende government in Chile in 1973. See Celia Wells and Juanita Elias, *Catching the Conscience of the King: Corporate Players on the International Stage*, in NON-STATE ACTORS AND HUMAN RIGHTS, *supra* note 58, at 141, 143–144; O. E. Udofia, *Imperialism in Africa: A Case of Multinational Corporations*, 14 J. BLACK STUD. 353, 360 (1984); OLIVIER DE SCHUTTER TRANSNATIONAL CORPORATIONS AS INSTRUMENTS OF HUMAN DEVELOPMENT (NOV. 2004), AT 14 (discussing "[w]ell-known historical episodes, such as the influence of the U.S.-based corporations ITT, Pepsi-Cola and the Chase Manhattan Bank in the coup d'Etat which put Pinochet into power in Chile or the role of the Union Miniere in the secession of Katanga from Congo" that demonstrate MNC interference an internal affairs of States in which they operate.).

[18] For a pertinent and penetrating discussion of the "leadership curse" that has plagued many resource-rich developing countries, see Emeka Duruigbo, *Permanent Sovereignty and People's Ownership of Natural Resources in International Law*, 38 GEO. WASH. INT'L L. REV 33 (2006).

[19] Plenary Theme Panel, *The Challenge of Non-State Actors: Remarks of Linda Mabry*, 92 PROC. AM. SOC'Y INT'L L. 20, 33 91,998). See also Addo, *Human Rights*, *supra* note 164, at 11. ("In the era of the global economy and the reduction of trading and investment barriers, the laws of one particular country will be inadequate in controlling corporate behavior.").

The internationalists, however, face a number of challenges. One area of concern is the enforcement of international rules on corporate accountability. An international tribunal or complaints mechanism set up for that purpose may be overwhelmed with an avalanche of petitions against the tens of thousands of MNCs operating in many countries across the world.

The SRSG has staked the argument that efforts should not be concentrated on the international plane as it carries the risk of frustrating the birth or stunting the growth of the necessary political and social structures for the protection of human rights in developing countries. Having functional domestic institutions would also ensure that all businesses—not just the multinationals—are held accountable for their human rights and environmental abuses. This is a cogent point, considering the glaring evidence "that firms operating in only one country and state-owned companies often are worse offenders than their highly visible private sector transnational counterparts."[20] Nevertheless, a strong counter-argument can also be made that the development of national institutions involves an immensity of time and expense. Thus, while developing them should not be ignored, to avoid continued corporate impunity, it may be more productive to establish international arrangements until the national organs take shape.[21]

The two arguments have considerable merit. Nonetheless, another approach that also needs to be considered is the role of institutions at the local or community level in checking corporate excesses and the importance of providing the right framework and tools for these institutions to emerge and thrive. Since these institutions would be more quickly and cheaply created, in view of the far smaller size of the areas

[20] *Mapping International Standards*, *supra* note 9, at para 3. See also *Latin America Consultation*, held by the special Representative of the Secretary-General on Human Rights and Transnational Corporations and Other Business Enterprises (Jan. 18 & 19, 2007), at 4 (stating that a State's discharge of its human rights obligations may be hampered where State-controlled corporations are involved).

[21] See INTERNATIONAL NETWORK FOR ECONOMIC, SOCIAL AND CULTURAL RIGHTS, *supra* note 13, at 28.

> While building the capacity of national governments to provide protection by 'regulating and adjudicating' the role of transnational corporations and other business enterprises is important, the SRSG should recognize that in reality in conflict-prone countries or in countries with poor human rights record this is not something that is achievable in the short-term. In the interim there is an urgent need for the international community to offer some means to protect the rights of the victims of corporate malpractice.

Id.

covered, they ought to be encouraged by both nationalists and internationalists. Richard Stewart, in the environmental context, examined some of the benefits of non-centralized decision-making, including fostering an opportunity for cost internalization, policy experimentation, and political self-determination.[22] Writing about the presumption in favor of local decision-making, the scholar states:

> This presumption serves utilitarian values because decisionmaking by state and local governments can better reflect geographical variations in preferences for collective goods like environmental quality and similar variations in the costs of providing such goods. Noncentralized decisions also facilitate experimentation with differing governmental policies, and enhance individuals capacities to satisfy their different tastes in conditions of work and residence by fostering environmental diversity. Important nonutilitarian values are also served by noncentralized decisionmaking. It encourages self-determination by fragmenting governmental power into local units of a scale conducive to active participation in or vicarious identification with the processes of public choice. This stimulus to individual and collective education and self-development is enriched by the wide range of social, cultural and physical environments which noncentralized decisionmaking encourages.[23]

Professor Stewart's arguments in favor of a local approach remain strong and arguably are applicable in the context of the general discussion of the virtues of local empowerment and the attendant benefits of forging innovation, effective representation, and efficient decision-making, leading to a government that serves the interest of all.[24] The next part hypothesizes that local empowerment holds a valuable key to effectively controlling the nefarious activities of corporations.

[22] Richard B. Stewart, *Pyramids of Sacrifice? Problems of Federalism in Mandating State Implementation of National Environmental Policy*, 86 YALE L.J. 1196 (1977).

[23] *Id.* at 1210–1211. See also David E. Adelman and Kristen H. Engel, *Adaptive Federalism: The Case Against Reallocating Environmental Regulatory Authority*, 92 MINN. L. REV. 1796, 1804 n.24 (2008).

[24] It should be noted that Professor Stewart favored federal regulation of intra-state environmental harms in some situations, especially where state action, which he said should generally be preferred, proves inadequate. See Adelman and Engel, *supra* note 23, at 1804.

3 A Theory of Local-Based Development and Accountability

Corporate unaccountability is primarily a feature of weak government zones.

This work theorizes that these States would become stronger, and therefore able to provide an environment in which corporate accountability is the norm, if local political communities are strengthened, economically and politically. Communities that are rich in natural resources present a good starting point for such fortification.

The nationalist and internationalist positions recognize affected local populations as victims of corporate environmental and human rights abuse and based on that understanding, stake out proposals for protecting them. This way of viewing the problem is not necessarily wrong. It is incomplete, however. Affected local populations need more than the paternalistic protection of national governments or the international system. They need to be empowered to be able to protect and defend themselves. Empowerment—legally, politically, and economically—will militate in favor of the local communities in two ways. First, it is only natural that attackers would avoid strong targets. If communities are strong, corporations will be reluctant to embark on activities that are inimical to the interest of the inhabitants of those communities. Second, even if corporations (with or without the connivance of the government) decide to engage in human rights abuse and environmental injustice, the empowered communities would be in a position to defend themselves from the attacks.

A perspicacious observation has been made that strong States and political representation emerged in Europe because strong local entities preceded them. The cooperation and interaction of these localities led to the formation of sovereign States and vibrant democratic institutions in Europe.[25] Political science professor Hendrik Spruyt has chronicled the transition from feudal lordship to sovereign, territorial statehood in Europe, attributing it to the importance of influential towns and

[25] See Kristopher W. Ramsay, NATURAL DISASTERS, THE PRICE OF OIL AND DEMOCRACY 7 (Rev'd September 2007), at http://www.princeton.edu/~kramsay/_private/oildemocracy4.0.pdf. Last visited May 13, 2008).

their need for political protection and desire for additional economic advantages.[26] According to the scholar:

> Given that towns had to contend with political opponents who wished to subject cities for their own benefit, for example, to gain revenue, towns would have to band together or seek territorial lords who were less predatorial than others. Hence, towns required either city leagues to pool their resources or high territorial lords who were willing to mitigate their exertions from rival lords. Furthermore, because these towns faced a competitive market environment where there were many suppliers and buyers and where profit margins were quite slim, they would benefit from a central authority which could override the drawbacks of the feudal system. Because of political fragmentation in the feudal environment, merchants had to engage in multiple overlord-peddler deals. In addition, the multiple jurisdictions with their tolls and different weights, measures, and coinage were highly inefficient. In economic terms, these towns would benefit from central organization which could lower transaction costs.[27]

Needless to say, in many oil-producing countries including Nigeria, the reverse is the case as reliance on oil revenues for running the country has resulted in the weakening of local entities by creating a system of dependence on the distribution of resource wealth from national leaders to the various localities and local leaders. It is necessary to re-think this arrangement and forge a stronger national union and effective state structures by first strengthening local governance.

The importance of strong local institutions in national political and economic development is underscored by the case of Botswana, another mineral-producing country in Africa but which has had dramatically different political and economic outcomes.[28] Botswana has risen from its position at independence in 1966 as one of the poorest countries in

[26] See Hendrik Spruyt, THE SOVEREIGN STATE AND ITS COMPETITORS: AN ANALYSIS OF SYSTEMS CHANGE (1996).

[27] *Id.* at 64–65.

[28] For a discussion of other factors that explain Botswana's exceptional performance, see Joseph Stiglitz, GLOBALIZATION AND ITS DISCONTENTS (2002) (discussing the interaction of a wise political leadership and assistance from experts from international institutions, such as the World Bank and Ford Foundation); Andres Marroquin Gramajo, *Where did the Miracle Come From? Exploring Institutional Formation in Botswana*, LAISSEZ-FAIRE 45, 52–53, at *fce.ufm.edu/publicaciones/laissez-faire/26–27/LF-26_Marroquin_.pdf*. Last visited September 16, 2008 (discussing foreign aid,

the world to its present position as an upper-middle-income country, in the process, recording one of the fastest growth rates in the world.[29] Botswana's success has been attributed to a combination of factors, including effective local institutions that facilitated the participation of the people in decision-making and served as a constraint on the political leaders during the pre-colonial period.[30] Through the local assembly or *kgotla*,[31] commoners were able to proffer suggestions and criticize chiefs.[32]

foreign human capital, ethnic homogeneity, relatively small population and effective enforcement of government's development plans.); Yoshio Wada and Ken Togo; DEVELOPMENT ASSISTANCE AND ECONOMIC GROWTH: A CASE STUDY OF BOTSWANA, Musashi University Discussion Paper No. 48 (February 28, 2008), at http://papers.ssrn.com/sol3/papers.cfm?abstract_id=1099080. Last visited September 16, 2008 (discussing the effectiveness of development assistance).

[29] THE WORLD BANK, AN ASSESSMENT OF THE INVESTMENT CLIMATE IN BOTSWANA 6 (Vol. 1: Main Report) (June 2007).

[30] Daron Acemoglu, Simon Johnson and James A. Robinson, AN AFRICAN SUCCESS STORY: BOTSWANA, Massachusetts Institute of Technology, Department of Economics, Working Paper Series, Working Paper 01–37 (July 2001), at 3; Daron Acemoglu, Simon Johnson and James Robinson, *An African Success Story: Botswana*, in IN SEARCH OF PROPENSITY: ANALYTICAL NARRATIVES ON ECONOMIC GROWTH 80 (Dani Rodrik ed. 2003).

[31] For a helpful description of kgotla and its several meanings, see Yonah Hisbon Matemba, *A Chief Called 'Woman': Historical Perspectives on the Changing Face of Bogosi (Chieftainship) in Botswana*, 1834–2004, JENDA: A J. CULTURE AFRI WOMEN STUDIES 1 (2005).

The term kgotla... first refers to all-powerful community institution where decisions are made. In Tswana culture, before important decisions are made an assembly or *kgotla* is called and people deliberate in a kind of parliamentary debate until a consensus is reached. The *kgotla* is also the place where rituals, trials, sentences, punishment are carried out. In another meaning of the term, the *kgotla* refers to the physical area (i.e. the courtyard) at the centre of a Tswana village where the chief sits in courts. In recent times the kgotla has evolved into part of the consultative machinery through which government policies are explained to the populace and through which the community can in turn pronounce on issues.

Id. at 3.

[32] Acemoglu et al., *supra* note 30, at 20. See also Scott Beaulier and J. Robert Subrick, THE POLITICAL FOUNDATIONS OF DEVELOPMENT: THE CASE OF BOTSWANA, 7 Mercatus Center, George Mason University, Global Prosperity Initiative, Working Paper 4 (September 2005), at http://www.scottbeaulier.com/Political_Foundations_of_Development4.doc. Last visited September 16, 2008. ("Within the tribe, kgotlas were the primary means of disseminating information to the community. At these assemblies, adult males would gather with the chief to discuss public issues. The chief received advice, criticism, and he was responsible for administering law and order.") For a

The fact that these institutions were not destroyed by the British during colonialism further ensured the survival of these institutions during the colonial and post-colonial eras, providing a check on the new political leadership.[33] The importance of constraints or checks to good governance cannot be overemphasized. Indeed, where "institutions limit the powers of rulers and the range of distortionary policies that they can pursue, good policies are more likely to arise."[34] In addition, constraints on political elites serve the useful purpose of reducing the political stakes and consequently contributing to political stability because the presence

critique, see FIONA TREGENNA, EXPLAINING BOTSWANA'S GROWTH: WITH A COMPARISON TO CHILE, POLICY INNOVATIONS 1, 9 (FALL 2006), at http://www.policyinnovations.org/idead/policy_library/data/01387. Last visited September 16, 2008.

Unlike most other authors who praise traditional institutions for their inclusivity and participatory nature, [Kenneth] Good is more critical. He characterizes pre-independence social relations in Botswana as highly stratified, sharply hierarchical, and with a concentration of wealth among the chiefs. While the *kgotla* functioned at one level as an indigenous form of popular participation, they essentially facilitated social control by the leadership by imbuing largely pre-determined policies with an appearance of consensus. Good actually argues that there has been a continuity in social control between the pre-colonial, colonial and independent political systems, and that the smoothness and brevity of the decolonization process (in contrast to the rest of the continent) also demonstrates this.

Id. See further Kenneth Good, *Interpreting the Exceptionality of Botswana*, 30 J. MOD. AFR. STUD. 69, 69 (1992) (arguing that "Botswana has achieved rapid growth with stability since independence in 1966, largely through the supportive interrelations between an open market economy and a system of elite democracy, successfully blending 'traditional' and 'modern' elements, and offering a range of fairly free and meaningful political choices.").

33 *Id*. See also *id*. at 23 ("Here again, the limited nature of colonial rule may have been important. Contrary to many other countries in Africa, colonial rule did not strengthen Botswana's chiefs and did not destroy the *kgotla* and other related institutions, nor did it introduce indirect rule with substantial power delegated to the political elites representing the British Empire.") The limited penetration of the British colonizers into Botswana (formerly known as Bechuanaland) has been attributed to a number of factors. According to Beaulier and Subrick:

Due to the perceived lack of natural resources in Bechuanaland, the high level of civil strife in South Africa and Rhodesia, and the relative strength of the Tswana tribes, British colonial involvement remained limited in Bechuanaland during the colonial period. The terrain inhibited the development of roads into Bechuanaland which further limited the ability of the British colonizers to influence the affairs of their colonists. No cost effective mechanism existed that would allow the British to monitor the events throughout Bechuanaland.

Beaulier and Subrick, *supra* note 13, at 9.

34 Acemoglu et al., *supra* note 30, at 21.

of constraints reduces the attractiveness of fighting to take the control of the state apparatus.[35] Also, constraints come with the implication that "other groups have less reason to fear expropriation by the elites, and more willing to delegate power to the state."[36]

The presence of strong local institutions provides at least a partial explanation for the different trajectories that Botswana and some other African countries took with their endowment with valuable mineral resources.[37] Some scholars have attributed Botswana's success to its toleration of dissent.[38] Comparing Botswana and the culturally identical neighbor, Lesotho, economics professors Daron Acemoglu, Simon Johnson, and James Robinson have made the following observation:

> It appears that [the] series of wars with the Boers is important in understanding why institutions that gave greater powers to the chiefs in general, and to the paramount chief in particular, emerged in Lesotho, but not in Botswana. As with Botswana the British invested practically nothing [in] Lesotho. However, the British did make a concerted attempt to foster the power of the paramount chief. To this end they created the Basutoland Council in 1910 which was dominated by the paramount and other chiefs as well as members appointed by the British. This policy seems to have undercut significantly the role of institutions such as the *kgotla,* further contributing to divergence in political institutions between Lesotho and Botswana. This difference in political institutions between the two countries appears to explain why the stakes in politics were higher and there were no effective constraints on political elites in Lesotho.[39]

The next part discusses a mechanism for the economic and political empowerment of local communities suffering, or with the potential to suffer, from corporate-related human rights abuse, namely community trusts established under the Petroleum Industry Act of 2021. This

[35] *Id.*

[36] *Id.*

[37] Atsushi Iimi, *Escaping from the Resource Curse: Evidence from Botswana and the Rest of the World*, 54:4 IMF STAFF PAPERS 663, 675 (2007) (echoing the sentiment that "Botswana's good institutions, particularly in the private property area, have stemmed from its precolonial political institutions, limited British colonialism, strong political leadership since independence, and the elite's motivation to reinforce institutions.").

[38] See e.g., George Ayittey, AFRICA BETRAYED (1992).

[39] Acemoglu et al., *supra* note 30, at 30.

arrangement favors an all-hands-on-deck approach in which community members take responsibility for the situation of things where they live. While corporate contribution to human rights and environmental abuses is incontrovertible, it cannot be gainsaid that the current situation is partly traceable to the activity of political actors and the passivity of the rest of the population. Almost everyone bears responsibility for the state of affairs and should share the responsibility for fixing it.

4 Community Trusts

This part discusses the concept of trusts and its recent application under new federal legislation in Nigeria. The community trusts to be created under the legislation provide a useful departure point to canvass for an increased level of rights and responsibilities for communities hosting oil and gas operations in Nigeria.

4.1 Concept of Trusts

A trust is an arrangement in law in which legal ownership of an asset, the *res*, is transferred to a trustee who becomes responsible for managing the *res* for the benefit of another person or persons, the beneficiaries.[40] In the case of the community trust funds established under the PIA, some of the revenue derived from oil exploration and production constitutes the trust assets which a board of trustees is empowered to manage for the benefit of the general population.

Trusts have generally emerged as a result of deficiencies in the legal mechanisms instituted for the management of the property.[41] Thus, the inadequacies attendant to oil revenue management in Nigeria make this a particularly attractive concept. Lately, trust funds have been attracting attention in academic and policy circles as pragmatic tools for addressing the unfortunate predicament generally manifesting in entities blessed with natural resource, especially oil.[42]

[40] See Marianne Guerin-McManus, Conservation Trust Funds, 20 UCLA J. Envtl. L. & Pol'y 1, 3 (2001).

[41] See *id.* at 5.

[42] See Stephen Krasner, TROUBLED SOCIETIES, OUTLAW STATES, AND GRADATIONS OF SOVEREIGNTY 41 (July 20, 2002), at www.sas.upenn.edu/browne cip/200304%20Papers/Krasner%20paper.pdf.

Utilizing trust funds to manage public properties, including natural resources, is not an entirely new phenomenon, nor is the creation of a trust wholly dependent on the mismanagement of resources.[43] A trust fund can be used to accomplish a variety of objectives including conservation of natural resources,[44] protection of the environment,[45] and development of communities.[46]

In centuries past, African societies have been able to devise trust-like institutions to address particular needs, such as the management of family or communal property.[47] Community trusts will directly confront and tackle the inadequacies of the existing community development arrangements present in some places. The opacity surrounding the current approaches to community development has provided ample room for corruption to become a way of life, cutting across different facets in

[43] See, e.g., *Tito* et al. *v. Waddel* et al. (No. 2) [1977] 3 All ER 129 (a dispute over whether the Crown was the trustee of the funds collected from phosphate sale royalties for the inhabitants of an island colony in the Western Pacific); Sir Joseph Gold, *Trust Funds in International Law; The Contribution of the International Monetary Fund to a Code of Principles*, 72 AM. J. INT'L. L. 856, 856 (1978).

[44] Guerin-McManus, *supra* note 40, at 8.

[45] Peter H. Sand, Trusts for the Earth: *New International Financial Mechanisms for Sustainable Growth*, in SUSTAINABLE DEVELOPMENT AND INTERNATIONAL LAW 160–70 (W. Lang ed., 1995).

[46] See Kyle W. Danish, *International Environmental Law and the "Bottom-Up" Approach: A Review of the Desertification Convention*, 3 IND. J. GLOBAL LEG. STUD. 133, 169 n.162 (1995).

[47] T.O. Elias, NIGERIAN LAND LAW 78 (4th ed. 1971); J.D. BAKIBINGA, LAW OF TRUSTS IN NIGERIA 5 (1989); Olayide Adigun, CASES & TEXTS ON EQUITY, TRUSTS AND ADMINSTRATION OF ESTATES 277 (1987); S.N. Chinwuba Obi, MODERN FAMILY LAW IN SOUTHERN NIGERIA 56–57 (1966); A. A. Utuama LAW OF REAL PROPERTY 7 (1989). Viscount Haldane's widely referenced statements on the issue are quite relevant:

The notion of individual ownership is quite foreign to native ideas. Land belongs to the community, the village or the family, never to the individual. All the members of the community, village, or family have an equal right to the land, but in every case the Chief or Headman of the community or village, or head of the family, has charge of the land, and in loose mode of speech is sometimes called the owner. He is to some extent in the position of a trustee and as such holds the land for the use of the community or family.

Amodu Tijani v. Secretary of Southern Nigeria, 2 A.C. 399, 404 (1921). Similar statements have been made regarding the same issue in other West African countries. See, W.C. Ekow Daniels, Some Principles of the Law of Trusts in West Africa, 6 J. Afr. L. 164, 168 (1962).

the oil-producing areas, including community leaders and corporate executives.

An important aspect of the community trust is the public's participation in decision-making. Under Nigerian customary law, the communal property is usually managed by those in a position of trust, with the active participation of the other community members who are co-owners of the property.[48] A major function of the trustees, through a management body and in close consultation with the respective communities, will be designing projects that are beneficial to the people and overseeing their proper completion.

4.2 Host Community Development Trust (HCDT)

The PIA provides for the establishment of a Host Community Development Trust in each community hosting oil activities in Nigeria and these trusts will establish trust funds for the communities. Explaining the nature and essence of these community trust funds, one commentator observes: "The relationship between oil and gas host communities in Nigeria has historically been very poor. The PIA aims to address this problem by creating the Host Community Development Trust Fund (HCDTF)."[49] The objectives of the community trust funds and associated arrangements under the PIA are to foster sustainable prosperity inside the host communities,[50] provide direct social and economic benefits from oil and gas operations to host communities,[51] enhance peaceful and

[48] M.G. Yakuba, LAND LAW IN NIGERIA 63 (1985). Yakuba states:

[E]very member of the community has the right to take part directly or indirectly in the management of the community land. The participation is direct where a member takes an active part in making decisions and in consultations on community land. It is indirect where he only takes part in selecting the Chief and other elders or councilors. It has been held that the requirement of consultation is a requirement of law and not just a matter of convenience by the Chief or elders to be observed or disregarded.

Id. (citation omitted).

[49] Kasirim Nwuke, *Nigeria's Petroleum Industry Act: Addressing Old Problems, Creating New Ones*, Brookings Blog (Nov. 24, 2021) at https://www.brookings.edu/blog/africa-in-focus/2021/11/24/nigerias-petroleum-industry-act-addressing-old-problems-creating-new-ones/ (accessed January 30, 2022).

[50] PIA, § 234 (1) (a).

[51] § 234 (1) (b).

harmonious coexistence between lessees or licensees and host communities,[52] and create a framework to support the development of these host communities.[53]

Every petroleum lessee or license holder or a collection of them ("settlor or settlors") shall establish a community trust in the community for which they are responsible.[54] In consultation with the host communities, the settlor shall appoint and authorize a board of trustees which shall be responsible for proposing and executing projects.[55] The HCDT shall establish a trust fund that will be funded primarily by the settlor through an annual contribution of an amount equal to 3 percent of the settlor's operating expenditure for applicable operations from the previous year.[56] The HCDT will be managed by a management committee, at least one of whose members will be a member of the host community.[57] The management committee will establish an advisory committee whose membership will include at least one member of the host community.[58] The relevant regulatory agency will make regulations pertaining to the community trusts.[59] The regulations shall include a grievance mechanism to resolve disputes between the lessees or licensees and the host communities.[60]

Oil-producing communities need an alternative economic base to replace what has been destroyed by the oil industry. They also need adequate institutions, such as well-equipped and properly functioning hospitals and schools, to take care of their immediate needs and prepare themselves for the kind of future that is suited to their new conditions as centers of major economic activities. This approach would be consistent with the aphorism that is better to teach a person how to fish than to give a person a fish.

Each community trust would be able to handle some smaller projects. It is suggested that neighboring community trusts should explore the

[52] § 234 (1) (c).

[53] § 234 (1) (d).

[54] § 235.

[55] Id.

[56] § 240.

[57] §§ 247 and 248.

[58] § 249.

[59] § 234 (2).

[60] § 234 (3).

option of pooling resources from multiple sources (including oil corporations and development institutions) to undertake bigger projects that ordinarily fall outside the capacity or scope of one community trust's budget. This scenario would result in a variance of what economists refer to as "coordination benefits," by which people find that it is in their greater interest to work together than going at it all alone.[61]

The community trusts established under the PIA are a good step forward. Yet, they should not be the terminal station for the journey toward community economic and political empowerment. A greater level of equity participation should be the next priority item. The current petroleum arrangement in Nigeria concentrates ownership of oil, gas, and minerals exclusively on the federal government. Landowners are dispossessed of their land the moment the oil is found there and they receive a completely incommensurate compensation from the government, not for the land but for the economic improvements on the land. The result has been stupendous wealth in the hands of political actors which frees them from concern for the people, engenders rent-seeking and corruption, and endangers the polity. A radical shift in paradigm and practice is probably the only pragmatic way of addressing the problem. This shift may incorporate a total transfer of ownership interests from the government to the people and communities that own the land. Such a proposal, which has been repeatedly made, is unrealistic in today's Nigeria despite its attractiveness, given the political and constitutional realities that confront it. A bridge between the status quo and the ideal situation should be considered in the form of equity participation by community members in natural gas infrastructure projects (including existing and proposed liquefied natural gas (LNG) and pipeline projects) and oil exploration and development projects.

5 Conclusion

Corporate accountability will remain a topical issue for the foreseeable future. Efforts to limit or eliminate corporate impunity for human rights and environmental abuses have spurned many proposals. This chapter joins the debate by arguing for politically and economically empowering

[61] For a discussion of coordination benefits, see Cary Coglianese, *Globalization and the Design of International Institutions*, in GOVERNANCE IN A GLOBALIZING WORLD 297, 289–300 (Joseph S. Nye Jr. & John D. Donahue eds., 2000).

communities to ward off corporate abuses or ensure effective redress when they occur. The Petroleum Industry Act 2021 provides for the establishment of community trusts that will be a part of this process. Efforts should go beyond this arrangement to provide for full community equity participation in oil and gas projects in Nigeria.

Community equity participation in oil and gas development projects, in which the government transfers a significant portion of its participating interests in natural gas infrastructure projects to communities in which the gas is produced or where the projects are located presents many advantages as well as attendant challenges. Careful structuring of the appropriate institutions and investment vehicles for accomplishing the purpose will help in confronting some of the envisaged problems.

Dividends from such investments will be paid to the community and managed by community-based institutions for the benefit of community members in accordance with their expressed needs. Each community should be able to determine its own priorities and decide whether to embark on brick-and-mortar development projects, rehabilitation of existing infrastructure, cottage industries, micro-credit schemes, or even cash payouts to mention a few items on the menu of available options. The advantage here is that the people are entrusted with their destiny and they are completely constrained to abide by the consequences of their choices—choice of projects and leadership selection. This arrangement is a marked departure from the current paradigm and practice that is marked by opacity in local governance and concentration of power on bureaucrats and politicians—including those far removed from the scene—to determine the needs of the people and design what they consider to be appropriate programs to address them.

The community trusts established under the Petroleum Industry Act 2021 are a good starting point. A more aggressive effort to further integrate communities in the ownership and management of their petroleum resources is needed to empower the host communities economically and politically. An empowered community will be better positioned to regulate corporate activities within the community. Such local regulation can be an effective check on multinational corporate activities and curtail some of the excesses of international business in developing countries.

CHAPTER 12

Judicial Misconduct: Analyzing the Code of Conduct for Judicial Officers in Nigeria

Ndubuisi J. Madubuike-Ekwe

1 Introduction

Inherent in Roscoe Pound's 1906 speech to the American Bar association is the basic premise that American courts and judges, as public institutions in a representative democracy must be responsive to the public and held accountable for their actions.[1] Only in a democracy would concerns over the cause of popular dissatisfaction with the administration of justice be given a public airing. Pound's speech was also premised on the notion that developments that compromised judicial independence, a basic tenet of American democracy would similarly erode public confidence in the courts.[2]

[1] James J. Alfini, Shailey Gurta-Brietzke and James F. McMartin IV, "Dealing with Judicial Misconduct in the States: Judicial Independence, Accountability and Reform", South Texas Law Review, Vol. 48 (2007) p. 889.

[2] Ibid.

N. J. Madubuike-Ekwe (✉)
Faculty of Law, Benson Idahosa University, Benin-City, Nigeria
e-mail: jekwe@biu.edu.ng

E. Duruigbo et al. (eds.), *International Law and Development in the Global South*, https://doi.org/10.1007/978-3-031-13741-9_12

Maintaining confidence in the judiciary anticipates that judges will be held to high standards of conduct. However, at the time Roscoe Pound delivered his 1906 speech to the American Bar Association, published standards, rules, or guidelines establishing ethical norms for the state judiciaries were virtually nonexistent.[3] One hundred years later, all state judiciaries are not only subject to officially adopted codes of judicial conduct or canons of judicial ethics but are also subject to modern disciplinary mechanisms for enforcing these ethics and standards. Although Pound might applaud this development in so far as it promised greater accountability, he might also have expressed concerns over the possibility that it might intrude on judicial independence.

Similarly, in Nigeria, judges occupy a very unique and sacred position in the society. Occupying this position means that a high level of integrity, honesty, and accountability is expected from judicial officers since they sit in judgment over the affairs and interactions of members of the society. This means that where a judicial officer violates or breaches any of the strict codes or standards of his exalted office, the society through relevant laws and structures must respond decisively to deal with such breach or violations that could be described as unbecoming of a holder of such a sacred and exalted office.[4] According to *Yusuf Dadem*, "judges are not immune from temptations which confront them daily as they undertake the tasks of adjudication and determination of disputes… pertaining to the civil rights and obligations of persons."[5] The exercise of judicial power[6] does not make the judges less accountable, rather it makes it imperative to hold them accountable if and when the need arises. Thus while there are mechanisms to ensure judicial independence, other mechanisms also exist for accountability and discipline of judges who fail to comply with the judicial ethics and Code of Conduct for judicial officers. Aside from international standards and conventions on Ethics and Code

[3] Ibid.

[4] Sokombaa Alolade, "The Discipline of judicial officers", The Lawyers Chronicle, 7 October 2016, at http://www.thelawyerschronicle.com/the-discipline-of-judicial-officers/. Accessed 12th February 2021.

[5] Yusufu Y. Dadem, "Removing the Judge: Challenges to Judicial Independence in Nigeria", The Nigerian Law Journal, Vol. 16. No. 1 (2013) p. 82.

[6] Section 6(6) of the 1999 Constitution of Nigeria.

for judicial conduct,[7] direct local codes of ethics are prescribed in the Constitution of the Federal Republic of Nigeria[8] and also by the National Judicial Council (NJC).[9]

The purpose of this chapter is to analyze the scope of the Code of Conduct for judicial officers and the concept of "Good behavior" as required by the Chief Justice of Nigeria. The chapter is divided into six Parts. Part I is the introduction. Part II discusses the role of the National Judicial Council (NJC) in the administration of the judiciary. Part III examines the scope of the Code of Conduct for judicial officers in Nigeria and the various categories of judicial ethics under the code. Part IV identifies the qualities and core values, i.e. good behavior, required of judicial officers. Part V discusses the NJC regulations which governs allegations of misconduct against judicial officers and Part VI concludes the chapter with a recommendation for a strict adherence to the process for discipline of judicial officers for misconduct and, also, for the NJC to conduct a speedy and transparent investigation of misconduct against a judicial officer.

2 The Meaning of Misconduct

Most of the complaints against judicial officers can be classified as "misconduct" complaints. Misconduct means bad or unethical behavior.[10] The *Blacks Law Dictionary* defines misconduct as "a dereliction of

[7] These include the Bangalore Principles of Judicial Conduct (2002); the Latimer House Guidelines (1998); the Beijing Statement on the Principles of Independence (1997); IFES and USAID Office of Democracy and Governance "Guidelines for promoting judicial independence and impartiality" ("Guidance Principles") and the International Bar Association, minimum standards of Judicial Independence (1982).

[8] The 1999 Constitution of the Federal Republic of Nigeria (Hereinafter, "the CFRN").

[9] The Code of Conduct for judicial officers in Nigeria was published in 1998; See, C. C. Nweze, "Judicial Ethics, Discipline and Conduct on and Off the Bench", NJI Law Journal (2009) p. 35; N. Tobi, "Code of Conduct and Professional Ethics for judicial officers in Nigeria", in J.O. Irukwu and I.A. Umezurike (eds.), *Judicial Excellence: Essays in Honor of Hon. Justice A.I. Iguh* (Enugu: Snaap Press Ltd, 2004) p. 38; Dadem, supra note 5.

[10] *Roget's 21st Century Thesaurus in Dictionary Form*, 3rd ed. (New York: Bantam Dell, 2006) p. 545.

duty, unlawful or improper behavior."[11] The 1999 Constitution defines misconduct as "breach of the Oath of allegiance or oath of office of a member or breach of the provisions of this constitution or a misconduct of such a nature as amounts to bribery or corruption or false declaration of assets and liabilities."[12] According to the Judicial discipline Regulations, misconduct includes "conduct prejudicial to the effect and expeditious administration of the business of the courts or any conduct described as misconduct in the Constitution and the Code of Conduct for judicial officers of superior courts."[13] The Code of Conduct for judicial officers construes misconduct as "violation of any of the rules contained in this Code... or misbehavior and may entail disciplinary action."[14]

3 The Role of the National Judicial Council

The Constitution of the Federal Republic of Nigeria vests in the National Judicial Council[15] the powers to exercise disciplinary control over judicial

[11] Black's Law Dictionary, 10th Edition, Bryan A. Garner, ed. Thomson Reuters (2014) 1149.

[12] Section 19, Part 1 of the Fifth Schedule of the 1999 Constitution of the Federal republic of Nigeria, as amended.

[13] See National Judicial Council Judicial Discipline Regulations 2014. Entered into force on 3rd November 2014.

[14] See Explanations (iii), Code of Conduct for judicial officers of the Federal Republic of Nigeria.

[15] The National Judicial Council (Hereinafter, "NJC") is one of the Federal executive bodies established for the Federation under Section 153 of the CFRN. The NJC comprises of the following members: the Chief Justice of Nigeria, the next most senior Justice of the Supreme Court, the President of the Court of appeal; five retired Justices selected by the Chief Justice of Nigeria from the Supreme Court or Court of appeal, the Chief Judge of the Federal high court; the President, National Industrial Court; Five Chief Judges of State to be appointed by the Chief Justice of Nigeria from among the Chief Judges of the States and of the High Court of the Federal Territory, Abuja in rotation to serve for two years; One Grand Khadi to be appointed by the Chief Justice of Nigeria from among Grand Khadis of the Sharia courts of appeal to serve for two years; one President of the Customary court of appeal to be appointed by the Chief Justice of Nigeria from among the Presidents of the Customary courts of appeal to serve in rotation for two years; five members of the Nigerian Bar association who have been qualified to practice for a period of not less than fifteen years at least one of whom shall be a senior advocate of Nigeria, appointed by the Chief Justice of Nigeria on the recommendation of the National executive Committee of the Nigerian bar association to serve for two years and subject to reappointment: Provided that the five members shall sit in the Council only for the purposes of considering the names of persons for appointment to the superior courts of record; and two persons not being legal practitioners, who ion the opinion of the Chief Justice of Nigeria, are of unquestionable integrity. See Section 20 of Part 1 of the Third Schedule to the 1999 CFRN, as amended.

officers against whom allegations of misconduct have been made[16] or for violation of any of the rules contained in the Code of Conduct for judicial officers.[17]

The National Judicial Council is very central to the administration of the judiciary in Nigeria.[18] It was established under the 1999 constitution; it never existed under past Constitutions.[19] According to Dadem, the reason for establishing the NJC was to reduce the control of the executive and legislative arms of government in the running of the affairs of the judiciary which was the case under previous regimes.[20] It was intended as an internal and self-governing body for administering the judiciary in Nigeria. The NJC is largely made up of persons with judicial and legal backgrounds.[21] Although the NJC has the power to recommend the appointment and removal of judicial officers, it has some other powers.[22]

The power of the National Judicial Council to discipline judicial officers is provided in Section 21 (b) of Part 1 of the Third schedule to the Nigerian constitution as follows:

> The National Judicial council shall have the power to:
>
> (b) Recommend to the President the removal from office of the judicial officers specified in sub-paragraph (a) of this paragraph and to exercise disciplinary control over such officers....

[16] See Part 1 of the Third Schedule of the 1999 CFRN as amended; See also, Section 2 of the National Judicial Council Discipline Regulations 2014.

[17] See Section 292 (1) and Section 21 of the Third Schedule to the CFRN; See also the code of conduct for judicial officers of the Federal Republic of Nigeria at http://www.nigeria-law.org/CodeofconductForJudicialofficers.htm. Accessed 20th August 2020.

[18] Dadem, supra note 4.

[19] The 1960, 1979, and 1989 Constitutions did not have the NJC. It was recommended by stakeholders in the justice sector during the 1994–1995 Constitutional conference but was equally rejected for failing the federalism test. However, it was later inserted in the 1999 Constitution. See Dadem, ibid.

[20] Dadem, ibid.

[21] See NJC, supra note 15.

[22] These include collecting, controlling, and disbursing all monies, capital, and recurrent, for the judiciary; advising the President and governors on any matter pertaining to the judiciary as may be referred to the council by the President or the Governors; appointing, dismissing, and exercising disciplinary control over members and staff of the Council; controlling and disbursing all monies, capital, and recurrent for the services of the council; and dealing with all other matters relating to broad issues of policy and administration; See Section 21 of Part 1 of the Third Schedule to the 1999 CFRN.

(d) Recommend to the Governors, the removal from office of the judicial officers specified in sub-paragraph (c) of this paragraph, and to exercise disciplinary control over such officers.

The NJC in the exercise of its disciplinary control over judicial officers can investigate any allegation of misconduct leveled against a judicial officer and can reprimand, suspend, advise, or recommend to the President or Governor for compulsory retirement, or dismissal as the case may be, where the judicial officer is found guilty. One instrument being used by the NJC to ensure discipline and accountability of judicial officers is the mechanism of judicial monitoring. In 2003, the NJC set up an Evaluation and Monitoring Committee to visit all courts of superior record on a quarterly basis to evaluate their performance and to ensure that provisions of the code of conduct are adhered to by judicial officers.[23] Since inception, the NJC has disciplined several judicial officers for one act of misconduct or another.

4 The Scope of the Code of Conduct for Judicial officers

In the Code the term "judicial officer" refers to the following judicial officers: the Chief Justice of Nigeria; Justices of the Supreme Court; President and Justices of the Court of Appeal; the Chief Judges and Judges of the Federal High Court, State High courts, and the High Court of the Federal Capital Territory, Abuja.[24]

Furthermore, the following judicial officers come within the meaning of the term: the Grand khadi or khadi of a sharia court of appeal of a State and of the Federal Capital Territory, Abuja, the President or Judge of a Customary Court of appeal of a State and of the Federal Capital Territory, Abuja. The Code also uses the term to include "the holder of a similar office in any inferior court whatsoever."[25]

[23] Rilwanu Salmanu Muhammad and Bobai Paul Ali, "Misconduct by a judicial officer in Nigeria: An Analysis of its Scope" A.B.U.J.P.L.L., Vol. 1. No. 7 (2015) p. 108.

[24] See "Explanations (1), Code of Conduct for judicial officers of the Federal Republic of Nigeria", at http://www.nigeria-law.org/CodeOfConductForJudicialOfficers.htm. Accessed 7th April 2021.

[25] Ibid; See also C.C. Nweze, supra note 9, p. 36.

5 Analysis of the Code of Conduct for Judicial officers

The broadest category of complaints against judges can be classified as "misconduct" complaints. As already noted, judicial misconduct has a very specific meaning under the Code: "violation of any of the rules contained in this Code...." The Code of conduct for judicial officers regulates the activities of judges on and off the bench.[26] The Code is a comprehensive statement of what constitutes judicial behavior and has been adopted by the National Judicial Council.

The code divides judicial ethics into several categories namely: judicial comportment, adjudicative duties, and extra-judicial activities.

5.1 Judicial Comportment

A judicial officer should avoid impropriety and the appearance of impropriety in all his activities.[27] A judicial officer should respect and comply with the laws of the land and should conduct himself at all times in a manner that promotes public confidence in the integrity and impartiality of the Judiciary.[28] Rule 1(2)(a) provides that a judicial officer must avoid social relationships that are improper or give rise to an appearance of impropriety, that cast doubt on the judicial officer's ability to decide cases impartially or that bring disrepute to the judiciary. According to Nweze, "this is part of the sacrifice required of the Officer so as to preserve judicial immunity from notoriety."[29] In England, for example, it is said that judges do not go into hotels or restaurants (except to a function in a private room) in a country in which they are sitting.[30]

A judicial officer should not be a member of any society or organization that practices invidious discrimination on the basis of race, sex, religion,

[26] Adelanwa Bamgboye, "CJN Outlines Core Values of a Good Judge", The Daily Trust, 23 June 2016 at http://www.dailytrust.com.ng/news/law/cjn-outlines-core-values-of. Accessed 7th April 2021.

[27] Rule 1, Code of Conduct for judicial officers.

[28] Rule 1(1).

[29] Nweze, supra note 9, p. 39.

[30] Ibid.

or ethnic origin or whose aims and objectives are incompatible with the functions or dignity of his office.[31]

6 Functions as a Judge

This covers three parts: his adjudicative duties, administrative duties, and his duties to observe the rule of natural justice as regards impartiality.[32]

6.1 Adjudicative Duties

A judicial officer should be true to the Constitution and the law, uphold the course of justice by abiding with the provisions of the constitution and the law and should acquire and maintain professional competence.[33] A judicial officer must avoid the abuse of the power of issuing interim injunctions *ex parte*.[34] This reason for this prohibition was stated by the former Chief Justice of Nigeria, Justice Mohammed Bello thus:

> The decision of some of our courts on ex parte injunction seem to put individual interest over and above the collective national interest in Nigeria. Public functionaries have been restrained without being given a hearing from performing their constitutional and statutory duties at the instance of an exuberant individual....[35]

A judicial officer should maintain order and decorum.[36] A judicial officer should be patient, dignified, and courteous to accused persons and litigants, assessors, witnesses, legal practitioners, and all others with whom he has to deal in his official capacity and should demand similar

[31] Rule 1(2)(b).

[32] See Rule 2(A–B) of the Code.

[33] Rule 2(A)(1), ibid.

[34] Rule 2(A)(2), ibid.

[35] See 1985 All Nigerian Judges Conference Papers, cited in A. Babalola, *Injunctions and Enforcement of Orders* (Ile-Ife: Obafemi Awolowo Press Ltd, 2000) p. 10; See also Nweze, supra note 8, p. 40 (describing how a Court in Nigeria restrained a University by order of *ex parte* injunction, from holding convocation to award degrees to over a thousand students because two students who had failed the examination had applied to court for a declaration that they too were entitled to be awarded degrees).

[36] Rule 2(A)(3), of the Code.

conduct of legal practitioners, his staff, and others under his direction and control.[37] Allegations of a judge's failure to maintain proper courtroom decorum and a judge's failure to be patient, dignified, and courteous may include rude, abusive, and improper consideration and treatment of a Lawyer, a party, a witness, a juror, the court staff, and others at the hearing; improper physical conduct; or persistent failure to dispose of court business promptly and responsibly.[38]

6.2 Administrative Duties

On administrative duties, a judicial officer should require his staff and other court officials under his direction and control to observe the standards of fidelity and diligence that apply to him.[39] Thus a judicial officer on becoming aware of reliable evidence of unethical or unprofessional conduct by another judicial officer or a legal practitioner should immediately take adequate steps to report the same to the appropriate body seized with disciplinary powers on the matter complained of.[40] Furthermore, a judicial officer should avoid nepotism and favoritism,[41] sexual harassment,[42] and should not be a member of a tenders' board or engage in the award of contracts.[43]

6.3 Impartiality/Disqualification

To maintain public confidence in the judicial process, the Code offers opportunity to judicial officers to disqualify themselves in the event of the occurrence or likely occurrence of such factors that suggest partiality.[44] Thus, Rule 2(C)(1) provides grounds for which a judicial officer may disqualify himself or be disqualified from presiding over a matter assigned

[37] Rule 2(A)(4), ibid.

[38] Rule 2(A)(6), ibid; See also Nweze, supra note 8, p. 48 (emphasizing the virtues of diligence in the discharge of duties and the maintenance of professional competence).

[39] Rule 2(B)(2) of the Code.

[40] Rule 2(B)(3), ibid.

[41] Rule 2(B)(4), ibid.

[42] Rule 2(B)(5), ibid.

[43] Rule 2(B)(6), ibid.

[44] Nweze, supra note 9, p. 50.

to him. The rule states that a judicial officer should disqualify himself in a proceeding in which his impartiality might reasonably be questioned, including but not limited to instances where:

1. He has personal bias or prejudice concerning a party or personal knowledge of facts in dispute;
2. He served as a legal practitioner in the matter in controversy,[45] or a legal practitioner with whom he previously practiced law served during such association as a legal practitioner concerning the matter or the judicial officer or such legal practitioner has been a material witness in the matter;
3. He knows that he individually or as a judicial officer or his spouse or child, has a financial or any other interest that could be substantially affected by the outcome of the proceeding;
4. He or his spouse or a person related to either of them or the spouse of such a person;
    1. Is a party to the proceedings, or an officer, director, or trustee of a party;
    2. Is acting as a legal practitioner in the proceedings;
    3. Is known by the judicial officer to have an interest which could be substantially affected by the outcome of the proceedings;
    4. Is to the judicial officer's knowledge likely to be a material witness in the proceedings.

7 Waiver of Disqualification

The rule on disqualification could, however, be waived. According to Rule 2(D) of the Code:

> A judicial officer disqualified by the terms of Rule 2(C) (1) or Rule 2 (c) (1) (d) may instead of withdrawing from the proceedings disclose on the record the basis of his disqualification. If based on such disclosure, the parties, their representatives and or their legal practitioners, independently

[45] See *Umenwa v. Umenwa* (1988) 4 NSWLR, 388 (In that case, the trial Judge had acted for the defendant while in private practice. Both the subject matter in the earlier suit and the parties were the same as the present case. Upon appeal by the plaintiff, the Supreme Court declared the judgment a nullity on grounds of bias); See Nweze supra note 8, p. 52.

of the judicial officer's participation, all agree that the judicial officer's relationship is immaterial or that the financial interest is insubstantial, the Judicial Officer is no longer disqualified and may participate in the proceedings. The consent by the parties, their representatives and/or their legal practitioners shall be recorded and shall form part of the record of proceedings.

Thus where the waiver provisions have been complied with, there can be no valid and rational grounds for impeaching the independence or impartiality of the judge.[46] In *Olue v Enewali*,[47] Nasir JSC (as he then was) stated that:

> The right to challenge or impugn proceedings of any court or tribunal which was tainted by the adjudicator being disqualified by interest or likelihood of bias may be lost by express or even by implied waiver of the right to object to the adjudicator at the first opportunity during the proceedings. There would, however, be no waiver or acquiesce unless the party entitled to take the objection was aware of the nature of the disqualification and had opportunity of so objecting[48]

7.1 Extra-Judicial Activities

The third and final aspect of the Code of Conduct enjoins the judicial officer to regulate his extra-judicial activities to minimize the risk of conflict with his judicial duties.[49] These judicial activities relate to vocational activities, civil and charitable activities, freedom of expression and association, non-acceptance of chieftaincy titles, business and financial activities, acceptance of gifts, and fiduciary activities (except for the estate, trust, or a member of his family) only if it will not interfere with his judicial responsibilities.[50] To combat corruption in the Judiciary, Rule 3(F)(1) of the Code prohibits a judicial officer and members of his family from accepting gifts, bequest, favor, or loan on account of anything done

[46] See *Olue v. Enewali* (1976) 2 SC 23; Nweze, supra note 8, p. 55.

[47] Ibid.

[48] See Nweze, ibid., p. 56.

[49] Rule 3 of the Code.

[50] Rule 3(A–G) of the Code.

or omitted to be done by him in the discharge of his duties.[51] Unfortunately, the Code does not expressly use the word "bribery" in describing corruption in the judiciary. According to Justice Nweze, this is rather an embarrassing omission in a Code targeted against corruption, the most conspicuous manifestation of which is the very vice of bribery. This omission must be addressed as a matter of urgency.[52]

However, Rule 3(F)(2) of the Code permits the acceptance of:

1. Personal gifts or benefits from relatives or personal friends to such extent and on such occasions as are recognized by custom;
2. Books supplied by publishers on a complimentary basis;
3. A loan from lending institution in its regular course of business on the same terms generally available to people who are not judicial officers;
4. A scholarship or fellowship awarded on the same terms applied to other applicants.

Finally, a judicial officer should not practice law or act as an arbitrator.[53]

8 The Core Values and Attributes of a Good Judicial Officer

Sometime in 2016, the former Chief Justice of Nigeria, Justice Mahmud Mohammed outlined the core values and attributes which all judges must possess to enable them do their job better.[54] The CJN noted that the qualities and core values of a good and eminent judicial officer includes:

[51] For example, Justice Matilda Adamu was dismissed in 2004 for receiving bribes to pass judgment in respect of a governorship petition tried by her and other judges. Similarly, Justice Chudi Nwokorie of the Federal High Court Katsina was dismissed for entertaining and making orders in respect of an election matter that had been tried by a court of Appeal. Both cases cited in Dadem, supra note 4, p.85.

[52] Nweze, supra note 9, p. 57.

[53] Rule 3(G) of the Code.

[54] Adelanwa Bamgboye, "CJN Outlines Core Values of a Good Judge", Daily Trust, 23 June 2015 at http://www.dailytrust.com.ng/news/law/cjn-outlines-core-values-of. Accessed 11th March 2021.

1. **Independence**: In this context independence means being free of any loyalties, duties, or interests that might inappropriately influence the performance of a judicial officer's functions. Judicial independence is not a privilege but a right to every court user in Nigeria that his or her cases are dealt with by a court whose independence is guaranteed in both qualification, nature, and character. Independence is therefore a core quality of an astute and eminent judicial officer.[55]
2. **Impartiality**: The next important attribute of a good and eminent judicial officer is impartiality which is closely aligned to independence. It lies at the heart of judicial function and it is reflected in the oath of office. All litigants must be treated equally. Likewise, where a judge is under a misapprehension in a case, it is not inappropriate to acknowledge the error and to thank the party that clarified the position. Such respect and cooperation strengthens the relationship between the Bar and the Bench and instills a sense of confidence in the humanity and integrity of the judiciary in the eyes of court users.[56]
3. **Communication skills**: Good communication skill is an essential requirement for a sound and erudite judicial officer. As judicial officers, you are constitutionally required to make rulings in the course of a trial and to give directions to litigants and witnesses. These rulings or judgments must be done in a manner and language that can be quickly understood by those who are expected to comply with them. Judicial officers are required to give written reasons for their decisions. Sometimes, the cases may involve complex factual and legal issues. The reasons must therefore be clear, succinct, and unambiguous so that the parties and other interested persons can understand them. Lack of good communication skills can be dangerous and devastating. Avoid too much Latin maxims that have no bearing on the positive Nigerian jurisprudence.[57]
4. **Courtesy**: This is not only a basic human quality but an important attribute for a judicial officer. In the past some judges regarded aloofness and gruffness as adding to judicial authority and to the

[55] Ibid.

[56] Ibid.

[57] Ibid.

mystique of office. Those days are gone. Everyone who comes before the Court is entitled to be treated with courtesy and respect, even those who are accused of heinous or despicable crimes deserve some respect. If litigants or counsel are throwing barbs at each other in offensive or disruptive manner, you must order them to stop. If a Counsel is shouting at a witness in a humiliating manner, you must order him to desist from doing that. After all, courtesy is not incompatible with effective advocacy or effective adjudication. Judicial courtesy bolsters the authority of the court, and earns the respect of the society it serves.[58]

5. **Cultural and Community Engagement**: Nigeria is a multi-ethnic nation. Most States of the Federation are made up of diverse ethnicities, languages, religions, and cultures. The success of such society depends on mutual understanding and respect. Equality before the law and respect for other people's rights are important elements of rule of law. As you move from one judicial division to another, you must treat all Court users with equal respect regardless of how different they are or how unpopular their cause may be. In the interpretation and application of customary and native laws, avoid assumptions that are based on cultural stereotypes. Negative cultural stereotypes strain harmony within the community and cause serious security breaches. Except where the adduced native law and custom is barbaric or offends the repugnancy test, every litigant is entitled to have his or her case decided based on then evidence that has been adduced and tested in open court in the course of trial rather than on any other extraneous considerations. For the Khadis of the Sharia court of Appeal, your applicable law is the Sharia. For the Judges of the customary court of Appeal, your applicable law is the customary laws of then litigants that come before you not the biblical or koranic injunctions. Your religious inclinations should not be brought to bear in your judicial decisions as a judge of the Customary Court of Appeal. No matter how you feel about the religious implications of such alleged customs, so long as they comply with requisite legal and judicial tests prescribed, you must apply them in relevant cases.[59]

[58] Ibid.

[59] Ibid.

6. **Sense of Humor**: The administration of justice is a serious business, with important obligations and responsibilities. Court cases involve tremendous stress for Court users and therefore the courtroom is not a place for judicial officers to try their hands at being comedians. That does not mean, however, that judicial officers must be perennially uptight and unhappy. No, the Courtroom is not a graveyard. A balanced lifestyle, interests outside the law, a down-to-earth personality, and a good sense of humor can increase a judicial officer's enjoyment of his judicial work. This can assist in ensuring that the mood in the courtroom is positive which in turn can ensure that the hearing is conducted in an efficient and harmonious manner.[60]
7. **Abiding by the Code of Conduct and Judicial Ethics**: This is the most important requirement of a judicial officer. Every judicial officer must abide by the Code of Conduct for judicial officers of the Federal Republic of Nigeria, and Judicial Ethics as expounded in the Bangalore principles of Judicial Conduct. Any judicial officer that does not abide by the code of Conduct may be discharged from the Nigerian Judiciary. "The National Judicial Council and the respective State's Judicial Service Commissions are adequately empowered to remove, with ignominy, any judicial officer or judicial staff that has chosen the path of dishonor to be lazy or refuse to abide by judicial ethics and Judicial Code of Conduct. The Code of Conduct covers all aspects of a judicial officers' lives both in and out of Court. It must be studied, digested and imbibed by all judicial officers in Nigeria."[61]
8. **Prompt Disposal of Cases**: This is a Constitutional requirement. A good judicial officer must dispose of matters before him promptly, efficiently, and diligently. The judicial officer must demonstrate due regard for the rights of the parties to have their cases heard and disposed of without unnecessary delay. He must be in control of his court to eliminate dilatory practices, avoidable delays, and unnecessary adjournments. "He must devote adequate time for court duties,

[60] Ibid.

[61] Ibid.

be punctual in attending court and expeditious in determining matters before him."[62]

> Thus the Chief Justice and the NJC has divined "good behavior" for judicial officers. Any judicial officers who fail to comply with the core values listed by the Chief Justice whether in or out of the Courtroom will be sanctioned by the NJC for misconduct.

9. **Making a Complaint About Judicial Misconduct**: Due to the position of judicial officers in the society, any formal complaint about a judicial officer should not be lightly made as it is a serious matter which affects the life of the judicial officer. It is hard to see how disagreeing with the outcome of a case could be a legitimate ground for complaint. For example, an appeal would normally be the appropriate way forward.

In light of this fact, the NJC enacted a regulation to govern allegations and complaints of misconduct against judicial officers.[63] The Revised Rules are aimed at curtailing frivolous petitions against judges and prevent judges from being distracted by vexatious and baseless allegations against them.[64] The Regulation set time limits within which a complaint must be made. Section 4 (1) of the regulation provides that:

1. A complaint must be made within six months of the event or matter complained of; provided that a complaint relating to a continuing state of affairs may be made at any time while that state of affairs continues or within six months from when it ends.

[62] The Former Chief Justice of Nigeria, Justice Mahmud Mohammed's speech at an induction course organized by the National Judicial Institute (NJI) for new judges; See Bamboye, ibid.

[63] See National Judicial Council, Judicial Discipline Regulations, 2014.

[64] C. J. Ubanyionwu, "The Revised Judicial Discipline Regulations of the National Judicial Council: A Clog in the Fight Against Judicial Corruption in Nigeria", Nnamdi Azikiwe University Journal of International Law and Jurisprudence, Vol. 6 (September 2015) p. 144.

Any complaint made outside the time limits must be dismissed by the Council upon report to the Council by the Secretary to the Council.[65] However, Rule 5(1) states that "the Chief Justice of Nigeria/Chairman of Council may extend a time limit under these regulations, whether or not the time has expired, where there is good reason to do so." Rule 5(2) provides that "a person who is refused an extension of time under paragraph 1, may make a representation to the Chief Justice of Nigeria/ Chairman of Council, asking the Chairman, within 14 working days of being notified of the refusal, asking him/her to refer the request for an extension of time to the Council." Failure to meet the time limit results in the dismissal of the complaint.[66] Under Rule 7(5)(a), "a complaint must be signed by the complainant and accompanied by a verifying affidavit deposed to by the complainant before a court of record."[67] To protect the integrity of the complaint process, the NJC enacted a National Judicial Policy which states that the institutions of judiciary concerned with the investigation of a judicial officer or implementation of decisions taken on a complaint shall cease where such complaints are leaked or discussed in the media.[68] Where such a leakage is occasioned after the submission of a complaint, then all investigations on the complaints shall be suspended and if such leakage is from the complaint or through other parties known to such a complaint, such a complaint should be discarded. This does not mean a total media blackout of information. The Policy however permits media report of such allegation after investigation is completed.

All these measures would protect the complaint process as well as the image and integrity of the judicial officers accused of judicial misconduct. This also will prevent a situation where judges whose arrests inundated the media would have been tarnished even when they are eventually not found guilty of the accusations leveled against them.

[65] Ibid., Section 4(2).

[66] Rule 6 of the Revised Judicial Discipline Regulations of the National Judicial Council, 2014.

[67] Ubanyionwu, supra note 76.

[68] Bridget Chiedu Onochie, "NJC, New Policy Guideline and Burden of Implementation", Guardian, 01 November 2016 at http://guardian.ng/features/njc-new-policy-guideline-and-burden-of. Accessed 13th March 2021.

9 Conclusion

The idea of enacting the Code of Conduct for judicial officers in Nigeria is a welcome development. Especially, in recent years, we have witnessed an unprecedented number of instances in which judges have been accused of criminal behavior and other serious acts of misconduct. However, it will be presumptuous for anyone to suggest a complete understanding of the notion of "good behavior" for judges or to claim a fully satisfactory prescription for the problem of judicial misconduct. The categories of prohibited acts are never closed. A judge's judicial and personal conduct should also be governed by general ethical standards. Hence, any other conduct unbecoming of a judicial officer may be punished if the National Judicial Council considers it a misconduct.

Section 291 and the fifth Schedule to the 1999 Constitution should be amended to state clearly the nature of misconduct that could warrant the exercise of disciplinary action against a judicial officer. The NJC should strive to give adequate time and opportunity to judges accused of misconduct with a view to confronting the allegations against them. To minimize the incidents of misconduct, the manner of appointment of judicial officers should be reviewed to prevent lawyers of questionable character or who lack the knowledge of law from finding their way to the bench. However, the NJC should continue to protect the integrity of the judiciary by conducting speedy and transparent investigation of allegations of misconduct against judicial officers.

CHAPTER 13

Development of International Commercial Arbitration in Virtual Reality During the COVID-19 Pandemic

Aileen Huang

1 Introduction

In 2020, nearly, all the countries in the world had to respond to the severe disruption caused by the "pandemic" (COVID-19), an infectious disease caused by a newly discovered coronavirus. The pandemic had posed enormous health and socioeconomic challenges for the world since it first

A. Huang (✉)
Golden Gate University School of Law, San Francisco, CA, USA
e-mail: aihuang@ggu.edu

E. Duruigbo et al. (eds.), *International Law and Development in the Global South*, https://doi.org/10.1007/978-3-031-13741-9_13

erupted in late December 2019.[1] As of the time of writing, it is not yet known when the pandemic will end.

The COVID-19 pandemic has exerted an unprecedented impact on individuals, entities, businesses, and states. Globally, judiciaries and arbitral institutions have been under great pressure to continue operating during the pandemic, notwithstanding the impact of social distancing, restrictions on movement, and other measures intended to suppress the pandemic.

In the "new normal" of wide-ranging travel advisories and restrictions, there is an emerging consensus to better integrate the use of technology with dispute resolution. Suggestions such as the increased use of electronic filings, virtual evidentiary hearings, and online case management have been widely discussed, and these mechanisms are now being applied at pace in international arbitrations. As with all others, arbitrators, lawyers, and arbitration centers adapted quickly to a reality in which personal contact in offices and hearing rooms risked infection with the pandemic.

The arbitration practitioners set out to hold hearings through virtual means, to sign decisions and awards electronically, and to introduce virtual technologies in all other aspects of the conduct and administration of the arbitration procedure. In order to offer faster arbitration and reduce costs, some arbitration institutions offered virtual hearings and other procedural support with the use of new technologies. In addition, the arbitration institutions themselves have adapted their internal operation to virtual

[1] See, e.g., Debra Cassens Weiss, *SCOTUS and Other Courts Are Restricting Visitors or Canceling Proceedings amid Coronavirus Concerns*, ABA J. (March 12, 2020), https://www.abajournal.com/news/article/one-federal-court-suspends-court-appearances-others-restrict-visitors-amid-coronavirus-concerns; Amanda Robert, *Quinn Emanuel Shuts Down New York Office After Partner Tests Positive for Coronavirus*, ABA J. (March 9, 2020), https://www.abajournal.com/news/article/quinn-emanuel-shuts-down-new-york-office-after-partner-tests-positive-for-coronavirus; Leigh Jones & Vanessa Blum, *Cancellations, Crisis Planning and Clorox: COVID-19 Strikes Legal Community*, LAW.COM (March 6, 2020), https://www.law.com/2020/03/06/cancellations-crisis-planning-and-clorox-covid-19-strikes-legal-community/; Amanda Robert & Stephanie Francis Ward, *Coronavirus and Law Schools: More Universities Shifting to Online Classes*, ABA J. (March 12, 2020), https://www.abajournal.com/news/article/coronavirus-and-law-schools-more-universities-shifting-to-online-classes; Karen Sloan, *Coronavirus Closures Hit Law Schools at Stanford, Columbia and Several Others*, LAW.COM (March 9, 2020), https://www.law.com/2020/03/09/coronavirus-closures-hit-law-schools-at-stanford-columbia-and-several-others/.

work. Most of this work is done through virtual office. The decision-making bodies of the arbitration institutions also hold their work sessions virtually.

The past year has witnessed an exponential acceleration of these developments toward the virtual practice of arbitration. The secretariats of most arbitration institutions, such as ICC, SIAC, HKIAC, and LCIA, have confirmed that they are still operational and that they continue to register and manage new and existing cases. Up to today, all arbitration institutions practically adapted their rules to the possibility that arbitrators can conduct the entire procedure remotely.

However, practice has also shown that sometimes, it is simply not possible to hold virtual hearings or other meetings between the parties and the arbitrators. It can be difficult to conduct witness hearings online in cases involving complex fact patterns. In such particularly complex cases, it may be justified to suspend or postpone the hearing.

In any case, many arbitration practitioners also confirm that the crisis has a great impact on the profession beyond the specific circumstances of the confinement. It seems that the use of technologies that allow virtual contact between people, while dispensing with personal contact and the time-consuming travel that this contact often requires, is something irreversible that will forever transform the way arbitral justice is delivered.

This chapter describes how international arbitration has been conducted in virtual reality under the pandemic by practitioners and arbitration institutions. It focuses on the new arbitration rules as to virtual proceedings implemented in some leading international arbitration centers in the world. The author gives an objective assessment of the advantages and disadvantages of the virtual operation by those institutions dealing with the new challenges under the pandemic. The author concludes with an outlook on international arbitration after the pandemic.

2 An Overview of the Operation of International Arbitration During the COVID-19 Pandemic

As observed in the introduction to this article, as of the end of 2020, the pandemic has already had a great impact on the legal fields globally including international arbitration practice. In order to continue the day-to-day practice of international arbitration but also deal with the mid-term phenomenon of new arbitrations being triggered by COVID-19 and the way state entitles, commercial entities, and individuals are dealing with these consequences.

Many arbitral bodies took precautionary steps shortly after COVID-19 received its pandemic status, to safeguard the health and well-being of their employees, as well as their users. The most common and obvious step taken has been to instruct all staff to work remotely, a measure that by now has also been taken by a significant number of legal entities and other companies. International arbitration institutions closed their premises, declared that they would not accept any further hand-delivery of documents and fled into home office. In some states, the legislature or government intervened by decreeing a national emergency, whereby limitation terms and forfeiture terms do not start to run and, if they have been running, are suspended throughout the duration of the state of emergency.[2] In general, most arbitral institutions assured their users, in a more or less credible manner that despite their closed premises they would remain fully operable.

International arbitration is often hailed as one of the most flexible forms of dispute resolution given the need often to accommodate parties from different jurisdictions across the globe. Either with the help of arbitral institutions or by themselves, the parties realized that the only way to safeguard a hearing at all was to run it virtually.[3]

As a result, the various arbitral centers are well used to providing for hearings taking place without the parties or the arbitrators together in the one place. For example, The International Chamber of Commerce ("ICC") has set up a COVID-19 response group and the Indian Council of Arbitration ("ICA") encourages all communications to take place via email. All hearings and other meetings scheduled to take place at the ICC Hearing Centre in Paris until 13 April 2020 are being conducted virtually where possible. The London Court of International Arbitration ("LCIA") expects to remain operational and its staff are working from home where possible. Requests for arbitration were already being filed

[2] See, e.g., Nestor Nestor Diculescu Kingston Petersen, *Arbitration in the Time of COVID-19. The Romanian Perspective*, LEXOLOGY (March 26, 2020), https://www.lexology.com/library/detail.aspx?g=c0b28431-4a84-45a6-ac88-9c54400015d4; Clyde & Co LLP, *Covid-19—Impact on Courts and Arbitration*, LEXOLOGY (March 22, 2020).

[3] See CMS Cameron McKenna Nabarro Olswang LLP, *Virtual Hearings: Are They Really the Answer?*, LEXOLOGY (April 17, 2020), https://www.lexology.com/library/detail.aspx?g=1f282802-62f6-4cc6-890a-6a5a8ee5ecee ("parties seem to have instinctively turned to [virtual hearings] as a replacement for face-to-face hearings").

electronically and cases managed remotely, predominantly through email correspondence. The LCIA system permits all documents to be uploaded online and accessed remotely. Online filing is therefore not a new concept for arbitration and to an extent, this is "business as usual" for the arbitral bodies, so that there should be no delay where parties are seeking the resolution of a dispute.

Arbitrators can conduct proceedings based on the documents alone; this often happens where an interim award is required, where the tribunal or arbitrator is asked to decide on specific issues. Such interim awards are commonplace and can reduce any delays parties may face. Where possible parties may be encouraged to consider using this method, particularly in the context of procedural matters where no evidence of factual witnesses is required.

Due to the international nature of many disputes and the location of the parties, procedural decisions are frequently made via telephone or video hearing, to avoid unnecessary travel costs and delays to proceedings. This familiarity with remote hearings can be complimented by the range of electronic legal tools which are now readily available, such as e-bundles and hosting platforms, which can provide private channels of communication for parties during hearings.

In addition to the shift to online platforms, the tribunals have, on a case-by-case basis and subject to the circumstances of any particular dispute, adjourned some hearings for a later date or have extended timelines for written submissions or witness statements. In some cases, parties have jointly requested for the suspension of the proceedings to hold without prejudice settlement talks. In less complex cases, parties have requested the tribunal to dispense with the oral hearing and decide the dispute based on documents alone.

In the last year or so, the pandemic has caused many jurisdictions to conduct proceedings online at least in part, for the first time, and accelerated the use of online proceedings in arbitration and mediation. The past year has witnessed a number of landmark decisions from various apex national courts,[4] reflecting the continued growth of international arbitration. Leading arbitral institutions also registered a record number of cases in 2019. The Singapore International Arbitration Center ("SIAC") registered 479 new cases involving parties from over 59 countries, its highest single-year caseload increase. The aggregate amount in dispute for SIAC-administered cases exceeded USD8 billion, a remarkable 14.6% jump from 2018. The LCIA similarly recorded its highest number of cases in 2019, with over 406 cases being referred to the institution, 346 of which specifically apply the LCIA Rules. The ICC also recorded 869 new cases in 2019, the second-highest number of newly recorded cases in any year by the ICC. The ICC also recorded its highest number of new cases involving states and state-owned entities (20% of new cases, featuring 212 state and state-owned entities).

3 The Reactions and Measures Taken by Some International Commercial Arbitration Institutions to Cope with the COVID-19 Pandemic

The environmental footprint of COVID-19 could be clearly measured.[5] As far as the international commercial arbitration realm is concerned, measures are not only taken to move the seat of arbitration conducting to

[4] The U.S. Supreme Court in GE Energy Power Conversion France SAS, Corp. v Outokumpu Stainless USA, LLC, et al. it affirmed the application of non-signatory theories in domestic law under the Convention on the Recognition and Enforcement of Foreign Arbitral Awards ("New York Convention"). The court held that state law principles of equitable estoppel could apply to bind non-signatories to arbitration agreements without running afoul of the Convention. The Court reversed the decision of the Eleventh Circuit that, in order to be bound by an arbitration agreement under the New York Convention, a party must have signed the agreement. In a unanimous ruling that reflects a robust approach to enforcing arbitration agreements, the Court held that the "text of the New York Convention does not conflict with the enforcement of arbitration agreements by non-signatories under domestic- law equitable estoppel doctrines" and that the Convention "contemplate[s] the use of domestic doctrines to fill gaps in the Convention."

[5] See Kerstin Schweizer, *Flip Side of the Coin: COVID-19 Gives Environment a Boost*, DW (April 15, 2020), https://www.dw.com/en/flip-side-of-the-coin-covid-19-gives-environment-a-boost/av-52981862 (arguing that pollution and Greenhouse gas emissions have gone down as countries try to contain the spread of the new coronavirus by lockdown and other national restrictions). See also the prophetic vision of T.C. Boyle in his short story *After the Plague*, *in* AFTER THE PLAGUE—AND OTHER STORIES 281 (2001).

home-office, but also to amend and enact new laws and rules regarding the arbitration proceedings.

In terms of arbitration rules, a number of arbitral institutions have commenced, and concluded processes to revise their rules.[6] Many guidelines had been released not long after the spread of the pandemic on the use of technology and the conduct of arbitral proceedings in a remote environment.[7] These soft law instruments complement preexisting guidelines on technology, date protection, and cyber security.[8]

Of course, international arbitration does not depend on the straight-jacket of national procurement laws but is more flexible in acquiring what is needed to run efficient arbitral proceedings. Parties and tribunals alike have also embraced the use of technology to facilitate proceedings. It is the increase in the use of remote hearings beyond case management and procedural conferences that has been remarkable. Now even complex multibillion-dollar disputes are now being heard on digital platforms.

The following are some noteworthy updates on arbitration rules and guidelines concerning virtual arbitration in different parts of the world.

First, at the international level, on April 9, 2020, the International Court of Arbitration at the International Chamber of Commerce (ICC) released its ICC Guidance Note on Possible Measures Aimed at Mitigating the Effects of the COVID-19 Pandemic ("ICC Guidance Note"). The ICC Guidance Note outlines a range of measures to help mitigate the effects of the COVID-19 pandemic on arbitral proceedings. In particular, it includes information on organizing virtual hearings, as well as two annexes: a checklist for protocol on virtual hearings, and suggested clauses

[6] LCIA unveiled its updated arbitral rules in August 2020. The rule span a spectrum of issues, including composite requests for arbitration, broader provisions on consolidation, the power of arbitral tribunals to order an early determination of claims or counterclaims that are manifestly without legal merit, the use of tribunal secretaries, and date protection and cybersecurity. The ICC and SIAC have also announced that revisions to their rules are forthcoming.

[7] Including the Seoul Protocol on Video Conferencing in International Arbitration and the Transnational Dispute Management Draft Procedural Order to Govern Virtual Arbitration Proceedings.

[8] Such as the ICCA-NYC Bar-CPR Protocol on Cybersecurity in International Arbitration and the draft ICCA-IBA Roadmap to Data Protection in International Arbitration.

for cyber-protocols and procedural orders dealing with the organization of virtual hearings.[9]

In international investment dispute resolution by arbitration, the International Centre for Settlement of Investment Disputes (ICSID) advised the party representatives of all pending ICSIS cases by email on 16 April 2020 about ICSID services and technology for virtual hearings. These include high-definition audio and video for up to 1,000 participants, with the ability to see and hear all tribunal members, counsel, experts and witnesses, robust security, real-time court reporting, simultaneous interpretation, and file sharing and virtual chat functions for correspondence between individuals or with all participants in the hearings.

Second, at regional level, in America, the American Arbitration Association-International Centre for Dispute Resolution (AAA-ICDR) has published (1) a Virtual Hearing Guide for Arbitrators and Parties, (2) a Virtual Hearing Guide for Arbitrators and Parties Utilizing Zoom, as well as (3) a Model Order and Procedures for a Virtual Hearing via Videoconference.[10]

In Europe, the London Court of International Arbitration ("LCA") published a services update on 18 March 2020, stating that it would be operating remotely from the following day and providing instructions to parties and arbitrators on how to communicate with the LCA.[11]

In Switzerland, after rounds of discussion that date back to 2017, the Swiss Parliament also approved amendments to the Private International Law Act in June 2020, which governs international arbitration seated in Switzerland. The amendments further strengthen Switzerland's robust approach to arbitration and its position as a leading arbitration jurisdiction. Among other things, the amendments empower the Swiss courts to appoint the entire tribunal in a multiparty dispute to preserve the equal

[9] See also INT'L CHAMBER COM., *ICC Guidance Note on Possible Measures Aimed at Mitigating the Effects of the COVID-19 Pandemic*, ¶ 22 (2020), https://iccwbo.org/content/uploads./sites/3/2020/04/guidance-note-possible-measures-mitigating-effects-covid-19-english.pdf [hereinafter ICC Guidance Note] ("*If a tribunal determines to proceed with a virtual hearing without party agreement, or over party objection, it should carefully consider the relevant circumstances, ... assess whether the award will be enforceable at law, ... and provide reasons for that determination*").

[10] See *Virtual Hearings*, AAA-ICDR, https://go.adr.org/covid-19-virtual-hearings.html (last visited May 22, 2020).

[11] See *LCIA Services Update: COVID-19*, LCIA (March 18, 2020), https://www.lcia.org/lcia-services-update-covid-19.aspx.

treatment of parties, simplify the form requirements for arbitration agreements and permit parties to file challenges against arbitral awards before the Swiss courts in English.[12]

In Sweden, The Arbitration Institute of the Stockholm Chamber of Commerce (SCC) offered the SCC Platform to ad hoc arbitrations globally, starting in May 2020. The SCC ad hoc Platform is supposed to be a secure digital platform for communication and file sharing between the parties and the tribunal.[13] Its uses will be free of charge for arbitrations commenced during the COVID-19 outbreak.

In Australia, the Australian Centre for International Commercial Arbitration (ACICA) published guidance on managing the impact of COVID-19 and the use of arbitration to mitigate risk, which sets out the advantages of arbitration and includes links to sample submission agreements and a sample procedural order.[14]

In Turkey, The Istanbul Arbitration Centre (ISTAC) issued online Hearing Rules and Procedures that are applicable to hearings conducted through teleconference or video conference and are subject to ISTAC Rules.[15]

In Singapore, The Singapore International Arbitration Centre (SIAC), one of the leading international arbitration institutions in Asia, provides regular COVID-19 updates on its websites.[16] In an open letter of 28 April 2020 by the SIAC Court President Gary Born, it was announced that: [I]n addition to our case administration work, we will also be hosting

[12] See *SCC Platform Made Available to Ad Hoc Arbitrations Globally*, SCC (April 23, 2020), https://sccinstitute.com/about-the-scc/news/2020/scc-platform-made-available-to-ad-hoc-arbitrations-globally/?link_id=GZORGcLaWyIa. Likewise, the Vienna International Arbitral Centre (VIAC) published a Checklist on Holding Arbitration and Mediation Hearings in Times of Covid-19 drawn up by Hafez Virjee and Maria Hauser-Morel (Hanefeld Rechtsanwalte).

[13] See *SCC Platform Made Available to Ad Hoc Arbitrations Globally*, SCC (April 23, 2020), https://sccinstitute.com/about-the-scc/news/2020/scc-platform-made-available-to-ad-hoc-arbitrations-globally/?link_id=GZORGcLaWyIa.

[14] See *Important Information for ACICA Users—COVID-19 Update*, ACICA, https://acica.org.au/important-information-for-acica-users/ (last visited May 19, 2020).

[15] See Paksoy, *Coronavirus Pandemic and International Arbitration Proceedings*, LEXOLOGY (April 28, 2020), https://www.lexology.com/library/detail.aspx?g=69d0aed4-ea20-45dc-a669-5530807c52fb.

[16] See *SIAC COVID-19 Updates*, SIAC, https://www.siac.org.sg/covid-19 (last visited May 19, 2020).

services of monthly webinars entitled "A dialogue on Covid-19 with the Secretariat" to address questions about the impact of COVID-19 on any aspect of SIAC arbitrations. The series will include Q&A sessions with the Secretariat, periodic panel discussions on best practices for virtual hearings and related issues, mock virtual hearings, and other events.

The Hong Kong International Arbitration Center ("HKIAC") serves a variety of different virtual hearing needs including fully virtual hearings in multiple locations and time zones handled by HKIAC remotely, thereby offering not only video and audio conferencing but also electronic bundle services, electronic presentation of evidence, transcription services, and interpretation services.[17] HKIAC has produced guidelines for conducting virtual hearings (HKIAC Guidelines for Virtual Hearings). They apply to hearings that are fully or partially virtual and deal with very practical, hands-on advice such as Rule 10.a. ("mute microphones unless speaking"), 10.c. ("avoid wearing a facemask when cameras that automatically track speakers by facial movement are being used.)[18]

The China International Economic and Trade Arbitration Commission ("CIETAC") has launched: Guidelines on Proceeding with Arbitration Actively and Properly during the COVID-19 pandemic (Trial).[19] These guidelines contain specific measures on using the outline case filing system, serving documents, and hearings. There is also an annex containing provisions on virtual hearings. The Guidelines came into force on 1 May 2020 and will cease to have effect when the pandemic is over.

Other jurisdictions that have embarked on legislative reform in the past year include India, New Zealand, Peru, and Tanzania. For example, Tanzania passed a new Arbitration Act that repeals its dated 1931 Arbitration Act. The act is not modeled after the UNCITRAL Model Law but nonetheless addresses a number of crucial issues, including the appointment of arbitrators, jurisdiction, the distinction between domestic and

[17] See *Virtual Hearings*, HKIAC (April 27, 2020), https://www.hkiac.org/content/virtual-hearings.

[18] *HKIAC Guidelines for Virtual Hearings*, HKIAC (2020), https://www.hkiac.org/sites/default/files/ck_filebro.wser/HKIAC%20Guidelines%20for%20Virtual%20Hearings_0.pdf.

See *LCIA Services Update: COVID-19*, LCIA (March 18, 2020), https://www.lcia.org/lcia-services-update-covid-19.aspx.

[19] See *CIETAC Launches Guidelines on Proceeding with Arbitration Actively and Properly During the COVID-19 Pandemic (Trail)*, CIETAC (April 28, 2020), http://www.cietac.org/index.php?m=Article&a=show&id=16919&l=en.

international commercial arbitration, and the enforcement of domestic and foreign awards. The act also creates a new Tanzania Arbitration Centre that will be responsible for the conduct and management of arbitration and the accreditation of arbitrators in Tanzania.

4 The Disadvantages and Concerns About the Virtual Hearings in International Commercial Arbitration Practice

Evidence has shown that arbitration does hold some significant advantages, particularly in the unrivaled flexibility available to all participants about where, when, and how hearings will be conducted.[20] The current president of the London Court of International Arbitration remarked: "*The technology also works beautifully and gave us an insight into the future world of virtual arbitration hearings there is no doubt that it can be done, and done very effectively.*"[21]

Sole arbitrator Timothy Cooke heard a case in March 2020 via video conference as well as six witnesses giving evidence from London, Sydney, and Taipei. He summarized his experience from this case as follows: "*The fact we were conducting a virtual hearing was almost forgotten as the matter got underway. Hearing oral argument was no different really from physical hearings.*"[22]

[20] *Can Arbitration Rescue Trials Stalled Due to Covid-19?*, GAR (April 28, 2020), https://globalarbitrationreview.com/article/1226196/can-arbitration-rescue-trials-stalled-due-to-covid-19.

[21] Alison Ross, *Virtual Vienna Vis Won by Indian University*, GAR (April 20, 2020), https://globalarbitrationreview.com/article/1225629/virtual-vienna-vis-won-by-indian-university.

[22] Ross, supra note x.

In general, it seems that the experience with virtual hearings was rather positive.[23] Nevertheless, for many arbitral institutions, counsel and arbitrators, it requires a big leap forward with respect to the use of technology and giving up well-loved habits.[24] More than that, it is discovered that many national courts lack the technological equipment to smoothly and rapidly switch from a physical hearing to video conferencing with party representatives, counsel, experts, and witnesses being physically located all around the globe.[25]

Practice has also shown that sometimes it is simply not possible to hold virtual hearings or other meetings between the parties and the arbitrators. It can be difficult to conduct witness hearings online in cases involving complex fact patterns. In such particularly complex cases, it may be justified to suspend or postpone the hearing.[26]

[23] Twenty Essex, *Arbitration in a Time of Covid-19: My Experience So Far*, LEXOLOGY (March 23, 2020), https://www.lexology.com/library/detail.aspx?g=fcb668cf-aa19-40b4-a475-4a6df5c083b6 ("[The] system worked very effectively. All lawyers and experts [were] able to gain a full understanding of what was taking place without any (actual or perceived) risk of infection"); Alison Ross, *Covid-19: Participants in SIAC Case Share Success of Virtual Hearing*, GAR (April 23, 2020), https://globalarbitrationreview.com/article/1225832/covid-19-participants-in-siac-case-share-success-of-virtual-hearing; Beale & Co., *Coronavirus Increases Use of Video Evidence in International Arbitration—Will It Become the Norm*, LEXOLOGY (March 21, 2020), https://www.lexology.com/library/detail.aspx?g=3f37fe36-3b20-4737-8e5d-392ba30b25df.

[24] See, e.g., William W. Park, *Arbitration and Fine Dining: Two Faces of Efficiency*, *in* THE POWERS AND DUTIES OF AN ARBITRATOR: LIBER AMICORUM PIERRE A. KARRER 251, 252 (Patricia Shaughnessy & Sherlin Tung eds., 2017) (arguing, that comparisons between arbitration and dining are not particularly apt, but that like dining, arbitral proceedings implicate proportionality and depend upon a multitude of factors which can make the experience better or worse).

[25] But see Marcia Coyle, *A Few Pauses, and 'Sorry, Chief,' But Supreme Court Pulls Off Historic First*, LAW.COM (May 4, 2020), https://www.law.com/nationallawjournal/2020/05/04/a-few-pauses-and-sorry-chief-but-supreme-court-pulls-off-historic-first/?slreturn=20200405031527 (reporting about the first time the U.S. Supreme Court heard arguments via teleconferencing on 4 May 2020); see also Cohausz & Florack, *BGH: Successful First Hearing of the Xth Civil Senate by Video Conference*, LEXOLOGY (May 6, 2020), https://www.lexology.com/library/detail.aspx?g=e9ed79f3-3c4a-467b-ae0c-a7f698cea8f2 (reporting about the first hearing via video conference by the highest German Court in Civil Matters on 23 April 2020).

[26] Cook County includes Chicago and the greater metropolitan area. In those days, Illinois was "*a pioneer in the use of video technology, but it was soon followed by other states.*" Shari Seidman Diamond et al., *Efficiency and Cost: The Impact of Videoconferenced Hearings on Bail Decisions*, 100(3) J. CRIM. L. & CRIMINOLOGY 869, 877 (2010).

Conducting hearings remotely (i.e., Zoom) will make it significantly harder to ensure that the testifying witness is not secretly being advised or reading from hidden documents without the knowledge of the tribunal or opposing party.[27]

Experienced practitioners warn that the quality of evidence provided by witness testimonies is likely to be negatively affected by online arrangements. In particular, during cross-examination, it is crucial for arbitrators to be able to see and analyze both the answers given by witnesses and their demeanor in order to assess their credibility.[28] Also, e-technical issues can cause delay and disruption.

Many arbitration rules explicitly stipulate that an arbitral tribunal shall hold a hearing if so requested by a party.[29] As described earlier, a virtual hearing is completely sufficient if only witnesses of minor importance are heard or even for whole arbitrations where the parties want to plead their case and enjoy their "day in court" but where the outcome of the case does not depend on the overall impression of a key witness or other factors which demand a physical hearing.[30] Of course, many arbitration rules provide for the possibility of arbitration without an oral hearing.[31] In particular, in cases that depend exclusively on legal issues, a "documents only" arbitration without a hearing is often most efficient and sufficient.[32]

[27] Id.

[28] Volterra Fietta, *The Impact of COVID-19 on Arbitration Proceedings and Due Process*, LEXOLOGY (April 9, 2020), https://www.lexology.com/library/detail.aspx?g=f82d0392-ba32-40ea-895d-422ad8104372.

[29] See, e.g., art. 24.1 of the SIAC Arbitration Rules 2016, art. 19.1 of the LCIA Arbitration Rules, art. 22.4 of the HKIAC Administered Arbitration Rules 2018 and art. 29.1 of the DIS Arbitration Rules. Not quite clear is art. 24.3 of the CAAI Arbitration Rules.

[30] See CMS Cameron McKenna Nabarro Olswang LLP, *Doing Arbitration Differently: Documents-Only Arbitration During the COVID-19 Pandemic and Beyond*, LEXOLOGY (March 26, 2020), https://www.lexology.com/library/detail.aspx?g=6b969224-c412-404e-858f-81d3a3f22d76.

[31] See, e.g., art. 26 of the ICC Arbitration Rules 2017 (in particular, in combination with art. 3.3 of the ICC Expedited Procedure Rules) and art. 22.4 HKIAC Administered Arbitration Rules 2018.

[32] See, in particular, Jörg Risse, *An Inconvenient Truth: The Complexity Problem and Limits to Justice*, 35 ARB. INT'L 291, 307 (2019).

Finally, there are reported issues around security and privacy of video conferencing applications, which have raised additional concerns about uninvited participants being able to join, intercept, or interfere with Virtual hearing.[33] In particular, Zoom, a well-known provider of video conferencing services, received a lot of criticism because of privacy issues.[34] Cyber fraud, e.g., in international arbitration has been a concern for the last few years. It might well be that COVID-19 will have an impact in this area. In fact, the prevalence of remote hearings is likely to increase cyber fraud.[35]

5 The Aftermath of the Pandemic and Potential Changes to International Commercial Arbitration

It has been confirmed by many arbitration practitioners that the crisis has a great impact on the profession beyond the specific circumstances of the confinement.[36] It has been witnessed that a new way of defining professional relationships between people seems to arise as all humanity is currently involved in the experiment of living confined to their homes and prevented from maintaining the hitherto usual professional and personal exchanges. COVID-19 gives arbitration practitioners cause to reflect not only on how to conduct their current cases but also on their entire way of life.[37] When COVID-19 passes by and will not be immediately replaced by a successor, the business of cross-border arbitration might

[33] See also Matt Reynolds, *Could Zoom Jury Trials Become the Norm During the Coronavirus Pandemic?* ABA J. (May 11, 2020, 8:00 AM), https://www.abajournal.com/web/article/could-zoom-jury-trials-become-a-reality-during-the-pandemic.

[34] Debra Cassens Weiss, *Another Lawsuit Is Filed Against Zoom over Alleged Privacy Problems*, ABA J. (April 14, 2020, 10:04 AM), https://www.abajournal.com/news/article/another-lawsuit-is-filed-against-zoom-over-alleged-privacy-problems (plaintiff alleges that Zoom failed to protect user data from Facebook and LinkedIn).

[35] *Questions and Answers on How Best to Deal with International Arbitration in the Face of COVID- 19*, HFW (2020), https://www.hfw.com/downloads/001977-HFW-How-best-to-deal-with-International-Arbitration-in-the-face-of-Covid-19-March-2020.pdf.

[36] Kathleen Lynn, *The Legal World Will Never Be the Same After COVID-19*, NYSBA (April 22, 2020), https://nysba.org/the-legal-world-will-never-be-the-same-after-covid-19/.

[37] See the almost prophetic article by Alison Ross, *The Coronavirus: What Impact?*, GAR (March 7, 2020), https://globalarbitrationreview.com/article/1215931/the-coronavirus-what-impact.

well continue as before—"but with heightened awareness of risk of overseas travel and the need to balance economic, commercial and legal imperatives with human ones."[38]

COVID-19 pandemic has shown that international arbitration is the more flexible dispute resolution mechanism in rapidly changing circumstances. International arbitration allows users to tailor the procedure to their needs. It also provides arbitrators and parties with flexibility to make adjustments as appropriate in the course of the proceedings.[39] Enthusiasts of virtual hearings even believe that virtual hearings are "the new normal,"[40] despite all the challenges of the new technology required in the practice of international arbitration.

COVID-19 has undoubtedly accelerated the use and acceptance of virtual hearings in international arbitration.[41] In the coming months and after the travel restrictions are eased, it is expected that users of arbitration will continue to refine and enhance the use of technology for virtual hearings. These hearings may become a "new normal" for cross-border disputes, at least for less complex cases, which may be better suited for online platforms. In that regard, it is not difficult to predict that in the post-corona period, there will be an increased use of e-trial systems. Document management systems and transcripts that can be assessed remotely will help to supplement the video hearing.[42]

A common question once posed by some practitioners: will the traditional arbitration conference survive in a post-COVID-19 world? For pure information purposes, a webinar might serve the purpose. However, a real arbitration conference with a real-world physical meeting of practitioners from different generations, jurisdictions, industries, and all levels

[38] Id., Ross.

[39] Linklaters LLP, *Arbitration in Times of COVID-19*, LINKLATERS (April 8, 2020), https://www.linklaters.com/en/insights/blogs/arbitrationlinks/2020/april/international-arbitration-in-times-of-covid-19.

[40] Janet Walker, *Virtual Hearings—The New Normal*, GAR (March 27, 2020), https://globalarbitrationreview.com/article/1222421/virtual-hearings-%E2%80%93-the-new-normal.

[41] Linklaters LLP, *Arbitration in Times of COVID-19*, LINKLATERS (April 8, 2020), https://www.linklaters.com/en/insights/blogs/arbitrationlinks/2020/april/international-arbitration-in-times-of-covid-19.

[42] Neil Kaplan, *Kaplan: How We Must Adapt to COVID-19*, GAR (March 30, 2020), https://globalarbitrationreview.com/article/1222179/kaplan-how-we-must-adapt-to-covid-19.

of expertise creates a platform for new formal exchange of information, to build up trust and confidence in other people and processes in a certain spirit which is necessary to nurture the idea of international arbitration. A webinar in an all-virtual arbitration world will never provide for opportunities to bump into arbitration celebrities at a buffet line and to build up shortlists and blacklists of arbitrator candidates simply by watching these candidates at a cocktail bar after the conference is over.

Kathleen Lynn published a programmatic article entitled *the legal world will never be the same after COVID-19* in April 2020. She writes that: "*because of ongoing social distancing measures, courts and lawyers are doing businesses by video, lawyers and legal staff are losing jobs, and new graduates can't start their careers—and these effects will probably persist for months, maybe years.*"

It is not hard to predict that once the legal profession makes it to the other side of the virus, there will be much greater use of technology.[43] Indeed, one long-term impact of COVID-19 will certainly be that the digitalization of international arbitration will speed up enormously. Neil Kaplan might certainly be right that, "surely video conferencing facilities should be the norm for all procedural hearings and case conferences."[44] Similarly, Ross expresses the hope for the future virtual hearing by saying: "Over all, a core piece of the new digitalized and virtual world of arbitration is the virtual hearing. Of course, the hope is with the virtual hearing, arbitration would become faster, cheaper and, maybe, even better in light of the lower ecological impact due to the lack of travel to the hearing venue and the paperless—in fact even almost contactless—arbitration."[45]

The author holds a position in agreement that COVID-19 has changed the way international arbitration is operated; some elements can take place

[43] Allen & Overy LLP, *Covid-19 Coronavirus: How the APAC Courts and Arbitral Institutions Have Adapted to the Change*, ALLEN & OVERY (April 3, 2020), https://www.allenovery.com/en-gb/global/news-and-insights/publications/covid-19-coronavirus-how-the-apac-courts-and-arbitral-institutions-have-adapted-to-the-challenge ("*Covid-19 has the potential to drive adaptions to arbitral and litigation proceedings that could have a much more lasting impact*").

[44] Neil Kaplan, *Kaplan: How We Must Adapt to COVID-19*, GAR (March 30, 2020), https://globalarbitrationreview.com/article/1222179/kaplan-how-we-must-adapt-to-covid-19.

[45] See Alison Ross, *Green Campaign Launches as Pandemic Forces Rethinking*, GAR (April 22, 2020), https://globalarbitrationreview.com/article/1225979/green-campaign-launches-as-pandemic-forces-rethinking.

in virtual reality, whereas some physical presence is and remains desirable or maybe even indispensable. The virtual practice will certainly not change the core elements of international arbitration—impartial, independent, fair, and just decision-making in disputes through a voluntary and flexible process.

CHAPTER 14

Recovery from International Trade Crisis

Ramesh Bikram Karky

1 Introduction

Since the birth of the multilateral trading system, the COVID-19 pandemic has brought the biggest crisis to international trade and regional trade. The COVID-19 pandemic not only disrupted the supply of goods and services but also eroded the fundamental values of the international trading system. Since the beginning of the pandemic, discrimination and unfair trade practices between trading states have become the new norm. To address and to recover from the trade crisis, in addition to other measures, we need to examine what kind of improvements are required within multilateral and regional trade agreements. To curb unfair trade and discriminatory practices, leveling the playing field is crucial to

R. B. Karky (✉)
School of Business, Conestoga College Institute of Technology and Advanced Learning, Kitchener, ON, Canada
e-mail: rkarky@conestogac.on.ca

School of Accounting and Finance, Adjunct Faculty at the University of Waterloo, Waterloo, ON, Canada

School of Law, Vrije Universiteit Brussel, Brussels, Belgium

E. Duruigbo et al. (eds.), *International Law and Development in the Global South*, https://doi.org/10.1007/978-3-031-13741-9_14

achieving the win–win situation in cross-border trade. It is essential to alleviate the international trade crisis through international cooperation. The international trade crisis demands global and permanent solutions and a holistic approach.

To recover from the pandemic crisis, we need to answer different questions. How do we address the crisis brought by the COVID-19 pandemic? Should we also address the challenges which were there in the international trading system before the commencement of the COVID-19 pandemic? Should we consider a temporary solution or try to find a permanent type of solution? Most probably, COVID-19 will remain the new normal in the future.

This paper reviews the international trade crisis faced by countries caused by the COVID-19 pandemic. To recover from the trade crisis, it provides a few recommendations for the improvement of multilateral agreements and regional agreements. This paper first covers the impact of COVID-19 on international trade and its legal implications. The paper further examines the subject matter of international trade, issues related to essential goods and services and means of livelihood, unfair imbalanced trade practices, and the impact of COVID-19 on globalization.

2 Impact of COVID-19 on International TRADE and Its Legal Implications

As of April 2020, 80 countries and separate customs territories have introduced export prohibitions or restrictions due to the COVID-19 pandemic.[1] The General Agreement on Tariffs and Trade (GATT)[2] Article XI prohibits export bans and restrictions. However, it allows members to apply them temporarily to prevent or relieve critical shortages of foodstuffs or other essential products. WTO rules also contain general exceptions. These general exceptions could be used to justify restrictions provided that they do not constitute a means of arbitrary or

[1] World Trade Organization, Export prohibitions and restrictions, Information Note, 23 April 2020, available at https://www.unescap.org/sites/default/files/Export%20Prohibitions%20and%20Restrictions_1.pdf (accessed 10 June 2020) [World Trade Organization, Export prohibition].

[2] General Agreement on Tariffs & Trade 1994, 33 I. L. M. 1153 (1994) [GATT 1994].

unjustifiable discrimination between countries, or a disguised restriction on international trade.[3]

When the GATT came into existence in 1947 the overall nature of trade and the environment of trade was different. As time passed by, GATT was considered out of date, and the WTO Agreement came into existence in 1995. Over the last 25 years, the international trading system has been facing many severe challenges, including the crisis brought by the COVID-19 pandemic. To address the new crisis caused by the COVID-19 pandemic, in addition to other means, we also need to examine what kind of changes are required within multilateral and regional trade agreements.

Article XVI:4 of the WTO Agreement states: "Each Member shall ensure the conformity of its laws, regulations and administrative procedures with its obligations as provided in the annexed Agreements."[4] Thus, article XVI:4 of the WTO Agreement deals with the requirement of bringing national legislation in conformity with the rules of the multilateral Agreements. Hence, we should not forget that multilateral trade agreements impact trade-related domestic laws. If we do not address new challenges within multilateral agreements, WTO Member countries will not be able to address the COVID-19 pandemic crisis within their domestic legal system.

Furthermore, the multilateral agreement plays a significant role in growing international trade. All countries have sovereign rights, and they have every right to prohibit the import of foreign goods or services into their jurisdictions. When states sign the multilateral agreement (WTO Agreement), they authorize the import of foreign goods or services into their jurisdictions. Countries sign multilateral agreements to achieve benefits from trade. A win–win situation between trading states is the prerequisite of the international trading system. Unfair trade is the enemy of the international trading system. Leveling the playing field is crucial to achieving a win–win situation in international trade and recovering from the trade crisis. Art. XXIII:1 of GATT has the concept of nullification or impairment of the benefit of trade. This provision is the central element of the whole GATT/WTO system. If any trade benefit accruing to any

[3] World Trade Organization, Export prohibition, *supra* note 1.

[4] Article XVI:4 of the Marrakesh Agreement Establishing the World Trade Organization, 33 I. L. M. 1144 (1994) [WTO Agreement].

WTO Member directly or indirectly under the WTO agreement is nullified or impaired, that Member has a right to a remedy under the WTO dispute settlement system.

The legal basis of regional trade agreements (RTA) is Article XXIV of the GATT, which is part of the WTO Agreement. The GATT provision of the regional trade agreement accepts discriminatory trade practices as an exception. This is an exception to the most-favored-nation treatment of the GATT/WTO Agreement. When an exception is overused, it may be considered as a general provision. The international trading system is well known as a non-discriminatory system, but unfortunately, its basic value is fading out. Protecting non-discriminatory practices and fair trading practices is one of the biggest challenges of our time, and the answers to these challenges can help recover from the crisis caused by the pandemic.

Because of the COVID-19 pandemic we have witnessed an unprecedented disruption of international trade.[5] The COVID-19 pandemic has also brought a new trend among countries. Countries are going to give preference to their local industries, local agriculture, local services, local means of livelihood, and local jobs, among others. Alan WM Wolff states:

> The COVID-19 pandemic poses a series of challenges for multilateralism. In some parts of the world, a move towards heightened nationalism and isolationism is threatened. The need for well-functioning global economic governance has become greater and more urgent than ever. … and updating and strengthening the World Trade Organization and its rules.[6]

Robert B. Zoellick says that trade has many benefits in the context of the current international trade crisis. International trade needs some safety valve, and, to address the current international trade, we need international cooperation.[7] In the same context, Pascal Lamy says that

[5] World Trade Organization, COVID-19 and world trade available at https://www.wto.org/english/tratop_e/covid19_e/covid19_e.htm (accessed 10 June 2020) [COVID-19 and world trade].

[6] Alan WM Wolff (WTO): Trade and peace are intimately related, 16 June 2020, available at https://www.wto.org/english/news_e/news20_e/ddgaw_16jun20_e.htm (accessed 17 June 2020). Alan Wm Wolff is current Deputy Director General of WTO.

[7] Robert B. Zoellick, Interview on what future for the global trading system? at Peterson Institute for International Economics, Washington, DC, 17 June 2020, available at https://www.youtube.com/watch?v=clKssKi-6w8 (accessed 22 June 2020). Robert B.

the European Union wants an open market system. Countries need to control state capitalism to level the playing field. International cooperation is required to fix the current international trade crisis.[8] "Fairness – in both the national-level distribution of benefits and in global competition – is essential for maintaining public support for trade and the open markets needed to get through and emerge from the crisis."[9]

Of course, after COVID-19, the same old international trade rules will not be able to address the new crisis. "Trade is essential to save both lives and livelihoods."[10] Among others, the new international trade rules should have provisions to address the challenges brought by unfair trade practices that are not covered under existing multilateral and regional trade agreements. Persistent trade imbalance is also a kind of unfair trade practice that is not covered by multilateral agreements. The trading countries' right to seek remedies to mitigate the harm caused by persistent trade imbalance should also be included in the multilateral agreements. It helps to level the playing field.

In addition, multilateral and regional trade agreements should include a provision of a boundary between areas of small businesses and multinational businesses. If you discourage multinational businesses to compete with individual or local small businesses, it will bring fairness in international trade. Similarly, in the absence of competition law, consumer protection law, and human rights law in multilateral and regional trade agreements, international trade rules will not be able to recover from the existing crisis. The recovery from the existing crisis is directly related to leveling the playing field in international trade.

The market economy has many benefits and virtues. The law of competition plays a significant role in making the market competitive and fair. Competition law also has an international dimension in the form of

Zoellick is the former United States Trade Representative and former President of the World Bank.

[8] Pascal Lamy, Interview on what future for the global trading system? at Peterson Institute for International Economics, Washington, DC, 17 June 2020 available at https://www.youtube.com/watch?v=clKssKi-6w8 (accessed 22 June 2020). Pascal Lamy is the former Director-General of World Trade Organization.

[9] OECD Policy Responses to Coronavirus (COVID-19), COVID-19 and international trade: Issues and actions, 12 June 2020, available at http://www.oecd.org/coronavirus/policy-responses/covid-19-and-international-trade-issues-and-actions-494da2fa/ (accessed 17 June 2020) [COVID-19 and international trade].

[10] *Id.*

the price-fixing and market-sharing arrangements that often spill across national borders. Abuses of a dominant position and corporate mergers etc. need to be simultaneously investigated by more than one jurisdiction.[11] The WTO Agreement has no provisions on competition law. In the absence of competition law, the benefits of multilateral trade agreements go to a handful of persons. The multilateral trade agreements can not protect the interest of weaker persons.

Similarly, in the absence of consumer protection law, consumers will be cheated, and there will be no protection for consumers. In the age of e-commerce, this is very vital. The WTO Agreement focuses on the interest of manufacturers and sellers, and it does not say anything about the interest of purchasers and consumers. Multilateral and regional trade agreements need to address this vacuum to recover from the crisis.

The following subchapter focuses on the need to determine the subject matter of international trade and provisions of essential goods and services and means of livelihood in the multilateral and regional trade agreement.

3 The New Deal to a Recovery: Subject Matter of International Trade and Provisions of Essential Goods and Services and Means of Livelihood

The right to international trade is not a fundamental right. International trade is a privilege given by sovereign countries by signing multilateral or regional trade agreements. In contrast, the right to livelihood is a fundamental right. The right to livelihood is related to the means of living. The Supreme Court of India in *Olga Tellis v. Bombay Municipal Corporation*, popularly known as the "Pavement Dwellers Case" states, "…An equally important facet of the right to life is the right to livelihood because no person can live without the means of livelihood."[12] Any trade which deprives people's right to livelihood is against the norms of human rights. Such types of international trade should be discouraged by multilateral trade agreements.

[11] OECD, OECD competition policy responses to COVID-19, available at https://read.oecd-ilibrary.org/view/?ref=130_130807-eqxgniyo7u&title=OECD-competition-policy-responses-to-COVID-19 (accessed 17 June 2020).

[12] Subodh Asthana/Avni Sharma, Extended Jurisprudence of Article 21 through the Lens of Right to Livelihood, iPleaders, February 2, 2020, available at https://blog.ipleaders.in/right-livelihood/ (accessed 18 July 2020).

The COVID-19 trade crisis has highlighted the importance of cross-border trade and its limitations. Crossing the border with every type of goods or services is not in the best interest of every society or country. Essential goods or services and means of livelihood need to be protected from the global competition. Domestic law alone cannot make such a provision. Article XVI:4 of the WTO Agreement requires bringing trade-related national legislation in conformity with the multilateral Agreements. To facilitate such provision in domestic law, the new multilateral and regional trade agreements should include such provisions.

"The world is in a mess. On the surface, the problem is the COVID-19 pandemic, but the root causes are deep-seated. Since World War II, global economic growth has been strong and widespread, but its benefits have been increasingly centralized near the top."[13] If we continue international trade as it is, one day, one person may have total global wealth (now eight persons have half of the worldwide wealth[14]). The end result of this process is creating a society of slaves. Under the current environment, individual or small businesses cannot compete with big companies. The big businesses cannot compete with multinational companies. Multinational companies cannot compete with China (in international trade, China is playing the role of a business company. China has 130,000 state-owned companies, and, in international trade, these companies have unfair advantages[15]).

There should be a clear demarcation between the area of big business (multinational business) and individual and small business. It will help to generate livelihood for everybody. Nowadays, relatively smaller businesses such as hair salons, restaurants, takeout food, etc., are run by multinational companies. Competition should be between equals. Protecting the interests of individual and small businesses is vital for the sustainability of society and livelihood. If we do not protect the interests of individual or

[13] James M. Boughton, It is finally time for a New Bretton Woods, CIGI, 22 June 2020, available at https://www.cigionline.org/articles/it-finally-time-new-bretton-woods (accessed 22 June 2020).

[14] OXFAM International, Press releases, Just 8 men own same wealth as half the world, 16 January 2017, available at https://www.oxfam.org/en/press-releases/just-8-men-own-same-wealth-half-world (accessed 25 July 2020).

[15] Frank Tang, South China Morning Post, 8 July 2020, available at https://www.scmp.com/economy/china-economy/article/3092339/china-approves-plan-boost-prominence-state-firms-despite (accessed 9 July 2020).

small businesses, ordinary people will have no purchasing capacity. If ordinary people have no purchasing power, international trade cannot grow. We have already witnessed this problem. Since 2014, the global trade of goods has been shrinking.

What an individual or small business can do should not be allowed to big businesses (multinational companies). An individual or small business cannot afford to build airplanes or trains or big ships or highways, etc. Only such types of businesses need to go to big businesses. If a multinational company sells "take-out food" or operates taxis in the neighborhood, it should not be considered fair. Generally, multinational companies go to others' areas of business and play foul games. For example, there is a case under consideration before the Supreme Court of Canada that will decide whether an Uber driver is an independent contractor or Uber employee.[16] In this case, the class action suit demands minimum wage, vacation pay, and other benefits protected under Ontario's Employment Standards Act. Uber claims that a driver is an independent contractor, and Uber is not under obligation to give benefits of employment. On June 28, 2020, in this case, the Supreme Court of Canada permitted class action litigation saying that the arbitration agreement clause requires to go to the Netherlands and paying fee CAD$14,500.00 for dispute settlement, which is unconscionable—so unfair to the driver that it cannot be enforced.[17] Pertinent here is the position of the Organization for Economic Cooperation and Development (OECD) expressed as follows:

> The OECD examines the trends and patterns in inequality and poverty for OECD and emerging countries. Its work analyses the multiple causes linked to growing inequalities, such as globalisation, technological change and changes in redistribution and policy fashion. It also assesses the effectiveness of social and labour market policies in tackling poverty and high inequalities.[18]

[16] *Uber Technologies Inc. v. David Heller*—SCC cases (Lexum), 28 June 2020, available at https://scc-csc.lexum.com/scc-csc/scc-csc/en/item/18406/index.do (accessed 29 June 2020).

[17] Ibid.

[18] OECD, Income inequality and poverty, available at http://www.oecd.org/social/inequality-and-poverty.htm (accessed 17 June 2020).

The OECD has also noted that "Fairness – in both the national-level distribution of benefits and in global competition – is essential for maintaining public support for trade and the open markets needed to get through and emerge from the crisis."[19]

Since the COVID-19 pandemic started, there have been tremendous losses of lives and wealth within a short period. Nobody knows how long this virus will last, or whether it will become the new normal. Our way of life has already changed. In the context of international trade, I predict that, for the next two to three decades, every country will focus on its people, health, and well-being. It means the areas of basic needs are not going to be the subject matter of international trade. Goods and services related to basic needs and means of livelihood will enjoy absolute protection. Most probably, in the areas of essential goods and services and means of livelihood, there will not be the national treatment provision between the domestic goods/services and imported goods/services and the same with the most-favored-nation treatment as well. "Goods and services may no longer flow around the globe as they used to. … In the new trade world "order," deals may count more than rules …."[20]

The General Agreement on Trade in Services (GATS)[21] has borrowed the idea of most-favored-nation treatment (MFN) and national treatment (NT) from the GATT. Now GATT may borrow some ideas from GATS, for example, schedules of specific commitment. Regarding trade in goods, there may not be a blanket type of non-discriminatory treatment. First, most probably countries will make a boundary between areas of domestic trade (relating to an individual or small business) and international trade. Within the fields of international trade, you can export your goods to a particular country if that country has opened those goods for importation. The Rule of GATS and its schedules of specific commitments may work as an example for trade in goods to address the new crisis. Under specific commitment of trade in goods, each country will identify the types of goods to which it will apply for market access, national treatment, and MFN treatment within that country's jurisdiction.

[19] COVID-19 and international trade, *supra* note 9.

[20] Hector Torres, The new world order, shaped by deals rather than rules, Opinion—GICI, 1 June 2020, available at https://www.cigionline.org/articles/new-world-order-shaped-deals-rather-rules. Hector Torres is a senior fellow at CIGI and a former executive director at the International Monetary Fund.

[21] General Agreement on Trade in Services, 33 I. L. M. 1167 (1994) [GATS].

In many situations, the persistent trade imbalance between two trading states causes poverty and unemployment in the state that has a trade deficit. The following subchapter deals with trade imbalance between trading partners.

4 Trade Imbalance as an Obstacle to Recovery

Trade is one of the means to achieve economic prosperity. Trade is important because it is a machine that generates economic activities and wealth. Trade itself is not an end or objective; the standard of life, happiness, and well-being of human beings are the objective. If any trade or trading system defeats these objectives, then such trade is a bad trade, not fair trade. International trade is justified when one country has a competitive or comparative advantage in specific products or services and another country does not have the same advantage. So, if these two countries trade-off such a product, both will be benefited from trade. For example, the United States has a comparative advantage in growing cotton on a large scale, whereas Bangladesh has no such advantage. Similarly, Bangladesh has a skilled workforce, and it has a competitive advantage in making clothes. There is a win–win situation when Bangladesh buys cotton from the United States, and the Unites States buys clothes from Bangladesh. This type of trade is fair trade, and is justified as international trade.

The purpose of international trade is to create a win–win situation between trading states. International trade is not based on zero-sum game theory. The unfair international trade practices distort conditions of competition between trading states. Hence, to be a justified international trade, it needs to meet the criteria of a win–win situation and fairness. Any international trade between two countries where only one country takes advantage of trade persistently and another country cannot, does not meet the requirements of justified trade. The GATT and the WTO Agreement have some provisions for unfair trade and its remedy.[22] Unfair dumping

[22] International Trade Centre and Commonwealth Secretariat, Business Guide to the World Trading System, the International Trade Centre UNCTAD/WTO and the Commonwealth Secretariat, 2nd ed., 1999, available at https://doi.org/10.14217/978 1848597044-en (accessed 18 July 2020). Also see: https://www.thecommonwealth-ili brary.org/commonwealth/trade/business-guide-to-the-world-trading-system/response-to-unfair-trade-practices-rules-on-the-use-of-countervailing-and-anti-dumping-duties_978184 8597044-14-en (accessed 18 July 2020).

can be addressed by imposing anti-dumping duties,[23] and foreign subsidies can be addressed by imposing countervailing duties.[24] The objective of these duties is to protect similar domestic industries from unfair foreign trade and level the playing field. Similarly, there is a provision of safeguard which protects the domestic industry from sudden import surge that is harmful to the local industry.[25] In addition to dumping and subsidies, there are many other types of unfair international trade practices that are not covered by multilateral and regional trade agreements. The persistent trade imbalance between two trading states, which causes domestic injury to one of them, is also not covered by multilateral or regional trade agreements. The recovery from the trade crisis is not possible without removing all kinds of unfair international trade practices.

The trade imbalance is related to trade surplus[26] and trade deficit[27] between two trading states. A trade deficit, as such, is neither bad nor good. It depends on the circumstances. Sometimes a trade deficit may have benefits, but it is not always. There are adverse effects of the trade

[23] Agreement on Implementation of Article VI of the General Agreement on Tariffs and Trade 1994, 1868 U. N. T. S. 201 [Anti-Dumping Agreement].

[24] Agreement on Subsidies and Countervailing Measures, 1869 U. N. T. S. 14 [SCM].

[25] Agreement on Safeguards, 1869 U. N. T. S. 154. GATT Article XIX permits Members to raise trade barriers to safeguard a domestic industry seriously injured or threatened with serious injury by import competition. If the conditions for imposing escape clause relief are fulfilled, a Member may suspend a GATT obligation in whole or in part, or withdraw or modify a tariff concession, on a temporary basis. *See* Art. 7:1 of the Agreement on Safeguards.

A Member imposing safeguard measures must not discriminate among sources of the imported product. *See* Art. 2:2 of the Agreement on Safeguards.

Voluntary Restraint Agreement may be considered as a de facto exception to the obligation of quantitative restrictions under GATT Article XI and XIII. The Agreement on Safeguards requires Members to phase out voluntary restraint agreement over a five years period and thereafter making them illegal unless they are concluded in strict observance of the rules laid down in the Safeguard Agreement. *See* Art. 11:2 of the Safeguard Agreement.

[26] "A trade surplus is an economic measure of a positive balance of trade, where a country's exports exceed its imports." *See* Will Kenton, Trade Surplus, Investopedia, 25 June 2019, available at https://www.investopedia.com/terms/t/trade-surplus.asp (accessed 19 July 2020).

[27] "A trade deficit occurs when a country's imports exceed its exports during a given time period. It is also referred to as a negative balance of trade (BOT). *See* Andrew Bloomenthal, Trade deficit, Investopedia, March 26, 2020, available at https://www.investopedia.com/terms/t/trade_deficit.asp (accessed 19 July 2020).

deficit as well. Joseph Stiglitz points out: "Countries running surpluses exert a 'negative externality' on trading partners, and pose a threat to global prosperity, far more than those in deficit."[28] Ben Bernanke argues in the context of European Union that "persistent imbalances within the euro zone are… unhealthy, as they lead to financial imbalances as well as to unbalanced growth. The fact that Germany is selling so much more than it is buying redirects demand from its neighbors (as well as from other countries around the world), reducing output and employment outside Germany."[29]

Andrew Bloomenthal writes:

> Trade deficits can create substantial problems in the long run. The worst and most obvious problem is that trade deficits can facilitate a sort of economic colonization. If a country continually runs trade deficits, citizens of other countries acquire funds to buy up capital in that nation. That can mean making new investments that increase productivity and create jobs. However, it may also involve merely buying up existing businesses, natural resources, and other assets. If this buying continues, foreign investors will eventually own nearly everything in the country.[30]

Along the same lines, Chris Somers has observed:

> To see how an unbalanced trade system works: Let's imagine just two countries, one is running a trade surplus and the other a matching trade deficit. The country with the trade surplus is exporting goods …. The country importing the goods now finds some of its investment or consumption goods are being supplied by imports so the demand for goods from its domestic economy will shrink and so the domestic economy will shrink. Unemployment will go up. … The exporting country is still saving too much, …. At the same time the importing deficit country has seen its economy shrink, because imports have replaced demand for

[28] Balance of Trade, Wikipedia, the free encyclopedia, https://en.wikipedia.org/wiki/Balance_of_trade (20 July 2020) [Balance of trade], See Joseph Stiglitz, Reform the euro or bin it", 5 May 2010, available at www.theguardian.com. See https://www.theguardian.com/commentisfree/2010/may/05/reform-euro-or-bin-it-greece-germany (accessed 20 July 2020).

[29] Balance of Trade, *Id*. See Ben S. Bernanke, Germany's trade surplus is a problem", retrieved 15 March 2018. https://www.brookings.edu/blog/ben-bernanke/2015/04/03/germanys-trade-surplus-is-a-problem/ (accessed 20 July 2020).

[30] Bloomenthal, *supra* note 27.

domestic goods, and so its economy no longer generates enough income to pay for those imports.[31]

It has become axiomatic that "Surplus countries get richer at the expense of deficit countries."[32] The current rules of international trade also do not provide any remedy that mitigates the harms caused by persistent trade imbalance.

Adam Smith argues in his book "An Inquiry into the Nature and Causes of the Wealth of Nations" that if a foreign country can supply us with a commodity cheaper than we can make it, it is better to buy.[33] This argument encourages international trade. The objective of international trade is to create a win–win situation for both trade partners. If one trade partner state is always in profit (trade surplus) and another partner state is consistently in loss (trade deficit), it is not justified trade between these two trade partners. The result of persistent imbalances (trade deficit) is poverty and joblessness in that country. "Trade deficits can create substantial problems in the long run. The worst and most obvious problem is that trade deficits can facilitate a sort of economic colonization."[34] Most importantly, the persistent trade imbalance nullifies or impairs the benefits of international trade, and thus cannot be justified as fair trade.

There is a very close relationship between international trade and globalization. However, international trade and globalization are not the same things. The following subchapter covers the impact of COVID-19 on globalization.

[31] Chris Somers, How economic imbalance lead to imbalances in trade, From Tone, 15 January 2017, available at https://fromtone.com/how-economic-imbalances-lead-to-imbalances-in-trade/ (accessed 19 July 2020).

[32] Balance of Trade, *supra* note 28.

[33] Legal Aspects of International Trade, Forum for International Trade Training, 6th ed., p. 42. *See* Adam Smith, *An Inquiry into the Nature and Causes of the Wealth of Nations* (W. Strahan and T. Cadell, London, UK, 1776).

[34] Bloomenthal, *supra* note 27.

5 Impact of COVID-19 on Globalization

The COVID-19 pandemic caused an unprecedented disruption to the global economy and trade.[35] There is also a prediction that the pandemic economic consequences may lead to outbreaks of violence and conflict, and it may impact peace.[36] Globalization was in trouble even before the COVID-19 pandemic.[37] In 2017, an OECD paper stated, "In the wake of uncertainty and tensions in the trading system today, alongside heightened public concerns about globalisation, open trade is under threat ...."[38] In addition to finance, technology, migration, etc., trade is only one component of globalization. Many people think that the current system is not fair and is not working for them.[39]

The recovery from the trade crisis is also related to the big picture and requires answers to many questions. Why are the rich becoming richer and the poor becoming poorer in every country? Why half of the world's wealth is in the hands of eight persons? Why are so many sovereign states in debt? Why are multinational (big) businesses successful, and why do individual or small businesses fail in every jurisdiction? Even in the United States (number one economy), currently, "More than 1 in 5 U.S. families

[35] COVID-19 and world trade, *supra* note 5, available at https://www.wto.org/english/tratop_e/covid19_e/covid19_e.htm (accessed 10 June 2020).

[36] Alan WM Wolff states, "...the pandemic, in particular its economic consequences, ... could lead to deterioration in Positive Peace and increase the risk of outbreaks of violence and conflict." *See* Alan WM Wolff (WTO): Trade and peace are intimately related, 16 June 2020, available at https://www.wto.org/english/news_e/news20_e/ddgaw_16jun20_e.htm (accessed on 17 June 2020). Alan Wm Wolff is current Deputy Director General of WTO.

[37] Has Covid-19 Killed globalization? The Economist, 14 May 2020 edition, available at https://www.economist.com/leaders/2020/05/14/has-covid-19-killed-globalisation (accessed on June 10, 2020).

[38] OECD (2017), *Making trade work for all*, OECD, Paris, https://www.oecd.org/trade/understanding-the-global-trading-system/making-trade-work-for-all (accessed 17 June 2020) [Making trade work for all].

[39] "But trade is only one element of a broader reaction to both globalisation – encompassing not only trade but also, for example, finance, technology and migration – and domestic economic and political systems in the wake of the global economic crisis. Many people, especially in some advanced economies, are expressing anger and frustration with an entire system that they no longer believe is delivering a better life for them and their families. They believe that the current system is unfair and is not working for them. There is increasing evidence that many of them may be right." See *Id.*

have zero or negative net worth, ..."[40] "When net worth is negative, it means that an individual or family's debts are greater than their assets."[41] Is it a domestic issue or an international trade issue? The WTO Agreement obligates every WTO Member to align their domestic trade laws, policy, and practices with the WTO Agreement.

Furthermore, the trade crisis has raised an important question of whether globalization is dead. Carmen Reinhart observes: "I think COVID-19 is the nail in the coffin of globalization."[42] Globalization was already not working fairly. For example, more than half of global wealth was in the hand of eight persons. Even in rich countries, few were becoming richer, and the majority were becoming poorer day by day. Globalization was a failure because people at large did not get the benefits of globalization.

The trade crisis also further raised an important question of whether international trade is dead. The answer is that international trade is not dead, and it will never die. "Trade is essential to save both lives and livelihoods."[43] But the norms or rules of international trade will change. Most probably, everything will not be the subject of international trade. If a country can produce a particular product inhouse, it will probably not buy such products from another country. If a country cannot produce certain goods or products, it will buy those goods or products from other countries. Therefore, the competitive price of certain products will not be the only determining factor of international trade. Instead, each country will examine other parameters, such as potential effects on local industries, local economy, local means of livelihood, jobs, etc. Most probably, areas of basic needs and services and livelihood means may not need to face global competition.

[40] Christopher Ingraham, The Washington Post, 4 June 2020, available at https://www.washingtonpost.com/business/2020/06/04/protecting-property-is-an-abstraction-growing-share-americans-who-own-nothing/ (accessed on 7 June 2020).

[41] *Id.*

[42] Carmen Reinhart, The Harvard Gazette, 20 May 2020, available at https://news.harvard.edu/gazette/story/2020/05/carmen-reinhart-named-chief-economist-at-the-world-bank/?utm_source=linkedin&utm_campaign=hu-linkedinuniversity-general&utm_medium=social (accessed on 6 June 2020). Carmen Reinhart is a Harvard Professor, Chief Economist and Vice-President at the World Bank.

[43] COVID-19 and international trade, *supra* note 9.

There is another opinion, which does not believe in deglobalization and believes that globalization will continue to grow; globalization was in transition for a while because of COVID-19; in fact, COVID-19 had brought disruption of supply particularly to products related to medicine and foods; and globalization is going to be restructuring.[44] On May 14, 2020, the G20 Trade and Investment Ministerial Meeting states that the long-term actions support the necessary reform of the WTO and the multilateral trading system, and work to ensure a level playing field to foster an enabling business environment, among others.[45]

6 Conclusion

The reality is that international trade alone did not cause all of the problems that concern so many people today, and international trade alone will not solve them either.[46] Against this background, to recover from the international trade crisis, there is a clear need to develop new international trade rules through international cooperation.

New multilateral and regional trade agreements need to determine the subject of international trade. Such new agreements need to give special recognition to essential goods and services and means of livelihood, and they should not be subject to national treatment. There should be a clear demarcation between the area of big business (multinational business) and individual and small business.

There are different types of unfair trade practices, and multilateral and regional trade agreements do not yet restrict some of them. Multilateral and regional trade agreements need to level the playing field by prohibiting all types of unfair trade between countries and providing remedies to mitigate the losses caused by unfair trade.

[44] Abdel-Hamid Mamdouh (Egypt), 2020 WTO DG Candidate, Press Conference, WTO, 15 July 2020, available at https://www.linkedin.com/video/live/urn:li:ugcPost:6689203449336213504/ (accessed 15 July 2020).

[45] G20 Trade and Investment Ministerial Meeting, Ministerial Statement, 14 May 2020, available at https://g20.org/en/media/Documents/G20SS_Statement_G20%20Second%20Trade%20&%20Investment%20Ministerial%20Meeting_EN.pdf (accessed 10 June 2020).

[46] Making trade work for all, *supra* note 38.

Acknowledgements The author would like to thank Professor Dr. Oded Tal and Dr. Larry Morgan for their valuable comments and feedback. The author, however, bears full responsibility for the Paper. The author also thanks the UN Policy Hackathon Team for inviting him to participate in the UN Policy Hackathon on Model Provisions for Trade in Times of Crisis and Pandemic in Regional and other Trade Agreements.

CHAPTER 15

Surrogacy, Religious Culture, and the Imperatives of the Law: Any Caveats for Law Makers?

Obiajulu Nnamuchi

1 Introduction and Preliminary Background

The term "surrogacy" has its origin in the Latin "surrogatus," which means to have been chosen as a substitute or to act in place of another.[1] It is an arrangement whereby a woman (surrogate mother) is commissioned to bear a child for another person or persons (commissioning parent or parents), who, upon birth, becomes the child's parents and assume all parental rights and obligations. Despite being rooted in antiquity, the practice is of relatively recent concern in most countries, especially in the developing world; yet, recent years have witnessed an astronomical rise in surrogacy arrangements as the number of couples unable

[1] WordSense.eu Dictionary, available at https://www.wordsense.eu/surrogatus/ (last visited April 30, 2021).

O. Nnamuchi (✉)
Faculty of Law, University of Nigeria, Enugu Campus, Enugu, Nigeria
e-mail: obi-nnamuchi@yahoo.com

E. Duruigbo et al. (eds.), *International Law and Development in the Global South*, https://doi.org/10.1007/978-3-031-13741-9_15

to beget children on their own and individuals eager to become single parents continue to soar. Strikingly, in most countries, there is no regulation governing surrogacy, the result being uncertainties regarding several aspects of the practice. These uncertainties have far-reaching implications and could, in some cases, operate to defeat the purpose of the transaction, leaving the parties emotionally and financially drained and frustrated. There is no gainsaying that uncertainties in this very important area of artificial reproductive technology (ART) hold nothing positive for anyone. Therefore, there is a need to address this challenge, the best way being through carefully crafted legal and/or policy frameworks.

An important task on the part of those charged with crafting these frameworks would be to devise a system that effectively responds to the needs of those whose conduct is sought to be regulated otherwise compliance would become problematic, which is a result nobody desires. The only way to guarantee compliance is to ensure that the regime (law or policy) is anchored on the lived experiences and realities of life in the jurisdiction concerned, on the cosmology, ethics, legal, and religious culture of the people. Religion, being at the core of cosmology, must undergird any regime to be unveiled for implementation. This is the basis for the focus of this chapter on the religious dimension of surrogacy, on how religious culture interfaces with and gives meaning (or otherwise) to surrogacy. A central contention of this chapter is that religious considerations must inform the crafting of the regime otherwise compliance would not be assured.

Aside from religion, there are, of course, other factors that should be taken into account in formulating legal and policy regimes to govern surrogacy such as ethics,[2] exploitation of vulnerable and marginalized women,[3] commodification or commercialization of women's reproductive capabilities,[4] the rights of affected children and the risks to which they are exposed such as abandonment and citizenship limbo,[5] and so forth. Although academic literature is replete with analysis of the interface between each of these factors and surrogacy, very scant attention has

[2] Obiajulu Nnamuchi, *Commoditizing Childbirth?—Maternal Surrogacy and the Ethicolegal Dimensions of Assisted Conception* 39 (4) MED. & L. 619–644 (2020).

[3] *Id.*

[4] *Id.*

[5] *Id.*

been paid by scholars to the religious component of the practice; yet, this is an important dimension that cannot be glossed over in the governance scheme of this aspect of human reproduction. This is a central thesis and the significance of this discourse.

Following this introductory section, Section 2 explores the two major genres of surrogacy, namely, traditional and gestational, and highlights the distinctions between them. In Section 3, the chapter investigates the position of the world's major religions on surrogacy. Those considered include Christianity (Catholic Church and Anglican Church/Church of England), Judaism, Islam, Hinduism, and Buddhism. This is critical. Latest Pew Research survey indicates that most people ascribe a high degree of importance to religion.[6] Excluding Europe, Canada, Asia, and the Pacific, the vast majority of people in other parts of the world point to religion as being very important in their lives—ranging from 53% (United States), 72% (Brazil and Egypt), 75% (South Africa), 88% (Nigeria) to 93% (Indonesia), 94% (Pakistan), and 98% (Ethiopia).[7] Taking into consideration the huge number of people whose lives and daily activities are impacted by religious creeds and practices, the conclusion—Section 4—is that it is important that these religious beliefs are taken into account in fashioning appropriate regulatory regime in the realm of surrogacy.

2 Categorizing Surrogacy: Traditional Versus Gestational

Surrogacy is classified into two major types, namely, traditional and gestational. The major distinction is the genetic origin of the egg.

2.1 Traditional Surrogacy

Traditional surrogacy (also called partial, natural, or straight surrogacy) involves the fertilization of the eggs of the surrogate with the sperm of the intended or commissioning father or a donor.[8] Because in this type of

[6] Pew Research Center, *The Age Gap in Religion Around the World: How Religious Commitment Varies by Country Among People of all Ages*, June 13, 2018, available at https://www.pewforum.org/2018/06/13/how-religious-commitment-varies-by-country-among-people-of-all-ages/ (last visited April 30, 2021).

[7] *Id.*

[8] Nnamuchi, *supra* note 2, at 623.

arrangement, the eggs used are those of the surrogate, she is the biological mother of the resulting child. Insemination may occur naturally or artificially. When the sperm of the commissioning father is used in the insemination, the resulting offspring will be genetically related to him and the surrogate.[9] Where, on the other hand, the sperm of a donor is used, the result will be a child that does not share genetic relationship with the commissioning parents.[10] In situations involving married couple, the preferred option is to use the husband's sperm so as to avoid legal problems. Although insemination typically takes place in doctors' offices or fertility clinics, the parties can perform the procedure themselves without external assistance, even by a physician.

2.2 Gestational Surrogacy

Gestational surrogacy (also known as host or full surrogacy),[11] which was first achieved in April 1986,[12] is the most common type of surrogacy. It involves using in vitro fertilization (IVF) technology to develop an embryo and subsequently transferring the same to the surrogate mother (gestational carrier). The embryo is created using the intended mother's (or donor's) egg and sperm from the intended father (or donor).

[9] Kalsang Bhatia, et al., *Surrogate Pregnancy: An Essential Guide for Clinicians* 11(1) OBSTET. & GYNECOL. 49–54 (2008).

[10] Bonnie F. Fremgen, MEDICAL LAW AND ETHICS 299 (2016) (explaining that because problems might arise where donor semen is used and the woman is married, some jurisdictions in the United States have enacted legislation in response thereof, the first being Oklahoma. A statute adopted by that state in 1967 stipulates that both husband and wife must consent in writing to the procedure. Part of the underlying rationale for this stipulation is to prevent the husband from alleging adultery against the wife on account of using a semen that was not his).

[11] Susan Imrie & Vasanti Jadva, *The Long-Term Experiences of Surrogates: Relationships and Contact with Surrogacy Families in Genetic and Gestational Surrogacy Arrangements* 29(4) REPROD. BIOMED. ONLINE 424–435 (2014).

[12] Bonnie Johnson, *And Baby Makes Four: For the First Time a Surrogate Bears a Child Genetically Not Her Own*, PEOPLE MAGAZINE, May 4, 1987, available at https://people.com/archive/and-baby-makes-four-for-the-first-time-a-surrogate-bears-a-child-genetically-not-her-own-vol-27-no-18/ (last visited May 10, 2021).

The difference between gestational surrogacy and the traditional type is that in gestational surrogacy, there is no biological or genetic connection between the surrogate and the child.[13] This is because, unlike in traditional surrogacy, which depends on using the surrogate's egg, gestational surrogacy involves using the egg of the commissioning parent or a donor.[14] Another distinction is that the gestational type relies on IVF technology—a procedure which became available in 1978 but continued to be considered experimental until the early 1990s.[15] Although IVF is usually associated with gestational surrogacy,[16] the technology can also be used in traditional surrogacy. Traditional surrogacy typically relies on artificial insemination (AI),[17] using intrauterine insemination (IUI).[18] A comparative advantage is that IUI is a far simpler method and does not subject the surrogate to as many fertility treatments prior to the procedure as does IVF.

Gestational surrogacy can take many forms, all of which will produce a child that is not related genetically to the surrogate[19]:

i. The embryo is created using the intended father's sperm and the intended mother's eggs.
ii. The embryo is created using the intended father's sperm and a donor egg.

[13] Lack of genetic relationship between the surrogate and the child is the reason this type of surrogacy has been described as "womb-leasing." See Marc Stauch, Kay Wheat & John Tingle, SOURCEBOOK ON MEDICAL LAW 414 (2002), quoting Gillian Douglas, *Law, Fertility and Reproduction* 141–144 (1991).

[14] Gestational surrogacy provides a treatment option for women with clearly defined medical problems such as absent uterus, recurrent miscarriage, repeated failure of IVF and other conditions. See Peter R. Brinsden, *Gestational Surrogacy* 9(5) HUM. REPROD. UPDATE 483 – 491 (2003).

[15] Carla Spivack, *The Law of Surrogate Motherhood in the United States* 58 AM. J. COMP. L 98 (2010). See also Fremgen, *supra* note 10, at 300.

[16] Gestational surrogacy is often called IVF surrogacy.

[17] Fremgen, *supra* note 10 at 298 (using the term "artificial insemination husband" (AIH) or "artificial insemination donor" (AID) in reference to a situation where the sperm used in AI originates from the husband or donor, as the case may be).

[18] Surrogate.com, *Traditional vs Gestational Surrogacy—What's Best for My Family?* https://surrogate.com/about-surrogacy/types-of-surrogacy/traditional-vs-gestational-surrogacy-whats-best-for-my-family/ (last visited May 10, 2021).

[19] The key factor is that the egg of the surrogate is not used.

iii. The embryo is created using the intended mother's egg and donor sperm.
iv. A donor embryo is transferred to a surrogate, such as where an excess embryo from others undergoing IVF[20] is donated to the surrogate and intending father, in which case, the resulting child will have no genetic relationship to the intended parent(s).[21]

3 Religious Perspectives on Surrogacy

A unique feature of human civilization is religion, a sociocultural system built on ideas and beliefs in God or a supreme being. Throughout history and continuing to the present, societies have tended to be organized along the lines of dominant values and principles, a large chunk of which are centered on religious beliefs and practices. The significance of religion to individual and collective existence, is demonstrated by the high number of people that identify with at least one religion. Of the global population, only a very small minority—about one-in-six (16%) people, numbering 1.1 billion, are religiously unaffiliated.[22] And even among this

[20] Ultimate disposition of excess embryo could be problematic in some instances such as where the couple are divorcing and there's no agreement as to custody. See, for example, *Davis v. Davis* 842 S.W.2d 588 (Tenn. 1992) (Tenn. Sup. Ct.):

> In summary, we hold that disputes involving the Disposition of preembryos produced by in vitro fertilization should be resolved, first, by looking to the preferences of the progenitors. If their wishes cannot be ascertained, or if there is dispute, then their prior agreement concerning Disposition should be carried out. If no prior agreement exists, then the relative interests of the parties in using or not using the preembryos must be weighed. Ordinarily, the party wishing to avoid procreation should prevail, assuming that the other party has a reasonable possibility of achieving parenthood by means other than use of the preembryos in question. If no other reasonable alternatives exist, then the argument in favor of using the preembryos to achieve pregnancy should be considered. However, if the party seeking control of the preembryos intends merely to donate them to another couple, the objecting party obviously has the greater interest and should prevail.

Id. at 604. The Court ruled that the preembryos should be destroyed. See also Fremgen, *supra* note 10, at 300.

[21] Brinsden, *supra* note 14.

[22] Pew Research Center, *The Global Religious Landscape: Religiously Unaffiliated*, December 18, 2012, available at https://www.pewforum.org/2012/12/18/global-religious-landscape-unaffiliated/ (last visited May 10, 2021).

number (religiously unaffiliated), many harbor some religious beliefs and some of them engage in certain kinds of religious practices[23]—meaning that very few of these people are completely unreligious in the sense of not having any belief in a higher power. The major religions include Christianity (with Catholic Church and Anglican Church/Church of England being the largest two), Judaism, Islam, Hinduism, and Buddhism. Just as the names differ, so also does the perspective of each of the religions regarding surrogacy. These differences are important and cannot be glossed over in countries committed to devising means of regulating the practice. Therefore, those charged with crafting legal and policy regimes must bear this in mind, and use the same as a basis for formulating appropriate governance regimes.

3.1 Catholic Church

The official position of Catholic Church regarding surrogacy is that it is immoral and incompatible with Catholic doctrine on birth, marriage, and life.[24] The Church's teaching on the morality of many modern

[23] *Id.*

[24] See Msgr. Charles Pope, *Why the Church Opposes Surrogate Motherhood and attempts to Legalize it in The District of Columbia*, June 19, 2013, available at http://blog.adw.org/2013/06/why-the-church-opposes-surrogate-motherhood-and-attempts-to-legalize-in-the-district-of-columbia/ (last visited May 10, 2021) (stating that surrogacy is forbidden to Catholics). This position seems to be representative of the position of other major Christian denominations. See Jennifer Roback Morse, *Why Everyone Should Oppose Surrogacy*, BLAZE MEDIA, May 4, 2016, available at https://www.theblaze.com/contributions/why-everyone-should-oppose-surrogacy (last visited April 30, 2021). In this thought-provoking article, Jennifer Morse offers critical arguments which should drive the opposition of the church to surrogacy. She categorizes the reasons under five headings, namely, prolife, prowoman, prochild, progressive, and proliberty—each with different set of motivations. Prolife opposition to surrogacy stems from the idea that the retrieved eggs which are fertilized outside the body are human beings, even if undeveloped. This involves aborting some of the babies when multiple eggs are implanted and more than required number survive (selective reduction). In addition, embryos which are not implanted are frozen indefinitely, destroyed or donated for research. Surrogacy promotes eugenics in that babies that do not meet the specifications of the intending parents are aborted. Pro-woman reasons to oppose surrogacy have three prongs; that is, broken bonds, objectifying women and fewer rights for the mother versus adoption. There is no attachment of importance to the bond between the gestational mother and the child once the child is delivered; once the womb of the gestational mother has been used for the agreed purpose, she is legally and emotionally discarded; and the attachment of the gestational mother to the child or concerns about the commissioning parents does not entitle

fertility procedures is contained in the document *Donum Vitae* (The Gift of Life), which was issued in 1987 by the Sacred Congregation for the Doctrine of the Faith.[25] While the Church is generally not condemnatory of contemporary techniques used in treating infertility, it wants it to be known that these techniques have profound moral implications, and this should guide people in making decisions about their use.[26] Catholics are under an obligation to examine each technique to determine its morality, in the sense of whether or not it is consistent with human good and human flourishing, and does no violence to the institution of marriage.[27] As affirmed by the Catechism of the Catholic Church, "Techniques that entail the dissociation of husband and wife, by the intrusion of a person other than the couple (donation of sperm or ovum, surrogate uterus), are gravely immoral."[28] The central concern of the Church is how these technologies impact innocent human life.[29] Its position is that a given medical

her to change her mind—a choice that is available to a mother who placed her child for adoption. There is a tripartite reason for prochild opposition to surrogacy. The procedure is psychologically risky for babies. It is known that infants attach to their mothers in the womb but not known whether the infant's attachment to the surrogate will transfer over to the commissioning mother. Surrogacy could be medically risky for babies. IVF children are at risk of premature birth, low birth weight, cerebral palsy, and other problems. Surrogate children are vulnerable to rejection for imperfection—that is, abandoning of the child by the commissioning parent on account of a birth defect. Progressive Christians' opposition to surrogacy derive from the belief that the procedure is economically exploitive. Affluent commissioning parents exploit poor women to satisfy their reproductive needs. Profit-making—the driving force of compensated surrogacy—commodifies the womb and baby-making. Regarding proliberty Christians, there are three arguments against surrogacy. First, it reduces the private realm by dragging baby-making, a private and intimate affair, into the realm of law. Second, it fosters artificial, state-created separations between parents and children in that surrogate, who carried a baby for nine months have no parental rights and responsibilities cognizable in law. Third, surrogacy creates a market in human beings by introducing financial gains into baby-making.

Morse, *id.*

[25] John M. Haas, *Begotten Not Made: A Catholic View of Reproductive Technology*, United States Conference of Catholic Bishops, available at http://www.usccb.org/issues-and-action/human-life-and-dignity/reproductive-technology/begotten-not-made-a-catholic-view-of-reproductive-technology.cfm (last visited May 10, 2021).

[26] *Id.*

[27] *Id.*

[28] Catechism of the Catholic Church, ¶ 2376, available at http://www.scborromeo.org/ccc/para/2376.htm (last visited May 10, 2021).

[29] Haas, *supra* note 25.

intervention is moral if it "helps or assists" the marriage act to achieve pregnancy but immoral when the intervention "replaces" the marriage act in order to engender life.[30]

The Church is vehemently opposed to IVF, which it considers immoral on account of the process that results in the baby. IVF supplants the natural means of achieving pregnancy (through act of love between husband and wife) with a laboratory scientist in which the husband and wife become mere sources of "raw materials"—that is sperm and egg—which are manipulated to produce embryos.[31] Several reasons underpin the disapproval of the Church. First, the use of donor eggs or sperm introduces a stranger to the marriage as one having genetic link to the child. There is a potential of a confusion when the child realizes that one of the parents raising him is not a biological parent.[32] Second, in cases where the donor of the sperm or egg is unknown, the child will not know his lineage, thereby depriving him of knowledge of genetic disposition to health problems. The knowledge void could also result in incestuous relationships—that is, marriage between brothers and sisters—when none of them is aware that the same sperm donor is their father.[33] Third, even when the egg and sperm come from husband and wife, there might still be serious moral problems. IVF often results in producing several embryos, some of which will be discarded due to deficiency in the sense of not showing promise of survival to term or simply in excess of the number the couple wants. Discarding embryos, which the Church considers to be human life, equates to murder—a serious offense against human life and God.[34]

Fourth, in order to improve the chance of success and hold down cost, doctors often implant multiple embryos in the woman's womb.[35] This may result in having more babies than actually wanted, putting emotional and psychological strain on the family.[36] Fifth is "fetal reduction" or

[30] *Id.*

[31] *Id.*

[32] *Id.*

[33] *Id.*

[34] *Id.*

[35] *Id.*

[36] *Id.* (reporting a case in Canada, where a woman gave birth to five children as a result of IVF. Because she had wanted only one, she sued her doctor for "wrongful life,"

"selective reduction." This involves destruction of babies in utero, those judged defective or not as healthy as others. Significantly, Catholic Church teaches that even when donor eggs or sperm are not used in the IVF process or there is no destruction of embryos and unwanted babies in the course of the pregnancy, there is still a moral problem with the procedure:

> The connection between *in vitro* fertilization and the voluntary destruction of human embryos occurs too often. This is significant: through these procedures, with apparently contrary purposes, [namely] life and death are subjected to the decision of man, who thus sets himself up as the giver of life and death by decree.[37]

For these reasons and others previously stated, the Church considers surrogate motherhood to be a lamentable practice, a bad policy that should not be supported in any form.[38]

3.2 *Anglican Church/Church of England*

There are major distinctions between the Catholic Church and Anglican Church (also known as "Church of England") on reproduction and contraception, and these differences have significant bearing on the way the two denominations view surrogacy. Unlike the Catholic Church, which forbids any interference with natural method of procreation and places an absolute prohibition on IVF, the Anglican Church allows contraception and, like other Protestant Churches, support the use of IVF by married couples.[39] It also permits physicians to use sperm obtained after masturbation.[40] Although the Anglican Communion was originally opposed to third-party donation of egg and sperm, seen as an intrusion

asking the court to order him to reimburse the cost of raising the four children she did not want).

[37] *Id.*

[38] Pope, *supra* note 24.

[39] H.N. Sallam & N.H. Sallam, *Religious Aspects of Assisted Reproduction* 8 (1) FACTS VIEWS VIS. OBGYN. 37 (2016).

[40] Agneta Sutton, *Three Christian Views on Assisted Conception and Marriage—The Roman Catholic Church, Church of England and Presbyterian Church of Scotland* 6 EUBIOS J. ASIAN & INT'L BIOETHICS 105–107 (1996), available at https://www.eubios.info/EJ64/EJ64H.htm (last visited May 15, 2021).

of third parties upon a sacred bond between husband and wife, its position has recently shifted. Extant teaching makes it permissible to accept gamete donation by third parties, although the decision remains personal, in the sense that individual members of the Church may decide against using donor gametes.[41]

Philosopher and bioethicist Agneta Sutton notes that following the publication of the Warnock Report of 1984,[42] the Anglican Church released two publications, one in 1984[43] and the other in 1985,[44] both of which attest to a wide diversity of opinion within the church. For instance, while the Church allows IVF within marriage, some members of the Committee that prepared the 1985 document were of the persuasion that IVF amounts to an unacceptable form of treatment of an evolving human life.[45] Referring to differences in opinion within the church regarding gametal donation, the document states that "[t]here are those who think that the genetic origins of a child are fundamentally important and those who think that what is more important is the loving nurture of the child in a stable relationship."[46] Moreover, while some are of the opinion that "if donation takes place within a stable marital relationship, it still has the status of a good," others believe that it "threatens marriage, as understood by Christians, and that it should be strongly discouraged."[47] Both documents reflect a general agreement to the effect that procreation ought to take place within marriage.

There are those who argue that because in gametal donation, such as artificial insemination by donor (AID), one of the spouses is replaced by

[41] *Id.*

[42] Formally known as "Report of the Committee of Inquiry into Human Fertilization and Embryology (1984)"—more commonly known as the "Warnock Report," so-named after the Committee Chairman, Mary Warnock.

[43] Board for Social Responsibility [Church of England] (1984): Human Fertilization and Embryology: The Response of the Board of Social Responsibility of the General Synod of the Church of England to the DHSS Report of the Committee of Inquiry, London.

[44] Board for Social Responsibility [Church of England] (1985): Personal Origins: The Report of a Working Party on Human Fertilisation and Embryology of the Board for Social Responsibility, London.

[45] Sutton, *supra* note 40, citing Board for Social Responsibility [Church of England] (1985) ¶ 118).

[46] *Id.* (citing Board for Social Responsibility [Church of England] (1985) ¶ 108).

[47] *Id.* (citing Board for Social Responsibility [Church of England] (1985) ¶ 108).

another person for the purpose of reproduction, the procedure constitutes a threat to the family.[48] The argument is based on the reasoning that even if the procedure does not rise to what would be considered adultery in the sense of sexual intercourse with a person other than one's spouse, it does inject a third party into the sacred nature of procreation and distorts family life.[49] Moreover, since British law protects anonymity of donors, the practice is objectionable on grounds that it intentionally deprives children of knowledge of their true genetic origins.[50] Although opinions differ regarding many aspects of assisted procreation, regarding surrogacy specifically, the position of the Church is that "surrogacy arrangements are unacceptable."[51] This position is connected with a number of concerns, namely, psychological trauma that often arises as a result of bonding between the surrogate mother and the child during the period of pregnancy; surrogacy contracts are often fraught with legal complications; and, the idea of receiving payment for womb-letting services is offensive to the dignity of the surrogate mother.[52]

3.3 Judaism

There is no uniformity of opinion in the Jewish community on the compatibility of surrogacy with Judaism. While some Jewish scholars and rabbis consider the procedure to be compatible with the tenets of Judaism, others veer toward a contrary direction. Those advocating that surrogacy is permissible under Judaism view it as providing a morally permissible method for Jewish women who are unable to conceive naturally to satisfy their religious mandate of procreation.[53] They anchor their position on the prescriptions of the Bible, chiefly Genesis 1:28, which commands the Jews to "Be fruitful, and multiply, and replenish the

[48] *Id.*

[49] *Id.* (citing Board for Social Responsibility [Church of England] (1985) ¶ 109).

[50] *Id.* (citing Board for Social Responsibility [Church of England] (1985) ¶ 108).

[51] *Id.*

[52] *Id.* (citing Board for Social Responsibility [Church of England] (1985) ¶ 126).

[53] Marni Besser, *Jewish Ethics and Surrogacy*, JEWISH INDEPENDENT, January 20, 2017, available at http://www.jewishindependent.ca/jewish-ethics-and-surrogacy/ (last visited May 20, 2021).

earth."[54] This is not seen as merely advisory, but an obligation on Jewish families, "the first of the 613 commandments of the Torah."[55] Signifying its importance, the commandment was restated after the depopulation of humanity by the great flood. Noah and his sons were enjoined in Genesis 9:1 to be "fruitful, and multiply, and replenish the earth."[56] The sweeping tone of this antediluvian injunction suggests that the duty to procreate and regenerate humanity is of utmost importance in Jewish tradition, as evident in recorded cases of polygamy and loose surrogacy among the people. It is on record that "Handmaids bore children, fathered by the patriarchs, when their wives suffered from infertility. The surrogates for the biblical matriarchs bore the children."[57] This position was affirmed by the Committee on Jewish Law and Standards, which in 1988 issued formal approval for surrogacy, holding that "the mitzvah of parenthood is so great that ovum surrogacy is permissible."[58]

Opposition by anti-surrogacy Jewish scholars and rabbis centers on the view that surrogacy is modern slavery, involving the exploitation of women's bodies and commodification of children.[59] Since there is a religious obligation to "actively engage in the redemption of those who are enslaved," it follows, therefore, that practices considered as involving human exploitation are subject to moral condemnation.[60] Prohibition of exploitation is explicitly spelt out in Leviticus 19:13: "You shall not oppress your neighbor." A major exponent of this view is Rabbi Immanuel Jakobovits, who argues that the act of using another person as an incubator and taking the child she carried and delivered for a fee is a repulsive

[54] Bible, KJV.

[55] Besser, *supra* note 53.

[56] Bible, KJV.

[57] Besser, *supra* note 53. Biblical precedent for surrogacy abound. In Genesis 16:2, Sarai (Sarah) invites Abraham to consort with her handmaid, Hagar. Abraham agrees and goes into Hagar who gives birth to Ishmael. Subsequently, in Genesis 30:3–8, Rachel asks Jacob to consort with her handmaid Bilhah so that she would bear him a child. Jacob took her as a concubine and she bore Jacob a son, whom Rachel named Dan. A second son was born by Bilhah and Rachel named him Naftali. In Genesis 30:9–13, Leah also took her handmaid Zilpah and gave to Jacob as concubine. The handmaid bore a son to Jacob and subsequently gave birth to another son. Leah named the first son Gad and the second one, Asher.

[58] Besser, *supra* note 53.

[59] *Id.*

[60] *Id.*

degradation of maternity and an affront to human dignity.[61] In support of this view is Rabbi Aaron Mackler.[62] He faults surrogacy on the basis, inter alia, that maternal status is determined by gestation and birth, which is not the case with surrogacy and, even worse, surrogacy involves exploitation and commodification of children.[63] Along similar trajectory, Rabbi David Golinkin advises childless couples to seek adoption, not surrogacy, asserting that for "anyone who raises an orphan in his home, [the] Scripture considers it as if he has given birth to that child."[64]

Another controversial issue regarding surrogacy among Jews is the issue of defining motherhood. The controversy revolves around three conflicting concerns, namely, whether the ovum donor is the mother; the surrogate is the mother; or the child has two mothers—both the ovum donor and the surrogate mother.[65] Although most scholars and rabbis consider the surrogate to be the mother, some ascribe motherhood to the ovum donor—an idea derived in part from the well-known passage in Sanhedrin 91b about Antoninus and Rebbe, which says that life begins at conception.[66] Still, there are notable Jewish scholars and rabbis such as Ze'ev Low and Rabbi(s)Avraham Steinberg and David Bleich holding the view that the child has two mothers—both the ovum donor and the surrogate mother.[67]

Not to be discounted is the issue of defining Judaism in the realm of surrogacy. According to Jewish Law, once a Jewish woman is the surrogate, the child is Jewish.[68] That much is settled. However, the issue becomes intensely polemized when the child is raised by a non-Jewish family and, as yet there is no agreement within the Jewish community on the subject.[69]

[61] Immanuel Jakobovits, JEWISH MEDICAL ETHICS 265 (1975).

[62] Besser, *supra* note 53.

[63] *Id.*

[64] *Id.*

[65] David Golinkin, *What does Jewish Law Have to Say about Surrogacy?* The Schechter Institutes 7(3) Responsa in a Moment (2012), available at https://schechter.edu/what-does-jewish-law-have-to-say-about-surrogacy/ (last visited May 25, 2021).

[66] *Id.*

[67] *Id.*

[68] *Id.*

[69] *Id.*

3.4 Islam

Islamic bioethics forbids surrogacy except between married couples and under certain conditions.[70] This represents the view of a vast majority of scholars, although some hold a contrary opinion. Two main considerations that make surrogacy unacceptable to adherents of the Islamic faith are their belief on the importance of protection of progeny, preservation of lineage—which is considered to be one of the five universals and objectives of Shariah,[71] and prohibition of adultery.[72] Surrogate motherhood is unacceptable because of its similarity to *zina* (adultery) in the sense that the fertilized egg the surrogate is carrying was fertilized by the sperm of someone who is not her husband.[73] In such a scenario, the resulting child would be considered illegitimate since the contracting man is not married to the surrogate.[74] In fact:

> Even if a husband gave written consent that his wife could act as a surrogate, there is a religious problem that would prohibit this. Islam prohibits the semen of one man to touch a fetus that is a product of another man's semen. Will we issue a law prohibiting husbands from exercising their legal right [to sexual relations] with their wives when they are pregnant

[70] Tawfique Al-Mubarak, *Surrogacy and Islam: Between Permissibility and Prohibition*, at 277, March 2014, available at https://www.researchgate.net/publication/284293479_Surrogacy_and_Islam_Between_Permissibility_and_Prohibition (last visited May 18, 2021) (citing the Fiqh Council of the Organization of Islamic Conference (OIC) in 1986).

[71] Hanafi Fiqh, *Islamic Position on IVF Surrogate Motherhood*, available at https://islamqa.org/hanafi/daruliftaa/7822 (last visited May 18, 2021).

[72] Sharmin Islam, et al., *Islamic Perspective Ethics of Surrogacy: A Comparative Study of Western Secular and Islamic Bioethics* 44(1) J. Islamic Medical Ass. of North America (2012), available https://www.ncbi.nlm.nih.gov/pmc/articles/PMC3708631/pdf/jima-44-1-05920.pdf (last visited May 18, 2021). See also Al-Mubarak, *supra* note 69 at 278 (basing the adultery concern of Islam on the Qur'anic verses al-Mu´minËn: 5–7, and al-Ma'arij: 29–31, which imposed an obligation upon the Muslims to preserve their chastity—implying that introduction of one's semen into the womb of another woman, unless it be his wife, is a violation of the Qur'anic injunction).

[73] Shaykh Mohammed Amin Kholwadia, *The Islamic Ruling on Surrogate Motherhood*, IlmGate, https://www.ilmgate.org/the-islamic-ruling-on-surrogate-motherhood/ (last visited May 18, 2021).

[74] Sharmin Islam, et al., *supra* note 71; Kholwadia, *id.* (making a logical argument that where "the product is *haram*, the means of acquiring the product (the surrogate's renting of her womb)" is "[equally] *haram*").

with another man's baby? And were such a law passed; how would it be enforced?[75]

Emphasizing this point, professor of obstetrics and gynecology Gamal Serour explains:

> The basic concept of Islam is to avoid mixing genes, as Islam enjoins the purity of genes and heredity. It deems that each child should relate to a known father and mother. Since marriage is a contract between the wife and the husband during the span of their marriage, no third party intrudes into the marital functions of sex and procreation. A third party is not acceptable, whether providing an egg, a sperm, or a uterus. Therefore, sperm donation, egg donation, and surrogacy are not allowed in Islam.[76]

The prohibitory thrust of Islamic teaching on surrogacy is so strict that even where a husband is married to two wives and an ovum is extracted from wife number one and fertilized with the sperm of the husband and implanted in the womb of wife number two, who carries it till birth, the child is not legitimate.[77] This is because there was an impermissible intrusion of the first wife (egg donor) into the marriage contract between the husband and the second wife; therefore, the child will belong to the second wife, the gestational mother, even though she is not the biological mother of the child.[78] Islamic law on this is very clear, "None can be their mothers except those who gave them birth."[79] This prescription allows a surrogate mother to claim to be the real mother even though it was the egg of another woman in her womb that produced the child.[80] The point is that even in that context, surrogacy is not allowed.[81]

This is consistent with the Declaration by the Council of the Islamic Fiqh Academy in 1986, namely, that surrogacy (in-vitro fertilization

[75] Islam, et al., *id.* (*quoting* Farag F. Al-Ahram Weekly On-line. 17–23 May 2001, Issue No. 534).

[76] Islam, et al., *supra* note 72.

[77] *Id.*

[78] *Id.*

[79] *Id.* (*quoting* The Qur'ān, Chapter 58, Verse 2).

[80] *Id.*

[81] *Id.* (*citing* Hathout H. Islamic perspectives in obstetrics and gynaecology. Cairo: Alam al-Kutub; 1988).

between the sperm and the eggs taken from the spouses, and subsequent implantation of the fertilized ovum into the womb of a volunteer woman) is prohibited—a prohibition targeted at preventing the consequences of lineage confusion and loss of motherhood.[82] It has been asserted that the benefit of having surrogacy babies pales in comparison to the harms resulting from the confusion and dispute thereby generated.[83] Not only will the child's birth give rise to perpetual stress for all the parties involved, the child himself will also be harmed; yet, a well-known maxim in Islamic law stipulates that "Harm is to be avoided before benefit is derived."[84]

There is another group of Islamic scholars who is united in repudiating the majority opinion, namely, that Islam prohibits surrogacy motherhood. They claim that one of the primary objectives of Islam is perpetuation of human species and, therefore, the pursuit of alternative methods of conceiving children by married couples is integrated within this primary objective.[85] According to this line of thinking, a married couple who is unable to conceive children should be allowed to use alternative means to override their inability to do so and if surrogacy is one of these methods, it should be allowed on grounds of *maslaha* (public interest).[86] The surrogate mother cannot be accused of adultery since the pregnancy did not result from sexual intercourse with a non-legal husband.[87] The fear of confusion of lineage of the child does not arise as the biological parents are already known. In surrogacy arrangement, they submit, the woman's womb can be said to be rented as an incubator, and this is analogous to hiring a woman to breastfeed a child (called wet nursing), which is permissible under Islamic tradition.[88]

Is wet nursing analogous to surrogacy and, therefore, permissible under Islam? The answer depends on who you ask, but those who argue that Islam permits surrogacy assiduously propagate and defend this view.

[82] Third session, held Amman, Jordan (October 11–16, 1986). See Islam, et al., *supra* note 71.

[83] Kholwadia, et al., *supra* note 73.

[84] *Id.*

[85] *Id.*

[86] *Id.*

[87] *Id.*

[88] *Id.*

Wet nursing arises when there is a mutual agreement between a mother and father to let another woman (wet nurse) to breastfeed their child because the child's mother is unable to breastfeed.[89] Such children are considered foster children of the wet nurse by virtue of suckling,[90] but does that rise to the level of what we know as surrogacy?

Islamic bioethicist Sharmin Islam provides this incisive response, using gestational surrogacy as an illustration. In gestational surrogacy, involving the fertilization in vitro of the sperm and ovum of a legally married couple and implantation in the womb of the surrogate, the woman who donated the ovum may be considered the real or biological mother because of the genetic link between her and the child while the woman who carries the fetus to term and gives birth becomes a foster mother.[91] But this analogy, argues, the bioethicist, is faulty. First, the wet nurse has no relationship with the father of the child she breastfed, but in a surrogacy contract, the woman is either artificially impregnated with the sperm of the father of the child or the embryo produced by the father's sperm is implanted in her womb and she carries it until she gives birth to it.[92] Furthermore, as important as the feeding function of the wet nurse is, it occurs only during infancy and does not establish any biological relationship with the child.[93] Along this line of thought, another scholar contends that the lineage of the child in wet nursing arrangement has been clearly established whereas in surrogacy, the lineage of the child cannot be established until it is born and DNA test results have proven it. In light of these distinctions, the conclusion, according to the scholars, must be that to claim that surrogacy is permissible on the analogy of wet nursing is baseless and must be dismissed.

[89] Shaheda Yashmin, *Islamic and Cultural Practices in Breastfeeding*, October 1, 2015, available at https://www.llli.org/islamic-cultural-practices-breastfeeding-2/ (last visited May 27, 2021).

[90] Islam, et al., *supra* note 72.

[91] *Id.*

[92] *Id.*

[93] *Id.*

3.5 *Hinduism*

Hindu religion permits surrogacy. Artificial insemination using the husband's sperm is allowed but not that of an unknown donor, reason being that the child would not know its lineage.[94] Unlike the other religions previously examined, Hindu scholars have not debated surrogacy extensively; nonetheless, a noted Indian reproductive biologist has stated that there is no inconsistency between Hinduism and assisted reproduction.[95] The idea of surrogacy among practitioners of the faith is rooted in mythology, one of which was said to have taken place in Bhagvata Purana, and suggests the practice of surrogate motherhood:

> Kan(sh) the wicked king of Mathura, had imprisoned his sister Devaki and her husband Vasudeva because oracles had informed him that her child would be his killer. Every time she delivered a child, he smashed its head on the floor. He killed six children. When the seventh child was conceived, the gods intervened. They summoned the goddess Yogamaya and had her transfer the fetus from the womb of Devaki to the womb of Rohini (Vasudeva's other wife who lived with her sister Yashoda across the river Yamuna, in the village of cowherds at Gokul). Thus the child conceived in one womb was incubated in and delivered through another womb.[96]

Another strand of thought derives support for surrogacy in Hinduism from the importance attached to children in Hindu families. Conception is viewed as divine, and children are seen as one of the key aspects of marriage.[97] These considerations drive the general acceptance of fertility treatments and surrogacy for growth of families.[98]

[94] Herencyclopedia, *Surrogacy and Hindu Mythology*, available at https://web.archive.org/web/20160607122542/https://herencyclopedia.com/2016/06/06/surrogacy-and-hindu-mythology/ (last visited May 27, 2021).

[95] T.C. Anand Kumar, *Ethical Aspects of Assisted Reproduction—An Indian Viewpoint* 14 (1) REPROD. BIOMED. ONLINE 140–142 (2007).

[96] Herencyclopedia, *supra* note 94.

[97] Anjana Chatterjee and Deepak Kotecha, *Hinduism's View on Infertility: What Is the Hindu Religions Stance on Infertility*?, available at https://www.beliefnet.com/faiths/hinduism/articles/hinduisms-view-on-infertility.aspx

[98] Montana Surrogacy, *Religion and Surrogacy*, March 6, 2018, available at https://www.montanasurro.com/blog/2018/2/28/religion-surrogacy (last visited May 23, 2021).

Surrogacy is also intertwined with notions of karma (the law of cause and effect or earned ethical reward) in Hindu tradition. Karma manifests in various degrees of social, psychological, and physical sufferings—all of which are considered pathologies in need of treatment.[99] One of these pathologies is infertility and, like other diseases, there is a general acceptance of medical intervention for its treatment in the Hindu community.[100] Treatment of infertility can take various forms such as assisted reproduction, including surrogacy.[101] Interestingly, surrogacy is not widely used as an option to treat infertility among Hindu women, although many of them serve as surrogates for Western commissioning couples.[102]

3.6 Buddhism

The compatibility of surrogacy with the teachings of Buddhism is far from settled. Nonetheless, the majority view is that the religion supports surrogacy, a position that is anchored on the fact that there is no condemnation of infertility treatments or surrogacy as immoral in any of the sacred texts of the religion.[103] Further support for surrogacy is underscored by the general view that the motivating factor is compassion for those battling infertility, compassion or *karuṇā* being a key component of spiritualism in the religion.[104] On the other hand, some Buddhist scholars have voiced opposition to surrogacy.[105] Opposition centers on the belief

[99] *Id.*

[100] *Id.*

[101] *Id.*

[102] *Id.*

[103] Herencyclopedia, *supra* note 94.

[104] GSE, *Evil and suffering,* BBC, available at https://www.bbc.co.uk/bitesize/guides/znxpr82/revision/4 (last visited May 23, 2021) (explaining, in response to the concern regarding how different religions respond to suffering, Buddhist followers are under obligation to lead lives that will help to relieve the suffering of others and describing *karuṇā* as "the understanding of, and the desire to help remove, harm and suffering from others").

[105] Jennifer Spirko, *Buddhist Beliefs About Surrogate Mothers*, https://classroom.synonym.com/buddhist-beliefs-about-surrogate-mothers-12087675.html (last visited May 23, 2021) (*citing* Shoji Mori, Professor Emeritus of Tokyo University, who contends that a central teaching of early Buddhist sutras was that "life begins with an element of intentionality, placing on us the burden of creating our own happiness," which he explains

in the concepts of karma (earned ethical reward)[106] and reincarnation (continuous cycle of rebirth).[107] The idea is that reincarnation is a natural manifestation of karma and is not open to interference such as the one interposed by surrogacy arrangements.[108]

Other Buddhist thinkers base their argument directly on the teaching of Buddha himself to the effect that trade in sentient beings, including humans, is immoral in the sense that it involves exploitation and suffering.[109] Echoing this view, Susumu Shimazono, professor of Religious Studies at the University of Tokyo, equates surrogacy to selling of organs, arguing that in such arrangements, the surrogate is consigned to a subservient position in that her womb becomes a "tool" to be exploited for the benefit of others.[110] This claim has been disputed by other Buddhist scholars who argue that so long as surrogate motherhood is primarily motivated by compassion, not profit, it cannot be assailed as exploitative and, therefore, morally objectionable.[111]

4 Conclusion

The postulations of the preceding section as to how each religion and its scholars conceptualize surrogacy may appear strange or even silly to some people; yet, such perceptions (of strangers to the religion) are immaterial to the subject of this chapter. Instead, what matters is the opinions, thoughts, and beliefs of the practitioners, the communities targeted for regulation. It is these people that should be the concern of the "wise men and women" charged with devising appropriate governance regime regarding surrogacy. In the vast majority of the countries throughout the

in a 2006 lecture to mean that the "state into which one is born results to some degree from past actions" and, therefore, there is no need for surrogate motherhood since to institutionalize it would amount to circumventing the workings of karma").

106 *Id.*

107 History Channel, *Buddhism*, available at https://www.history.com/topics/religion/buddhism (last visited May 23, 2021).

108 Spirko, *supra* note 105.

109 Daily Enlightenment, *Is Surrogacy Right in Buddhism?*, January 27, 2015, available at https://thedailyenlightenment.com/2015/01/is-surrogacy-right-in-buddhism/ (last visited May 23, 2021).

110 Spirko, *supra* note 105.

111 Daily Enlightenment, *supra* note 109.

world, one or more of the religions discussed in this work dominate the cultural life and are encoded into the moral ethos, as the principal determinant of what is right and wrong, the path to the good life. Any action, whether clothed in a legal or policy garb, that is incompatible with this moral ethos risks upending existing order, peace, and harmonious coexistence in the affected countries—and for this reason alone, is likely to be met with resistance and noncompliance. This was the point canvassed by historian and political theorist Gabriel Olusanya in a 1986 paper, *to wit*, "[f]or any law to grow and be productive, it must be rooted in the culture and tradition as well as the realities of the people for whom it is made."[112] To be successful, therefore, future regulatory action on surrogacy must be anchored on these realities, at the forefront of which is religion.

Acknowledgements For their insightful questions and comments, which significantly improved the quality of this paper, I thank my health law, bioethics and human rights graduate students and, of course, AdaObi Nnamuchi, my able assistant. The usual caveats apply.

[112] G. O. Olusanya, *African Charter on Human and Peoples' Rights, History and Development*, Paper Presented at the Seminar Marking the Centenary of Legal Profession in Nigeria, Lagos, February 21, 1986, *cited* in Olusola Ojo, *Understanding Human Rights in Africa*, Paper Presented at the Preparatory Conference on Human Rights: Individual Rights or Collective Rights, University of Limburg, Maastricht, The Netherlands, September 18–20, 10 (1987); Rhoda E. Howard, *Group Versus Individual Identity in the African Debate on Human Rights* in HUMAN RIGHTS IN AFRICA: CROSS-CULTURAL PERSPECTIVES 159, 168 (Abdullahi Ahmed An-Na'im & Francis M. Deng eds.,1990).

CHAPTER 16

A Case for the Application of Strict Liability in Oil and Gas Pollution Cases in Nigeria

Sunday Gozie Ogbodo and A. Chinwe Umadia

1 Introduction

Nigeria is one of the world's leading exporters of crude oil. Since 1956, when oil was discovered in commercial quantity in Oloibori, Bayelsa State, the extractive and productive activities of the multinational oil companies (MNCs) have resulted in grave environmental degradation and pollution of the Nigerian environment, particularly, in the oil-producing region, generally classified as the Niger Delta region. The incidents of environmental degradation have arisen from oil spills and gas flaring, which are symbiotically inherent from the extractive and productive activities of the oil industry. Incidents of oil pollution in the Niger Delta region

S. Gozie Ogbodo (✉)
Enugu, Enugu State, Nigeria
e-mail: gozie.ogbodo@yahoo.com

A. C. Umadia
Faculty of Law, Godfrey Okoye University, Enugu, Nigeria

E. Duruigbo et al. (eds.), *International Law and Development in the Global South*, https://doi.org/10.1007/978-3-031-13741-9_16

have arisen accidentally and also as a result of intentional acts and negligent actions of the culprits. Accidentally, it has been reported that about 4,835, oil spills occurred between 1976 and 1996, resulting in the spillage of about 2,446,332 barrels of oil. From the total barrels spilled, it is estimated that 1,896,930 barrels of oil were lost to the Niger Delta environment alone.[1] The intentional acts which resulted in oil spillage included the vandalization of oil pipelines by the Niger Delta youths, violent attacks on oil company facilities and stations, etc. With respect to gas flaring, presently it is estimated that Nigeria flares about 2.5 billion cubic feet of associated gas every day, second to Russia in gas flaring, worldwide.[2]

Many of these cases of degradation and pollution have resulted in severe health implications for the citizens, like asthma, dysentery, diarrhea, etc. In extreme cases, many citizens lose their lives as well as the lives of their family members as a consequence of pollution from the oil and gas industry.

As a result of the environmental and economic consequences of oil pollution, particularly, in the Niger Delta region of Nigeria, "the oil that was expected to be a blessing to the region has turned out to be a curse."[3] In frustration, the youths of the region engaged in violent acts like pipeline vandalization, destruction of oil facilities, and hostage-taking of oil workers, particularly, the expatriates. These disruptive activities caused the country to produce at a lower level than its daily production capacity thereby resulting in billions of dollars in lost and unearned revenues. It was estimated that Nigeria lost over US $16 billion as a result of the militancy crisis in the Niger Delta region.[4]

[1] The Price of Oil: Corporate Responsibility and Human Rights Violations in Nigeria's Oil Producing Communities (New York: Human Rights Watch, 1999).

[2] *Country Analysis Brief Overview: Full Report (Nigeria)*, U.S. Energy Information Administration (December. 2013), http://www.eia.gov/countries/analysisbriefs/Nigeria/nigeria.pdf

[3] S. Gozie Ogbodo, The Human Rights Implications of Oil Pollution in Nigeria's Niger Delta Region, *ESUT Law Journal*, Vol. 1, No. 1, 2012, 89.

[4] See Energy Information Administration: Country Brief Analysis, available online at http://www.eia.doe.gov/emeu/cabs/nigeria/oil.html, accessed 5/10/2012. Thanks to the then President Yar'adua for initiating the Amnesty programme aimed at the demilitarization of the Niger Delta region with a view to ending the crisis. Under the programme, the militants were encouraged to surrender their arms in exchange for training in a skill acquisition programme, both locally and abroad.

The Nigerian Constitution[5] guarantees the right to life as a fundamental human right under Section 33. The section provides categorically as follows:

> Every person has a right to life, and no one shall be deprived intentionally of his life, save in execution of the sentence of a court in respect of a criminal offence of which he has been found guilty in Nigeria.

Despite this guarantee of the right to life by the Nigerian Constitution, which is the *grundnorm,* many Nigerian lives have been, and is still being lost as a result of the polluting activities of the multinational oil companies in Nigeria. It is, therefore, our contention that this amounts to a grave violation of the fundamental right to life of the citizens of Nigeria, particularly, those resident in the Niger Delta region.

Although the present Constitution of Nigeria blazed the trail as the first Nigerian Constitution since independence in 1960 to expressly incorporate environmental protection, it nevertheless, fell short of providing maximum support to the victims of environmental pollution. Section 20 provides as follows:

> The state shall protect and improve the environment and safeguard the water, air and land, forest and wild life of Nigeria.

This section of the Constitution falls under Chapter 2 which is categorized as Fundamental Objectives and Directive Principles of State Policy. All the twelve sections[6] under this category have been rendered non-justiciable by the same Constitution and reinforced by the Nigerian courts in a plethora of judicial decisions.[7] Section 6 (6) (c) of the Constitution provides as follows:

The judicial powers vested in accordance with the foregoing provisions of this section—

[5] Otherwise referred to as the 1999 Constitution of the Federal Republic of Nigeria (as amended).

[6] The twelve sections span from Section 13 to Section 24.

[7] See the case of Attorney General, Ondo State V. Attorney General of the Federation (2000) 6 NWLR Pt 660, p. 228.

(c) Shall not, except as otherwise provided by this Constitution, extend to any issue or question as to whether any act or omission by any authority or person or as to whether any law or any judicial decision is in conformity with the Fundamental Objectives and Directive Principles of State Policy set out in Chapter 2of this Constitution.

As we posited elsewhere[8], this has resulted in a Constitutional mirage since the same Constitution effectively erased the Constitutional hope which it heralded. What it gave with one Constitutional hand, it took with another Constitutional hand. Again, we ask[9]: what kind of life can a Nigerian citizen be expected to enjoy devoid of clean water, air and land? Are those not the basis upon which lived is lived and enjoyed?

As a result of the foregoing, the next in the hierarchy of Environmental laws in Nigeria is the National Environmental Standards and Enforcement Agency Act (NESREA Act), which is the flagship law on Nigeria's environment. The NESREA Act expressly criminalized pollution and stipulated fines and imprisonment for convicted offenders under the relevant sections dealing with air pollution, water pollution, noise pollution and land pollution.

Under the Act, in order for an environmental offender to be fined or imprisoned, such a penalty must be subsequent to conviction by a Nigerian court. The standard of proof under Nigerian Criminal law is proof beyond a reasonable doubt. In other words, any prosecution of a crime which does not meet this high threshold of beyond a reasonable doubt will fall short of the standard for conviction. For the avoidance of doubt, the NESREA Act provides in Section 32(4) that the Criminal Procedure Act (CPA) or the Criminal Procedure Code (CPC), depending on the venue of the suit, shall apply in respect of the trial of an offence under the Act or its subsidiary regulations to the same extent as they apply to general offences in Nigeria. This provision of the Act cements the requirement of proof of *mens rea* in the prosecution of environmental offences under the Act[10]. Such prosecution, as required for all criminal

[8] *Supra,* note 3.

[9] Ibid.

[10] In order for a prosecutor to secure a conviction of a crime, he must prove beyond a reasonable doubt both elements of *actus reus* and the *mens rea* of the crime. With respect to the element of *actus reus,* see *Powell v State of Texas* (1968) 392 US 514 and *Gibbons v. Proctor* (2004) 1 Cr. App. R. With respect to the element of *mens rea,* see *Idiok v. The*

prosecutions in Nigeria, shall be done by the Attorney General or with his consent and is subject to his *nolle* powers[11]. Curiously, the same NESREA Act excluded oil and gas pollution from some of its primary functions[12].

A complementary law to the NESREA Act with respect to the enforcement of oil and gas pollution in Nigeria is the National Oil Spill Detection and Response Agency (Establishment) Act, 2008. The NOSDRA Act also criminalized any contravention of the provisions of the Act[13], in conformity with the classification by the NESREA Act. Additionally, the Associated Gas Re-Injection Act[14] regulates the incidence of gas flaring in Nigeria.

In a country where the majority of rural citizens who form the bulk of the victims of environmental pollution are illiterate, poor, lack access to justice, incessant delay by the courts, etc., it is tantamount to an uphill task for the prosecutor to meet this standard of proof in environment pollution cases. Moreover, the majority of environmental offenders in the category of oil and gas polluters are the multinational oil companies. To prove *mens rea* on the part of the officers of the company or the company itself is an uphill task. It has been argued that this explains the reluctance of the United States in employing criminal prosecution in the enforcement of environmental protection laws[15].

The thesis of this paper is that environmental pollution is a threat to the fundamental right to life of the Nigerian citizens under the Nigerian Constitution. Therefore, an application of strict liability will better protect that most cherished right when threatened by environmental pollution whether arising from air pollution, water pollution, noise pollution or land pollution.

State (2006) 12 NWLR (Pt. 993) and *Ubani v. The State* (2003) 18 NWLR (Pt. 851) 224.

[11] Section 32(3), NESREA Act.

[12] See Section 7 (g), (h), (j), (k), (l).

[13] Section 28(2) of the NOSDRA Act provides: "Any person who contravenes the provision of any regulations made under this Act is guilty of an offence and is liable on conviction to the penalties specified in the regulations.".

[14] Associated Gas Re-Injection Act, Cap (A25), LFN, 2004.

[15] See Niki Tobi, "Judicial Enforcement of Environmental Laws in Nigeria," (2005), 1 *Environmental and Planning Law Journal (EPLJ)*, p. 94.

2 Clarification of Concepts

2.1 Environment

The National Environmental Standards and Regulations Enforcement Agency Act[16] defines environment as including water, air, land and all plants and human beings or animals living therein and the interrelationships which exist among these or any of them.

2.2 Enforcement

The Black's Law Dictionary defines enforcement as the act or process of compelling compliance with a law, mandate, command, decree or agreement.

2.3 Pollution

Section 37 of the NESREA Act also defines pollution as man-made or man-aided alteration or chemical, physical or biological quality of the environment beyond acceptable limits and "pollutants" shall be construed accordingly.

2.4 Standard of Proof

The Black's Law Dictionary defines the standard of proof as the degree or level of proof demanded in a specific case, such as "beyond a reasonable doubt" or "by a preponderance of the evidence"; a rule about the quality of the evidence that a party must bring forward to prevail.

2.5 Strict Liability

The Black's Law Dictionary defines strict liability as liability that does not depend on proof of negligence or intent to do harm but that is based instead on a duty to compensate the harms proximately caused by the activity or behavior subject to the liability rule. Prominent examples of strict liability involve the rules governing abnormally dangerous activities and the commercial distribution of defective products.

[16] Section 37, NESREA Act.

2.6 *Pollution Under the NESREA Act*[17]

The Act made elaborate provisions for pollution under the following categories: air pollution[18], noise pollution[19], water pollution[20] and land pollution[21]. Inexplicably, the same Act specifically removed oil and gas sector from the oversight functions of the Agency[22]. By so doing, the National Oil Spill Detection and Remediation Agency Act became the complementary law with respect to oil pollution in Nigeria.

2.7 *Air Pollution*

The Act empowers the Agency to "make regulations setting specifications and standards to protect and enhance the quality of Nigeria's air resources, so as to promote the public health or welfare and the natural development and productive capacity of the nation's human, animal, marine or plant life"[23]. Specifically, the Agency shall regulate.

1. Minimum essential air quality standards for human, animal, marine or plant health;
2. The control of concentration of substances in the air which separately or in combination are likely to result in damage or deterioration of property or of human, animal, marine or plant health;
3. The most appropriate means to prevent and combat various atmospheric pollution;
4. Control of atmospheric pollution originating from energy sources, including that produced by aircraft and other self-propelled vehicles, industries, factories and power generating situations or facilities;

[17] For a comprehensive reading and comparison of the NESREA Act and the repealed FEPA
Act, see S.Gozie Ogbodo, HANDBOOK ON THE NATIONAL ENVIRONMENTAL STANDARDS AND REGULATION ENFORCEMENT ACT, 2007, Ambik Press, 2010.

[18] Section 20, NESREA Act.

[19] Section 22, NESREA Act.

[20] Section 23, NESREA Act.

[21] Section 24, NESREA Act.

[22] See note 8.

[23] Section 20 (1), NESREA Act.

5. Standards applicable to emissions from any new mobile or stationary source which in the Agency's judgment causes or contributes to air pollution which may reasonably be anticipated to endanger public health or welfare, and
6. The use of appropriate means to reduce emissions to permissible levels

The Act specifically provides that any violation of the regulations made pursuant to this section amounts to a crime. Where such a violation is committed by an individual, upon conviction, the court shall impose a maximum fine of N200, 000 or imprisonment for a maximum term of one year or to both fine and imprisonment[24]. In addition, the court may impose additional fine of N20,000 for every day the offence continues[25]. With respect to a violation by a corporate body, the Act provides that upon conviction of the corporate body, the court shall impose a maximum fine of N2,000,000 and an additional fine of N50,000 for every day the offence continues[26].

2.8 Noise Pollution

The Act empowers the Agency to make Regulations with respect to noise pollution. Specifically, the Agency shall[27]:

1. Identify major noise sources, noise criteria, and noise control technology; and
2. Make regulations on noise, emission, control, abatement, as may be necessary to preserve and maintain public health and welfare.

Further, the Act empowers the Agency to "enforce compliance with existing regulations and recommend programmes to control noise originating from industrial, commercial, domestic, sports, recreational, transportation or other similar activities"[28].

[24] Section 20 (2), NESREA Act.

[25] Ibid.

[26] Section 20 (3), NESREA Act.

[27] Section 22 (1), NESREA Act.

[28] Section 22 (2), NESREA Act.

Again, the Act specifically provides that any violation of the Regulations made pursuant to this section amounts to a crime. Any individual who violates the Regulations shall, upon conviction, be liable to a maximum fine of N50,000 or to a maximum imprisonment of one year or to both fine and imprisonment[29]. Additionally, the court may impose an additional fine of N5,000 for every day that the offence continues[30]. If the violation is committed by a body corporate, upon conviction, it shall be liable to a maximum fine of N500,000 and an additional fine of N10, 000 for every day the offence continues.

2.9 Water Pollution

The Act empowers the Agency, in collaboration with other relevant agencies, to make regulations with respect to Federal water quality standards with a view to protecting public health or welfare[31]. The Act mandates the Agency, in enforcing this law, to take into consideration the use and value of public water supplies, propagation of marine and wildlife recreational purposes, agricultural, industrial and other legitimate use[32].

The Act specifically provides that any individual who violates the regulations shall, upon conviction, be liable to a maximum fine of N50,000 or to a maximum imprisonment of one year or to both fine and imprisonment[33]. An additional fine of N5,000 may be imposed for every day the offence continues[34]. Further, the Act provides that a violation by a body corporate, upon conviction, shall be liable to a maximum fine of N50,000, and an additional fine of N10,000 for every day it continues[35].

2.10 Land Pollution

The Act empowers the Agency to "make regulations, guidelines and standards for the protection and enhancement of the quality of land resources,

[29] Section 22 (3), NESREA Act.

[30] Ibid

[31] Section 23 (1), NESREA Act.

[32] Section 23 (2), NESREA Act.

[33] Section 23 (3), NESREA Act.

[34] Ibid.

[35] Section 23 (4), NESREA Act.

natural watershed, coastal zone, dams and reservoirs including prevention of flood and erosion"[36]. Further, the Act directs the Agency, in the formulation of the "proposals for such regulations, guidelines or standards, to take into consideration the Zoning Acts, Municipal Development Guidelines and Building Codes to prevent sitting of essential facilities on flood plain"[37].

Specifically, the Act provides that any individual who violates the regulations pertaining to this section, has committed a crime. Upon conviction, the individual shall be liable to a maximum fine of N200,000 or sentenced to a maximum imprisonment of one year or to both fine and imprisonment[38]. The Act empowers the court to impose an additional fine of N10,000 for every day the offence continues[39]. If the violator is a corporate body, upon conviction, it will be liable to a maximum fine of N1,000,000 and an additional fine of N50,000 for every day the offence continues[40].

2.11 Environmental Right as a Fundamental Right

Human rights are encompassing as life and connote everything that assures an individual's dignity, security and well-being. These rights are by and large inherent in life and inalienable. While they may be enshrined in Constitutions and Codes, and thus acquire justiciability in some cases, they are not gifted and therefore cannot be taken away. As societies develop, so do human rights. New rights emerge while existing rights undergo qualitative change. This is inherent in social and technological progress. Rights are entitlements (not) to perform certain actions or be in certain state or entitlements that others (do not) perform certain actions or be in certain states[41].

They are legal and moral entitlements to do or refrain from doing something, or to obtain or refrain from obtaining an action, thing or recognition in civil society. Rights dominate most modern understandings

[36] Section 26 (1), NESREA Act.

[37] Section 26 (2), NESREA Act.

[38] Section 26 (3), NESREA Act.

[39] Ibid.

[40] Section 26 (4), NESREA Act.

[41] Stanford Encyclopedia of Philosophy.

of what actions are proper and which institutions are just. They structure the forms of our governments, the contents of our laws, and the shape of morality, as we perceive it[42]. To accept a set of rights is to approve a distribution of freedom and authority, and so to endorse a certain view of what may, must and must not be done[43].

The traditional definition of the concept of rights was that they maintain individual autonomy. Human rights are classified into negative and positive rights. Negative rights are those held against the government only while positive rights are those to be awarded some benefit[44]. The classical conception of rights was that their purpose was to maintain individual autonomy. It was clearly necessary to have some level of organized government to maintain the framework of law required to enable individuals to pursue their own ends without coercion by others. The powers necessary to achieve this, however, could also be used to threaten individual autonomy[45].

The term "human rights" indicates both their nature and their source. They are the rights that one has simply because one is human. They are held by all human beings irrespective of any rights or duties individuals may (or may not) have as citizens, members of families, workers or parts of any public or private organization or association. If all human beings have them because they are human, human rights are held equally by all. And because being human cannot be renounced, lost or forfeited, human rights are inalienable.

When human rights are enshrined in the Constitution of any country and acquires the legal toga of justiciability, it is distinguished as a fundamental human right, in contrast with other socially recognized human rights. Under the Nigerian Constitution 1999 (as mended), all the rights enshrined in Chapter 4 are deemed justiciable, while the ESC rights under Chapter 11 are deemed to be non-justiciable.

One of the critical fundamental human rights is the right to life. We had canvassed elsewhere that "the growing trend now, both internationally and locally, is that environmental pollution and spoliation are

42 Ibid.

43 Ibid.

44 Robertson, B, "The Problem with Economic Rights", Quadrant, July 1, 1998, available at http://www.highbeam.com

45 Ibid.

regarded as an affront to fundamental rights especially the right to life enshrined in the Constitution. Therefore, an individual may institute an action in an effort to enforce his fundamental right to life and environmental right to clean air, water and environment that is benign and aesthetically pleasing[46]". The Nigerian *locus classicus*[47] on the enforcement of environmental right as a justiciable fundamental human right is *Jonah Gbemre v. Shell Petroleum Development Company Ltd and Ors*[48]. In the suit, the applicant was granted leave to institute these proceedings in a representative capacity for himself and for each and every member of the Iweberekan community in Delta state, and to apply for an order enforcing or securing the enforcement of their fundamental human right to life and human dignity as provided by Section 33(1) and 34(1) of the 1999 Constitution and reinforced by Articles 4, 12 and 16 of the African Charter on Human and Peoples' Right[49]. The court held that these constitutionally guaranteed rights inevitably include the rights to a clean, poison-free and pollution-free healthy environment. The judge further declared that the actions of the respondents (Shell and NNPC) in continuing to flare gas in the course of their oil exploration and production activities in the applicant's community, is a violation of their fundamental rights.

[46] S. Gozie Ogbodo & H.U. Agu, Issues and Challenges in Enforcement of Environmental Laws and Standards in Nigeria, *Journal of Contemporary Law*, University of Nigeria, Vol. 2 (2013—June 2014), 56.

[47] B.A. Oloworaran, "*The Right to a Clean Healthy Environment and the Fundamental Human Rights Provisions of the Constitution of the Federal Republic of Nigeria, 1999,*" *Nigerian Journal of Petroleum*, Natural Resources and Environmental Law (NJPNREL), Vol. 2, No. 1 (2010), p. 53. See also *Okpara v. Shell Petroleum Development Company Ltd and Ors,* Suit No FHC/PH/CS/518/2005, with similar facts having arisen also from gas flaring.

[48] (2005) Suit No. FHC/B/CS/53/05, (unreported).

[49] Cap. A9 LFN, 2004.

3 Impediments to Enforcement of Environmental Laws

3.1 *Conflict of Interest by the Nigerian Government*

The Nigerian government plays a dual role in the oil and gas sector as both a regulator and a key business stakeholder through its regulatory agency, the Department of Petroleum Resources (DPR) which works hand-in-glove with the Nigerian National Petroleum Company (NNPC)[50]. The NNPC is a party to the joint venture agreements between the multinational oil companies and the Nigerian government. As a majority shareholder in such joint venture agreements, the priority of the government is more to maximize profit and loss to strictly enforce consequential environmental law violations, which could, and invariably perpetuate violations of human rights[51].

The World Bank has warned that the dual role played by the Nigerian government both as a regulator and a partner in the oil industry "...has resulted in the government regulating oil pollution while at the same time being party to much of the oil-related environmental problems of the Niger Delta[52]".

Given the close business relationship and the prevalence of corruption in Nigeria, the government officials become susceptible to corrupt practices and bribery by the multinational companies.

[50] See J.G. Frynas, *Corporate and State Responses to Anti-Oil Protests in the Niger Delta,* 100 AFR. AFFAIRS 27, 52 (2001), cited in E.O. Ekhator, *Public Regulations of the Oil and Gas Industry in Nigeria: An Evaluation, Annual Survey of International & Comparative Law,* Vol. XXI, 2016, 64.

[51] Amnesty Int'l, *Nigeria: Petroleum, Pollution and Poverty in the Niger Delta,* 42 (2009), http://www.amnesty.org/en/library/asset/AFR44/017/2009/en/e2415961-da5c-44f8-a73c-a7a4766ee21d/afr440172009en.pdf

[52] Industry and Energy Operations Division West Central Africa Department, *World Bank Defining an Environmental Development Strategy for the Niger Delta,* Vol. II 45 (May 25, 1995), cited in Amnesty Int'l, *supra* note 46. The authors acknowledge these citations from E.O. Ehkator, *Public Regulations of the Oil and Gas Industry in Nigeria: An Evaluation.*

3.2 Poverty

Majority of the inhabitants of the Niger Delta region earn their livelihood from their environment either as farmers or fishermen. The degradation caused by oil and gas pollution in the region has exacerbated the poverty level of the inhabitants of the region[53]. Majority of the activities of the multinational companies take place in rural areas which is mainly inhabited by poor rural dwellers. When these poor people suffer damages from the activities of the multinational companies, they lack the financial resources to retain a lawyer. In the rare cases where the public agency like NESREA or NODSRA prosecute the environment polluter, these poor people who are expected to come and testify in court may not be able to afford the high cost of transportation to the nearest court. Without the testimony of the victims, the prosecution of the polluter will be weak and ineffective.

3.3 Illiteracy

In a country where majority of the citizens, particularly, in the rural areas are illiterate, their ability to know their rights as well as how to assert them becomes limited. With respect to enforcing their environmental rights, many of them do not know that they are entitled to any environmental right, neither do they know how to enforce such rights. Combined with poverty[54], they would rather live in their environmentally degraded communities due to lack of knowledge and awareness.

3.4 Lack of Technological Equipment

In order to determine the extent and quantum of environmental damage caused by the oil and gas industry, high-powered technological equipments are necessary. These equipments are very expensive to procure either by the government agencies or by individuals. In the absence of such equipment, the agencies and the individuals may not be able to prove the extent and quantum of the environmental damage, particularly, in the oil and gas industry.

[53] UNDP, Niger Delta Human Development Report, 2006.

[54] Ibid.

As a result, the polluter may limit the extent and quantum of damage caused by their oil and gas activities knowing that the claimants and the environment agency lack the technological equipment to prove otherwise.

3.5 Delay in the Judicial Process

Nigerian judicial process is notorious for delay in the speedy dispensation of justice. The court dockets are replete with many cases lasting for years. So many factors account for judicial delay in Nigeria. These include poor investigation, poor prosecution, lack of facilities in the courts, corruption, etc.

These factors discourage potential environmental litigants from seeking legal redress when they suffer environmental harms. Further, the determined litigants often lack the financial resources to retain top-class lawyers who can match the top-class lawyers who represent the multinational companies.

3.6 Standard of Proof

According to the Black's Law Dictionary, standard of proof is the degree or level of proof demanded in a specific case, such as "beyond a reasonable doubt" or "by a preponderance of the evidence"; a rule about the quality of the evidence that a party must bring forward to prevail. Under the Nigerian law, standard of proof is provided for by Section 134 of the Evidence Act, 2011[55]. Section 135 of the Evidence Act, 2011, provides that the standard of proof in criminal proceedings is proof beyond reasonable doubt. In a plethora of cases, the Nigerian courts have insisted that the prosecution, in order to secure conviction, must meet that degree or level of proof demanded in a criminal case[56]. Section 136 of the Evidence Act, 2011, however, provides that the standard of proof in civil proceedings is by a preponderance of evidence[57].

55 Mogajin v. Odofin Bello (1978) 4 SC 91.

56 Ezekwe v. Otomewo (1957) W.R.N.L. 130; Ikoku v. Okoli (1962) 1 All NLR 194; Nwankwere v. Adewunmi (1967) NMLR 45.

57 However, there are exceptions to the rule of balance of probabilities as follows: (a) Allegation of crime in civil case under Sect. 135(1) of the Evidence Act, 2011. See Benson Ikoku v. Enochi Oli (1962) All NLR 194 pp 199 & 200; Torti v. Ukpabi (1984) SCNLR

As earlier stated, environment pollution in Nigeria is a crime. In order for a prosecutor to secure conviction for a crime in Nigeria, the prosecutor must prove the case beyond a reasonable doubt. This is a very high standard of proof in contrast to the standard of the preponderance of evidence in civil cases.

Given the poverty and illiteracy of the majority of rural dwellers who are the likely victims of oil and gas pollution, it is always an uphill task to meet the high threshold of proving their case beyond a reasonable doubt. As a result, many multinational oil companies successfully defend their liabilities in Nigerian courts.

It is our view that of all the factors which impede the effective enforcement of environmental laws in Nigeria, the ability of the claimants to meet the standard of proof is the greatest impediment to environmental enforcement in Nigeria. Hence, our thesis that the application of strict liability in such cases will greatly enhance environmental enforcement in Nigeria.

3.7 Strict Liability

Strict liability is liability without fault. It is liability founded on injury *per se*, whether or not the liable party intended to cause the injury or not. In strict liability, liability attaches automatically to the offender once the tort is committed. The intendment of the law of strict liability is to hold liable anyone who by his conduct causes harm to another person by bringing on to his land a non-natural user. The principle of strict liability states that an offender is liable for the damage caused by the wrong done once it occurs, whether it was intentional, negligent or not.

In order to successfully prove strict liability, *mens rea* or a guilty mind is not an element to prove in order to succeed. This is a result of the fact that liability attaches once the prohibited act is done and damage occurs as a result of the act. This position was succinctly highlighted when Salmon canvassed that where a man acts at his peril, he is responsible for accidental harm, independently of the existence of either wrongful intent or negligence.[58]

214; Nwobodo v. Onoh (1984) SCNLR 1 (b) Where special damages are claimed. See Khawan v. Akinkugba (2002) FWLR (PT 109) 1574.

[58] JW Salmond & RFV Heuston, Salmon on the Law of Torts. London: Sweet & Maxwell, 1961.

The concept of strict liability was first developed in common law and then expounded through the courts in several cases, including *Tubervil v. Stamp*[59]and *Tenant v. Goldwin.*[60] However, it was in the case of *Rylands v. Fletcher*[61] that the concept and elements of strict liability were fully developed. In that case, the defendant–appellant who was the owner of a mill hired contractors to build an underground reservoir that would supply water to his mill. While the construction was going on, the contractors noticed some abandoned mine shafts and passages in the line of the reservoir. The contractors failed to exercise due care by investigating the discoveries and ensuring that the passages and mine shafts were blocked. Once the construction was completed and the underground reservoir was filled with water, the water overflowed and flooded the plaintiff's coal mine and caused damages. The plaintiff sued. The lower court found for the plaintiff, thereby holding the defendant–appellant responsible. On appeal, the House of Lords confirmed the judgment of the lower court. In his judgment, Lord Cairns improved on the already established principle by adding that for the offender to be liable, the thing that caused the damage must be a non-natural user (that is, something not occurring naturally on land) that escaped. By extension, the case heralded the application of the principle to environmental issues.

The rule states as follows:

> A person who for his own purposes brings on his land and collects and keeps there anything likely to do mischief if it escapes, must keep it at his peril, and if he does not do so, is prima facie answerable for all the damage which is the natural consequence of the escape.

From the foregoing, therefore, in order to succeed in an action for strict liability, the plaintiff must prove that the defendant brought on to his land or kept on his land a thing which is not naturally occurring on the land. Secondly, that the thing which was brought on the land or accumulated is likely to cause mischief if it escapes. Thirdly, that the non-natural user which was kept on the land by the defendant escaped. Fourthly, that damage was done to the plaintiff as a result of the escape of the non-natural user that was brought on the land by the defendant.

[59] (1697) 90 ER 846.

[60] (1704) 91 ER 20.

[61] (1868) UKHL 1, (1868) LR 3HL, 330.

The rationale for the principle is to balance the right of a landowner to enjoy his land with the right of another not to be harmed by the enjoyment of the other person. A person is entitled to own and hold property as long as others are not harmed by the consequences of how he uses his property. The Rule in *Rylands v. Fletcher* has been expanded to cover damages which occur as a result of several things accumulated or brought on the land that escapes. Such things could be electricity as in the case of *Northwestern Utilities Ltd. v. London Guarantee & Accident Co*[62], water as in the case of *Rylands v. Fletcher*[63], fire as in the case of *Tubervil v. Stamp*[64] and oil spillage as in the case of *Umudje v. Shell Petroleum Development Company Ltd*[65].

In the case of *Umudje v. Shell Petroleum Development Company Nigeria Ltd,* the defendant while exploring for oil, blocked the Utefe stream and allowed crude oil to escape, thereby polluting the plaintiff's ponds. The court held, relying on the rule in Rylands v. Fletcher, that the defendant was liable for the escape of crude oil that caused the damage.

It is worthy of note that the rule permits of several defences which include the act of God. A defendant can plead that the escape of the non-natural user was caused by an act of God. This is a general defence in the law of torts when a defendant can claim that he did not have control over the thing that happened which resulted in the damage. In other words, when such an act of God occurs, no foresight could have prevented the act and the resultant damage, for example, a tornado or earthquake. Another permissible defence is contributory negligence. In this case, the defendant's defence will be anchored on the plaintiff's behavior as a major contributor to the injury or harm. Also, a defendant can plead the defence of the acts of a third party. In other words, the defendant's defence will be anchored on the fact that third parties contributed immensely in causing the harm complained about.

It is noteworthy that the application of strict liability in Nigerian environmental law is not novel. The Harmful Waste (Special Criminal) Provisions Act adopted strict liability by imposing liability on any person who deposits, dumps or imports harmful waste, except where the damage

62 (1936) AC 108.

63 (1868) UKHL 1, (1868) LR 3HL, 330.

64 (1697) 90 ER 846.

65 (1975) 2 SC 155.

was caused wholly as a result of the fault of the person who suffered it or by a person who voluntarily accepted the risk thereof[66]. Also, in the Oil Pipelines Act[67] and the Petroleum Act[68], the rules of strict liability were adopted.

4 Justification for the Application of Strict Liability

In the light of the impediments faced by both the prosecutor as well as the victims of oil and gas pollution in Nigeria, particularly, with respect to meeting the high standard of proof beyond a reasonable doubt, the following are some of the justifications for the application of strict liability:

4.1 Death of the Victims

Oil and gas pollution, particularly in the oil-producing Niger Delta region of Nigeria, result in the death of the rural dwellers of that region. The chemical components of oil and gas which include carbon, hydrogen and nitrogen, diesel particulate matter, pose serious health challenges to the victims of the pollution. Due to prolonged exposure to these chemical components from oil and gas activities, many victims of the pollution eventually die from complications arising from such exposure. Residents with preexisting health challenges are more susceptible to die from the prolonged exposure to oil and gas pollution.

As a result, many deaths occurring in the Niger Delta region are directly or indirectly caused by the polluting effects of oil and gas activities in the region. These avoidable deaths violate the Constitutional right to life enshrined in the Constitution of Nigeria[69] and are outside the scope of the permissible exceptions provided under Subsection 2 of Section 33[70].

[66] Section 12, HWSCP Act.

[67] Section 11(5) (c).

[68] Paragraph 36 of the schedule 1 to the Petroleum Act, Act P10 LFN, 2004.

[69] Section 33(1) of Nigeria's Constitution, 1999 (as amended).

[70] These exceptions include death arising from the use of force to defend any person from unlawful violence or for the defence of property; in order to effect a lawful arrest or to prevent the escape of a person lawfully detained; or for the purpose of suppressing a riot, insurrection or mutiny.

4.2 *Serious Health Challenges*

In addition to causing death, oil and gas pollution cause serious health challenges to the residents of the host communities. As a result of the hazardous nature of the chemical makeup of oil and gas, the inherent health risks include fatigue, noise and asthma. The health challenges also include chronic exposure to toluene, carcinogene, benzene, which individually and collectively may result in serious health challenges.

Consequently, many residents of the region suffer serious health consequences which include heart damage, immune system defects, death, etc.

4.3 *Poverty*

Majority of both male and female adults in Nigeria's Niger Delta region earn their major source of livelihood from farming, fishing and logging. When their rivers and fish ponds are polluted with the hazardous chemicals from oil, it results in the death of thousands of fishes as well as render their water inconducive for fish farming.

In the same vein, when 40 million litres of oil are spilled annually, substantial quantity pollute the land which is the foundation for agricultural productivity. A polluted land is not conducive for any farming activity, whether crop farming or animal husbandry. Also, massive pollution of the region from oil and gas impedes productive logging activity. It makes it extremely difficult to access heavy logs in the densely forested region with any logging truck or machinery.

As a natural consequence of the foregoing, poverty is exacerbated in the region. It is estimated that the poverty head count for most of the Niger Delta states range from 19.2% to 33.1%.

4.4 *Environmental Degradation*

Environmental degradation arising from oil and gas activities negatively impact land, air and water. They manifest in acid rain, groundwater contamination, poor water quality and poor air quality. It is estimated that about 40 million litres of oil are spilled every year across the Niger Delta region. Air, land and water have all been contaminated as a result of the huge quantity of oil spilled into the water sources of the Niger Delta region.

Gas flaring is another major source of environmental degradation arising from oil and gas activities. Nigeria is presently ranked as one of the major emitters of gas worldwide. Gas flaring produces acid rain which pollutes the air and worsens the air quality of the region.

4.5 *Benefits Derivable from the Application of Strict Liability*

The application of strict liability in the enforcement of oil and gas pollution cases will, no doubt, guarantee the following benefits for both the multinational oil companies and the victims.

4.6 *Fast Resolution of Pollution Claims*

The few cases filed in Nigerian courts which arose from oil and gas pollution span many years before resolution. In some situations, the litigant may die before the case is resolved due to the incessant delays arising from the prosecution of such cases. It is pertinent to highlight that the delay may be caused by one of the following impediments to a successful prosecution of a criminal case in Nigeria. They include incompetent charge or information, filing the charge or information in the wrong court, improper arraignment, failure to present credible evidence and corruption[71].

Under the Nigerian law, a "charge" is defined as the statement of offence or statement of offences with which a defendant is charged in a trial whether by way of summary trial or trial by way of information before a court. The law vests jurisdiction on the Federal High with respect to environmental pollution cases. As a result, all criminal proceedings at the Federal High Court are prosecuted by the process of information[72].

Of all the impediments to a successful prosecution of oil and gas pollution cases in Nigeria, the ability of the prosecutor to present credible evidence which will meet the high threshold of proving the case beyond a reasonable doubt is the philosopher's stone of this paper. In order to

[71] For further reading, see C.C. Ani, Loopholes in Investigation and Prosecution: *Raison D'Etre* for Dead on Arrival Cases, in An Amazon in the Pinnacle of Justice: Essays in Honour of Hon. Justice N.P. Emehelu, Chief Judge of Enugu State, C. O. Ajah and C. A. Ogbuabor (ed), Chenglo Ltd., 337–354.

[72] Such prosecutions are handled by the Attorney General of the Federation or on his behalf under Sect. 174(2) of the 1999 Constitution (as amended).

ameliorate the situation and offer a more reasonable prosecutorial alternative, this paper canvasses for the application of strict liability in such a case.

4.7 Decongestion of Court Dockets

The application of strict liability will facilitate the speedy resolution of such cases in the Nigerian courts, which will invariably result in the decongestion of the court dockets. Once the issue of liability is determined, the court will proceed to determine appropriate compensation, thereby concluding the matter expeditiously.

This will serve as a win–win situation for both the court and the parties. By so doing, the judicial system will become more efficient and deliver justice faster. In the same vein, the parties will be saved the high cost of litigation occasioned by prolonged judicial delays.

The victim party who is typically a poorer than the multinational oil company will be relieved of paying high legal fees as a result of incessant judicial delays. Contrariwise, the deep-pocket multinational will prefer a speedy resolution of the matter in order to save the huge legal fees paid to their high-prized lawyers and focus on the growth of their business.

4.8 Harmonious Relationship

Currently, there exists a hostile relationship between the oil-producing communities and the multi-national oil companies. Such a relationship is inimical to business growth and development as can be seen from the cat and mouse relationship existing between the oil-producing communities and the multinational companies.

In the recent past, there was increased restiveness by the Niger Delta youths who unleashed attacks on the oil installations and engaged in different acts of sabotage against the multi-national companies operating in their communities. These attacks were manifested by the destruction of oil pipelines and installations as well as the kidnapping of oil workers for ransom payment. During this period of violence in Nigeria's oil-producing Niger Delta region, it was reported that Nigeria lost billions of naira as a result of decreased oil productivity and export.

4.9 Increased Productivity/Earnings

Every business thrives in a peaceful and harmonious business environment. This is particularly desired by multi-national oil companies which are foreign-owned companies which are operating in a different business environment from their home country.

Prolonged litigation and the inherent high legal fees paid to high-priced lawyers are sufficient to adversely impact the productivity and earnings of any company. Further, when the host community is hostile and antagonistic to the multi-national company, it results in less business productivity and less earnings.

The cost of engaging more security personnel to protect the lives and property of the company staff and equipment, as well as the recurring cost of replacing damaged equipment pose a drain on the financial resources of the company.

4.10 Poverty Alleviation

Oil and gas pollution degrades the environment and results in the impoverishment of the inhabitants of the host communities. Oil spillage results in the pollution of the water sources and rivers of the host community. Since many of inhabitants are professional fishermen and women, their source of livelihood is greatly impaired as a result of water pollution.

Gas flaring results in both air and land pollution, thereby causing health challenges like asthma and bronchitis. An unhealthy man or woman will be unfit to engage in the strenuous activities of farming, fishing or wood logging, which are the major sources of income of the rural inhabitants of the oil-producing Niger Delta region of Nigeria.

In a situation where they are expeditiously compensated by the application of strict liability, they will be financially made whole and their rate of poverty will be alleviated.

4.11 Clean/Healthy Environment

The application of strict liability will compel multinational oil companies to be more compliant with the safety and hazard codes in order to avoid reckless pollution incidents in their oil and gas exploration and production activities.

Presently, there is a palpable perception by the rural inhabitants of the oil-producing communities that the multinational companies are reckless in their oil and gas activities in view of the stringent judicial hurdles which impede fast compensation of the victims of oil and gas activities.

Less pollution of the environment of the oil-producing community by multi-national oil companies in their oil and gas activities will result in a clean and healthy environment.

5 Conclusion

This work has interrogated the present and recurring challenges in the enforcement of oil and gas pollution cases in Nigeria. Despite the grundnormic nature of the right to life as enshrined in Nigeria's 1999 Constitution (as amended), the incessant pollution arising from oil and gas activities continue to deprive innocent citizens of their right to life. Further, the flagship Environmental law in Nigeria, the NESREA Act, classified such environmental pollution as a crime. The NOSDRA Act, which deals specifically with oil and gas pollution in Nigeria, also classified any violation of any provision of the Act as a crime.

In Nigeria's judicial system, in order to secure conviction of any crime qua crime, the prosecutor must prove the case beyond a reasonable doubt by satisfying both elements of *actus reus* and *mens rea*. Hence, oil and gas pollution which qualifies as a crime, should also be proved beyond a reasonable doubt. The standard of proving a crime beyond reasonable doubt is a very high prosecutorial standard which should be reserved for heinous criminal charges. Due to the high standard of proof required in order to succeed in the prosecution of any crime, most multi-national oil companies escape liability for very egregious environmentally degrading activities. This has caused youth restiveness in the Niger Delta region of Nigeria and soured the relationship between the youths of the host communities and the multi-national oil companies.

In the light of the foregoing, this paper canvasses the application of strict liability in oil and gas pollution cases in Nigeria. This proposal will tremendously facilitate a fast resolution of environmental cases resulting from oil and gas pollution between the host communities and the multi-national companies; reduce the court dockets; enhance harmonious working relationship; enhance increased productivity/earnings; ensure poverty alleviation and guarantee clean/healthy environment.

The application of strict liability will serve as a win–win situation for both the host communities and the multinational oil companies.

In order to effectuate the foregoing proposal, the following recommendations are proffered:

1. Amendment of the Environmental law framework

There is an urgent need to amend the legal framework governing Environmental law in Nigeria, particularly, with respect to the classification of environmental violation as a crime with the attendant hardship in prosecuting the offence beyond a reasonable doubt. As earlier discussed, the key legal framework governing oil and gas pollution in Nigeria classified such pollution as a crime, thereby establishing a command and control enforcement system which has failed to effectively protect the Nigerian citizens, particularly, those resident in the Niger Delta region from the degradation occasioned by the reckless pollution of their environment from the oil and gas activities of the multi-national companies.

We, therefore, strongly recommend the replacement of oil and gas pollution as a 'crime' with "strict liability", for the very many reasons already adduced.

Another area which demands urgent amendment is with respect to penalties imposed on violators, particularly, the financial sanction. Penalties imposed by the NESREA Act on violators who committed air pollution (Section 20), noise pollution (Section 22), water pollution (Section 23), and land pollution (Section 26), are so low and devoid of any deterrence flavor for the multinational oil companies. For example, the highest penalty for all the classes of pollution was imposed by Section 20(4) under air pollution by a corporate body in the sum of Two million naira (N2,000,000) which is currently equivalent to Four thousand dollars ($4,000). This amount is paltry to any multi-national oil company. These penalties should be increased to such amounts that would serve as a good deterrence to the multinational companies.

2. Expanding standing in environment lawsuit

Standing is the legal capacity of a party to sue for a breach of a legally recognized right. In order to ensure better protection of the Nigerian environment and better protect the rights of victims of environmental abuse, the Nigerian courts should expand their interpretation of who has the standing to sue for environmental abuse. The more liberal the interpretation of standing, the more encouraged victims will become to pursue their environmental rights in courts. Perhaps, this will discourage the youthful victims of environmental abuse from resorting to unlawful vandalism and self-help as earlier discussed.

Another aspect of liberalization of standing is the encouragement of ADR processes and citizen suits in the enforcement of environmental rights. ADR processes which include arbitration, mediation, negotiation, etc., facilitate speedy resolution of disputes and will tremendously serve both the potential environmental violator and the victim faster and better. Also, citizen suits will complement the role of the environment agencies and law enforcement agencies in the onerous task of enforcing environmental laws across the entire country.

Citizen suits encourages a person or group of persons or an organization to bring a civil suit against any environmental protection agency for failure to perform non-discretionary duty. It also encourages individuals to enforce statutory, regulatory and permit requirements through suits seeking compliance orders and/or penalties.

3. Increase funding for Environment agencies

Environmental agencies are poorly funded and lack the equipment to effectively carry out their oversight functions. For example, the NOSDRA Agency is empowered to carry out surveillance, reporting, alerting and other response activities with respect to oil spillage throughout the country. Yet, the agency does not have enough manpower, the logistics and the equipment to effectively carry out its mandate throughout the expansive geographic spread of Nigeria.

4. Good governance

At the heart of effective environmental enforcement is good governance, which is devoid of corruption. Unfortunately, corruption has become very pervasive in Nigeria and negatively impacts governance in the country. Under Sect. 6(2), the NOSDRA Act empowers the agency to impose a penalty of N2,000,000 for each day that an oil spiller fails to report to the Agency, within 24 h, after the occurrence of an oil spill.

As laudable and deterrent as this provision appears, the multi-national companies would rather bribe an agency official with less amount than pay the huge penalty of N2,000,000 for each day that they failed to report the spill to the agency.

CHAPTER 17

Nganjiwa V Federal Republic of Nigeria—Judicial Contrivance of Immunity for Judges?

Osita Nnamani Ogbu

1 Introduction

On 11th December, 2017, the Court of Appeal, Lagos Division, delivered a judgment in the case of *Hon. Justice Hyeladzira Ajiya Nganjiwa v Federal Republic of Nigeria*.[1] The case has been popularly and frequently cited with approval by the Nigerian Bar Association (NBA) and many legal minds and it is fast assuming the status of a *locus classicus*. It has therefore become imperative to critically examine the decision which touches on many fundamental principles of Nigerian constitutional law.

[1] (2017) LEPELR-4339 (CA).

O. N. Ogbu (✉)
Faculty of Law, Enugu State University of Science and Technology (EUST), Agbani, Enugu State, Nigeria
e-mail: ositaogbu2005@yahoo.com

E. Duruigbo et al. (eds.), *International Law and Development in the Global South*, https://doi.org/10.1007/978-3-031-13741-9_17

2 Facts of the Case

The appellant was charged for offences ranging from unlawful enrichment by a public officer to giving false information contrary to Section 82(a) of the Criminal Law of Lagos State, No. 11 2011 and Section 39(2)(a) of the EFCC (Establishment) Act, 2004. The Appellant upon being served with the information filed a notice of preliminary objection challenging the jurisdiction of the trial court to hear the case against him mainly on the ground that conditions precedent to the filing of the information had not been fulfilled. In its ruling delivered on June, 2017, the trial Court dismissed the preliminary objection. Dissatisfied with the ruling, the appellant appealed to the Court of Appeal.

3 Issues for Determination Adopted by the Court of Appeal

The Court of Appeal apparently adopted the following two issues for determination formulated by the Respondent's counsel:

1. Whether the lower court can validly exercise criminal jurisdiction over a sitting judicial officer (the Appellant) whilst still occupying such office without first satisfying the condition precedent of subjecting such judicial officer to the disciplinary jurisdiction of the National Judicial Council as provided for in the Constitution of the Federal Republic of Nigeria, 1999 (as amended).
2. Whether in view of the constitutionally guaranteed doctrine of independence of the judiciary, the lower court is right in reaching the conclusion that the executive arm of government (acting through the EFCC or any other authority can directly prosecute a sitting judicial officer without first following due process as provided for in the Constitution by first referring the matter by way of petition to the National Judicial Council.

4 Decision of the Court on the Issues

The lead judgment in the case was delivered by His Lordship, Abimbola Osarugue Obaseki-Adejumo, J.C.A. The honorable Justice of the Court of Appeal considered the two issues together. In the opinion of the Court, a cumulative reading of the provisions of Section 153(1) and 158(1), and paragraph 21(b) of Part 1 of the Third Schedule to the 1999 Constitution (as amended) is to the effect that the National Judicial Council (NJC) is the sole body with authority to recommend to the President the appointment and removal of any Judicial Officer at the federal level and also to exercise disciplinary control over judicial officers. In line with paragraph 21(h)&(i) thereof, the NJC has the power to collect, control, and disburse all monies for the judiciary and to deal with all other matters relating to policy and administration, and it is in this regard that the National Judicial Policy of April, 2015; Judicial Discipline Regulations of 9th March, 2017; Revised Code of Conduct for Judicial Officers of the Federal Republic of Nigeria of February 2016; Revised NJC Guidelines & Procedural Rules for the Appointment of Judicial Officers of all Superior Courts of Record in Nigeria of 3rd November, 2014 were all formulated.

The Court referred to the Revised Code of Conduct for Judicial Officers of February, 2016 which provides: "Violation of any Rules contained in this Code shall constitute judicial misconduct and or, misbehavior and shall attract disciplinary action." The Court observed that the Appellant, who was then a judge of the Federal High Court, was charged vide Criminal information for conduct/acts which are tantamount to a breach of his oath of office and breach of the Revised Code of Conduct of February, 2016 and which are at the same time offences under the criminal law. The Court on this premise held that as a serving Judge, the Appellant is under the management, control, and disciplinary "jurisdiction" of the NJC as envisaged under Paragraph 21(b) part 1 of the Third Schedule to the 1999 Constitution. According to the court, this proposition has been affirmed in a host of judicial authorities including *Elelu-Habeeb & Anor v A.G. Federation*[2]; *Opene v NJC*[3]; *Abdullahi v Governor, Kano State.*[4]

In the reasoning of the Court, whenever a breach of judicial oath occurs, it is a misconduct itself, and then the NJC is the appropriate body to investigate such breaches by the judicial officer and if found to be so, such judicial officer shall face disciplinary action and the NJC may recommend the removal of such a judicial officer to the appropriate authority which is either the President in the case of a Federal judicial officer or the

[2] (2012) 13 NWLR (pt. 1318) 423.

[3] (2011) LPELR (CA/A/324/07).

[4] (2014) 16 NWLR (pt. 1433) 213 at 256.

Governor of the State in the case of a State judicial officer and/or take other actions appropriately. When this is done and accepted by the appropriate authority in compliance with the provisions of the Constitution, then the relevant law enforcement agent or agency is at liberty to make the said judicial officer face the wrath of the law. Continuing, the Court of Appeal held that any act done by the law enforcement agent or agency in violation of the above is tantamount to denying the NJC the powers to discipline judges in accordance with the provisions of Section 153(1) and paragraph 21 part 1 of the Third Schedule to the 1999 Constitution. On this premise, recourse to the NJC is a condition precedent "as clearly set out by the Constitution," and any attempt by any Agency of Government to bypass the Council will amount to failure to observe the condition precedent which constitutes a flagrant violation of the Constitution.

The Court noted that the charge is mainly made up of 13 allegations of corruption allegedly committed by the Appellant as a sitting Judge of the Federal High Court and that the last count relates to a statement made to the EFCC during investigation. To the Court, it is obvious from the various counts that the Appellant is purportedly being charged with "unlawful enrichment by public officer ..." while being a Judge of the Federal High Court.

Curiously, his Lordship observed that if a judicial officer commits theft, fraud, murder or manslaughter, arson, and the likes, which are crimes committed outside the scope of the performance of his official functions, he may be arrested, interrogated, and prosecuted accordingly by the State directly without recourse to the NJC. To his Lordship, these classes of criminal acts are not envisaged and captured by the provisions of paragraph 21, Part 1 of the Third Schedule.

In the opinion of his Lordship, if any Judicial Officer commits a professional misconduct within the scope of his duty and is investigated, arrested, and subsequently prosecuted by security agents without a formal complaint/report to the NJC, it will be a usurpation of the latter's constitutionally guaranteed powers under Section 158 of, and paragraph 21 Part 1 of the Third Schedule to, the 1999 Constitution, thereby inhibiting and obstructing the NJC from carrying out its disciplinary control over erring judicial officers as clearly provided by the Constitution, which in the opinion of the Court, will amount to a violation of the constitutionally guaranteed independence of the judiciary.

The Court further observed that in most known democracies, the judiciary is always accorded the freedom to conduct its affairs without fear of interference, intimidation, threat, or ill-will from any other arm of Government; and that it is in order to ensure that this is done that the NJC was established under the Constitution and specifically given the power to discipline any of its judicial officers who misconducts himself in accordance with the provision of paragraph 21(b) Part 1 of the Third Schedule to the 1999 Constitution.

Therefore, as it relates to the instant case, and with specific reference to the powers of the NJC to exercise disciplinary control over the Appellant, a Judicial Officer, it is quite plain that the Constitution endows the NJC with the responsibility of recommendation for appointment and disciplinary control over judicial officers and not the Executive through its agents. In support of this proposition, the Court cited with approval the pronouncement in the case of *Elelu Habeeb & Anor v A.G. Federation*[5] to the effect that:

> … it is in the spirit of the Constitution in ensuring checks and balances between the three arms of Government that the role of the Governor in appointing and exercising disciplinary control over the Chief Judge of his state is subjected to the participation of the National Judicial Council and the House of Assembly of the State in the exercise to ensure transparency and observance of the rule of law.[6]

In his concurring judgment in the *Nganjuwa* case, Hon. Justice Mohammed Lawal Garba. J.C.A. agreed with the reasoning and conclusion that the provisions of the EFCC Act empowering the Respondent to investigate and prosecute the named offences in the Act, are subject to the provisions of the Constitution which empower the National Judicial Council to discipline serving judicial officers in the country for misconduct which may involve some form of the offences the Respondent may investigate and prosecute. In a similar tone like the lead judgment, His Lordship emphasized that the Constitution does not exempt, by way of immunity, serving judicial officers from investigation and possible prosecution for offences which the EFCC is vested with the requisite authority and power to investigate and prosecute. The Constitution only provides for the procedure to be followed and complied with in the investigation and before possible prosecution of serving judicial officers.

[5] (2012) 13 NWLR (pt. 1318) 423.

[6] (2012) 13 NWLR (pt. 1318) p. 423.

Another concurring Justice, Hon. Justice Yargata Byenchit Nimpar, J.C.A., not only agreed with the reasoning and conclusion in the lead judgment but rendered a longer concurring judgment. To his Lordship, the main issue to be determined is whether or not the lower court had the jurisdiction to sit over the prosecution of the appellant prior to all necessary and constitutional steps by the NJC. According to His Lordship, the Appellant, a serving judicial officer, was charged for offences ranging from unlawful enrichment by a judicial officer to giving false information. These are criminal allegations which also constitute breach of the judicial code of conduct. In any case, his Lordship distinguished the instant case from the case of judicial immunity and observed that the issue of judicial immunity does not arise in the instant case.

His Lordship observed that the Criminal Laws of Lagos State and the Economic and Financial Crimes Commission (EFCC) Act, 2004 provides for the prosecution of any person suspected to have committed the offences brought against the Appellant. However, to his Lordship, the Appellant being a serving judicial officer is primarily under the Constitutional disciplinary powers of the NJC. This is a body specifically created under the Constitution with strictly specified responsibilities, which includes the disciplining of a judge. The implication of the constitutional provisions particularly paragraph 21(b) Part 1 of the Third Schedule to the 1999 Constitution is that the Constitution gives the NJC the power to exercise disciplinary control over erring judicial officers where there is breach of the Code of Conduct. According to his Lordship, the judicial Code of Conduct made pursuant to a constitutional power is a subsidiary legislation and therefore has the force of law. Accordingly, if there is any allegation of misconduct brought against a judge in the execution of his official duties which is a breach of the Code of Conduct, it must first go through and be dealt with by the NJC before any other step is taken by anybody or person with other powers and who still desires to proceed against such a judicial officer.

To his Lordship, the role of the NJC is synonymous to being the glory or cover for judicial officers. How then does one intend to attack its members without first going through it? A standard procedure has been set for the discipline of judicial officers which should be strictly complied with; else, the gates will be open for all sorts of intimidation and threats against judicial officers who refuse to bow to the whims and caprices of those who believe they have authority to also deal with judicial officers.

His Lordship also referred to and purported to rely on the case of *Elelu Habeeb & Anor v A.G. Federation*[7].

In further support of his opinion, his Lordship referred to the case of *Opene v NJC & Ors*[8] and stated that although the above authority deals with the removal of a judicial officer, the principles raised are also applicable to the disciplining of a serving judicial officer. In the opinion of his Lordship, the Respondent must first report any infraction to the NJC to carry out its Constitutional and disciplinary control over the Appellant to establish a case before criminal proceeding.

5 Nganjinwa Precedent Religiously Followed by the Courts

The Nigerian courts have no hesitation in following the Nganjinwa precedent. Hon. Justice Sylvester Ngwuta, Justice of the Supreme Court of Nigeria, was discharged by Justice John Tsoho of the Federal High Court Abuja in a money laundering charge brought against His Lordship by the Economic and Financial Crimes Commission on the ground that a condition precedent to filing the charge, that is, prior investigation by the NJC, has not been complied with. The prosecution then said that a petition would be sent to the NJC to formally place the alleged charge before the Council.[9]

Nobody heard about the case again until the demise of Justice Ngwuta in 2021. A similar objection was brought and sustained in the charge against Hon. Justice Ofili-Ajumogobia.[10]

6 Comments on the Case

In this comment, we will address the two issues for determination in the case which are somewhat similar. In addition, we shall consider whether it constitutes a violation of the doctrine of separation of powers for

[7] (2012) 13 NWLR (pt. 1318) 423.

[8] 2011 (LPELR) 4795 C.A.

[9] See guardian.ng/news/court discharges-Justice-Ngwuta-of-money-laundering-charge (accessed on 12 April 2021).

[10] See guardian.ng/news/drama-as-efcc-rearrests-ofili-ajumogobia-for retrial (accessed on 12 April 2021).

executive agencies to investigate and/or prosecute allegations of crime involving misconduct or breach of the judicial code of conduct against a judge.

6.1 Whether Criminal Jurisdiction can be exercised over a Sitting Judicial Officer without first subjecting such Judicial Officer to the Disciplinary Jurisdiction of the NJC

On this issue, we agree with the judgment that the constitutional immunity within the meaning of Section 308 of the 1999 Constitution does not avail judicial officers and that the issue of judicial immunity does not arise in the case. Section 308(2) of the 1999 constitution expressly provides that the immunity conferred by Section 308(1) "applies to a person holding the office of President or Vice-President, Governor or Deputy Governor." There is nowhere in the constitution that a similar immunity is conferred on a judge, even the Chief Justice of Nigeria. It is a principle of statutory interpretation that the express mention of one thing means the exclusion of another (*expressio unis est exclusio alterius*). In other words, the express mention by the Constitution of offices that enjoy immunity means that those not mentioned do not enjoy immunity.[11]

It is pertinent to observe that even in respect of the offices that enjoy immunity, the Supreme Court has held that immunity does not preclude investigation of the occupant of the offices for crime by the law enforcement agencies. In *Fawehinmi v I.G.P.*[12] the Supreme Court held that although public officers covered by the immunity clause cannot be arrested or prosecuted, they are not immune from investigation for corruption and other criminal offences. In the words of Uwaifo, J.S.C.:

> The evidence may be useful for impeachment purposes if the House of Assembly may have need of it. It may no doubt be used for prosecution of the said incumbent Governor after he has left office. But to do nothing under the pretext that a Governor cannot be investigated is a disservice to the society.

[11] Please see *Udoh v Orthopaedic Hospital Management Board* (1993) 7 NWLR (pt.304) 139.

[12] (2002) WRN 1.

The decision in the *Nganjiwa* case is in conflict with the Supreme Court decision in the *Fawehinmi* case. *Ngangiwa* constitutes a qualification of the power of investigation of allegation of crime against a sitting judge where the allegation involves judicial misconduct or breach of the Judicial Code of Conduct contrary to the decision of the Supreme Court in the *Fawehinmi* case. As the Supreme Court observed in the *Fawehinmi* case, a crime by persons enjoying immunity may also constitute a misconduct for which the person can be impeached by the legislature, yet this does not preclude the power of security agencies to investigate the allegation prosecution will follow on the expiration of the immunity. The decision in the *Nganjiwa* case has qualified the power of investigation and prosecution of the crime of corruption against sitting judges notwithstanding that they do not enjoy immunity from the criminal process.

Under the principle of *stare decisis* it is mandatory for the Court of Appeal to follow the decision of the Supreme Court. In any case, the *Fawehinmi* case was not cited to the Court of Appeal in the *Ngangiwa* case and the Court of Appeal did not advert to it. In effect, the decision in the *Ngangiwa* case can be considered to have been given *per incuriam.* In *Alhaji Karimu Adisa v Emmanuel Oyinwola & 4 Ors.,*[13] the Supreme Court maintained that a case is decided *per incuriam* where a statute or rule having statutory effect or other binding authority which would have affected the decision had not been brought to the attention of the court.

It must be noted that because of the important functions or objects of criminal law,[14] priority is always given to the criminal process as against the civil process let alone the domestic process. This has given rise to the Rule in *Smith v Selwyn*. According to the Court of Appeal in *Attorney*

[13] (2000) IV NWLR (pt. 674) 116.

[14] The Wolfenden Committee in England defined the function of the criminal law to include "To preserve public 'order or decency', to protect the citizen from what is 'offensive or injurious'...." Home Office, Report of the Committee on Homosexual Offences and Prostitution (1957). See also the Model Penal Code of the U.S.A. which provides that the general purpose of the provisions governing the definition of offences include "to forbid and prevent conduct that unjustifiably and inexcusably inflicts or threatens substantial harm to individual or public interests."

General of the Federation & 4 Ors v Idowu Dawodu & 7 Ors[15] in its undiluted form, the Rule in *Smith v Selwyn*[16] says that an action for damages based upon a felonious act on the part of the defendant committed against the plaintiff is not maintainable so long as the defendant has not been prosecuted or a reasonable excuse shown for his not having been prosecuted, and that the proper course for the court to adopt in such a case is to stay further proceedings in the action until the defendant has been prosecuted.[17]

As observed by Aderemi, J.C.A. in *Alao v NIDB*[18] the intendment of the Rule in *Smith v. Selwyn* is primarily to avoid the compounding and the concealment of a felony hence it dictates a hold on further proceedings in an action for damages founded on a felonious act alleged to have been committed by the defendant against the plaintiff until the defendant has been prosecuted or a reasonable excuse offered for his non-prosecution.

It must be noted that the criminal jurisdiction vested on the State High Court by Section 272 of the 1999 constitution is not made subject to the NJC procedure where the criminal charge against a sitting Judge also borders on breach of the Code of Conduct for Judicial Officers. As the Constitution makes it very clear in the case of the Code of Conduct for Public Officers, criminal trial and trial of a person for breach of the Judicial Code of Conduct can go on concurrently.

6.2 *Whether it is Contrary to the Doctrine of Separation of Powers or against the Independence of the Judiciary for the Executive to Prosecute a Sitting Judicial Officer without First Petitioning the NJC*

To address this issue, a pertinent question is whether the NJC has any role in criminal investigation of a sitting judge or any judge at all. It has become necessary to consider the constitutional powers and functions of the NJC. Section 153 of the 1999 constitution established the NJC as one

[15] (1995) 2 NWLR (pt. 380) 712.

[16] (1914) 3 K.B. 98.

[17] For elaboration of the Rule, see Ogbu, O.N. *Modern Nigerian Legal System 3rd edn* (Enugu: SNAAP Press, 2013) p. 39. It is important to note that in the *Nganjinwa* case, counsel to the Appellant alluded to the Rule without expressly mentioning it.

[18] (1999) LPELR 6673 (CA) pp. 8–16.

of the Federal Executive Bodies. The powers of the NJC as contained in Part I of the Third Schedule to the Constitution are as follows:

> 21. The National Judicial Council shall have power to—
> (a) recommend to the President from among the list of persons submitted to it by—
> (i) the Federal Judicial Service Commission, persons for appointment to the offices of the Chief Justice of Nigeria, the Justices of the Supreme Court, the President and Justices of the Court of Appeal, the Chief Judge and Judges of the Federal High Court, and
> (ii) the Judicial Service Committee of the Federal Capital Territory, Abuja, persons for appointment to the offices of the Chief Judge and Judges of the High Court of the Federal Capital Territory, Abuja, the Grand Kadi and Kadis of the Sharia Court of Appeal of the Federal Capital Territory, Abuja and the President and Judges of the Customary Court of Appeal of the Federal Capital Territory, Abuja;
> (b) recommend to the President the removal from office of the judicial officers specified in sub-paragraph (a) of this paragraph and to exercise disciplinary control over such officers;
> (c) recommend to the Governors from among the list of persons submitted to it by the State Judicial Service Commissions persons for appointments to the offices of the Chief Judges of the States and Judges of the High Courts of the States, the Grand Kadis and Kadis of the Sharia Courts of Appeal of the States and the Presidents and Judges of the Customary Courts of Appeal of the States;
> (d) recommend to the Governors the removal from office of the judicial officers in sub-paragraph (c) of this paragraph, and to exercise disciplinary control over such officers.
> (e) collect, control and disburse all moneys, capital and recurrent, for the judiciary;
> (f) advise the President and Governors on any matter pertaining to the judiciary as may be referred to the Council by the President or the Governors;
> (g) appoint, dismiss and exercise disciplinary control over members and staff of the Council;
> (h) control and disburse all monies, capital and recurrent, for the services of the Council; and
> (i) deal with all other matters relating to broad issues of policy and administration.

It is thus clear that the NJC is an executive body though with judicial character but without any power of criminal investigation. When it exercises its powers in relation to disciplining judicial officers, it becomes a quasi-judicial tribunal. Even in that garb, it is still not a Court and therefore does not exercise judicial power. The question then is, can the NJC investigate allegations of crime against a judge or try such allegations even when such allegations involves a misconduct or breach of the judicial code of conduct. A similar question arose before the Supreme Court in *Garba v The University of Maiduguri*.[19] One of the issues that arose in that case was whether a domestic tribunal which is not a court can try a person for allegations involving a crime. The Supreme Court held that the implication of the constitutional guarantee of fair hearing is that offences which are against the criminal law of the land can only be tried by a law court. The exception to this rule is where a person has confessed to committing the offence.

The Supreme Court decision in the *Garba* case was purported to be based on the application of Section 33(1) and (4) of the 1979 Constitution (now Section 36(1) and (4) of the 1999 Constitution) to the case. In arriving at that decision the Supreme Court relied heavily on the decisions in *Denloye v Medical and Dental Practitioners Disciplinary Committee*[20] and *Sofekun v Akinyemi*.[21] In the latter case, Section 22 of the 1963 Constitution, which is in *pari materia* with Section 36 of the 1999 Constitution, was in issue. It was held that the implication of the fair hearing guaranteed in that section is that once an allegation involves a crime, only a court of law has jurisdiction to hear the matter. In the *Denloye* case, the Supreme Court held that where professional misconduct of a practitioner amounts to a crime, it is a matter for the court to deal with and once the court has found a practitioner guilty of an offence, then the tribunal may proceed to deal with him under the Act. This principle was restated by the Supreme Court in *Baba v NCATC*[22] where it held that once an allegation against a person involves a crime, the hearing body cannot be anything less than a judicial body vested with criminal

[19] (1986) 1 NWLR (pt. 18) 550.

[20] (1968) 1 All NLR 306.

[21] (1980) 5–7 S.C. 1.

[22] (1991) 5 NWLR (pt. 192) 388.

jurisdiction. A similar decision was equally reached in the earlier case of *Federal Civil Service Commission v Laoye*[23].

The import of the above principle is that a domestic tribunal or any other tribunal which is not a court, including the NJC, cannot even look into or investigate any allegation involving a crime until the criminal aspect has been investigated and a court makes a pronouncement on it. In other words, if we follow these decisions, the NJC cannot even begin to take any action against a judge alleged to have committed a criminal offence, whether or not misconduct or breach of the code of conduct for judicial officers is involved, until the criminal aspect has been investigated and the judge tried for the crime where a prima facie case has been established against the judge.

This position was, however, criticized by some legal minds, including Nwabueze[24] and the present writer.[25] Nwabueze contended, rightly in our view, that disciplinary proceedings and criminal trial operate on completely different planes and serve entirely different purposes.[26]

In any case, in the subsequent case of *Yusuf v Union Bank of Nigeria Ltd*[27] the Supreme Court shifted from its position and held that it is not necessary under the common law nor is it a requirement of Section 33 of the 1979 Constitution that before an employer can summarily dismiss his employee from his service, the employee must be tried before a court of law where the accusation against the employee is for gross misconduct involving dishonesty bordering on criminality. The import of this decision is that trial for misconduct per se does not amount to criminal trial. Thus, a non-judicial tribunal can try a person for a misconduct involving allegation of crime but only a court of competent jurisdiction can try a person for the crime. A similar decision was reached by the Supreme Court in the case of *Arinze v First Bank of Nigeria*[28]. It is pertinent to observe that in the two latter cases, the Supreme Court did not overrule *Garba*

[23] (1989) 2 NWLR (pt. 106) 652 at 679.

[24] Nwabueze, B. O. *Military Rule and Constitutionalism* (Ibadan: Spectrum Law Publishing, 1992) 186. Nwabueze is an eminent Professor of Law and perhaps the leading constitutional lawyer in Africa.

[25] Please see "Ogbu, O.N. "Fair Hearing, Domestic Tribunals and Allegations Involving a Crime" (2003) 1 N.B.J. 236.

[26] Nwabueze *op. cit.*

[27] (1996) 6 NWLR (pt. 457) 632.

[28] (2004) All FWLR (pt. 217) 668.

v the University of Maiduguri. The decision in the instant case constitutes a reversal by the Court of Appeal of the principles established by the Supreme Court in the foregoing cases in relation to sitting judges.

It is interesting that in the case under review, the Court of Appeal cited and purported to rely on the Court of Appeal case of *Justice Okwuchukwu Opene v National Judicial Council*[29]. In that case, it was contended, relying on the *Garba* case, that the National Judicial Council cannot investigate or punish the appellant since the allegations against him bordered on criminality. The Court of Appeal in dismissing the appeal refused to follow the *Garba* case and followed the decision in *Yusuf v Union Bank of Nigeria Ltd*[30] to the effect that what the NJC did was to take action in respect of judicial misconduct without trying the criminal aspect of the case. The Court refused to follow the *Garba* case because the *Yusuf* case is later in time. If the *Opene* case was rightly interpreted in the instant case, all that it means is that trial for misconduct by the NJC has no relationship with criminal trial. Of course, criminal investigation is a precursor to criminal trial.

Okonkwo, has pertinently observed that "there is no special intrinsic characteristic of criminal conduct distinguishing it from non-criminal conduct. We can only say that it is a crime if, after having enquired whether it is prohibited by law, it is also attended by the requisite legal procedure"[31]. The learned Professor went further to say that:

The legal definition of an offence is essentially a definition in terms of procedure. As far as the courts are concerned, it is criminal procedure which marks out a crime from a civil wrong, and we may note a few of the distinguishing characteristics of that procedure... Most important of all, a finding of guilt leads to a passing of sentence by the court and may lead to punishment[32].

Thus a trial which is not for the purpose of penal sanction at the instance of the state cannot be said to be a trial for a criminal offence.

[29] (2011) LPELR 4795.

[30] (1996) 6 NWLR (pt. 457) 632.

[31] Okonkwo and Naish, *Criminal Law in Nigeria* 2nd edition (London: Sweet & Maxwell, 1980) p. 2.

[32] *Ibid*. p. 19.

Section 36(4)-(12) of the 1999 Constitution makes provision for situations in which a person is formally charged with a criminal offence before a court or a judicial tribunal.

In *Bamgboye v University of Ilorin*[33] where the appellant was dismissed from the University for examination malpractices, Uwaifo, JSC was forthright in saying:

> The allegations made against the appellant were amply supported by evidence. It is true they have some connotation of criminality. But what the council would be concerned about is whether the appellant acted in abuse of his office.[34]

It is very clear that the NJC cannot try a judge for a crime because it is not a court or a judicial tribunal. In relation to judges, the NJC can be likened to the Legal Practitioners' Disciplinary Committee which is a tribunal for trial of lawyers for misconduct but not a court. In *Eke Umazi Ndukwe v The Legal Practitioners Disciplinary Committee & Anor*[35] the Supreme Court held that the Legal Practitioners Disciplinary Committee is neither a court of law exercising jurisdiction in criminal matters nor is it a pre-trial investigator. Rather, it is an administrative tribunal created by statute and vested with quasi-judicial jurisdiction to consider and determine cases charging legal practitioners with misbehavior or breach of the code of conduct for legal practitioners. Similarly, the NJC is not a court of law exercising criminal jurisdiction or a pre-trial investigator of criminal allegations.

In the *Nganjinwa* case, the Court of Appeal purported to anchor its position on the doctrine of separation of powers also. It must be noted that arrest, investigation, and prosecution of persons for offences are executive functions and not judicial functions. The control of criminal prosecutions and *ipso facto* criminal investigations, according to

[33] (2001) FWLR 12 S. C.

[34] at p. 74.

[35] (2017) 5 NWLR (pt. 1026) 1 at 30. The Supreme Court in that case stated that the word "charge" used in Rule 4 of the Legal Practitioners (Disciplinary Committee) Rules refers to any process by which all the essential elements of any allegation against a legal practitioner are brought to his or her notice before commencement of disciplinary proceedings against the legal practitioner.

Nwabueze, is one of the great powers exercised by the executive government in the administration of a state.[36] Following the common law tradition the 1999 Nigerian constitution vests the control of criminal prosecution on the attorneys general. Sections 174 and 211 of the 1999 constitution provide for the powers of the Attorneys General of the Federation and of the States respectively, which include the power to undertake, takeover, or discontinue criminal prosecution. Judicial power does not extend to criminal investigation or prosecution. Judicial power, according to Chief Justice Griffith of the High Court of Australia in *Huddart, Parker & Co Proprietary Ltd v Moorehead*[37]:

> means the power which every sovereign authority must of necessity have to decide controversies between its subjects, or between itself and its subjects, whether the rights relate to life, liberty or property. The exercise of this power does not begin until some tribunal which has power to give a binding and authoritative decision (whether subject to appeal or not) is called upon to take action.

This definition of judicial power was adopted without reserve by the Judicial Committee of the Privy Council in the Australian case of *Shell Co. of Australia v Federal Commissioner for Taxation*[38] and the Nigerian Supreme Court in *Bronik Motors Ltd. v Wema Bank Ltd.*[39] The term judicial power is thus co-extensive with the power of the state to administer public justice. Judicial power may be exercised by a court or tribunal. Investigation or prosecution of a sitting judge by executive agencies does not constitute a violation of the principle of separation of powers or checks and balances. It is only after investigation and prosecution that judicial power will come into play.

With all due respect, it is submitted that all the authorities their Lordships cited in support of the proposition that executive investigation or prosecution of sitting judges for corruption without first petitioning the

[36] Nwabueze, B. O. *Nigeria's Presidential Constitution 1979–83: The Second Experiment in Constitutional Democracy* (London: Longman, 1985) p. 308.

[37] (1909), C.L.R. 330 at 383.

[38] (1931) A.C. 275 at 295 and 283.

[39] (1983) I SCNLR.

NJC constitutes a violation of separation of powers are irrelevant to the *Ngangiwa* case.[40]

Moreover, the NJC does not have the capacity and the machinery for criminal investigation. It is obvious that the constitutional functions of the NJC does not include or extend to criminal investigation.

It has already been shown that the NJC cannot investigate or try a criminal offence but can investigate cases of alleged misconduct against judicial officers notwithstanding that the allegations also involve criminality. The 1999 Constitution makes the position clearer when it provides in relation to the Code of Conduct for Public Officers as follows:

The sanctions mentioned in subparagraph (2) hereof shall be without prejudice to the penalties that may be imposed by any law where the conduct is also a criminal offence.[41]

The Code of Conduct for Nigerian Public Officers is contained in the 5th schedule to the constitution. By Section 172 and 209 of the constitution, persons in the Federal and State public services are required to conform to and observe the Code of Conduct.

By part II paragraph 5 of the Fifth Schedule to the constitution, a Public Officer for the purpose of the Code of Conduct include "all judicial officers and all staff of court of law." Under paragraph 12 of the Code of Conduct for Public Officers, any allegation that a public officer has committed a breach of or has not complied with the Code of Conduct shall be made to the Code of Conduct Bureau. In *Ahmed v Ahmed*[42] the Supreme Court held that any allegation that a public officer has committed a breach of, or has not complied with the provisions of the Code of Conduct for Public Officers shall be made to the Code of Conduct Bureau which has established its tribunal with exclusive jurisdiction to deal with any violations of any provisions under the Code.

In effect, the NJC ought not investigate any allegation of breach of the Code of Conduct for Public Officers. If, however, such breach also amounts to judicial misconduct, the NJC can investigate and punish for the misconduct without purporting to investigate or punish for breach of the Code of Conduct for Public Officers.

[40] Pronouncement on separation of powers in the following cases were cited in the leading judgment: *A.G. Federation v Guardian Newspapers Ltd* (1999) LPELR 3162 (SC); *Goyang Kaili v Esly Yilbuk & Ors* (2015) LPELR 24,323 (SC).

[41] Paragraph 18(3) of 5th Schedule to the 1999 Constitution.

[42] (2013) 15 NWLR (pt. 1377) 274.

It is interesting that His Lordship observed in the leading judgment that if a judicial officer commits theft, fraud, murder or manslaughter, arson, and the likes, which are crimes committed outside the scope of the performance of his official functions, he may be arrested, interrogated and prosecuted by the State directly without recourse to the NJC. To his Lordship, these classes of criminal acts are not envisaged and captured by the provisions of paragraph 21, part 1 of the Third Schedule to the 1999 Constitution.

It is submitted with utmost respect that the classification of offences into those in which the NJC has a role and those in which the NJC has no role on the ground that the former relates to the performance of judicial function while the latter does not, is without legal basis. Commission of any crime by a judicial officer amounts to a misconduct. Rule 1(1) of the Code of Conduct for Judicial Officers provides that a Judicial Officer should respect and comply with the laws of the land.[43] Commission of criminal offence is an infraction of the laws of the land. There is no crime that is within the scope of the duties of a judge. For instance, a judge handling a case who receives bribe in respect of the case acted outside the scope of his duties. His Lordship Aderemi, J.C.A. pertinently observed in *Alao v NIDB*[44] that proof of a criminal matter is quite different from proof of a civil matter and there is really no justifiable reason why the two should be so related in terms of prosecution." Criminal procedure, including investigation and prosecution, has no room for NJC intervention.

The proposition that investigation of sitting judicial officers for corruption without recourse to the NJC undermines the independence of the judiciary of the judiciary does not hold water. Independence of the judiciary does not mean that the judiciary should be an island unto itself. It does not connote impunity. Corruption constitutes a subversion of the rule of law. Corruption actually means that things are not done according to law. In fact, a corrupt judiciary is not independent. Independence of the judiciary does not mean only independence from executive or legislative interference. It also connotes independence from any sort of external influence.

[43] Rule 1.3 of the National Judicial Council Revised Code of Conduct for Judicial Officers of the Federal Republic of Nigeria contains a similar provision.

[44] (1999) LPELR 6673 (CA) pp. 8–16.

7 Conclusion

The decision in the *Ngangiwa* case amounts to conferring or contriving partial immunity from the criminal process on sitting judges. Applying Hofeld's paradigm, the effect of immunity is to disable a person who otherwise has a right to proceed against the person enjoying the immunity. Immunity and disability are thus considered to be jural correlatives.[45] The decision tries to disable executive agencies from investigating or prosecuting sitting judges save with the consent of the NJC.

It has been shown that the decision was given *per incuriam*. In that case, the Court of Appeal gave tendentious and wrong interpretation to the existing case law in order to arrive at a pre-determined conclusion. The decision violates the rule of law in more ways than one. In the first place, it assigns to the NJC powers which no law or the constitution conferred on the body. The rule of law, according to Dicey's second meaning of the concept, means equality before the law. In the words of Dicey, "... 'the rule of law' in this sense excludes the idea of any exception of officials or others from the duty of obedience to the law which governs other citizens or from the jurisdiction of the ordinary tribunals ...." In other words, every person should be equal before the law interpreted by the ordinary courts.[46]

Principles of law or statutory provisions ought not be interpreted to protect abuse of office or corrupt practices. This proposition was eloquently and unambiguously pronounced by Nweze, J.S.C. in relation to the Public Officers Protection Act in *CIL Risk & Asset Management Limited v Ekiti State Government & 3 Ors.*[47] His Lordship said:

> The Public Officers (Protection) Act is designed to protect the officer who acts in good faith and does not apply to acts done in abuse of office and with no semblance of legal justification. The Act will not apply if it is established that the defendant abused his position for purposes of acting maliciously. In that case, he has not been acting within the terms of statutory or other legal authority. He has not been bona fide in endeavouring

[45] Hofeld, W. N. *Fundamental Legal Conceptions as Applied in Judicial Reasoning* cited in Lloyd, D. *et. al. Introduction to Jurisprudence 5th edn* (London: Sweet and Maxwell, 1985) p. 54.

[46] Dicey, A.V. *An Introduction to the Study of the Law of the* Constitution *10th* edn (New Delhi: Universal Law Publishing Co. Pvt. Ltd, 1994) pp. 202–203.

[47] (2020) 12 NWLR (pt. 1738) 203.

> to carry it out. In such a state of facts, he has abused his position for the purpose of doing a wrong and the protection of the Act never could apply to such a case. Thus, abuse of office and bad faith are factors that can deprive a party of the protection of section 2(a) of the Public Officers (Protection) Act that he would otherwise have been entitled to. The protection enjoyed by public officers under the Public Officers (Protection) Act is not automatic. The law does not automatically protect any public officer who had abused his position. Therefore, a court should not immediately dismiss an action on the ground only that the action commenced against a pubic officer was filed outside three months from the date of accrual of the cause of action. The court has to be satisfied that the act executed by the public officer was not done in bad faith or did not amount to abuse of office, that is to say using the power to achieve personal gain, to show undue favour to another or to wreak vengeance on an opponent, or exercised in breach of his statutory or constitutional duties.

In the golden era of the Nigerian judiciary, there was no immunity for sitting judges from criminal investigation or prosecution. The integrity of judge was his immunity outside the normal judicial immunity which as rightly observed in the *Nganjiwa* case is inapplicable to the case.

When the judiciary starts interpreting the constitution wrongly in favor of itself as in the *Ngangiwa* case, it will affect public confidence in the judiciary.

CHAPTER 18

A Critique of the Nigeria National Security Strategy 2019

M. Ozonnia Ojielo

1 Introduction

In 2019, the Nigerian government adopted a National Security Strategy. This is only the third time that Nigeria was producing and adopting a national security strategy.[1] The rationale for a strategy rested on the recognition of myriad national, regional and international challenges, which the authors acknowledge, called for a robust, dynamic and proactive national security framework and infrastructure capable of dealing time.[2] The author further acknowledges that notions of security have shifted from contemporary ideas of state-centric security to a comprehensive focus on human security.

[1] The first national security strategy was the grand national security strategy 2000 by President Obasanjo in reaction to the Niger Delta crisis while the President Goodluck administration adopted a Nigeria security strategy in 2014.

[2] See the preface to the Strategy.

M. O. Ojielo (✉)
United Nations System, Bishkek, Kyrgyz Republic
e-mail: ozonnia.ojielo@un.org

E. Duruigbo et al. (eds.), *International Law and Development in the Global South*, https://doi.org/10.1007/978-3-031-13741-9_18

As I write this paper, at least 30 out of the 36 states in Nigeria are under national peacekeeping operations. In the Northeast of the country, Boko Haram and the Islamic State in West Africa continue to attack communities and infrastructure. The best efforts of the Nigerian security forces have prevented them from holding territory. However, their ability to attack at will in any part of that region has not diminished. In the Northwest of the country, armed bands of bandits and kidnappers are roaming the region carrying away hundreds of school children in the forests and holding them for ransom. In the first six months of June 2021, there were 1405 security incidents, resulting in 12,743 deaths and 830 kidnap incidents in the region.[3] In the Northcentral and Southeast regions, bands of herders, most of them well armed are engaged in violent confrontations with communities.

In the Southwest region, the state governments came together to establish a regional security architecture known as Amoetekun, recruiting and deploying hundreds of young men to communities across the region.

The South-South region had been on the boil since the commencement of the 4th Republic in 1999. Efforts made by previous governments to grant amnesty to the militants in the region, and to reskill some of them so that they can engage in productive economic activities were largely successful. However, as with conflict causation processes, the opportunity and feasibility offered by widespread violence and insecurity in other parts of the country resulting in the thin presence of the security agencies across the country created openings for the escalation of maritime piracy in Nigeria. The Gulf of Guinea is now noted as the most dangerous maritime highway in the world.[4]

The development of a National Security Policy and Strategy are therefore important responses to these developments and to the worsening security situation in the country. Both documents should represent not only the philosophy and principles behind the national approach to

[3] Eons Intelligence, "Analysis of Nigeria Insecurity Challenges: From June 2011 to June 2021". Lagos, June 2021. The Government of Zamfara state had in 2019 set up a committee for ending banditry and armed violence perpetrated by herders and other armed groups. The committee reported that between June 2011 and May 2019, at least 6,319 people had been killed in the state, 3,672 kidnapped, and 3,587 houses burnt. See *New Telegraph Newspaper*, 12 October 2019.

[4] Nigeria National Security Strategy 2019. See also Peacebuilding Commission, "Ambassadorial-Level Meeting of the Peacebuilding Commission: Piracy in the Gulf of Guinea". New York: June 2021.

security but also the operational pathway out of the situation, which should then serve as a complement to and be read together with the national approach to politics, peace and socio-economic transformation for sustainable development to be realized in the country.

The present writer searched long and hard to locate the policy framework underpinning the new national security strategy. Apparently, Nigeria has not developed a national security policy in more than 50 years or ever. A policy represents the principles that guide present and future decision-making. It is a strategic effort to translate an institutional or national ambition on a particular issue by defining the goals or results sought to be achieved and the ways that build synergy, complementarity and linkages so as to attain the desired results. In a sense, a policy sets the direction of travel. A strategy is a pathway that leads to the end results, by identifying specific actions and activities the totality of which can lead to those results. A strategy is assessed at the output level through the specific activities sought to be implemented while a policy is assessed at the outcome level through the results that are achieved by a combination of all the activities. In the absence of a national security policy, it is not clear what the broader goals are nor when a determination could be made that the implementation of the strategy has resulted in the realization of the policy objectives. It is therefore doubtful how the results from the implementation of the strategy should be assessed.

Part of the challenges posed by the absence or lack of a national security policy is that the national security strategy was drafted as separate but complementary to the National Counter Terrorism Strategy; the Cybersecurity Policy and Strategy; the National Defence Policy, and the Economic Recovery and Growth Plan among others. Nigeria's national security relies on sectorial strategies which were developed as responses to different threats to Nigeria's national interests and therefore are reactive in conception and implementation.[5] All of these strategies and policies should be part and parcel of a national security policy. A national security policy would have elaborated how all these policies and strategies cohere and the nature of the interface that should exist among them. The national security strategy would then become the operational benchmark for the coherent implementation of all the policies and strategies, rather than being read or presented as a separate but complementary initiative to

[5] Saleh Bala and Emile Ouedrago "National Security Strategy Development—Nigeria Case Study" Working Paper (unpublished) July 2018.

these others as is the present case. Given this absence or lack of a national security policy, the national security strategy in some sections reads more like a policy document, and in other sections reads like a wish list. More importantly, with the national security strategy being presented as a separate initiative from the others, it is probable to expect confusion, overlap or clashes over mandates and responsibilities of the various institutions, leading to gaps or delays in implementation or in response to threats until the overlaps are clarified.[6]

1.1 Human Security

The national security strategy made reference to being based on a human security framework. Apart from this reference, there is nowhere in the document where the concept of human security in the Nigerian context was explored or explained, and how the combination of different policies and strategies would lead to the attainment of human security in Nigeria. More importantly, the document does not contain any reference or mechanism to how the combination of efforts in these multiple approaches would be assessed to come to a conclusion that human security in Nigeria would have been realized. What is left therefore are provisions that refer to aspects of human security. Unfortunately, the connections are missing. In the end, the provisions on human security come across as aspirations.

Human security is the paradigm for understanding and responding to vulnerabilities by shifting the frames of reference from traditional notions of security through military security to a focus on the human being as the unit of analysis. Human security has been referred to as human right, referring to the security of people and communities as distinct from the security of states. It includes several dimensions related to feeling safe such as freedom from fear, freedom from want and freedom to live in dignity.[7]

In its groundbreaking 1994 Human Development Report[8], the United Nations Development Programme (UNDP) argued that the

[6] Different experts at the 2nd Umaru Shinkafi Intelligence and Security Summit 2021, "The Socio-Economic Implications of Kidnapping and Banditry in Nigeria" lamented the competition, overlapping mandates and working at cross purposes that still hallmark the work of the police, the security and the intelligence agencies in the country.

[7] GPPAC, "Human Security" accessed at https:www.gppac.net on 28th May 2021.

[8] United Nations Development Programme, *Human Development Report*. New York: 1994.

world can never be at peace unless people have security in their lives. It further predicted that future conflicts would be more intra-state and often triggered by socio-economic disparities among other deprivations. It argued that the search for security must therefore lie in development, not in arms. With several nations experiencing different types of fragility and disintegration, due to a myriad of sources: ethnic, religious and political, the underlying drivers have often been traced to inequality and a sense of relative deprivation evidenced by limited participation of people in any such progress.

In elaborating a new concept of human security, the report argued that it was time to move away from the notion of security shaped by the potential for conflict between states to a feeling of insecurity that arises more from worries about daily life than from the dread of a cataclysmic world event. Job security, income security, health security, environmental security, security from crime, have become the emerging concerns of human security all over the world. It redefined security to mean safety from the constant threats of hunger, disease, crime and repression. It also means protection from sudden and hurtful disruptions in the pattern of daily lives-whether in the homes, jobs, in communities or in the environment.

In his seminal report, "In Larger Freedom, Towards Development, Security and Human Rights for All"[9], then UN Secretary General Kofi Annan enunciated the principles which have since given rise to the new paradigm of human security. He argued that, "we will not enjoy development without security, we will not enjoy security without development, and we will not enjoy either without respect for human rights".[10] Human security therefore refers to the human condition in all its dimensions, as opposed to state-centric notions of safety and stability.

Twenty-seven years after the elaboration of the concept of human security, every development indicator and report (MDG reports, SDG reports, peace and social cohesion indexes, African Governance Reports, African Peer Review Mechanism Reports, Report of the High-Level Panel on Post-2015 development, etc.) identified conflict and violence as the major threats to the achievement of human security. In response, the High-Level Panel on Post-2015 went ahead to propose Goal 16: the

[9] United Nations, "In Larger Freedom: Towards Development, Security and Human Rights for All, A/59/2005: Report of the UN Secretary General". Five-year progress report on the implementation of the MDGs. New York: 2005.

[10] See paragraph 17.

attainment of "peaceful societies" as one of the sustainable development goals (SDGs).[11] Annual reports of the Geneva Declaration on Armed Violence and Development[12] consistently highlight the massive amounts of money and other development costs lost by countries that have experienced conflict and violence. The annual Global Peace Indexes of the Institute of Economics and Peace demonstrate the economic costs of war and showed that one US dollar spent in conflict prevention and peacebuilding saves several hundred dollars more spent on peacekeeping, peace enforcement and the rebuilding of destroyed infrastructure.[13]

Across Nigeria, a major narrative in political and social discourses is of inequality and relative deprivation of ethnic and other groups. While these narratives may be perceptual, they detract the government's attention from the over-arching developmental challenges the country faces.

It will be important then to interrogate how the National Security Strategy proposes to achieve freedom from fear, freedom from want and freedom to live in dignity for Nigerians. We will now summarize the key components of the strategy and apply the human security framework to the contents of the strategy.

1.2 Elements of the National Security Strategy

The strategy is composed of eight chapters, apart from the forward and the preface. In Chapter 1, "National Values, Interests and Objectives", the strategy refers to certain values which undergird the Nigerian way of life and the pursuit of collective prosperity and progress. These include

[11] United Nations, "A Global Partnership: Eradicate Poverty and Transform Economies through Sustainable Development. Report of the High-Level Panel of Eminent Persons on the Post 2015 Development Agenda". New York, 2013:9.

[12] Geneva Declaration Secretariat, *Global Burden of Armed Violence 2015: Every Body Counts*. Cambridge, Cambridge University Press: 2015. See also Luigi De Martino, "Reducing Armed Violence: Enabling Development". Research Note No 19. Armed Violence, Small Arms Survey and Geneva declaration Secretariat, 2012; and Robert Muggah, *Armed Violence in Africa: Reflections on the Costs of Crime and Conflict*. Geneva, UNDP: 2008.

[13] Institute of Economics and Peace, *Economic Value of Peace 2021: Measuring the Global Economic Impact of Violence and Conflict*. Sydney January 2021: 4. This IEP publication used a comprehensive methodology that includes 18 indicators to cover the direct and indirect costs of violence and the expenditures to contain and prevent violence.

freedom, equality and justice, the sanctity of human life and enhancement of human dignity. Peace, security and prosperity in the country is acknowledged as resting upon the foundations of democracy, rule of law, free enterprise, respect for human rights including women and minority rights, and the need to create an enabling environment for the full expression of the potentials of the people in the form of political inclusion, economic empowerment, social integration, equal opportunity and access to justice.

On national objectives, the document cites the need to protect Nigerian people and territory, economic interests and way of life through deploying the full spectrum of national power to ensure a safe and secure nation. On promoting Nigeria's prosperity and sustainable development, the strategy states that the objective is a broad-based prosperity that leaves no one behind while providing social security investments that protect the poor, vulnerable and unemployed to ensure a just and equitable distribution of wealth.

The national objective to promote national unity and peaceful co-existence recognized that the ethnic, linguistic, religious and cultural diversity are sources of national strength which would be harnessed as cardinal requirements of national security and to reinforce social cohesion.

The strategy is silent on how the national values will be promoted and sustained and accountability for their assimilation. Values define a society. They define the rules of governance and politics. They are not just mere statements of aspiration. They are the foundation on which societal coexistence is anchored. Given the evolution of politics in Nigeria over the last couple of decades, it is unfortunate that this most important section of the strategy received the least treatment.

Chapter 2 contains an overview of Nigeria's geostrategic environment, beginning with an assessment of the domestic situation. The strategy sees Nigeria's 250 ethnic groups and the three predominant religions (Christianity, Islam and traditional worship) as platforms of competition expressed through divisive ethnic loyalties, religious intolerance, violent extremism and political acrimony which impede development. The response should be to forge bonds beyond ethnicity and religion through strength in the national diversity. The strategy also sees possibilities from the current under utilization of the national demographic of 201 million citizens out of which 55.9% are within the age bracket of 15–64.

From the external environment, the strategy identifies the shrinking of Lake Chad in the Northeast region as a threat which contributes to a scramble for the diminishing water and other resources. This threat is accentuated by challenges of climate change which is creating environmental and related agitations that have enabled the spread of the activities of Boko Haram and the Islamic State in West Africa Province. From the coastline, the Gulf of Guinea is a major threat area, associated with different economic infrastructure and activities including ports, coastal infrastructure, shipping, fishing, sea-borne trade, offshore energy assets, undersea pipelines and cables among others.

Chapter 3 of the strategy is an in-depth review of the national security threats. There are multifaceted threats blurring the distinctions between internal and external risk factors. The chapter discusses the following security threats: terrorism and violent extremism, armed banditry, kidnapping, militancy and separatist agitations, pastoralists-farmers conflicts, transnational organized crime, piracy and sea robbery, porous borders, cybercrimes, technological challenges; socio-political threats, fake news and hate speech; environmental threats, public health challenges; economic challenges, regional and global security challenges, and their various impacts and consequences. On armed banditry and kidnapping, the strategy infers that trend analysis suggests a correlation between armed banditry, militias groups, kidnapping and cattle rustling showing a convergence of illegal networks. Militancy and separatist agitations cover the Niger Delta, the South East and South West and therefore represent significant threats to national stability. Climate change, population explosion and growth of new settlements are impacting and accelerating the quest for land, grazing routes, water and other resources thereby exacerbating pastoralists and farmers conflicts. The situation is compounded by other threats, including organized crime, piracy and sea robbery, porous borders which are inadequately manned, cybercrimes and technology challenges.

The chapter also discussed socio-political threats, noting that political stability and social cohesion are foundational for sustainable, socio-economic growth and stability. The chapter highlighted political intolerance, electoral malpractices, fake news, hate speech and violence as threats to constitutional order and social cohesion. It further referenced Nigeria's youth demographic as both a threat and an opportunity to stability. Noting that the youth population is severely impacted by poverty, inadequate health and education services. Environmental threat, public health and economic challenges were also examined, including energy deficits, crude oil-related crimes, unemployment and poverty, regional and global economic and security challenges. While the chapter acknowledged some regional security challenges, it was completely silent on regional economic issues which could impact Nigeria. It failed to note the fact of the increasing migration of Nigerians to countries in the subregion as economic migrants, and Nigeria's dominance of trade between countries in the subregion, which dominance is attracting resentment and regular protests against Nigerian traders in their host countries, and of legislation and restrictions by countries in the region, in spite of ECOWAS protocols, to restrict the involvement of Nigerians in their local economies.

The challenge with broad sweeps of analysis as is contained in this chapter is that they lack the specificity and peculiarities of context that enable a reviewer to situate the national security strategy and its appropriateness. The situation described in the chapter could apply to any other African country with a coastline and an oil economy. Perhaps in the desire to keep the document short and readable, quality has been sacrificed for brevity.

1.3 The National Security Response

Chapter 4 of the National Security Strategy could be understood as providing the overarching framework for the response approaches examined in the subsequent chapters of the strategy document, as well as articulating the security response. It comes across as being embedded in a prevention conceptual framework, even though the issues discussed in the chapter do not seem to fully articulate or explain how the prevention architecture is conceived or will be enabled. The rest of this paper will therefore be devoted to analysing Chapter 4 and other subsequent chapters which discuss the various response approaches to respective threats contained in the strategy document.

Chapter 4, focusing on security threats, begins by highlighting the dominant themes in the national security threat analysis, as a result of which the strategy has focused on "all categories of security threats". However, the chapter lists the threats as terrorism and violent extremism, armed banditry, kidnapping and militancy, cybercrimes, transnational organized crime, insecurity in other domains, potential threats from chemical, biological, radiological, nuclear and explosive (CBRNE) agents and national disasters.

Promoting Crisis Response and Resilience: To promote crisis response and resilience therefore, the main organs of response will be the National Security Council, the National Defence Council and the National Emergency Management Agency which deals with both security and national disasters. It needs to be noted that crisis could be man-made and/or natural. Man-made crisis could be social, political, economic or environmental. This section should have started with a broader definition of crisis and crisis response, which would provide the foundation for examining the interconnectedness between the various response approaches and how they are designed to complement each other. The use of the word "resilience" in this part of the document can only be understood to mean that whatever the threat level, the expectation is that the range of actions taken by the state and the various institutions should result in outcomes that don't do harm or cause further harm, minimize the impact on the public and restore the situation to a much better level than was previously the case. Such an expectation cannot be guaranteed only by hard security operations.

To define a strategy of crisis response and resilience by providing for combat or hard security operations from the get-go misses the opportunities inherent in preventive possibilities and planning for them even where it seems that military action is inevitable. To therefore have security-related agencies as the main foci for dealing with all types of crisis is an acknowledgement of a physical security-driven approach to crisis resolution.

It is important to restate that security agencies should be the last options of response in any crisis situation. The only exception is where violence may be imminent. In such a situation a preventive security deployment may be appropriate. But once the violence is prevented, averted or contained, the security institutions should take the backseat and prominence given to civic institutions and other groups with capacity and mandate to engage in mediatory processes to enable amicable resolution of the issues in conflict. A security approach is not appropriate for issues that have social, political, economic or environmental origins and dimensions. In such contexts, a national institution with responsibility for reconciling and mediating differences among conflicting parties is the most appropriate response mechanism. Such institution is complemented by various civic, religious and traditional institutions which play similar roles. It is unfortunate that the National Security Strategy did not contemplate the creation/transformation of such an institution or the complementary roles various groups of actors in the civic sphere can play in the implementation of the strategy as part of the national crisis response architecture.

What we are left within this section of the strategy document is the instrumentalization of the security and intelligence agencies, as the main institutions of response, early warning, intelligence gathering and response. It is further not surprising that the strategy then takes an ad hocish approach to crisis response through the proposal for case-specific strategic level crisis management teams, based on unified command, control, intelligence, communication and coordination structures, which represents a classic military and security approach. A national security strategy focused on prevention, as the strategy document suggests is the preferred approach, begins with an identification of the resilience and preventive capacities, and details how they will be enabled, promoted and sustained to engage in early analysis, early warning and anticipatory actions in response, to prevent the occurrence of the perceived threat. The approach cannot be reactive to cases as they occur, which is what is suggested in the strategy document.

Internal Security: The goal of internal security in the strategy document is to create a safe and secure environment for the pursuit of peace, personal well-being, prosperity and development. It defined internal security as a "complex multi-sectorial national endeavour which calls for concerted, proportionate, open, flexible and effective application of political, economic, social, informational, diplomatic, intelligence, law enforcement and military response where they become inevitable". Internal security is to be promoted by an enabling political environment hinged on good governance, rule of law, human rights and both credible and peaceful political transitions. When there is a disjunct in their application, insecurity, violence and resistance are inevitable. According to the EONS Intelligence Timeless Insight, "Analysis of Nigeria Insecurity Challenges", from June 2011 to June 2021 reported deaths due to insecurity amounted to 77,850 persons[14] with a preponderance of the deaths occurring in the three northern zones of Northwest, Northeast and Northcentral. From January to June 2021, there were a total of 2943 kidnapped

[14] EONS Intelligence Timeless Insight, "Analysis of Nigeria Insecurity Challenges from June 2011 to June 2021", Lagos, Nigeria, July 2021.

from 4069 attacks from a combination of Boko Haram, Kidnapping, robbery, bombs, guns, machetes and suicide bombing incidents.[15]

It is therefore not surprising that Nigeria ranks 146 out of 163 countries in the 2021 Global Peace Index[16], which measures peacefulness across three domains: safety and security, ongoing conflict and militarization. While the Index noted the decline in the number of deaths since 2015, it highlighted that the total number of conflicts has continued to rise including state-based violence, non-state violence and one-sided violence. The average intensity of internal conflict also continued to rise.[17] The strategy document asserted that internal security in Nigeria will be measured by improved public perception of security, public confidence and trust in the security agencies particularly the Nigeria Police Force, drastic reduction in the incidence of crime and all forms of insecurity. In the 2020 Ibrahim Index of African Governance, Nigeria was ranked 34th out of 54 African countries with a score of 45 out of a maximum of 100 on overall governance.[18] More importantly, Nigeria's ranking showed "increasing deterioration" in three out of the four major categories of measurement.[19] The goal of internal security as envisaged in the National Security Strategy still remains an aspiration with no clear path towards its realization.

1.4 Promote Nigeria's Prosperity and Sustainable Development

Chapter 5 of the National Security Strategy captures the elements of the economic response, noting the need to harness the economic opportunities arising from the human and natural resource endowments of the country and investing in human development as part of the overall agenda of national security. The strategy document notes that "the overall national security agenda including sustainable development, prosperity and external influence is dependent on a viable and prosperous economy"

[15] ibid.

[16] Institute of Economics and Peace, *Global Peace Index 2021: Measuring Peace in a Complex World*, Sydney, June 2021.

[17] ibid.

[18] Mo Ibrahim Foundation; *2020 Ibrahim Index of African Governance-Index Report*. London, 2021: 21.

[19] The categories assessed in the Index are security and rule of law; participation, rights, inclusion and gender; foundations for economic opportunity, and human development.

and that the strategy would integrate the economic potential and opportunities with other components of national security for the prosperity of the people.

It is important to quote the political and economic analysis of Nigeria by the Economist Intelligence Unit in full so as to appreciate the gravity of the situation, and how far off the mark the aspirations in the National Security Strategy have become:

> The Economist Intelligence Unit expects the president, Muhammadu Buhari, to remain in power until his second (and final) term expires in 2023, but the security situation in many parts of Nigeria is in a state of continuous deterioration. The president will be under immense pressure to stabilize Nigeria, but myriad security threats will prove unmanageable, with the military and police overstretched and unable to tackle simultaneous security crises. Emergencies will be triaged, with military resources deployed to whichever is considered the most pressing. There will be unceasing conflict in the north-east, particularly in Borno state, between the military and two Islamist terrorist groups, Boko Haram and the Islamic State of West Africa Province, which will consolidate forces to some extent after the death of Boko Haram's leader in mid-2021. The government will be unable to regain full dominion over the north-east, and more recently Boko Haram has expanded into central Nigeria, not far from the capital, Abuja. Although central Nigeria—an agricultural heartland—has for several years been affected by violent conflict between farmers and herdsmen over land and water resources, it is newer territory for Boko Haram. Our belief is that Nigeria's federal government will nonetheless be able to assert control over "core" regions, such as Abuja, and other areas of economic or political importance, at the expense of "periphery" regions that have been mired in conflict for many years. This system is resilient enough to keep the government in power but will leave many parts of Nigeria highly dysfunctional. Security challenges will be pronounced in numerous areas of the country, with unrest in the south-east attributed to Biafran secessionist groups and a broader surge in kidnappings by organized criminal networks. Banditry and violent crime will remain pervasive, and other areas of Nigeria could begin to resemble the north-east as, in essence, "no-go" zones. Neglect of the periphery could eventually reach an implosion-point for overall stability, but we do not expect this within the 2021-25 forecast period. The near- to medium-term outlook is made more uncertain by the scars of recession in 2020 and by rising unemployment (at about 33%—one of the highest levels in the world) and poverty. Declining living standards arguably prolonged protests over police brutality that broke out

in cities across southern Nigeria in October 2020. The risk of fresh bouts of protest will be elevated in the near term by a ban on Twitter, a social media platform, which was enforced in June and can be viewed as an attempt by the government to gag public opinion at a time of mounting censure over governance failings, notably deepening instability. The risk of internet regulation being a precursor to wider authoritarianism is low—the state is too frail to depart extensively from the democratic social contract. As a restoration of petrol and electricity subsidies in 2021 (temporarily reduced in 2020) has demonstrated, the Buhari administration is inclined towards concession making, and is expected to capitulate on any issue that leads to major protests.[20]

1.5 Promote National Unity and Peaceful Co-Existence

Chapter 6 of the strategy noted the importance of effective management of Nigeria's diversity in order to achieve peace, security and development. It defined the objective of political security to include aggregating and unifying the aspirations of individuals and groups in the federation through reasonable distribution of power as well as wholesome generation and equitable distribution of resources. It pledged that deliberate measures would be taken to overcome the challenges of managing diversity through such measures as promoting unity and national cohesion by fostering a culture of civility and inclusive public discourse, promoting non-discrimination among all Nigerians irrespective of gender, religion or ethnic origin, engaging sectional and factional groups in constructive dialogue to address agitations, and continuing to adhere to the constitutionalized principle of federal character by ensuring that appointments into public service institutions fairly reflect the linguistic, ethnic, religious and geographic diversity of the country, among other objectives.

If anyone needed an assessment of how well the National Security Strategy has been responding to the challenges of the Nigerian context, the answer was provided by the House of Representatives when it convened a National Security Summit in June 2021. In his opening statement at the Summit, the Speaker Hon. Femi Gbajabiamila stated as follows, " at this time of our national history, when insecurity threatens the authority of the state and the foundations of our nationhood with the activities of insurgents, bandits, and criminals of every stripe impede

[20] Economist Intelligence Unit, "Country Report, Nigeria," London: 20 July 2021.

our efforts at progress and prosperity we must confront the realisation that our previous and current approaches to addressing the challenges of insecurity have not yielded desired result".[21]

2 Conclusion

There is undeniable logic in wanting to anchor the Nigeria National Security Strategy on a framework of human security. The Nigeria National Security Strategy has made a tepid effort in that regard. The conference convened by the House of Representatives presents additional complements for a review and strengthening of the strategy. Most importantly, security provisioning cannot be instrumentalized as an end in itself. It is part of the process of governing. If other governing mechanisms and processes are inadequate as reflected in the Ibrahim Index of African Governance, then the best-written security strategies are bound to fail. Herein lies the lesson for Nigeria's policymakers.

[21] Femi Gbajabiamila, "Welcome Speech" National Security Summit Report. Full Report of the Special Summit on National Security, Abuja June 2021.

CHAPTER 19

The American Judiciary and Judicial Institutions on Trial

Ifeanyi Innocent Onwuazombe

1 Introduction

The American Judiciary and judicial institutions are currently on trial. Following the change in administration on January 20, 2021, will the American judiciary and judicial institution, with its well-developed structures, and rich precedent be able to redress, and sanction the crimes, monumental wrongs, misdeeds, misconduct of the past five years? These include interference in criminal investigation and criminal cases, suppression of criminal investigation using key Department of Justice (DOJ) personnel, police brutality, politicization of judicial appointment and the courts, voter suppression legislations, Capitol Hill insurrection, politicization and brazen weaponization of the Department of Justice, etc. Can the Judiciary recover from the wreckage of the past five years, be truly independent, and uphold justice without partisan flavor, respect the Constitution and the rule of law? Only time will tell the appropriateness

---

I. I. Onwuazombe (✉)
Golden Gate University School of Law, San Francisco, CA, USA
e-mail: onwuazombelaw@yahoo.com

E. Duruigbo et al. (eds.), *International Law and Development in the Global South*, https://doi.org/10.1007/978-3-031-13741-9_19

or otherwise of the United States approach to these issues and response to the nagging questions.

The United States of America has an enviable reputation and is recognized and adored as the leader of the free world. In almost all the fields of human endeavors, be it science, medicine, agriculture, technology, intellectual property, law/judiciary, human rights, corporate governance, human resources, engineering, environmental protection, etc., American standards and procedures are revered and viewed as the benchmark, being copied by nations across the globe. But recent shameful events and embarrassing developments in the country diminish the stature of the country and put to question its moral authority as the conscience and police of the world.

America as widely acclaimed is a nation of laws. The Constitution of the United States is the oldest active codified constitution. "Written in 1787, ratified in 1788, and has been in operation since 1789, the United States Constitution is the world's longest surviving written charter of government."[1] The United States enjoys a representative form of government, shaped by three separate coequal branches, the Legislature, Executive, and Judiciary, as established by the Constitution. A system of checks and balances, which the Constitution also set forth, limits the powers of each branch. Executive lawlessness experienced in the most recent past bulldozed the walls separating the three tiers of government and rendered the principles of checks and balances almost impotent.

1.1 Champion of the Global Crusade for the Spread of Democracy and Democratic Governance:

The United States has been in the forefront of the crusade for global spread of the ideals of democracy and democratic governance. "Democracy promotion has been a key aspect of U.S. identity and foreign policy, though Washington also has a long history of supporting non-democratic forms of governance; it has both consolidated democratic regimes and intervened to overthrow democratically elected governments."[2]The United States annually invests huge amounts of money

[1] United States Senate, "Constitution Day," available at https://www.senate.gov.

[2] David Ryan and Liam O'Brien, "Democracy Promotion and US Foreign Policy," Oxford Research Encyclopedias, https://oxfordre.com/politics/politcs/view/10.1093//acrefore/9780190228637.001.0001/acrefore-9780190228637-e-361.

and human resources toward the promotion and fostering of democratic governance abroad through targeted foreign aid and assistance. Given its self-characterization as a shining "city on a hill," democracy promotion is one of the component parts of U.S foreign policy.

The global promotion of democracy has emerged, according to the Bush administration, as the defining mission of contemporary American foreign policy.[3] Speaking in lofty and eloquent tones in his second Inaugural Address, President George W. Bush insisted that it would henceforth be "the policy of the United States to seek and support the growth of democratic movements and institutions in every nation and culture, with the ultimate goal of ending tyranny in the world."[4] Insisting that, "America's vital interests and deepest beliefs are now one," the president claims that the expansion of freedom is the imperative of America's security, indispensable to the survival of liberty at home and the achievement of world peace.[5] This position has fairly been consistent over time.

1.2 Leader of the Fight for Human Rights Promotion, Protection, and Enforcement:

Similarly, the United States has been in the forefront of the crusade and often time champions the promotion, protection, and enforcement of human rights across the globe. America is very vocal on issues concerning abuses and violation of rights to life, freedom of expression, freedom of religion, peaceful assembly, health, equal protection of the law, dignity of the human person, development, source of livelihood, freedom from discrimination on the basis of race, nationality, gender, etc. Also associated with fundamental rights are economic, social, and political rights which the nation is known to have fought to promote and protect through their national policies and actions. Ironically, some of these rights the United States has spearheaded the crusade to protect and promote at the global level, are denied many American citizens in their own country.

[3] David C. Hendrickson and Robert W. Tucker, "Mini Teaser: Promoting Democracy is Not only Alien to American Diplomatic Tradition, it could Jeopardize Our National Security," The Freedom Crusade, September 1, 2005, available at www.nationalinterest.org

[4] *Id.*

[5] *Id.*

1.3 Voter Suppression:

The Civil Rights Movement, a struggle for social justice and equality for African Americans that took place in the 1950s and 1960s led to legislation during Reconstruction that sought changes for equality and the right to vote. The 14th Amendment to the Constitution in 1868 gave Black people equal protection under the law while in 1870, the 15th Amendment granted Black American men the right to vote. "Although the Civil Rights Act of 1957 granted all Americans the right to vote many southern states made it difficult for Blacks citizens. They often require prospective voters of color to take literacy tests that were confusing, misleading and nearly impossible to pass."[6] Other similar legislation include the Civil Rights Act of 1964 and the Voting Rights Act of 1965. "Jim Crow" laws beginning in the late nineteenth century introduced segregation of Blacks in public facilities, schools, restaurants, trains, buses, etc.

In a landmark decision of the U.S. Supreme Court regarding the constitutionality of two provisions of the Voting Rights Act of 1965: Section 5, requiring certain states and local governments with a history of discrimination to submit any proposed changes in voting procedures to the U.S. Department of Justice or a federal district court in D.C.—before it goes into effect—to ensure the change would not harm minority voters thus requiring a federal preclearance to be obtained before implementing any changes to their voting laws or practices; and Section 4(b), which contains the coverage formula that determines which jurisdictions are subject to preclearance based on their histories of discrimination in voting. The United States Supreme Court in a 5–4 vote, struck down the formula at the heart of the Voting Right Act in 2013. According to the apex Court:

> The coverage formula in Section 4(b) of the Voting Rights Act—which determines which jurisdictions are covered by Section 5—is unconstitutional because it is based on an old formula. As a practical matter this means that Section 5 is inoperable until Congress enacts a new coverage formula, which the decision invited Congress to do.[7]

[6] Civil Rights Movement, www.history.com.

[7] Shelby County vs. Holder 570 U.S. 529 (2013); 133 S. Ct. 2612; 186 L Ed 2nd 651. See also Brennan Center for Justice, www.brennancenter.org.

The power of the Voting Right Act was in the design that the Supreme Court gutted—the court struck down a formula at the heart of Voting Rights Act—henceforth, voters who are discriminated against bear the burden of proving they are disenfranchised.[8] As a matter of fact, this ruling actually opened the flood-gate for anti-democratic and voter suppression bills especially in the south as witnessed after the 2020 presidential election.

Soon after the decision, republican lawmakers in Texas and North Carolina earlier covered by the law, moved to enact new voter ID laws and other restrictions. A federal court later struck down the North Carolina law on the grounds that it was designed to target African Americans "with almost surgical precision,"[9] but Republicans are still pushing a new voter ID law. Starting in 2014, Alabama and Mississippi enforced a law requiring photo ID. Following the decision in Shelby, Texas Republicans resurrected SB 14—a strict voter ID bill that required that voters show one of a handful of government-issued IDs to vote. Prior to Shelby's decision, the justice department refused to approve the law, but after the decision, Texas announced the law would "immediately" be in effect. Years later, the law was found to be discriminatory against Black and Latinx communities, and struck down again. But eventually, lawmakers created a new version of the bill, SB 5, with minor adjustments, which passed in 2017.[10]

Voter ID laws have long been found to disenfranchise people of color and marginalized, who are less likely to have the kinds of ID states require to vote. Justice Ruth B. Ginsburg in her dissenting opinion for the court in Shelby's case noted that, "throwing out pre-clearance when it has worked and is continuing to work to stop discriminatory changes is like throwing away your umbrella in a rainstorm because you are not getting wet."

According to the Brennan Center for Justice, "ten states are considering new voter ID requirements, including six states that do not currently require voters to present ID at the polls. Two states, Mississippi and New Hampshire are considering placing new limits on the kind

[8] Sam Levine and Ankita Rao, The Guardian, June 25, 2021, available at theguardian.org. See also, Brennan For Justice.

[9] *Id.*

[10] *Id.*

of ID that can be used." There are currently 106 pending bills across 28 states that would restrict access to voting, according to data. Brennan's Center found that[11]:

1) More than a third of the bills would place new restrictions on voting by mail;
2) Pennsylvania has 14 pending proposals for new voter restrictions, the most in the country. It's followed by New Hampshire (11), Missouri (9), and Mississippi, New Jersey, and Texas (8);
3) There are seven bills across four states that would limit opportunities for election day registration;
4) There are also 406 bills that would expand voting access pending across 35 states, including in New York, (56), Texas (53), New Jersey (37), Mississippi (39), and Missouri (21).

Also, there are reports that "in 43 states across the country, Republican lawmakers have proposed 253 new laws that would limit mail, early in-person and election day voting with such constraints as stricter ID requirements, limited hours or narrower eligibility to vote absentee."[12] If all these proposed bills are passed into law, it is feared that this could result in a historic contraction of voting rights like we have not seen in recent memory. Republicans across the country responded to record voter turnout in more than a century by unleashing a flurry of legislation aimed at restricting ballot access citing concerns over unfounded allegations of rampant voter fraud that they themselves stoked for months.

Georgia is the ground zero or epicenter of voter suppression legislation, and the leading edge to enact new state laws aimed directly at the suppression and or disenfranchisement of minority voters. Efforts to roll back voting rights targeted to undermine Black voters in the state include

[11] Brennan Center for Justice, www.brennacenter.org, Sam Levine, "Republicans Considering more than 100 Bills to Restrict Voting Rights," The Guardian, Thursday January 28, 2021, https://amp.theguardian.com.

[12] Amy Gardner, Kate Rabinowitz, and Harry Stevens, "At least 250 New Laws have been Proposed in 43 States to Limit Mail, Early In-Person and Election Day Voting, March 11, 2021, Washington Post, March 11, 2021. See also, Igor Derysh/Salon," 253 Bill in 43 States: How Republicans are Using Trump's "Big Lie" to Enact a Tidal Wave of Voter Suppression, February 28, 2021, https://www.alternet.org,

bill #SB 241. This bill supports new voting restrictions for the state with provisions:

> To end no-excuse absentee voting, limits absentee voting to people 65 and older, those with physical disability and those out of town on election day, require more ID from absentee voters, and have their ballot signed by a witness for the vote to count, and constrain the use of ballot drop boxes. The bill would also mean a court order would need to go into effect to extend voting hours and it gives the state legislature the powers to block emergency voting changes. Earlier in March 2021, Georgia House of Representative passed bill #HB 531 which could reduce weekend voting hours and would include the same ID requirements.[13]

Pre-election voting on Sunday is also under attack because that is disproportionately used by African Americans. Church congregations organize parishioners to travel by bus to voting booths after services. If this bill with other racist anti-democratic bills become law, that will roll back and restrict voting access for Georgia voters. Washington Post called the measures "the most sweeping contraction of ballot access in the United States since the end of Reconstruction."[14] It is unthinkable that America is spearheading the crusade for spreading the ideals of democracy and protection of minority's economic, social and political rights across the world while within, in the states of Georgia, New Hampshire, Pennsylvania, Mississippi, Missouri, New Jersey, and Texas, minority voting rights is brazenly under severe attack, constricted and restricted through laws, policies, and other state measures. Where lies the U.S. moral authority to call-out, or lecture China on grave human rights violation against the minority Muslims and suppression of political rights in Hong Kong, Tibet or chastise Russia, Syria, Saudi Arabia, Cuba, Myanmar, Cuba or North Korea, etc., for police brutality and violation of the rights of its citizens?

It is equally worthy of note that Oregon lawmakers are considering a bill that would allow convicted felons to vote while they are in prison. If passed and adopted, Oregon would join Maine and Vermont as the only two states in the country and the District of Columbia that allow

[13] Keydra Manns, "Georgia Senate Passed Sweeping Voter Restriction Bill Following Democratic Election Wins," March 9, 2021, thegrio, https://news.yahoo.com.

[14] Amy, Kate & Harry, *supra* note 12.

this. "Lebron James, Michael Jordan helped join Michael Bloomberg's $27 million effort to help clear fines and fees for about 40,000 in the state/Florida so that they can vote in the 2020 presidential election."[15] This is a welcome development though the state of Florida unfortunately tried to put some obstacles to frustrate this noble and democratic gesture.

1.4 *Proof of Citizenship:*

A controversial restriction was implemented by Arizona Republicans in 2013—a new system requiring residents to show proof of U.S. citizenship in local and state elections. However, the Supreme Court had earlier in that year held that Arizona previously covered by the Voting Rights Act, could not require proof of citizenship to vote in federal elections. But Arizona attorney general and secretary of state said that they could still require it for state and local elections. Alabama and Georgia have citizenship proof laws passed before the Shelby County decision, but neither state is currently implementing the law. "A Kansas law requiring proof of citizenship to register to vote, estimated to have affected 30,000 people was blocked by the federal courts. In 2020, Texas attempted to question the citizenship status of 100, 000 registered voters, before admitting its claim was based on false data."[16]

1.5 *Closure of Polling Centres:*

According to a report from the Leadership Conference on Civil and Human Rights, there were 1,688 polling place closures between 2012 and 2018, in states previously covered by section five of the Voting Rights Act. Georgia, a state previously covered by the Voting Rights Act had two hundred and fourteen of those closures. Prior to the Shelby County decision, local officials would have had to submit these changes for federal review and show they were not discriminatory. But post Shelby County decision, local officials are free to make those changes under the radar without analyzing the discriminatory impact of the closures. They no

[15] Ryan Young, "Lebron James, Michael Jordan among celebrities Paying Court Fees to Help Felons Vote," Tampa Bay Times, November 2, 2020. See also, Veronica Stracqualursi, "Lebron James' Voting Rights Group to Help Florida's Ex-Felons who Owe Fines and Fees Register to Vote,' CNN Saturday July 25, 2020.

[16] Sam Levine and Ankita Rao, *supra* note 8.

longer had to submit such proposed changes for review to the federal government.

Some of the legislative and judicial gains of the two decades of the Civil Rights Movement came under severe attack during the administration of Donald J. Trump with the intent to reversethem back to the *status quo.* His administration in many defiant moves pushed to disenfranchise the colored minority using the instrumentality of the law and the courts. In many of the states controlled by the ruling Republican Party, several bills that placed near insurmountable hurdles or obstacles were passed into law, making it very difficult and or impossible for people of color to vote in an election. As at present, following the resounding defeat of the Republican Party in the 2020 presidential election, 43 GOP-controlled state legislatures and governors have come up with more than 100 bills to restrict voting rights.

These hurdles for suppression of votes in certain areas of voting blocks were in form of voters' identification, proof of written residential address, etc. Efforts to stave off the wave of voter suppression legislations across the nation were met with stiff resistance through the courts wherein the bench is populated by conservative justices sponsored by conservative groups with vested interest.

Many are of the view that these "restrictions come on the heels of an election in which there was record turnout and Democrats and Republicans election officials alike said there was no evidence of widespread wrongdoing or fraud"[17] despite the torrents of misinformation and conspiracy theories propagated and disseminated by key political leaders and their allies/supporters. There were multiple recounts, audits, and lawsuits across many states to back up those assurances. Federal and state officials called the election "the most secure in American history." America as one of the oldest democracies serves as a benchmark and an example to the world. It is rather strange that in the United States, the Republicans' response to a record high voter turnout and widespread participation of citizens would be a historic surge of anti-voting legislation. This is in sharp contrast with the widely acclaimed principles of American participatory democracy: "that every citizen has the right

[17] Sam Levine, "Republicans Considering more than 100 Bills to Restrict Voting Rights."

to vote and to have their vote counted,"[18] which the U.S. espouses, preaches, and exports to nations across the globe.

1.6 Weaponization of the Judiciary:

By constitutional design, and as intended by the framers of the American Constitution the judiciary is supposed to be and should be independent from the Executive and the Legislature. The American Judiciary is a well-developed institution, rich in precedents, has a long history tainted with racial bias and prejudice. Although not yet perfect, over the years, judicial practices have evolved standards, regulations, norms, and procedures for fair and equitable dispensation of justice. But the Executive in the last five years (2016–2020) made no pretenses about its interference in the internal affairs and unyielding push to weaponize and manipulate the institution to achieve selfish personal and political goals.

The Trump Administration deftly loaded the Department of Justice with appointees and cronies that "were ever willing to flout norms to achieve their ends, a weapon to advance majority (ruling) party preferences," many have the notion that altering judicial assignments to achieve certain results might not be beyond them.[19] Under the leadership of William Barr as the head of the DOJ, firing and reassignment of career professionals in the department whose mandate requires that they remain politically independent was rampant during this period to clear the coast for unwholesome judicial practices.

The former Attorney General William Bill Barr's era at the DOJ was marked by political drama, starting with the mischaracterization, distortions, and misrepresentation of the special counsel Robert Mueller's Report on Russian Collusion with the Trump's Campaign to interfere in the U.S. 2016 presidential election. The Working Group of the University of Pennsylvania Center for Ethics and Rule of Law, found that "Barr distorted both law and facts, placing a spin on his own actions, the actions of the DOJ, or the actions of the president's political rivals in a way that

[18] Fred Wertheimer's "Weekly Note," H.R.1 Vs. GOP State Voter Suppression Efforts, March 12, 2021, https://democracy21.org.

[19] Jacob Finkel, 'Trump's Power Won't Peak for Another 20 Years, The Atlantic, www.theatlantic.com.

was not faithful to reality and seemingly motivated by political considerations"[20]; pushed the special counsel Durham to produce at least a partial report on his findings on early aspects of the FBI investigation into the Trump's Campaign before the 2020 presidential election[21]; interfered in criminal proceedings of Roger Stone and Michael Flynn, leading to the resignation of a career prosecutor and withdrawal of all the four prosecutors from the case due to undue interference and pressure from Barr.

Furthermore, Barr twisted and shredded the age-long policies, and broke a 40-year protocol/memo to inject his office and the DOJ into election politics and petition to enable Trump to use the DOJ to challenge the outcome of the 2020 presidential election.[22] After Barr gave federal prosecutors the green light to investigate "any substantial allegations" of election irregularities, Richard Pilger who worked in the Public Integrity Section noted as follows, '"fter I familiarized myself with the policy and its ramifications... I must regretfully resign from my role as director of Election Crime Branch."[23]

Instead of staying above the fray of partisan politics, the former Attorney General, acting more or less as the president's personal defense lawyer/campaign manager, echoed Trump's mantra on Cable News Network (CNN) that mail-in voting that was highly utilized because of the COVID-19 pandemic was akin to "playing with fire and could easily be subject to fraud and coercion,"[24] thereby enabling the advancement of the former president's unfounded allegations of electoral fraud and conspiracy theories.

[20] Report of the Working Group of the Center for Ethics and the Rule of Law, University of Pennsylvania, Report of the Department of Justice and the Rule of Law Under the Tenure of Attorney General William Barr, October 12, 2020, p. 8, available at law.upenn.edu.

[21] Katelyn Polantz and Evan Perez, 'John Durham is Looking at FBI's Launch of Trump Campaign Probe,' CNN.

[22] Michael Balsamo, "Barr Tells DOJ to Probe Election Fraud Claims, if they Exist," Associated Press, Monday, November 9, 2020.

[23] Katie Benner and Michael S. Schmitdt, "DOJ Official In-charge of Voter-Fraud Probes Quits Post after Barr's Memo," *New York Times*, November 9, 2020.

[24] Katelyn Polantz and Caroline Kelly, 'Barr Says Voting by Mail is Playing with Fire,' September 2, 2020, CNN.

The rot was apparent even at the most senior levels of the Department of Justice wherein they were used as henchmen to fight Trump's opponents and to help his allies. Time-tested rules, regulations, protocols, and ethics were willfully disregarded in order to achieve certain or desired partisan outcomes. Senior DOJ officials were used to stop or quash criminal investigation, slow down, frustrate and or interfere with ongoing criminal investigation or case. By the active connivance and complicity of the most senior DOJ official, Michael Cohen, former Trump's lawyer and fixer turned ardent critic was unjustly hounded and sent back to prison in a clear retaliatory prosecution and personal vendetta to stop him from completing and publishing a book critical of the president he was writing. The cases of Michael Flynn and Roger Stone were despicable judicial debacles of epic proportion unbecoming of even the so-called banana republics or tyrannical dictatorships, but it happened here in the United States in the twenty-first century of all times.

It has been revealed that the head of the Criminal division was used to frustrate, quash, or stop criminal investigation of friends and allies of former President Trump. Criminal investigation of Rudy Giuliani and search warrant were blocked by officials of the justice department. Again, in the waning days of the Trump administration, the Department of Justice "declined to pursue a criminal investigation of the Transportation Secretary Elaine Chao, who is married to the former Senate majority leader, Mitch McConnel, despite the extensive report from her agency's Inspector General recommending that cause of action."[25] The DOJ's Criminal and Public Integrity Division both refused to launch official probes of her conduct. Chao, who declined to participate in the Inspector General's investigation, abruptly resigned on January 7, citing the previous day's Capitol insurrection as her motivation.

On the other hand, the criminal and civil divisions and the office of the deputy attorney general launched retaliatory investigations with full force against the former president's critics and foes. According to the report of the Working Group of the Center for Ethics and Rule of Law, University of Pennsylvania, "using law for political ends or as a weapon against

[25] Reed Richardson, Trump DOJ Reportedly Refused to Pursue Criminal Probe of Transportation Secretary Elaine Chao Despite IG's Recommendation,' www.msn.com. See also, Paul LeBlanc, "Elaine Chao: Transportation Department Watchdog Asked DOJ to Consider Criminal Probe of then- Secretary over concerns," CNN.

political enemies poses a lasting threat to not only to the integrity of the Department of Justice, but also a threat to the rule of law itself."[26]

Such apparent double standard in the administration of criminal justice and abuse of civil procedures extensively damaged the credibility and reputation of the department as an unbiased umpire/arbiter. Political operatives put in sensitive areas shed any pretense of decency and decorum to the principles of and observance of the rule of law, flouted norms, protocol, rules, and regulation with impunity in their mediaeval pursuit of unequal justice. Thus, the department was weaponized for the sole purpose of serving partisan interests and achieving political gains and advantage.

What happened at the DOJ in the past five years is a mind-boggling assault on due process, and the rule of law. This should be roundly condemned, and perpetrators/actors should be brought to justice and sanctioned in accordance with existing laws. In order to restore public confidence in the Department of Justice, the civil populace and the rank and file should be assured that the department would no longer face undue pressures/influences to attack the president's enemies and protect his allies. The battered credibility of the DOJ and American's civil rights and civil liberties should be redressed immediately. Clean up of the damage done to the department and its remake is absolutely necessary. Otherwise, a dangerous precedent would have been set and it will not take long for history to repeat itself.

1.7 Politicization of the Judiciary and the Courts:

"The Working Group of the Center for Ethics and Rule of Law University of Pennsylvania came to the reluctant conclusion that Barr was using the powers of the DOJ as a vehicle for supporting the political objectives of President Donald Trump which created the ethos of politicization of the Department of Justice." And because the DOJ plays a vital role

[26] Report of the Working Group of the Center for Ethics and the Rule of Law, University of Pennsylvania, Report of the Department of Justice and the Rule of Law Under the Tenure of Attorney General William Barr, October 12, 2020, p. 8, available at https://www.law.upenn.edu.

in securing and protecting the rule of law, its continued politicization is dangerous to our system of democratic governance.[27]

It is on record that in at least one instance, "Bill Barr gave orders to federal officers to use tear gas and pepper spray as well as other physical force on peaceful protesters so the president could have a political photo op of himself outside a church in Washington, DC,"[28] whereas the same administration failed to muster enough courage and basic competence to coordinate and order federal officers to defend and protect Congress men and women during the January 6, 2021 insurrection. An irony of fate indeed.

Also, the DOJ under Barr "manipulated loopholes in the law to justify use of federal officers for violent crackdown on dissidents, including in Portland Oregon and Lafayette Park in the District of Columbia where federal troops were used against peaceful protesters."[29] The double standard in the Police and National Guard rapid deployment in full combat readiness to crush civil protests be it in Portland Oregon, Minneapolis, Minnesota, or Lafayette Park, Washington DC, compared with the police lack of preparedness on January 6 during the Capitol Hill insurrection—not properly equipped/armed, out-numbered, unexplained confusion and botched reinforcement—despite being put on notice earlier about the potentials for violence on January 6, 2021 and Trump's December 20, 2020 tweet, urging his supporter to participate. "Big protest in DC on January 6th. Be there, will be wild."[30] Will the perpetrators of the incitement and masterminds of this treasonous attempt to stop the certification of the 2020 presidential election and peaceful transfer of power in the UnitedStates be ever held to account by the DOJ and the Courts?

On the other hand, another effort to politicize the judiciary is through an intense "court capture operations." There have been concerted campaigns toward capturing the courts by both the conservatives and the liberals. But it is worthy of note that "court capture" operation has been ongoing for a while but it gained fierce momentum in the past five years. The past administration powered by well-funded secret special

[27] Report of the Working Group of the enter for Ethics and Rule of Law, note 17 supra at p. 8.

[28] Report of Working Group note 12 supra at p. 11.

[29] Report of Working Group note 12 supra at p. 11.

[30] Steve Holland, Jeff Mason, and Jonathan Landay, "Trump Summoned Supporters to "Wild" Protest, and Told them to Fight. They Did," Reuters, Thursday January 7, 2021.

interests pursued the operation for court capture with a breathtaking speed and commitment. The ulterior motive behind this hot race for the control of the judiciary and the courts is not far-fetched—consolidation of power and control of the polity through compromised judicial processes. Trump's administration, to this end, appointed a record-breaking two hundred and twenty-four (224) judges, three Supreme Court justices that radically shifted the balance of conservative and liberal-leaning justices to 6:3, fifty-three Appeal Court judges, and one hundred and sixty-eight District Court judges within a four-year period.

The key criteria for the appointment of judges, namely, knowledge of the law, courage, character, and experience, in many cases, were supplanted with parochial group ideology like pro-life conservatism, gun advocacy by the conservative groups to whom the then ruling party farmed out the shortlisting of conservative nominees. Consequently, ten out of the 224 judges appointed to the courts in the intervening period were adjudged "not qualified" by the American Bar Association for lack of meaningful trial experience—some have never tried a case, civil or criminal.

The case of Kathryn Kimbell Mizelle stands out. Mizelle 33, "lacked experience, with less than 12 years of experience practicing law; never tried a case-civil or criminal-as lead attorney or co-counsel and lacked meaningful trial experience."[31] Besides, "more than 220 national human rights and civil rights groups opposed Mizelle's confirmation, citing her 'stunning lack of experience,' along with her involvement in civil rights rollbacks at Trump's Justice Department."[32] Nevertheless, with their majority in the Senate then, the ruling Republican Party rammed through her confirmation to a lifetime seat on the United States District Court for the Middle District of Florida.

Others include Judge Lawrence VanDyke, as reported to the Senate, there were concerns about his temperament. One interviewee said that, "Mr. VanDyke is arrogant, lazy, an ideologue, and lacking in the knowledge of the day-to-day practice including procedural rules."[33] They felt that he "lacks humility, has an 'entitlement' temperament, does not have

[31] Jennifer Bendery, 'Republicans Confirm Another One Trumps Unqualified Court Picks,' Microsoft News.

[32] *Id.*

[33] Samantha Cyrulnik-Dercher, "The Truth about Trump's Judges," Leadership Conference on Civil and Human Rights, www.civilrights.org.

an open mind, and does not always have a commitment to being candid and truthful."[34] He currently has a lifetime seat on a powerful U.S. Court of Appeals for the Ninth Circuit.

The case of the nominee to the U.S. District Court for the District of Columbia, Mathew Petersen was more absurd. He was so inexperienced that he could not answer basic questions about legal procedure. "During his confirmation hearing, after admitting that he had never tried a case or even argued a motion in state or federal court, he could not define a motion *in limine*, a motion frequently used at pre-trial hearing and during trial in both state and federal courts. Petersen eventually removed himself from consideration for judgeship."[35] Most of these judges are known to be members of the Federalist Society, a conservative organization, and tends to hold extreme conservative opinion and have records of being hostile to abortion rights, LGBTQ rights, voting rights, and the Affordable Care Act.

2 Conclusion

Five years of diligent maneuvers and deliberate weaponization of the DOJ with the attendant perversion of justice and trampling of the rule of law is an epic moment of national shame and embarrassment to the United States that should have not happened in the first place and should not be allowed to repeat itself. The general public and the whole world are watching with keen interest and are anxiously awaiting the final verdict or outcome of this trial, expecting justice not only to be done but seen to be done. There is a compelling need to restore public confidence and faith in the judiciary and the courts. The nation will have to reassure the public and the global community that America is still a nation of laws by prosecuting and bringing to justice all that are directly or remotely involved in crimes against the state, groups, or individuals. Sweeping all the egregious crimes and misconducts of the past five years under the carpet is not a palatable option as doing so will do further damage to the image and reputation of the nation, especially before the international community.

[34] *Id.*

[35] *Id.*

The nation's reputation in the world is already under a severe challenge. In other to reclaim its leadership position in the world stage, and cleanse its reputation of the rot and decadence of the past five years, sanctions in accordance with the subsisting laws should be evenly applied to all perpetrators of crimes (domestic terrorism, obstruction of justice, interference in criminal cases and investigation, human rights abuses and violation, etc.) irrespective of economic status, political affiliation or connection to the corridors of power. Else, the nation will be viewed from the prism of the so-called "banana republic" in the light of some unbecoming events of the recent past. The Judiciary has a huge and complex task at hand, the way and manner it will redress, cleanse and remake the DOJ and the courts from the wreckage of the past five years and will determine the way forward to the restoration to a benchmark tone of justice in the nation, public faith, its acceptability, and the overall integrity of judicial pronouncements locally and offshore. But should the nation miss this singular opportunity to redeem the image and reputation of the judicial institutions, it will have a far-reaching effect and implications in the larger society and beyond.

CHAPTER 20

The Unconformity of California's Gender Quota Law with the Contractual Theory of Corporate Law

Murat Can Pehlivanoğlu

1 Introduction

Historically, gender equality has been defended mainly in the legal arenas of constitutional law and employment law.[1] However, social and economic progress has required corporate law to provide gender equality on corporate boards. Recently, following the trend in Europe,[2] the State of California enacted a law requiring every publicly held corporation based in California to have women on its board of directors. The law made California the first U.S. state to mandate a corporate gender quota.

[1] Richard Leblanc, The Handbook of Board Governance: A Comprehensive Guide for Public, Private and Not-for-Profit Board Members (1. Ed., 2016).

[2] EC 2019 Report on Equality available at https://op.europa.eu/en/publication-detail/-/publication/f3dd1274-7788-11e9-9f05-01aa75ed71a1/.

M. C. Pehlivanoğlu (✉)
İstanbul Kent University, Istanbul, Turkey
e-mail: can.pehlivanoglu@kent.edu.tr

E. Duruigbo et al. (eds.), *International Law and Development in the Global South*, https://doi.org/10.1007/978-3-031-13741-9_20

According to a March 2020 report issued by the California Secretary of State, most of the surveyed publicly held corporations appear to be in compliance with the gender quota law.[3]

Public policies supporting competitiveness and inclusivity are not objectionable. In fact, international conventions such as the United Nations Convention for the Elimination of All Forms of Discrimination against Women reflect the international agenda to remedy gender inequality. However, the chosen method for implementing such policies is critical. In the case of California's gender quota law, scholars not only argue that the law is unconstitutional, but also suggest that alternative methods such as shareholder activism offer a superior approach.[4] While pending lawsuits will show the fate of the law in terms of its constitutionality,[5] this paper, criticizes the California legislature's method under U.S. corporate law.

The contractarian view of corporate law is dominant in U.S. jurisprudence.[6] This paper opines that the conformity of gender quota law with contractarian theory is questionable. After all, under the contractarian theory, the role of corporate law is to facilitate private contracting and only intervene when there is an empirically demonstrable need.[7] Accordingly, this paper discusses and provides that a mandatory gender quota law may not be justified on contractarian theory grounds and therefore is not in conformity with the principles of U.S. corporate law.

2 California Corporate Gender Quota Law

California corporate gender quota law is codified as Sec. 301.3 and Sec. 2115.5 of the California General Corporation Law (i.e., California

[3] CA Secretary of State Office, Woman on Boards, March 2020 Report, available at https://www.sos.ca.gov/business-programs/women-boards/.

[4] Joseph A. Grundfest, *Mandating Gender Diversity in the Corporate Boardroom: The Inevitable Failure of California's SB 826*, Rock Center for Corporate Governance Working Paper Series No. 232, 12 (2018), available at https://ssrn.com/abstract=3248791.

[5] See, Meland v. Padilla, Case Number: 2:2019cv02288 US District Court for the Eastern District of California.

[6] Michael Klausner, *The Contractarian Theory of Corporate Law: A Generation Later*, 31 J. Corp. L. 779, 780 (2006).

[7] J.A.C. Hetherington, *Redefining the Task of Corporation Law*, 19 U.S.F.L. REV. 229, 260 (1985).

Corporations Code) and is also known as "S.B. 826." The purpose of the gender quota law is explained as ensuring women's high-level involvement in corporations and achieving gender equity in the workplace and throughout the society. It is envisioned that such proactive policy will achieve a gender parity result which will otherwise take up to 50 years to obtain.[8] In light of public history, the law represents a signal that corporate law is being used for public purposes, particularly to improve social welfare.[9] It is one big step further in terms of gender diversity when compared with federal securities law's "comply or explain" approach.[10]

Since the gender quota law is a matter related to corporate governance, it is necessary to define the related concepts used in this paper, prior to the discussion of the law itself. First of all, the term "corporation" refers to a corporation organized under California Corporations Code and to any other corporation to the extent it is expressly included in a particular provision of the code (GCL Sec. 162). Secondly, whereas a "close corporation" is defined as a corporation with the number of shareholders not exceeding thirty-five (GCL Sec. 158), a "publicly held corporation" is defined as a corporation with its outstanding shares listed on a major U.S. stock exchange (GCL Sec. 2115.5(b)).

Thirdly, GCL Sec. 164 defines "Directors" as "natural persons designated in the articles as such or elected by the incorporators and natural persons designated, elected or appointed by any other name or title to act as directors, and their successors." Accordingly, California corporate law requires directors to be natural persons, and defines it irrespective of any gender, race, or any other specification. There is no cap on the number of seats a corporate board may have (Sec. 301.3(a)).

2.1 Corporations Code Sec. 301.3 and Sec. 2115.5

Gender quota law is applicable to corporations that are domestic (corporations incorporated in California) publicly held corporations and foreign publicly held corporations (corporations not incorporated in California)

[8] S.B. 826, 2017–2018 Leg. Reg. Sess. (Cal 2018).

[9] Ben Taylor, *Why California Senate Bill 826 and Gender Quotas Are Unconstitutional: Shareholder Activism as a Better Path to Gender Equality in the Boardroom*, 18 Fla. St. U. Bus. Rev. 117, 118 (2019).

[10] See, SEC Regulation S-K Item 401 and Item 407.

whose principal executive offices are located in California[11] The location of a corporation's principal executive office is determined pursuant to the respective corporation's SEC 10-K form (GCL Sec. 301.3(a)). In this regard, the statute applies to foreign publicly held corporations to the exclusion of the law of the jurisdiction in which the corporation is incorporated (GCL Sec. 2115.5(a)).

A corporation is deemed a "publicly held corporation" when its outstanding shares are listed on a major U.S.stock exchange (GCL Sec. 301.3(f)(2) and Sec. 2115.5(b)). In this sense, a corporation would not be deemed a publicly held one if its shares are listed on a stock exchange outside the United States. Likewise, a closely held corporation or a publicly held corporation whose shares are not listed on a stock exchange but only exchanged between purchasers in secondary market, would not be covered by the statute. Furthermore, a corporation incorporated in a jurisdiction outside the United States would be covered by the statute if its principal executive office is located in California and its shares are listed on a major stock exchange in the United States[12]. Therefore, it can be said that the statute has a selective extraterritorial effect.

GCL Sec. 301.3(a) provides that no later than the close of the 2019 calendar year, covered corporations shall have a minimum of one female director on its board; and GCL Sec. 301.3(b) provides that no later than the close of the 2021 calendar year, covered corporations are required to satisfy the number of female directors articulated by the statute in connection with the number of directors the corporation has on board. The envisioned quota system decreases as boards get beyond six members and gives corporations less time to implement the quota than other jurisdictions did.[13] Since board members can be removed, resign or lose legal capacity even after election, it is noted that a female director having held

[11] Before S.B. 826, the term "foreign corporation" was used to mean any corporation other than a domestic corporation and does not include corporations chartered under the laws of the United States (Sec. 171). S.B. 826 amended this definition in the areas covered by the amendment.

[12] Unlike Sec. 301.5's "listed corporation" definition requiring shares to be listed on the New York Stock Exchange, NYSE Amex, NASDAQ Global Market and NASDAQ Capital Market; Sec. 301.3's publicly held corporation definition only mentions major stock exchanges. Accordingly, stock exchanges not listed in Sec. 301.5 are also taken into the coverage of Sec. 301.5.

[13] Darren Rosenblum, *California Dreaming?*, 99 Boston University Law Review, 1435, 1444 (2019).

a seat for at least a portion of the year shall not be a violation (GCL Sec. 301.3(e)(3)).

"Female" for the purposes of the section, means an individual who self-identifies her gender as woman, without regard to the individual's designated sex at birth (GCL Sec. 301.3(f)(1)). The wording of the statute suggests that persons with "male" gender designated at birth may be elected to satisfy the rule as long as the person self-identifies her gender as woman. While this wording may be used as a gateway to circumvent the rule, it is nevertheless a contemporary approach on the public policy regarding gender identity issues in California[14]

2.2 Ensuring Compliance

In the context of publicly held corporations, election of the board of directors is finalized following a proxy contest. A proxy contest "is an election contest pursuant to which shareholders nominate and run a slate of directors different from those nominated and supported by management."[15] However, even if the proxy contest is pursued in a quota-complying manner, the result of the board of directors' election will depend upon shareholders' reaction.

It is a well-known principle that the business and affairs of the corporation shall be managed, and all corporate powers shall be exercised by or under the direction of the board of directors (GCL Sec. 300(a)). Under California law, directors are elected at each annual meeting of shareholders (GCL Sec. 301(a)). If the shareholders of a corporation are deadlocked so that they cannot elect the directors at the annual meeting of shareholders, the superior court of the proper county may appoint directors upon petition of shareholders (GCL Sec. 308(b)). In shareholders meetings, the affirmative vote of a majority of the shares represented either in person or by proxy and voting at a duly held meeting at which a quorum is present shall be the act of the shareholders (GCL Sec. 602(a)).

Since the election of directors for the board is an affirmative action requiring shareholder voting, it is necessary that the shareholders of the

[14] Teal N. Trujillo, *Do We Need to Secure a Place at the Table for Women? An Analysis of the Legality of California Law SB- 826*, 45 J. Legis. 324, 328 (2018).

[15] Lisa M. Fairfax, *All on Boards? Board Diversity Trends Reflect Signs of Promise and Concern*, 87 George Washington Law Review, 1032, 1049 (2019).

respective corporation choose to elect women directors. In case the shareholders choose not to elect any woman on board, then the corporation may face monetary penalties (GCL Sec. 301(e)). While it may be said that this violation may be avoided by nominating only women candidates for boards, it is important to note that it is among shareholders' statutory rights under California law to nominate directors at shareholders' meetings[16] (GCL Sec. 709). Therefore, election of male board members cannot be prohibited under the current wording of the gender quota law.

The method of sanctioning noncompliance suggests that choosing a male director to a seat which should be allocated to women would not automatically invalidate the shareholder vote or the election itself. In other words, an election with an outcome contrary to GCL Sec. 301.3 will be still deemed valid. Therefore, it is likely that some corporations will prefer to pay the monetary fines rather than comply with the rule.[17] This kind of sanction preference is a reflection of the fact that shareholder voting process is accepted as the exercise of the free will of parties through a contractual scheme.[18] After all, a comprehensive theory of corporate legitimacy perhaps rests on capacity of the corporation to conduct itself pursuant to a democratic society standard.[19]

The opinion set forth by the court in *Meland v. Padilla*[20] supports the analysis above. In *Meland v. Padilla*, Meland brought the suit against Alex Padilla, California's Secretary of State, as a shareholder of a company subject to S.B. 826. The Plaintiff alleged that S.B. 826 impairs his right to vote for the company's board of directors in violation of the Equal Protection Clause, but the court granted the defendant's motion to dismiss based on lack of standing grounds. The court has, among others, specifically explained that the plaintiff is not injured by S.B. 826's requirements since the law places the obligations on the corporation and does not force the plaintiff to vote in a particular manner. The court further explained that while S.B. 826 may influence the way the plaintiff chooses to vote at

[16] Stephenson v. Drever, 16 Cal. 4th 1167 (1997).

[17] In Norway, where a similar law is in effect, the penalty for noncompliance is dissolution (Darren Rosenblum, *Feminizing Capital: A Comparative Imperative*, Berkeley Business Law Journal Vol 6.1., 57 (2009)).

[18] Sec. 194 defines "vote" as "authorization by written consent".

[19] Michael E. Murphy, *The Nominating Process for Corporate Boards of Directors: A Decision—Making Analysis*, 5 Berkeley Bus. L. J. 131, 192 (2008).

[20] Meland v. Padilla, 2020 WL 1911545.

a shareholders meeting, that influence is merely incidental to the injury caused to the corporation by the law itself.

3 Contractual Theory of Corporate Law

The historical background of the contractual theory is related to the economic analysis of corporate law. In a nutshell, the economic analysis provides that firms arise to reduce transaction costs and self-interested post-contractual behavior among persons who otherwise would be engaged in market transactions.[21] A corollary to this point is that the corporation itself is seen as a nexus amongst the corresponding relationships mainly consisting of executives, directors, creditors, suppliers, customers, employees, and shareholders[22] Accordingly, it is said that corporate law should focus on facilitating these relationships in the most efficient manner.[23]

Contractarians argue that since corporations involve private contractual relationships, there should be no regulation constraining the parties' liberty to contract freely.[24] After all, the main function of contracts law is to let parties the contract to reallocate their resources, and corporate law should indeed be no different.[25] Of course, even when the corporation is accepted as a contract, the state has the power to regulate it at least to the extent it regulates other contracts.[26] Therefore, it is asserted that concepts central to contract law such as capacity, duress, undue influence, misrepresentation, fraud, unconscionability, and public policy may be the doctrines which may justify regulating corporate law to some extent.[27]

[21] Grant M. Hayden & Matthew T. Bodie, *The Uncorporation and the Unraveling of "Nexus of Contracts" Theory,* 109 Mich. L. Rev. 1127, 1129 (2011).

[22] These parts are the contractual relationships between the various parties involved with the firm: executives, directors, creditors, suppliers, customers, and employees. The corporation itself doesn't really exist; it is merely the nexus (or connection or link) amongst these various corresponding relationships.

[23] Hayden & Bodie, at 1130.

[24] Joseph F. Morrissey, *A Contractarian Defense of Corporate Regulation*, 11 Transactions: Tenn. J. Bus. L. 135, 136 (2009).

[25] Hetherington, at 256.

[26] Larry E. Ribstein & Erin Ann O'Hara, *Corporations and the Market for Law*, U. Ill. L. Rev. 661, 722 (2008).

[27] Morrissey, at 140.

Since the interests of the parties are the primary justification for the obligations arising from the contract, the promotion of those interests is the basic goal[28]. However, it is said that just like contract law does not give primacy to a particular group of participants in general, corporate law should not give primacy to any single group as well.[29]

Under the contractarian theory, corporate law plays an important role by providing a standard form contract reducing the transaction costs associated with reaching and adhering to optimal contracts[30] Especially, since the publicly held corporation environment creates prohibitively high transaction costs, parties cannot use private contracting to achieve efficient results and this justifies imposing legal rules as a substitute for private contracting.[31] Ideally, the standard form will match the results of costless bargaining.[32] Accordingly, its function is to reduce bargaining costs.[33] As a normative matter, contractarians defend that corporate law should be generally comprised of default rules which may be departed from, rather than mandatory rules.[34]

4 Justifying Gender Quota Law Mandate

In the legal literature, there are normative and functionalist arguments made in support of corporate gender quotas[35] The functionalist approach is connected with the "business case" for women representation.[36] On

[28] Lewis A. Kornhauser, *Contractual Freedom in Corporate Law*, 89 Columbia Law Review, 1449, 1451 (1989).

[29] Melvin A. Eisenberg, *The Conception That the Corporation Is a Nexus of Contracts and the Dual Nature of the Firm*, 24 J. Corp. L. 819, 833 (1999) (The Conception).

[30] Henry N. Butler, *The Contractual Theory of the Corporation*, George Mason University Law Review Vol. 11 No. 4, 99, 119 (1989).

[31] Bainbridge, at 865.

[32] Cheffins, at 787.

[33] Harry G. Hutchison, *Choice, Progressive Values and Corporate Law: A Reply to Greenfield*, 35 Del. J. Corp. L. 437, 448 (2010).

[34] Stephen M. Bainbridge, *Community and Statism: A Conservative Contractarian Critique of Progressive Corporate Law Scholarship*, 82 Cornell L. Rev. 856, 861 (1997).

[35] Peta Spender, *Gender Quotas on Boards—Is it Time for Australia to Lean In?* Deakin Law Review Vol. 20 No. 1, 95, 106 (2015).

[36] Spender, at 106.

the other hand, the normative approach is connected with moral considerations. While the prior suggests that giving women opportunity will get businesses richer, the latter provides that equality, parity, and democratic legitimacy are the reason for its requirement.[37] The functionalist argument is dominating the literature and practice, since it "appeals to a culture steeped in shareholder value as the metric for corporate decision making."[38] As the discussions by the California legislature regarding the law's justification has taken a functionalist form,[39] this paper will rely on this mainstream justification when related.

4.1 Distinguishing Between the Types of Rules

The legal nature of corporate law rules is generally categorized under three groups, namely (1) enabling rules, (2) default (or suppletory) rules, (3) and mandatory rules. While enabling rules group gives legal effect to principles that are adopted by the parties, the default rules group governs issues unless the parties adopt other rules.[40] On the other hand, the mandatory rules group governs issues prohibitively that cannot be varied by the parties.[41] It should be noted that U.S. corporate law consists largely of default rules.[42]

The subject matter of corporate law rules is categorized under another set of groups, namely (1) structural rules, (2) distributional rules, and (3) fiduciary rules.[43] Structural rules govern the decision-making power and process among corporate organs and agents, distributional rules govern the asset distributions to shareholders (as well as to the board of directors and creditors), and fiduciary rules govern the duties of managers and

[37] Spender, at 108.

[38] Deborah L. Rhode and Amand K. Packel, *Diversity on Corporate Boards: How Much Difference Does Difference Make?* 39 Delaware Journal of Corporate Law 377, 383 (2014).

[39] See, S.B. 826, 2017–2018 Leg. Reg. Sess. (Cal 2018).

[40] Melvin Aron Eisenberg, *The Structure of Corporation Law*, 89 Colum. L. Rev. 1461, 1461 (1989) (The Structure).

[41] Eisenberg, The Structure, at 1461.

[42] Jens Dammann, *The Mandatory Law Puzzle: Redefining American Exceptionalism in Corporate Law*, 65 Hastings L.J. 441, 448 (2014).

[43] Eisenberg, The Structure, at 1462.

shareholders.[44] While some of these rules are articulated in the articles of association and bylaws of the corporation, the rest of them remain in the statutory and case law.[45]

Pursuant to the abovementioned categorization of corporate law rules, it can be agreed that California gender quota law would be categorized under mandatory rules and structural rules groups. After all, gender quota law regulates the appointment of the board of director members and it is mandatory in nature. However, such law does not readily satisfy the rationale of the structural mandatory rules under the contractarian theory of corporate law in the context of publicly held corporations. On the contrary, the immunity of close corporations from the scope of such law can be satisfied by the rationale of the structural mandatory rules under the contractarian theory.

4.2 *Traditional Justifications for Structural Mandatory Corporate Law*

The depiction of the firm as a contract-based private entity advanced the notion that regulatory intervention in those private agreements is unnatural.[46] The American academic literature[47] generally provides three reasons in support of mandatory corporate law: the existence of externalities (interest of third parties), imperfect pricing of corporate charters, and the prospect of opportunistic midstream charter amendments.[48] A mandatory regime is generally justified in issues concerning investor protection, midstream corporate changes, and market uncertainty.[49] Since

[44] Eisenberg, The Structure, at 1462.

[45] Murat Can Pehlivanoglu, *Involuntary Dissolution: Theory and Operation in Publicly Traded Corporations*, Annual Survey of International and Comparative Law Vol. 23 Iss. 1 Article 2, 9–15 (2019).

[46] Rory Van Loo, *The New Gatekeepers: Private Firms As Public Enforcers*, 106 Virginia Law Review, 467, 495 (2020).

[47] In comparative legal literature, different justifications are provided for different countries. See, Klaus J. Hopt, *Directors' Duties and Shareholders' Rights in the European Union: Mandatory and/or Default Rules?*, ECGI Working Paper No. 312/2016 (2016).

[48] Jens Dammann, *Homogeneity Effects in Corporate Law*, 46 Ariz. St. L. J. 1103, 1138 (2014) (Homogeneity).

[49] Jonathan R. Macey, *Corporate Law and Corporate Governance: A Contractual Perspective*, 18 J. Corp. L. 185, 187 (1993).

the subject matter of gender quota law, as a structural rule, is not related to the externality or opportunistic midstream charter amendment issues, only the imperfect pricing (corollary, the investor protection issue) reason deserves a specific discussion.

Imperfect pricing of corporate charters, a reason given in support of mandatory rules, represents a basis for a frequently offered justification: paternalism for the sake of investor protection. It is claimed that investors cannot be expected to understand the full implications of the provisions they agreed to by purchasing shares of the corporation[50] In this sense, markets may be pricing charter terms imperfectly[51] and mandatory terms protect investors who cannot protect themselves. This theory may be extended to claim that mandatory rules protect third parties such as creditors, judiciary as well as other corporations.[52] However, it is unlikely to envision that a gender quota law reduces the transaction costs or information asymmetry concerning the understanding of a corporate charter. There is no empirical research, to the best knowledge of this author, which provides that a gender quota law is helpful to protect investors' investment.[53]

Still, just like many parts of the law, there are contract-defeating rules which are accepted as inherent in corporate law and these cannot be generalized.[54] For example, corporate law rules such as the ones dealing with insider trading and tender offers which are not representing any reciprocal arrangements, are mandatory.[55] These rules may be justified by the necessity to standardize contract terms through the use of mandatory legal rules in order to reduce the information costs for the investors

[50] Edward P. Welch & Robert S. Saunders, *Freedom and Its Limits in the Delaware General Corporation Law*, 33 Del. J. Corp. L. 845, 862 (2008).

[51] Dammann, Homogeneity, at 1137.

[52] Welch & Saunders, at 862.

[53] Likewise, while uncertainty about terms of the corporate relationship may reduce the value of the corporation and increase the transaction costs for investors interested in investing since they will spend time to obtain and analyze the terms (Welch & Saunders, at 867), the rationale mentioned above can be asserted in connection with this reason as well.

[54] Frank H. Easterbrook & Daniel R. Fischel, The Economic Structure of Corporate Law, 22 (1996).

[55] Eisenberg, The Conception, at 823.

and enforcement costs for the judicial system.[56] Likewise, proxy for board election issue is seen as among the mandated limitations on private ordering since effectuation of some statutory rights of the shareholders requires its regulation.[57]

It is important to recognize that different arguments can be made in support of mandatory rules depending on the close or publicly held nature of the corporation. After all, publicly held corporations and close corporations are dissimilar in terms of the main needs for their organizations. In fact, the abovementioned arguments are based on the common theme of widely dispersed ownership.[58] Before analyzing the situation of the California gender quota law, the close corporation and publicly held corporation contexts will be evaluated separately below through the lens of justification reasons referred above.

Close Corporation Immunity

Operations of close corporations are different than publicly held corporations. First of all, while the investors of close corporations anticipate an active role in the affairs of the corporation, the opposite is applicable in publicly held corporations.[59] Secondly, free transferability of shares is almost a necessary precondition for the publicly held corporations, but this is not a characteristic specifically desired in close corporations[60] Thirdly, the presence of a ready market for shareholders dissatisfied with their investment in publicly held corporations eliminate the necessity of providing a judicial relief for lock-up situations which are likely probable in the case of close corporations.[61] These operational differences result in different justifications for mandatory rules in the context of close corporations.

Since gender quota law is a structural mandatory rule, it is necessary to discuss the situation of structural rules specifically. In closely

[56] John C. Coffee, Jr., *The Mandatory/Enabling Balance in Corporate Law: An Essay on the Judicial Role*, 89 Colum. L. Rev. 1618, 1678 (1989).

[57] SEC Facilitating Shareholder Director Nominations Final Rule, at 17.

[58] John C. Coffee, Jr., *The Future as History: The Prospects for Global Convergence in Corporate Governance and Its implications*, 93 Nw. U. L. Rev. 641, 691 (1999).

[59] Henry G. Manne, *Our Two Corporation Systems: Law and Economics*, Virginia Law Review Vol. 53 No 2, 259, 278 (1967).

[60] Manne, at 278.

[61] Manne, at 280.

held corporations, shareholders generally prefer to bargain for at least some of the structural rules.[62] As the number of shareholders are small and to a reasonable extent know each other in close corporations, each shareholder acts as a fully informed party considering his own utility in actions concerning the corporations.[63] This factual reality supports the contractual view of corporate law, since it is easier to envision close corporations' formation and operational process as private bargaining between the parties. Some states' policy to permit the parties to alter the corporate structure by agreement in the context of close corporations is an implicit recognition of their contractual nature.[64]

It is said that corporate law's duty should be enforcing the bargain according to its terms and this is why such rules should be enabling or default, rather than mandatory. This sounds particularly rational for close corporations. However, a corporate relationship is a long-term one in which many disputes arise in the course of its operation. As transaction costs prohibit estimation of all contingencies concerning long-term relational contracts, corporate law has taken the position to prevent opportunism and protect the reasonable expectations of the shareholders through some mandatory rules as well.[65]

Accordingly, if a gender quota is something that the shareholders bargained for, then corporate law will (through mandatory rules such as involuntary dissolution) be able to provide a remedy to avoid the frustration of shareholders' reasonable expectations.[66] However, apart from this specific case, corporate law should not mandatorily impose a gender quota rule on close corporations since this will have nothing to do with reducing the transaction costs for an initially underestimated contingency regarding the contractual relationship between the parties. This analysis justifies why close corporations should be left out of the gender quota law, from the lens of contractual theory.

[62] Eisenberg, The Structure, at 1463.

[63] Eisenberg, The Structure, at 1463.

[64] Hetherington, at 254.

[65] Eisenberg, The Structure, at 1466.

[66] See, Murat Can Pehlivanoglu, Controlling the Non-Pecuniary Private Benefits of Influencing Shareholders in Publicly Traded Corporations Through Judicial Dissolution (2018) (unpublished S.J.D. dissertation, Golden Gate University School of Law) (on file with author).

Publicly Held Corporations' Coverage
Historically, managerial abuse of power and its implications on the investing public has been the main concern in the context of publicly held corporations[67] Therefore, structural rules, to which the gender quota law belongs, were likely to be subject to specific rules in publicly held corporations. Accordingly, the critical analysis of corporate law measures was focused on this aspect, at least on federal level.[68] However, state laws were mostly unresponsive to the approach requiring more restrictions on management for the sake of investor protection.[69]

Due to a large number of shareholders, most of who do not know each other or the managers personally, a direct bargaining for the structural rules is not possible for the investing public. Likewise, shareholders are generally underinformed than the managers.[70] Therefore, corporate law measures are much more necessary to determine the details of the corporate relationship. As a corollary, its nature and limits should be determined, to a large extent, in accordance with the fact that top managers may be self-interested, and the market forces may be insufficient to control the corporations' structural operations' impact.[71] Especially, the divergence of interest between corporate managers and shareholders justifies mandating structural rules under a mandatory rule regime.[72] Still, it is unlikely to envision gender quota as a measure eliminating managerial abuse.

On the other hand, the imperfect pricing justification referred above has a plausible basis for publicly held corporations. The efficient capital market hypothesis provides that securities prices accurately reflect all publicly available information about the security, including any changes in legal rules.[73] Accordingly, shareholders accept the corporate contract by buying shares of the company with a price implicitly reflecting the rules applicable to its governance.[74] However, structural rules reflected in the

[67] Hetherington, at 237.

[68] Hetherington, at 237.

[69] Hetherington, at 244.

[70] Easterbrook & Fischel, p. 1.

[71] Eisenberg, The Structure, at 1471.

[72] Eisenberg, The Structure, at 1473.

[73] Butler, at 122.

[74] Klausner, at 783.

corporate contract may be open to managerial abuse and the market may not value such openness accurately, thus its pricing may be imperfect. In this case, shareholders would be buying an ownership interest from a price they would normally not buy due to a structural defect. To support the efficient pricing of the marketplace, mandatory rules can be useful. However, there is no reason to believe that a mandatory gender quota rule would be helpful in curing the pricing failures.

California Gender Quota Law's Unconformity

Since justifying a mandatory rule for publicly held corporations is more likely under contractarian theory than justifying for close corporations, gender quota law's conformity with the contractarian theory should be further investigated. Irrespective of the justifications discussed above, the first issue in determining whether a rule should be mandatory or not concerns whether the benefits of mandating such principle outweighs the costs associated with it.[75] It is important to note that, costs of mandatory rules may be high not just because of uniformity costs but also due to the concerns regarding the design of mandatory norms.[76]

In terms of gender quota law, if there is a negative (or no positive) relationship between the gender diversity and firm performance (or its regulatory control), the cost of inclusion of women directors will become a demotivating factor in the implementation of such public policy favoring women inclusivity.[77] The best way of evaluating the desirability of such mandatory regime is by examining the relevant empirical evidence.[78] In the absence of such evidence, its desirability may be assessed by searching whether the effect of a mandatory rule may be reached through the market forces themselves.[79]

[75] Macey, at 187.

[76] It is pointed out that such norms will have less quality where the political process is corrupt, lawmakers are incompetent, and lobbying is problematic (Dammann, at 487).

[77] David A. Carter, et al., *The Gender and Ethnic Diversity of US Boards and Board Committees and Firm Financial Performance, Corporate Governance: An International Review* 18(5) 396, 397 (2010).

[78] Macey, at 207.

[79] Ross Grantham & Charles Rickett, Corporate Personality in the 20th Century 221 (1998).

In the context of publicly held corporations, the basic premise is that investors will prefer maximum aggregate gain.[80] Much debate about gender quotas has focused on the "business case" for quotas.[81] While there are empirical researches suggesting firms with women in leadership generate better return on equity, the existing literature does not uniformly support a positive correlation between gender diversity and improved corporate performance.[82] In this sense, the research on the effect of board diversity on firm performance is inconclusive and the outcomes are dependent on the adopted methodology.[83] In fact, the firms required to comply with the gender quota law experienced a large negative stock market reaction at the signing of the law.[84] Together with the absence of the empirical evidence in support of the rule, the market forces have also showed that such a rule is actually not desired. Accordingly, it is likely that the rule's costs will outweigh its benefits.

The second issue to discuss is that some mandatory rules, as commentators insist, are in fact voluntary since those would be adopted irrespective of whether they are required by law. While the same indication can be asserted for default rules as well, the distinction between making such a rule mandatory or default would be again based on a cost and benefit analysis referred above. Therein, the duty of loyalty is given as an example by indicating that no shareholder would agree to permit managers to steal corporate assets in any case.[85] Likewise, shareholder oppression doctrine reduces the need for expensive ex ante bargaining and allows parties to proceed with an incomplete agreement.[86] However, the same thinking

[80] William W. Bratton, *The Economic Structure of the Post-Contractual Corporation*, Northwestern University Law Review Vol. 87 No. 1, 180, 199 (1992).

[81] Much debate about sex quotas has centered on the 'business case' for quotas. A body of empirical research suggests that firms with woman in leadership positions generate higher profits, return- on- equity, share prices, or other financial benefits for a firm.

[82] Rosenblum& Roithmayr, at 902.

[83] Rhode & Packel, at 390.

[84] Daniel Greene, Vincent J. Intintoli & Kathleen M. Kahle, *Do Board Gender Quotas Affect Firm Value? Evidence from California Senate Bill No. 826*, Journal of Corporate Finance 60, 32 (2020).

[85] Roberta Romano, *Contractual Freedom in Corporate Law*, 89 Colum. L. Rev. 1599, 1602 (1989).

[86] Benjamin Means, *A Contractual Approach to Shareholder Oppression Law*, 79 Fordham L. Rev. 1161, 1194 (2010).

may not be applied to gender quota law, since to the best knowledge of this author, there is no empirical research showing that the parties would have agreed on employing a gender quota even when it is not the law,[87] if the transaction costs were not prohibitive. Therefore, irrespective of any justification basis discussed above, a mandated gender quota law does not fit in the contractual theory of corporate law.

5 Conclusion

When the corporation is accepted as a nexus comprising voluntarily associating individuals, it is rational to accept that it pursues the private purposes of the contracting parties, therefore, it should not be made a part of public purposes.[88] Therefore, justifying a mandatory regime of gender quota law should be chased through a different set of reasoning. Under the contractarian theory, the role of corporate law is to facilitate private contracting and only intervene when there is an empirically demonstrable need. However, it is neither possible to demonstrate this need nor use other justification grounds in the literature for gender quota law.

While California gender quota law is controversial due to concerns other than the general principles of corporate law, this paper provides that the law presents an unconformity with the legislation it is put in. In order to preserve the general rationale of corporate law through the contractual theory, it is necessary to envision the rule as a non-corporate mandatory rule and to displace it. Otherwise, the rule will remain as a provision which is not properly justified since contractual theory does not embody it. It is likely that this unconformity will pose an increased threat to the rule's legacy, given the pending lawsuits against its validity.

[87] While boardroom diversity may be suggested to play a role in solving agency problems, it is generally agreed that there is no strong support for this conclusion (Carter et al., at 399).

[88] William W. Bratton Jr., *The "Nexus of Contracts" Corporation: A Critical Appraisal*, 74 Cornell L. Rev. 407, 434 (1989).

CHAPTER 21

The Role of the Judiciary in Development of an ISDS Mechanism in Vietnam

Chau Huy Quang

1 Introduction

This article aims to address how important the judiciary's role is in the course of developing a feasible mechanism for investment dispute resolution in Vietnam and seeks to argue that such judicial reforms are essential.

2 Overview of the Judiciary and Roles of Key State Organs in Vietnam

Vietnam's judicial system has been active for over 70 years, commencing on September 2, 1945,[1] promulgated to include courts, prosecutors,

[1] The date on which President Ho Chi Minh declared the independence of the Democratic Republic of Vietnam from France.

C. H. Quang (✉)
Saigon Centre, Ho Chi Minh City, Vietnam
e-mail: quang.chau@lctlawyers.vn

E. Duruigbo et al. (eds.), *International Law and Development in the Global South*, https://doi.org/10.1007/978-3-031-13741-9_21

investigative authorities, and enforcement authorities. Development of the judicial system is based on fundamental criteria set out in the Constitution of Vietnam, amended in 1946, 1959, 1980, 1992, and 2013.

The Constitution of Vietnam (1992) (as amended on March 12, 2001) is an important legal instrument with respect to judicial reform. It redefined functions, duties, competences, organizational structure, and fundamental principles. The courts were divided into specialized functional courts (e.g., economic, labor, and administrative courts). Prosecutors were bestowed the right to prosecute and independently supervise judicial activities. The functions of the investigative authorities were strengthened. The civil enforcement agencies were granted the right to perform several activities and strengthen the quality of execution of civil cases.[2]

Fundamental to the constitutional composition of the modern State is the concept of judicial power and its exercise solely through the judiciary. The judiciary possesses the powers to rule on violations of laws, including the Constitution, to settle disputes or conflicts of rights and obligations arising from social relationships, and to recognize the legality of events or acts and change or terminate rights and obligations of individuals, entities, and State organs accordingly. Vietnam recognized judicial power as one of three prongs of political power which constitute the centralized power of the State, the others being legislative and executive.[3]

There is a divergence of views as to the precise scope of judicial power. The State's judicial power is exercised through judgments with

[2] See Prof Dr Le Minh Tam, The Judicial System of Vietnam since the Revolutionary Period of 1945 August to Present, The Law Magazines, No. 1/2003.

[3] Article 102 of the Constitution of Vietnam (2013) states:

1. *The People's Courts are the judicial bodies of the Socialist Republic of Vietnam, exercising the judicial power.*

2. *The People's Courts comprise the Supreme People's Court and other courts established by law.*

3. *The People's Courts are responsible for the protection of justice, human rights, citizen's rights, socialist regime, interests of the State and legal rights and interests of organizations and individuals.*

discrete rulings gradually accreting. In the aggregate, the judiciary creates a consistent body of law setting out the correctness and legitimacy of certain acts, resulting in a unified body of law mediating social relationships and balancing the rights and interests of individuals, legal entities, and State organs. From this legal perspective, judicial power is solely the power exercised by the courts in the course of judicial activities. In this context, justice is regarded as a field of State power exercised through judgments and judicial review of the legitimacy of legal acts and decisions in the context of disputes over the rights and interests of the law.[4]

Judicial authority refers to courts' jurisdiction as stated in Article 97 of the original Constitution (1946).[5] Customarily by international standards, judicial organs are understood only as including courts. However, since the 1959 Constitution, Vietnam's concept of judicial organs is broader and not only includes courts (as ordinarily understood) but also State bodies such as prosecutors and police investigators.

The taxonomy and appropriate nomenclature for State judicial organs are unclear. This has practical consequences. Such taxonomical slipperiness leads to controversies and debates over judicial authorities' independence and whether judicial activities and bodies[6] are subject to the leadership of the Communist Party of Vietnam ("CPV"), raising questions as to how judicial powers are to be meaningfully distinguished from executive and legislative powers. These questions remain in flux with various contending views as the Vietnamese legal system remains in a State of transition.[7]

Article 4.3 of the Constitution (2013) stipulates that "*all Party organizations and the Party Members operate within the legal framework of the Constitution and the law.*" This is commonly interpreted as reflecting the State's desire to enhance the rule of law in Vietnam under which all people are equal before and only subject to the law. One corollary

[4] Nguyen Dang Dzung, The Judicial Institutions in the Rule of Laws, The Judicial Publishing House, 2004, p. 11.

[5] Art. 97 states "*The Supreme People's Court of the Democratic Republic of Vietnam, the local people's courts, and the military courts are judicial organs of the Democratic Republic of Vietnam.*"

[6] XXX.

[7] Penelope (Pip) Nicholson & Nguyen Hung Quang, The Vietnamese Judiciary: The Politics of Appointment and Promotion, 14 Pacific Rim Law and Policy Journal 1, 2 (2005).

of this is that the State can only govern based on the Constitution and constitutionally sound laws.

Given such legislative framework, the judicial bodies of Vietnam comprise the "People's Courts."[8] Within the network of these judicial bodies is the Supreme People's Court ("SPC"), the highest-level judicial body of Vietnam. It has general supervision over the judicial functions of the other courts.[9]

3 The Notion of Judicial Independence

In principle, under the Law on Organization of the People's Courts,[10] the courts are "*independently organized*" in accordance with adjudicative jurisdiction. However, while this notion suggests an unequivocal carve-out of the judiciary from Vietnam's other State organs—particularly, the legislative and the executive arms of government as prescribed in the Constitution (2013)[11]—the overarching reality is that the National Assembly has "*power of supreme oversight*" with respect to the judiciary (among other State bodies).[12] At the local level, in Vietnam's 64 provinces and centrally run cities, the "*people's councils*" oversee lower judicial organs.[13]

This is also leaving aside the uncertain role of the CPV,[14] which is to be the "*vanguard*" of the working class, the people, and the State, and, accordingly, their representatives.[15] The interrelationship between the National Assembly, which has been constitutionally enshrined as the highest representative body of the people and highest body of State power

[8] Constitution of Vietnam (2013), Article 102.

[9] Constitution of Vietnam (2013), Article 104.

[10] Law on Organization of the People's Courts No. 62/2014/QH13, The National Assembly of Vietnam, November 24, 2014 (the "Law on Organization of the People's Courts (2014)"), Article 5.

[11] Constitution of Vietnam (2013), Article 2.3.

[12] Constitution of Vietnam (2013), Article 70.2; Law on Organization of the People's Courts (2014), Article 19.

[13] Law on Organization of the People's Courts (2014), Article 19.

[14] Nicholson, Quang, supra, note 7, at 280.

[15] Constitution of Vietnam (2013), Article 4.1.

of Vietnam,[16] and the CPV remains abstract with no definitive hierarchy. However, that the CPV has a certain influence in the way the State is run is indisputable—the extent of which is commonly understood as the CPV being tasked with a leadership role, and the State (with power vested in the National Assembly) being tasked with a management role.[17]

The manifestation of the CPV's driving influence can be seen in lawmaking[18] as the CPV has a function to steer State policies.[19] For the judiciary, the CPV's role is also likely extended to cover policy-related matters (e.g., promulgation of policies or guiding instruments for the SPC).[20] As a result, with the judiciary being an apparatus of the State under the National Assembly,[21] the political doctrine of separation of powers has not been entrenched as it is generally understood in Western democracies.[22]

Despite the absence of such separation of powers, from the lawmakers' perspective, the Constitution (2013) explicitly prescribes that during a trial, judges and assessors[23] are to be independent and only obey the law. Agencies, organizations, and individuals are prohibited from interfering in a trial by judges and assessors.[24] This is reflected in the

[16] Constitution of Vietnam (2013), Article 70.2.

[17] John Gillespie, Changing Concepts of Socialist Law in Vietnam. In John Gillespie & Pip Nicholson (Eds.), *Asian Socialism and Legal Change: The Dynamics of Vietnamese and Chinese Reform*. ANU Press, 2005.

[18] Nicholson, Quang, supra note 7, at 4.

[19] Law on Promulgation of Legislative Documents No. 80/2015/QH13, Articles 31–33.

[20] Luu Tien Dung, Judicial Independence in Transitional Countries, United Nations Development Program—Oslo Governance Centre: The Democratic Governance Fellowship Programme, 32, 2003.

[21] Nicholson, Quang, supra note 7, at 6.

[22] Penelope (Pip) Nicholson, Judicial Independence and the Rule of Law: The Vietnam Court Experience, 3 Australian Journal of Asian Law 37, 37 (2001).

[23] The term, "*assessors*" used in the Constitution of Vietnam (2013) refers to the people's jurors or laypersons who are appointed to adjudicate certain disputes at lower level people's courts (provincial level or district level courts)—akin to the function of a jury in other jurisdictions. Law on Organization of the People's Court (2014), Articles 7–9. Nicholson, supra note 7, at 42. In this book, it will not be necessary to address the adjudicative functions of these assessors.

[24] Constitution of Vietnam (2013), Article 103.2. This is also prescribed under the Law on Organization of the People's Court (2014), Article 9. While the Vietnamese language

respective procedural rules of the courts, granting the judiciary a degree of independence.

However, what the judiciary is formally independent from remains a controversial question.[25] The mandatory observation of the law as stipulated in these instruments leads to spillage by the legislative arm over the judiciary. There is no authoritative stipulation that the judiciary is an independent, standalone institution.[26] The extent of independence enshrined in these instruments is likely a reference to the judiciary being the only body with the competence[27] to handle judicial matters.[28] It is difficult to reconcile the first aspect, as the People's Courts have a constitutional duty to safeguard the interests of the State.[29]

This presents a dilemma: when faced with a matter that may adversely affect the interests of the State, a question arises as to what extent the People's Court will be able to preserve authentic independence while respecting constitutional duties. Notably, Vietnam does not have a constitutional court or equivalent.[30] It follows that until the courts are faced with such situation, or the National Assembly is able to provide some comfort to the judiciary (e.g., certain immunity), such dilemma will remain unsolved.

is translated to refer to independence during the "*trial*" only, it is uncertain as to whether it is also intended to apply to the entire adjudicative process, and not just the hearing. However, this scope has never really been seriously and publicly tested in Vietnam. Dung, supra note 7, at 32.

[25] Nicholson, supra note 7, at 40.

[26] Dung, supra note 7, at 32.

[27] The judiciary having the freedom to implement the will of the people as specified in the laws to which the judges are to obey, and that, as opposed to the common notion of judicial independence attached to a separation of powers, is divided into the following two limbs: external independence in which the judiciary is to be independent of any outside institutions (including other state agencies or otherwise other forces outside of the judiciary that have the capacity to encroach on the judiciary's independence); and internal independence in which the judges (or others tasked with adjudicative functions) are to be independent of colleagues and other parties that can impact individual adjudicative competence.

[28] Dung, supra note 7, at 13.

[29] See generally Nicholson, Quang, supra note 7 "*The People's Courts have the duty to safeguard justice, human rights, citizens' rights, the socialist regime, the interests of the State, and the lawful rights and interests of organizations and individuals.*" Furthermore, the CPV has a hand in steering (or vetting) the appointment of judges in Vietnam.

[30] Nicholson, supra note 7, at 42.

In practice, the judiciary is vulnerable to external elements, including from State agencies and CPV leaders, which undermines perceived independence.[31] Further, if a judge were to depart from duties prescribed under law, the consequences can be severe, particularly:

a judge can be dismissed for committing a violation in the course of adjudicative functions, settling matters, or otherwise committing an "illegal act;"[32] and

a judge can be prosecuted and be subject to criminal sanctions, including up to ten years' imprisonment, if an "illegal" judgment is rendered.[33]

The People's Procuracies, State agencies that have been specifically appointed to prosecute and supervise judicial activities,[34] constitute a "check and balance" mechanism against judges' procedural powers by providing strict supervisory functions. The Procuracies follow a similar hierarchical system to the People's Courts, the determination of which corresponds to their supervisory competence. Like the SPC, the highest-level People's Procuracy, the People's Supreme Procuracy, is appointed by and answerable to the National Assembly.[35]

[31] U.S. Department of State, Bureau of Democracy, Human Rights and Labor, Country Reports on Human Rights Practices for 2017—Vietnam, http://www.state.gov/j/drl/rls/hrrpt/humanrightsreport/index.htm?year=2017&dlid=277131 (last accessed November 18, 2018).

[32] Law on Organization of the People's Court (2014), Article 82. Whether "*illegal act*" in this context refers to a crime (i.e., violation of the Criminal Code), or a mere violation of duties enshrined in other legislative instruments, remains undefined.

[33] Criminal Code No. 100/2015/QH13, The National Assembly of Vietnam, November 27, 2015, Article 370, as amended by Law No. 12/2017/QH14 on amendments to the Criminal Code No. 100/2015/QH13,The National Assembly of Vietnam, June 20, 2017. What constitutes "*illegal*" in the context of this provision is not legally defined and therefore, its interpretation will be subject to the sole discretion of the competent state agencies. However, it is arguably ambiguous and general enough to cover an instance in which the judge renders a judgments against the interests of the State in breach of his or her constitutional duties.

[34] Constitution of Vietnam (2013), Article 107.1. Law on Organization of the People's Procuracies No. 63/2014/QH13, The National Assembly of Vietnam, November 24, 2014, Article 2.1.

[35] Constitution of Vietnam (2013), Article 70.

Accordingly, the supervisory function enables these procuracies to "*supervise the lawfulness of acts and decisions committed or made by agencies, organizations and individuals in judicial activities.*"[36] In view of the above functions, there is limited room for departure of adjudicative functions by a judge as in the settlement of court cases (including recognition of foreign arbitration awards), the Procuracies shall represent the State before, during, and after the trial's phases at all levels.[37]

Therefore, on balance of both upper level pressure and the severe implications for "defiance," judges may be reluctant to pass down a decision that would adversely impact the interests of the State. Even if the National Assembly created stronger mechanisms for impartial adjudication, doing so without regard to the State's interests would remain a challenge.

4 Role of the Courts in Resolving Investment Disputes

Generally, foreign investors[38] are not comfortable in domestic courts where there is an investment dispute with the host State, particularly if such judiciary is not independent from State political power.[39] For resolution of international investment disputes, almost none of the BITs to which Vietnam is a signatory require a dispute to be decided in a local court of the host State as a precursor to commencing international arbitration. However, so-called "fork-in-the-road" provisions are common in which foreign investors are afforded a decision to select either one of (i) the host State's administrative or judicial authorities or (ii) investment arbitration for final adjudication.

[36] Law on Organization of the People's Procuracies (2014), Article 4.1.

[37] Law on Organization of the People's Procuracies (2014), Article 27.4.

[38] Since the advent of Vietnam's Economic Reform period beginning in 1986, and in particular since the National Assembly passed the first (substantive) Law on Foreign Investment in 1987, there has been a 30-

[39] Kamal Huseynli, Enforcement of Investment Arbitration Awards: Problems and Solutions, 31 Baku State University Law Review 40, 2017, at 63. And for Vietnam, the fact that the judiciary is inherently partial towards safeguarding the interests of the state.

Under the Civil Procedure Code (2015) (the "CPC"), the courts have competence to adjudicate investment disputes alongside natural jurisdiction over civil and commercial disputes.[40] However, such a route is rarely (if ever) employed, perhaps understandably because, by the time an investor has reached the point of considering mounting an investment dispute against the State (typically after a mandatory negotiation or consultation period), such investor already has international arbitration as a viable option.

5 The Extent of the Court's Interference During Arbitration Proceedings

The question then becomes the extent to which the State can intervene if the investor elects to pursue the dispute through arbitration. Save for ICSID arbitrations, this depends on the seat or the legal place of the arbitration, typically determined by the arbitration tribunal. Particularly:

a. In an ICSID arbitration, there is no seat, and the proceedings are "*delocalized*" from domestic procedures such that the local courts are barred from intervening in the ICSID process,[41] made possible by the contracting states' ratification of the ICSID Convention enshrining such delocalization commitment.
b. For non-ICSID arbitrations, such as arbitration under the UNCITRAL Arbitration Rules or the ICSID Additional Facility Rules, unless the ISDS provision stipulates or there is an agreement otherwise, the tribunal will typically determine this. However, seldom is an investment arbitration seated in the jurisdiction of a disputant (especially of the host state) as this would compromise the extent of any neutrality that international arbitration is to attract.[42]

[40] Civil Procedure Code (2015), Article 30. "*Investment*" disputes fall under the broader umbrella of "*business and trade disputes*".

[41] ICSID, Process Overview, ICSID World Bank, https://icsid.worldbank.org/en/Pages/process/Overview.aspx (last accessed October 18, 2018).

[42] Muruga Perumal Ramaswamy, Enforcement of ICSID and Non-ICSID Arbitration Awards and the Enforcement in BRICS, 15 International Journal of Business, Economics and Law 15, 75.

It follows that the determination of a seat impacts the extent to whether Vietnamese courts would intervene in the arbitration process. As addressed below, it may also impact visibility in the process of recognizing and enforcing a resultant arbitration award. This is because the only courts that should become involved in the arbitration process are those at the seat.[43]

This is to avoid the situation where the court may attempt to intervene in an investment or other international arbitration with a seat domiciled outside of Vietnam. Such an attempt, should it be carried out, would be futile from both legal and procedural perspectives, while enforceability would see the State depart from international commitments. It would not be acceptable to the international investment community if a national court is conferred with powers to review the awards in the context of national laws.[44]

However, to the extent that the seat is in Vietnam, the judiciary has been known to intervene. One well-known example of such intervention involved a case before the ICC International Court of Arbitration in 2012 between a Japanese construction contractor (as claimant) and a State body, the People's Committee of Ho Chi Minh City (as respondent). While the arbitration in question was not filed directly against the Government of Vietnam, it was filed against a local authority which administers State power.[45] The case was particularly notable as it saw the People's Court pass a decision (on an *ex parte* basis) to nullify the tribunal's partial award on jurisdiction—an award of which would permit the tribunal to continue adjudicating the arbitration against the People's Committee. As such, it called into question (i) the impartiality of and due process afforded by the court and (ii) the extent to which the People's Committee had played a role in driving the issuance of the decision. The result was that the tribunal ultimately refused to acknowledge being bound to the court's decision. From the perspective of international legal practitioners, this is controversial.

Particularly, it undermines the intended message to existing and potential foreign investors, which is that Vietnam upholds a legal regime to

[43] Julian D M Lew, Does National Court Involvement Undermine the International Arbitration Process, 3 American University International Law Review 24, 494.

[44] Huseynli, supra note 39, at 64.

[45] The Constitution of Vietnam (2013), Article 114.

protect the interests of investors and is an investment-friendly jurisdiction. The impact is particularly significant, as the dispute concerned a project in Vietnam's economic hub of Ho Chi Minh City. After the conclusion of the case (despite arbitration being inherently private), a large number of foreign construction companies were aware of the proceedings and the attempts of the court to frustrate the same.[46] Investors have taken note that an investor having a dispute adjudicated overseas does not necessarily preempt judicial intervention or influence.

6 Recognition and Enforcement of Foreign Arbitral Awards in Vietnam

Given the limited extent of intervention afforded to the host State's judiciary during the arbitration process, the judiciary's role primarily comes into play at the point in which the arbitral award is rendered, and the investor pursues measures to recognize and enforce it against the host State. In this circumstance, in non-ICSID arbitration, any challenge against the award's recognition will be subject to the law of the seat of arbitration.[47] If the seat of arbitration is not the host State (as is often the case), then the standards and procedures for judicial review in that State will not ordinarily be of concern (and, of course, it is typically in the investor's interest to champion a seat that is perceived to be "neutral" in the interest of an independent and impartial judicial review).[48]

However, notwithstanding such seat, the provisions of the New York Convention 1958 that prescribe a general obligation on the member State to recognize arbitration awards as binding, the extent of recognition can still be subject to the member State's national laws. Any arbitral award in which a seat is designated in a jurisdiction outside of Vietnam's territory will be considered a "*foreign arbitration award*" which may be interpreted as encompassing investment arbitration awards. Accordingly, such

[46] This has become apparent that many of the construction contractors with whom he spoke were well-aware of the arbitration, despite there being no press coverage or other official public notices regarding the same.

[47] Ramaswamy, supra note 42, at 75.

[48] Id.

award will likely be subject to the recognition procedures set forth under the CPC.[49]

These regulations apply to any international treaty and are arguably extendable to the ICSID Convention as well. Where no such treaty exists (e.g., a foreign award issued in a State that is not a member of the New York Convention), then recognition shall be done on a "*reciprocity*" basis. To date, there is no clear guidance as to the elements of such reciprocity.[50]

7 Grounds for Non-recognition, and the "Basic Principles of the Laws of Vietnam"

One main attributing cause of practical inefficiencies is often the consideration by the court of factors that may allow it to refuse recognition of a foreign arbitration award. Particularly, the court must not recognize a foreign arbitration award if the award debtor provides sufficient evidence to the court establishing any of the following cases,[51] among others[52]:

1. The parties do not have capacity to conclude an arbitration agreement according to the law applicable to each party;
2. The arbitration agreement is not legally effective according to the law of a country which is chosen to be applied or according to the law of where the award is made if the parties cannot choose which law applies to such agreement;
3. The foreign arbitrator's award had not taken mandatory legal effect against the parties; or the enforcement of the foreign arbitrator's award has been cancelled or terminated by a competent agency of the country where such award is made or the home country of the law that is applied;

[49] Civil Procedure Code (2015), Chapter XXXV, Part VII.

[50] It is likely, however, that the competent court will consider the extent to which the relevant state has recognized or enforced an arbitration award issued in Vietnam—in other words, whether that state has reciprocated in such process.

[51] Civil Procedure Code (2015), Article 459.1.

[52] The composition of the foreign arbitrator and/or procedures for settling the disputes adjudicated by the foreign arbitrator does not comply with the arbitration agreement or to the law of the country where the foreign arbitrator's award has been made (in case the arbitration agreement does not provide such matters).

4. The award debtors being agencies, organizations, or individuals are not promptly and sufficiently notified of the appointment of the arbitrator/tribunal or of procedures for adjudicating the dispute through foreign arbitration, or due to other plausible reasons, such agencies, organizations, or individuals are unable to exercise their procedural rights; or
5. The foreign arbitrator's award was in respect to a dispute that neither disputing party had requested to be settled or exceeds the request of the parties.[53]

While the burden of proof lies with the award debtor to establish the above, such that the court would and should take the foreign arbitration award at face value, in practice courts have been known to employ inquisitorial powers in shifting the onus on the award creditor to establish that the foreign award does not fall within the above cases. Considering the extensive scope of these cases, this has, at times, proven to be overwhelming to a judgment creditor. The court can also otherwise refuse to recognize a foreign arbitration award if[54]:

1. the dispute was not capable of being adjudicated by arbitration under Vietnamese law; and/or
2. recognition and enforcement in Vietnam of such foreign arbitrator's award would be contrary to the "*basic principles of Vietnamese law.*"

Annulments on the grounds of violating "*basic principles of Vietnamese law*" have drawn attention. It is distinguishable from the public policy provision under the New York Convention[55] but modeled on a similar concept.[56] While each State would have its own concept of "public policy" in the context of the New York Convention, many civil law

[53] If it the relevant (infringing) sections in the arbitration award can be carved out or separated from the remainder of the award, the remaining portions may be recognized and enforced in Vietnam.

[54] Civil Procedure Code (2015), Article 459.2.

[55] New York Convention, Article V.2(b). "*Recognition and enforcement of an arbitral award may also be refused if the competent authority in the country where recognition and enforcement is sought finds that...the recognition or enforcement of the award would be contrary to the public policy of that country.*"

[56] Blanco et al., supra note 239, at 39.

jurisdictions, such as Switzerland or Germany, have recognized them as reflecting fundamental legal principles.[57]

The term has typically been associated with a narrow interpretation.[58] Vietnam has not enacted a specific definition for "*basic principles of Vietnamese law*," resulting in inconsistent application. This has led to some courts applying it broadly to the point of considering any inconsistency in the findings with a provision of Vietnamese law to constitute a violation of "*basic principles*" (even if the substantive law is not of Vietnam). In 2014, the SPC promulgated guidance to the People's Courts on interpreting such provision, defining such principles as meaning "*the arbitral award violates the effective basic rules for formulation and implementation of the laws of Vietnam.*"[59]

However, such guidance was largely ineffective in practice, as it layered upon another undefined term, creating uncertainty as to what such "*basic rules*" comprised. It did not resolve the complete discretion that was afforded to the courts in determining the extent of "*basic principles of the laws of Vietnam.*" The implications of this discretion were notorious among the legal and business communities as it became the most cited grounds on which Vietnamese courts refused to recognize a foreign arbitration award, leading to a variety of outcomes.[60]

8 Sovereign Immunity, the Choice of Enforcement, and the Judiciary's Track Record

While no recent statistics are publicly available, according to the SPC, between 2000 and 2014, only 24 out of 52 petitions for recognition of

[57] Alan Redfern & Mark Hunter, Law and Practice of International Commercial Arbitration, Sweet & Maxwell, 2004, at 41.

[58] Blanco et al., supra note 239, at 39.

[59] Resolution No. 02/2014/NQ-HDTP providing guidelines for the Law on Commercial Arbitration, Council of Judges of the Supreme People's Court, March 20, 2014, Article 14.2(dd).

[60] Nadia Dridi, The Enforcement of Foreign Arbitration Awards in Vietnam: Overview and Criticisms 59 Harvard International Law Journal (2017). Online journal, available at http://www.harvardilj.org/2017/12/the-enforcement-of-foreign-arbitration-awards-in-vietnam-overview-and-criticisms/ (last accessed October 19, 2018).

a foreign arbitration award were successful.[61] The reasons for this track record, despite the supposed effect of the New York Convention, and leaving aside the enablement of discretion of the domestic laws, may be attributed to two major reasons[62]:

1. Vietnamese courts tend to only apply domestic law and neglect international law; and
2. Vietnamese courts have traditionally maintained a conservative view, electing to refuse recognition to protect the interests of Vietnamese entities.[63]

These statistics do not just capture data from awards of investment disputes, but generally any foreign commercial arbitration awards. Considering the potential impact of investment treaties to FDI inflows as well as the court's general reluctance to avoid direct application of international law, there is a fear that many of the recognition and enforcement mechanisms set forth by these treaties may go disregarded.

A concern that is seldom addressed in Vietnam is the prospect of the State enlivening sovereign immunity to prevent a forced attachment on its sovereign assets—the result being the award creditor being left with a favorable award on paper but without any monetary value in practice.[64] Although a State will have waived its jurisdictional sovereign immunity on agreeing to investment arbitration, it remains arguable that a State can still maintain immunity over sovereign assets at the enforcement stage.[65]

[61] Ministry of Justice, Hội nghị tổng kết 20 năm thực hiện công ước New York năm 1958 về công nhận và cho thi hành quyết định của trọng tài nước ngoài [English translation: Review of Conference on 20 Years of Implementing the New York Convention on the Recognition and Enforcement of Foreign Arbitral Awards], http://moj.gov.vn/qt/tintuc/Pages/hoat-dong-cua-lanh-dao-bo.aspx?ItemID=2052, November 21, 2014 (last accessed October 19, 2018).

[62] Blanco et al., supra note 239, at 40, 41.

[63] Dzung, Trang, supra note 65, at 291.

[64] Yue, Ma, The ICSID Review and Enforcement Mechanisms and the Backlash against the Investor-State Arbitration, Central European University Electronic Thesis And Dissertations.

[65] Jacob A. Kuipers, Too Big to Nail: How Investor-State Arbitration Lacks an Appropriate Execution Mechanism for the Largest Awards, 39 Boston College International And Comparative Law.

In Vietnam, this is regarding the fact that "...property managed or invested in by the State are public property owned by all the people, and represented and uniformly managed by the State."[66] However, the treaties that govern investment arbitration and domestic law are silent as to the extent to which Vietnam has execution or enforcement immunity (and whether there are any specific limits). While it has not yet been encountered in practice, such type of immunity could theoretically be raised by Vietnam under the New York Convention,[67] particularly pursuant to Article III (on public policy or "basic principles") and/or Article V(2)(b). However, for the former, it is difficult to reconcile that a seizure of sovereign assets would constitute a breach of "basic principles of Vietnamese law."

For most rendered investment awards, respondent States have nevertheless typically complied with orders voluntarily. In the event this does not occur, the award creditors are presented with few options[68] to pursue recognition and enforcement of the award in the host State. If recognition is successful, there remain potential bureaucratic obstacles if the quantum of the claim is sizeable.

Furthermore, while civil judgment enforcement authorities are under the auspices of the Ministry of Justice,[69] the Law on Enforcement of Civil Judgments does not identify the competent body to enforce arbitration awards rendered against the State. The investor may pursue recognition and enforcement of the award in an offshore jurisdiction where the procedures for recognition and enforcement may be subject to the seat of the arbitration.

For recognition and enforcement of arbitral awards in Vietnam, unless there is a specialized international instrument (e.g., the ICSID Convention) or if the investor is not a member state of the New York Convention, the award creditor will be subject to recognition procedures pursuant to the CPC, which incorporated the provisions of the New York Convention. Foreign investors are then faced with challenges, inter alia judicial independence, and general discretionary powers of judges which may result

[66] Constitution of Vietnam (2013), Article 48.

[67] Huseynli, supra note 309, at 52.

[68] Huseynli, supra note 309, at 45.

[69] Law on Enforcement of Civil Judgments, Chapter VIII.

in non-recognition of an award. The question of whether the State can enliven enforcement immunity also comes into play.

9 Gaps in Judicial Divergence

Despite current legislation and (binding) international instruments, there is a shortcoming in the judiciary's implementation—a legislative and judicial divergence. In the context of investment disputes (and, particularly, arbitration), two key concerns can be identified:

1. a conflict between judiciary independence and the inherent and overarching duties to safeguard the interests of the State; and limited technical knowledge of the judiciary regarding investment disputes and Vietnam's international commitments, which has led to inconsistencies in the application of the law (and diverging and unpredictable results).

Such challenges have not gone unnoticed by the Government. In 2002, in recognition of certain failings of the judiciary, the CPV passed Resolution No. 08-NQ/TW to initiate judicial reform.[70] Among the criticisms were conservativeness and lack of technical knowledge of judges.[71] What followed were a series of reforms to legal instruments which resulted in greater procedural uniformity among the judiciary and broader education and training regimes.[72] Efforts have been made by the State in

[70] Pip Nicholson, Vietnamese Jurisprudence: Informing Court Reform. In Gillespie, John, Nicholson, Pip (Eds.), *Asian Socialism and Legal Change: The Dynamics of Vietnamese and Chinese Reform*. ANU Press, 2005, at 159. Resolution No. 08-NQ/TW on targeting matters regarding judicial work for the future, The Politburo, January 2, 2002 ("Resolution 08-NQ/TW").

[71] Id.

[72] Id.

availing of international cooperation (or "donors") to assist in the reform process,[73] which has resulted in gradual development.[74]

On June 14, 2016, Decision No. 1063/QD-TTg of the Government[75] recognized a deficiency in the knowledge and capacity of public sector officers in international investment disputes and promulgated a "roadmap" to address such deficiency. Whereas conventional ISDS mechanisms generally left enforcement to the sole discretion of the courts in interpreting the New York Convention, the ISDS provisions in the EVIPA suggest a recent breakthrough toward reform—going so far as to potentially pave the way for the State's ratification of the ICSID Convention.

Particularly, the EVIPA stipulates that the enforcement of investment arbitration awards against Vietnam as a State respondent would be subject to the New York Convention.[76] However, this is caveated by the transitional provision that such regime will only be in force for a five-year extendable grace period, after which an "*automatic*" enforcement regime will come into effect. This has imposed upon the State a deadline toward stripping the judiciary of gatekeeper functions in which it has certain discretionary powers for refusing recognition and creating a process in which civil judgment enforcement authorities would need to handle awards directly.[77] Although, considering investment awards issued under the EVIPA are "foreign awards" and court recognition is required prior to enforcement, it remains to be seen whether Vietnam will abolish such recognition process.

[73] Pip Nicholson & Cait Storr, The Vietnamese Courts and Reform Dynamics. In Christoph Antons, *Routledge Handbook of Asian Law*. Routledge, 2006. For example, as one of its cooperation projects in Vietnam, the Japan International Cooperation Agency ("JICA") has been providing technical assistance to the MOJ, the Supreme People's Court and the Supreme People's Procuracy in connection with its judicial system reform programme. See Japan International Cooperation Agency, Activities in Vietnam—Technical Assistance Project for Legal and Judicial System Reform, https://www.jica.go.jp/vietnam/english/activities/activity09.html (last accessed November 18, 2018).

[74] Id.

[75] Decision No. 1063/QD-TTg to approve the project for capacity building for officers of ministries in the field of international law and in the settlement of international investment disputes for the 2016–2020 period, Government Office, June 14, 2016 ("Decision No. 1063/QD-TTg").

[76] EVIPA, Article 3.57(3).

[77] EVIPA, Article 3.57(3).

While the fact that this provision has been maintained in the EVIPA reflects Vietnam's reluctance to recognize most investment arbitration awards, it also suggests that the Government of Vietnam has recognized such judicial challenges. Together with more than 60 existing BITs and FTAs which Vietnam is a signatory, should the EVIPA be ratified with such grace period in place, such ratification could be the catalyst that Vietnam needs to expedite judicial reform with respect to a feasible mechanism for investment dispute settlements.

CHAPTER 22

In-Country Processing as a Solution to the International Refugee Crisis: The Example of the CAM Program

Giulia Rettagliati

1 Introduction

Under international refugee law, "[i]t is a general requirement for refugee status that an applicant who has a nationality be outside the country of his nationality. There are no exceptions to this rule. International protection cannot come into play as long as a person is within the territorial jurisdiction of his home country."[1]

Thanks to the Central American Minors (or "CAM") program, certain Central American minors can be processed for refugee protection and receive immigration status in the United States before leaving their

[1] UNHCR, *Handbook on Procedures and Criteria for Determining Refugee Status and Guidelines on International Protection Under the 1951 Convention and the 1967 Protocol Relating to the Status of Refugees*, 25 (Apr. 2019), HCR/1P/4/ENG/REV. 4.

G. Rettagliati (✉)
Law Offices of Marco Ambron, San Francisco, CA, USA
e-mail: g.rettagliati@gmail.com

E. Duruigbo et al. (eds.), *International Law and Development in the Global South*, https://doi.org/10.1007/978-3-031-13741-9_22

country. As a solution to the current international refugee crisis, this chapter advocates for the global adoption of national programs that should follow the model of the CAM program in the United States.

First, the chapter conducts an analysis on the lack of means of protection under international refugee law for individuals who have not yet left their home country, where their lives are in danger.

Then, the chapter examines the experience of the CAM program in the United States and the beneficial consequences arising from processing certain qualifying migrants within their own country to award them refugee protection in the United States.

Finally, the article recommends for national States to follow the model of the CAM program and it examines the advantages of implementing national in-country refugee processing programs.

2 A Void in International Law

2.1 The Global Refugee Problem

Migration flows are rising worldwide: in the past ten years, the number of forcibly displaced persons has doubled and the number of refugees has almost doubled.[2] Currently, about 82.4 million people worldwide, many of whom are children,[3] are forced to leave their homes after suffering serious human rights violations.[4] Generally, migrants have to undertake a highly dangerous trip to seek protection.[5] They take extremely dangerous paths in order not to be noticed by the authorities and returned to their country of origin.[6] Along the migration routes, migrants are at risk

[2] American Immigration Council, *An Overview of U.S. Refugee Law and Policy*, Fact Sheet (Sep. 20, 2021).

[3] Omer Karaspan, *Sharing the Burden of the Global Refugee Crisis*, Brookings (Jan. 27, 2020).

[4] UNHCR, *Global Trends Forced Displacement in 2020*, 2 Report (June 18, 2021).

[5] See e.g. Olivia Ruiz Marrujo, *Los riesgos de cruzar. La migración centroamericana en la frontera México-Guatemala*, vol. 13, no. 25 (Jan.–June 2001); International Crisis Group, *Easy Prey: Criminal Violence and Central American Migration*, [hereinafter International Crisis Group, *Easy Prey*] 10–14 Latin America Report n° 57, (July 28, 2016).

[6] Anastasia Moloney, *Seeking New Routes, Central American Migrants at Risk of Trafficking*, Thomson Reuters, http://www.reuters.com/article/us-mexico-human-trafficking/seeking-new-routes-central-american-migrants-at-risk-of-trafficking-idUSKCN0ZA364 (posted on June 24, 2016, 10:33 a.m.); Nina Lakhani, *Central American Migrants*

of harm, exploitation, and trafficking, especially at the hands of violent criminal organizations.[7] However, they still consider it safer to face this dangerous trip than to remain at home.[8]

The COVID-19 pandemic exacerbated the refugee problem: for some people, the spread of the virus was a triggering factor in their decision to flee their homes.[9] The measures adopted to reduce the spread of the virus made it much more difficult than before to reach safety for individuals in need of international protection.[10] Despite the current global health crisis, it is necessary to offer protection to victims of human rights violations; at the same time, it is necessary to reduce as much as possible the travels needed to seek and receive protection to reduce the spread of the COVID-19 pandemic. However, international law offers no protection to people who would like to seek refugee status unless they move outside of their own country.[11]

2.2 The Refugee Convention and Protocol

The Convention Relating to the Status of Refugees[12] (or "Refugee Convention") and the Protocol relating to the Status of Refugees (or "Protocol")[13] are the most important international law documents that

Desperate to Reach US Risk New Dangers at Sea, The Guardian, https://www.theguardian.com/global-development/2016/sep/15/migrants-mexico-human-trafficking-us-immigration-crackdown (posted on Sep. 15, 2016 at 6:00 a.m. EDT); International Crisis Group, *Easy Prey*, supra n. 5.

[7] Jo Tuckman, *Migrants Risk Life and Limb to Reach the US on Train Known as the BEAST*, The Guardian, https://www.theguardian.com/world/2014/aug/23/migrants-mexico-train-the-beast-fleeing-poverty (posted on Aug. 23, 2014, 4:13 p.m. EDT); International Crisis Group, *Easy Prey* supra n. 5; *MS 13*, InSight Crime, http://www.insightcrime.org/el-salvador-organized-crime-news/mara-salvatrucha-ms-13-profile (accessed Oct. 18, 2021).

[8] International Crisis Group, *Easy Prey* supra n. 5 at 10.

[9] Eric Reidy, *One Year On: How the Pandemic Has Affected Refugees, Asylum Seekers, and Migration*, The New Humanitarian (Mar. 10, 2021).

[10] Ibid.

[11] See supra n. 1.

[12] UNGA, *Convention Relating to the Status of Refugees*, 28 July 1951, U.N.T.S., vol. 189, p. 137.

[13] UNGA, *Protocol Relating to the Status of Refugees*, 31 January 1967, U.N.T.S., vol. 606, p. 267.

spell out the rights of refugees and impose international obligations to guarantee their protection.[14] Under the Refugee Convention and the Protocol, States agreed to provide two main forms of protection to individuals in need: asylum and resettlement.

2.3 *Asylum*

International human rights law guarantees the right to seek and enjoy asylum in other countries for individuals who fall within the definition of "refugee."[15] Article 1 of the Refugee Convention defines a "refugee" as follows:

> [...] any person who [...] owing to well-founded fear of being persecuted for reasons of race, religion, nationality, membership of a particular social group or political opinion, is outside the country of his nationality and is unable or, owing to such fear, is unwilling to avail himself of the protection of that country; or who, not having a nationality and being outside the country of his former habitual residence as a result of such events, is unable or, owing to such fear, is unwilling to return to it. In the case of a person who has more than one nationality, the term "the country of his nationality" shall mean each of the countries of which he is a national, and a person shall not be deemed to be lacking the protection of the country of his nationality if, without any valid reason based on well-founded fear, he has not availed himself of the protection of one of the countries of which he is a national.[16]

Thus, the right to asylum is available only for individuals who are located outside their country of nationality.

[14] See *Convention Relating to the Status of Refugees*, supra n. 12, *Protocol Relating to the Status of Refugees*, supra n. 13.

[15] See generally IJRC, *Asylum & the Rights of Refugees* https://ijrcenter.org/refugee-law/#:~:text=Article%2014(1)%20of%20the,enjoy%20asylum%20in%20other%20countries.&text=The%201951%20Convention%20establishes%20the,to%20those%20granted%20refugee%20status (accessed Oct. 18, 2021).

[16] *Convention Relating to the Status of Refugees*, supra n. 12 at art. 1.

2.4 *Resettlement*

The principle of *non-refoulement* is one of the key principles of international refugee law[17] and it is largely considered to be a rule of *jus cogens*.[18] According to article 33(1) of the Refugee Convention, "[n]o Contracting State shall expel or return ('refouler') a refugee in any manner whatsoever to the frontiers of territories where his [or her] life or freedom would be threatened on account of his [or her] race, religion, nationality, membership of a particular social group or political opinion."[19] Consistently with the international principle of *non-refoulement*, some countries implemented programs to regulate the resettlement within their territory of refugees from a third country.[20] Similarly, to the right to asylum, the principle of *non-refoulement* only applies to individuals who fall within the definition of refugees.[21] In conclusion, the principle of *non-refoulement* only protects persons who already left their own country; therefore, resettlement is only available for individuals who are able to reach a country different than their country of nationality.

2.5 *International Issues*

The lack of tools of protection under international refugee law for people who have not left their own country is deeply troubling for various reasons: first, it completely excludes from international protection individuals who are already disadvantaged and often materially unable to undertake a dangerous journey. Subjects like minors, elderly people, and persons with disabilities are completely cut out of international refugee law protections if their condition does not allow them to travel out of their country with their own resources. When national States fail

[17] *See* UNHCR, *Advisory Opinion on the Extraterritorial Application of Non-refoulement Obligations Under the 1951 Convention Relating to the Status of Refugees and Its 1967 Protocol* (Jan. 26, 2007).

[18] See e.g. Jean Allain, *The Jus Cogens Nature of Non-refoulement*, Vol. 13, Int'l J. of Refugee L., 533–558 (Oct. 1, 2001); Alice Farmer, *Non-refoulement and Jus Cogens: Limiting Anti-terror Measures that Threaten Refugee Protection*, 23 Geo. Immigr. L.J. 1, 18–22 (2008).

[19] *Convention Relating to the Status of Refugees*, supra n. 12 at art. 33(1).

[20] Karen Musalo, Jennifer Moore & Richard A. Boswell, *Refugee Law and Policy: A Comparative and International Approach* 75 (4th ed. Carolina Academic Press, 2011).

[21] *Convention Relating to the Status of Refugees*, supra n. 12 at art. 33(1).

to protect the rights of the members of the above-mentioned vulnerable groups, they are shamefully failing their international human rights obligations.[22]

Second, the lack of eligibility for international refugee protections of people who reside within their own country, independently from the existence of situations of immediate life danger for them, encourages people to migrate to seek protection.[23] As a result, States have little control over the overwhelming flows of migrants all over the world.[24] Along their path, migrants who are already vulnerable when they are running away from life-threatening situations are exposed to the danger of being further victimized by criminals.[25]

Third, forcing people to travel to be eligible for international protection furthers the need for otherwise unnecessary travels, in contrast with the international effort in preventing and containing the spread of the COVID-19 pandemic.[26]

Overall, the lack of international refugee law mechanisms for the processing and admission of refugees to different countries from within their home country encourages unlawful and uncontrolled migration flows. As a solution to the issues examined above, the author proposes

[22] *See* UNGA, *Convention on the Rights of the Child*, 20 November 1989, United Nations, Treaty Series, vol. 1577, p. 3; UNGA, *Convention on the Rights of Persons with Disabilities: Resolution/Adopted by the General Assembly*, 24 January 2007, A/RES/61/106; UNGA, *United Nations Principles for Older Persons Adopted by General Assembly*, 16 December 1991, A/RES/46/91; UNGA, *Implementation of the International Plan of Action on Ageing and Related Activities: Resolution/Adopted by the General Assembly*, 16 December 1991, A/RES/46/91.

[23] See e.g. UNHCR, *Global Trends Forced Displacement in 2020*, Report (June 18, 2021); American Immigration Council, *An Overview of U.S. Refugee Law and Policy*, Fact Sheet (Sep. 20, 2021).

[24] See e.g. Migration Data Portal, *Irregular Migration*, https://www.migrationdataportal.org/themes/irregular-migration (accessed Oct. 20, 2021); Eurostat, *Migration and Migrant Population Statistics*, https://ec.europa.eu/eurostat/statistics-explained/index.php?title=Migration_and_migrant_population_statistics#Migrant_population:_23_million_non-EU_citizens_living_in_the_EU_on_1_January_2020 (accessed Oct. 20, 2021).

[25] See e.g. IRC, *The Human Stories of the World's Most Dangerous Migration Route*, https://www.rescue.org/article/human-stories-worlds-most-dangerous-migration-route (accessed Oct. 18, 2021); The New Humanitarian, *Risky Journeys*, https://www.thenewhumanitarian.org/migration/risky-journeys (accessed Oct. 18, 2021).

[26] Korin Miller, *American Tourists Are Being Urged to Stay Home*, Verywell Health (Sep. 7, 2021).

the global adoption of national programs to screen and evaluate refugee claims of persons still residing within their own country. After being awarded refugee status within their country of nationality, these individuals could then travel safely and lawfully enter their country of refuge. The next chapter analyses the CAM program in the United States and underlines its strengths to propose the global adoption of analogous in-country processing refugee programs worldwide.

3 The CAM Program

3.1 Overview

The CAM Program is an in-country processing program that allows certain qualifying Central American minors to travel safely to the United States.[27] Starting in 1979, the United States implemented various in-country processing programs as a response to humanitarian crises.[28]

The CAM process starts with the application of a qualifying United States-based parent or legal guardian.[29] To be eligible, the children must be unmarried under twenty-one years old nationals of El Salvador, Guatemala, or Honduras residing within their own country.[30] After various steps—involving the International Organization on Migration—minors receive a determination by the United States Citizenship and Immigration Services ("USCIS").[31]

[27] US DHS, *In-Country Refugee/Parole Program for Minors in El Salvador, Guatemala, and Honduras with Parents Lawfully Present in the United States*, Fact Sheet (Nov. 14, 2014); USCIS, *Central American Minors (CAM) Refugee and Parole Program*, https://www.uscis.gov/CAM (accessed Oct. 18, 2021); US DHS, *Central American Minors (CAM) Program*, https://www.state.gov/refugee-admissions/central-american-minors-cam-program/ (accessed Oct. 20, 2021).

[28] Faye Hipsman and Doris Meissner, *In-Country Processing in Central America: A Piece of the Puzzle*, 9 Migration Policy Institute (Aug. 2015).

[29] USCIS, *Central American Minors (CAM) Refugee and Parole Program*, https://www.uscis.gov/CAM (accessed Oct. 18, 2021); US DHS, *Central American Minors (CAM) Program*, https://www.state.gov/refugee-admissions/central-american-minors-cam-program/ (accessed Oct. 20, 2021).

[30] Ibid.

[31] Ibid.

There are three possible outcomes of the CAM process: a grant of refugee status, a grant of parole status, or denial of any status.[32] The procedure for appealing in case of denial of refugee status is called a request for review.[33]

3.2 CAM Refugee Program

To qualify for refugee status, minors have to be admissible to the United States, located outside of the United States territory and they have to demonstrate that they fit within the definition of "refugee"[34]—except for the requirement of being outside their country of nationality. Minors who qualify for refugee status through CAM receive a high range of benefits, such as a loan to support the traveling expenses necessary to be reunited with their United States-based parent or guardian, resettlement assistance, the possibility to include certain persons as derivatives on their application for immigration status, and eligibility for employment authorization.[35] One year after being awarded refugee status, children can adjust to legal permanent residency.[36] Five years after being designated as refugees, children are eligible to apply for U.S. citizenship.[37]

[32] See Ibid.

[33] Ibid.

[34] Ibid. The definition of refugee in the United States under INA § 101(a)(42) reflects the international definition of refugee given by art. 1 of the Refugee Convention.

[35] US DHS, *Central American Minors (CAM) Program*, https://www.state.gov/refugee-admissions/central-american-minors-cam-program/ (accessed Oct. 20, 2021); US DHS, *In-Country Refugee/Parole Program for Minors in El Salvador, Guatemala, and Honduras with Parents Lawfully Present in the United States*, Fact Sheet, Nov. 14, 2014.

[36] US DHS, *Central American Minors (CAM) Program*, https://www.state.gov/refugee-admissions/central-american-minors-cam-program/ (accessed Oct. 20, 2021); 8 C.F.R. § 209.1.

[37] US DHS, *Central American Minors (CAM) Program*, https://www.state.gov/refugee-admissions/central-american-minors-cam-program/ (accessed Oct. 20, 2021); *See* 8 C.F.R. § 316.

3.3 CAM Parole Program

Parole status is awarded for urgent humanitarian reasons or significant public benefit.[38] USCIS officers evaluate if the applicant deserves a favorable exercise of discretion.[39] Among the elements for establishing if there are urgent humanitarian reasons for children in the CAM program, USCIS takes into account the following factors: "[w]hether or not the circumstances are pressing; the effect of the circumstances on the individual's welfare and wellbeing; and the degree of suffering that may result if parole is not authorized."[40] Minors who receive parole status through the CAM program are allowed to be temporarily lawfully present in the United States and are eligible to apply for work authorization, but parole is not a pathway to residency or citizenship.[41] Once paroled in the United States, minors can access legal representation and apply for any other possible immigration relief that they may be eligible for under U.S. immigration law. At the expiration of the term for parole, which currently may be of up to three years, minors can apply for renewal.[42]

3.4 Legislative History

In December 2014, the Obama administration first implemented the "In-Country Refugee/Parole Processing for Minors in Honduras, El Salvador and Guatemala (Central American Minors – CAM)" as a response to the 2014 surge of immigrant children from the Central American Northern

[38] INA § 212.5.

[39] INA § 212(d)(5)(A).

[40] USCIS, *Humanitarian or Significant Public Benefit Parole for Individuals Outside the United States*, https://www.uscis.gov/humanitarian/humanitarian-or-significant-public-benefit-parole-individuals-outside-united-states (accessed Oct. 18, 2021).

[41] US DHS, *Central American Minors (CAM) Program*, https://www.state.gov/refugee-admissions/central-american-minors-cam-program/ (accessed Oct. 20, 2021); USCIS, *Central American Minors (CAM) Refugee and Parole Program*, https://www.uscis.gov/CAM (accessed Oct. 18, 2021); US DHS, *In-Country Refugee/Parole Program for Minors in El Salvador, Guatemala, and Honduras with Parents Lawfully Present in the United States*, Fact Sheet (Nov. 14, 2014).

[42] 9 FAM 202.3-2(B)(U); USCIS, *Central American Minors (CAM) Refugee and Parole Program*, https://www.uscis.gov/CAM (accessed Oct. 18, 2021).

Triangle.[43] During the life of the program, nearly 5000 children living in situations of danger were reunited with their families in the United States.[44] About 69% of the minors who took part in the CAM program were granted parole, 1% were denied status, and the rest were granted refugee status.[45]

In 2017, the Trump administration first terminated the CAM parole program[46] due to its adoption of a different policy to secure the border.[47] Among the explanations provided, the administration attributed to immigrant children the gang problem affecting the United States, even though experts find that immigrant minors are generally victims of gang activities.[48] The termination of the CAM parole program affected 2714 minors who were already approved parole status but could not carry out the final step of the process and lawfully join their parents in the United States.[49]

The termination of the CAM parole program did not directly affect the CAM refugee program,[50] but it certainly made its cancellation foreseeable. Indeed, the Trump administration shortly after terminated the CAM refugee program as well as part of the "U.S. Refugee Admission

[43] US DHS, *Central American Minors (CAM) Program*, https://www.state.gov/refugee-admissions/central-american-minors-cam-program/ (accessed Oct. 20, 2021); National Immigration Forum, *Fact Sheet: Central American Minors (CAM) Program*, Fact Sheet (Mar. 19, 2021).

[44] US DHS, *Restarting the Central American Minors Program*, Media Note (Mar. 10, 2021).

[45] Tal Kopan, *DHS Ends Program for Central American Minors*, CNN, http://www.cnn.com/2017/08/16/politics/trump-ending-central-american-minors-program/index.html (posted on Aug. 16, 2017 at 5:19 p.m. EDT).

[46] *Termination of the Central American Minors Parole Program*, Federal Register Volume 82, Number 157, Department of Homeland Security (Aug. 16, 2017).

[47] USCIS, *Central American Minors (CAM): Information for Parole Applicants*, https://www.uscis.gov/humanitarian/humanitarian-parole/central-american-minors-cam-information-parole-applicants (accessed Oct. 18, 2021).

[48] Tal Kopan, *DHS Ends Program for Central American Minors*, CNN, http://www.cnn.com/2017/08/16/politics/trump-ending-central-american-minors-program/index.html (posted on Aug.16, 2017 at 5:19 p.m. EDT).

[49] KIND, *Thwarted Potential*, 2 (Nov. 2, 2020); David Nakamura, *Trump Administration Ends Obama-Era Protection Program for Central American Minors*, The Washington Post (Aug. 16, 2017).

[50] Federal Register Volume 82, Number 157 (Aug. 16, 2017).

Program for FY 2018."[51] The reason provided for the termination of the CAM Program was related to the limited number of children admitted as refugees through the program.[52] The Department of State communicated that, from November 9, 2017, it would stop accepting new CAM applications and that USCIS officers would continue interviewing minors only until January 31, 2018.[53] The termination of the CAM refugee program, following the termination of the CAM Parole program, in practical terms meant the end of the entire CAM program.[54] Many Central American children, who after being victimized by the gang members often are "virtual prisoners inside their homes, having abandoned school and work as a result of the threats and beatings,"[55] were left out of lawful avenues to reach safety in the United States. Consequently, the end of the CAM program was heavily criticized[56] and caused the filing of a complaint with the Northern District of California in S.A. v. Trump, 18-cv-03539.[57]

As stated by Lisa Frydman, Vice President for International Programs at Kids in Need of Defense (or "KIND"), when interviewed by the author:

> It is really the administration abandoning children, more than anything, who are potential refugees. The explanation given by the administration, which is that this Program has helped a small number of refugees, it is unsatisfactory, in significant part because the way in which this Program

[51] US DoS, US DHS, US DHH, *Proposed Refugee Admissions for Fiscal Year 2018*, 43 Report to the Congress (2017).

[52] Ibid.

[53] USCIS, *Status of the Central American Minors Program*, https://www.uscis.gov/archive/status-of-the-central-american-minors-program (accessed Oct. 19, 2021).

[54] *See* US DoS, US DHS, US DHH, *Proposed Refugee Admissions for Fiscal Year 2018*, 43 Report to the Congress (2017).

[55] Nina Lakhani, *Thousands of Young Central Americans at Risk as Refugee Ban Halts Key Program*, The Guardian https://www.theguardian.com/us-news/2017/feb/02/central-america-young-refugees-cam-trump-travel-ban?CMP=share_btn_fb (posted on Feb. 2, 2017 at 6:00 a.m. EST).

[56] See e.g. David Nakamura, *Trump Administration Ends Obama-Era Protection Program for Central American Minors*, The Washington Post (Aug. 16, 2017); Latin America Working Group, *CAM Program Parole Termination: Latest Sign of the Administration's Intent to Harm Children & Families from Central America*, Statement (2017).

[57] *S.A. v. Trump*, Case No. 18-cv-03539-LB (N.D. Cal. Mar. 1, 2019).

> was set up is what part of the problem is. [...] Essentially this is saying to me that the administration has determined that there is not a need for refugee protection for Central American children, and that is not true at all. Rather, what the administration should be doing is looking to see what other ways could improve the Program to bring in more individuals as refugees.[58]

In March 2021, the Department of State announced the reopening of the CAM program,[59] and in mid-September 2021, the Biden-Harris administration opened the CAM program for new applications.[60] The new administration had the merit of reopening the CAM program as part of a comprehensive migration management strategy that includes the expansion of legal pathways to enter the United States and the treatment of migrants with humanity and respect.[61]

3.5 Strengths of the CAM Program

In general, in-country programs aim to improve access to humanitarian protection and regulate refugee and humanitarian admissions to the United States under conditions of extreme danger and sizeable flows. However, in-country programs have been controversial throughout their history, and have been strongly criticized by even some immigrants—and human—rights advocates. Several key factors determine how effective in-country programs are and how they are viewed—the reason for establishing the program, the admission criteria, how the application process is structured, how long it takes for cases to be adjudicated, and whether the program can adequately protect applicants.[62]

[58] Telephonic Interview with Lisa Frydman, Vice President for International Programs, Kids in Need of Defense (or "KIND"), San Francisco (Nov. 20, 2017).

[59] US DHS, *Restarting the Central American Minors Program*, Media Note (Mar. 10, 2021).

[60] US DHS, *Joint Department of State and Department of Homeland Security Rollout of the Application Process for the Central American Minors (CAM) Program*, Media Note (Sep. 13, 2021).

[61] US DHS, *Restarting the Central American Minors Program*, Media Note (Mar. 10, 2021).

[62] Faye Hipsman and Doris Meissner, *In-Country Processing in Central America: A Piece of the Puzzle*, 1 Migration Policy Institute (Aug. 2015).

Some aspects of the CAM program can certainly be improved: the lengthy processing time for applications—it takes about one year for the process to be completed—should be reduced, particularly because minors who qualify for the CAM program are generally in situations of immediate danger[63]; the CAM program should be extensively advertised—in particular between the communities of potentially eligible parents and guardians—to ensure widespread access to it[64]; the involvement of UNHCR child protection officers would bring more attention to the circumstances of the minors[65]; providing access to legal representation for minors throughout the process would improve its fairness.[66]

Despite its weaknesses, the strengths of the CAM program examined below make it an example worthy of global attention as a possible measure to adopt as part of a strategy for tackling the international refugee crisis.[67] The highest merit of the CAM program is that, in case of a positive USCIS determination, it provides "a safe, legal, and orderly alternative to the dangerous journey that some children are currently undertaking to the United States."[68] Thanks to the CAM program, minors with a successful claim do not have to face the dangerous trip to reach the U.S. border, which puts them at risk of being victims of violence and abuse.[69]

[63] Maria Soledad Silva Benitez, *Immigrant Children Despair: The Central American Minors Program (CAM) as the U.S. Response to the Humanitarian Crisis of Unaccompanied Immigrant Children,* [hereinafter Maria Soledad Silva Benitez, *Immigrant Children Despair*] 36 Duke University Graduate Liberal Studies (Apr. 3, 2018).

[64] See id. at 38–39; "At KIND, we were trying to urge the Department of State and USCIS from the beginning that they needed to be out in the Latino community publicizing the Program, talking to legal services providers, talking to social services providers, so that the organization could tell their clients about the Program." Telephonic interview with Lisa Frydman, supra n. 58.

[65] Telephonic interview with Lisa Frydman, supra n. 58.

[66] Ibid; Maria Soledad Silva Benitez, *Immigrant Children Despair*, supra n. 63 at 40.

[67] *See* American Immigration Council, *An Overview of U.S. Refugee Law and Policy,* Fact Sheet (Sep. 20, 2021); Faye Hipsman and Doris Meissner, *In-Country Processing in Central America: A Piece of the Puzzle*, 14 Migration Policy Institute (Aug. 2015).

[68] U.S. DoS, *In-Country Refugee/Parole Program for Minors in El Salvador, Guatemala, and Honduras with Parents Lawfully Present in the United States*, Fact Sheet (Nov. 14, 2014).

[69] See e.g. IRC, *The Human Stories of the World's Most Dangerous Migration Route*, https://www.rescue.org/article/human-stories-worlds-most-dangerous-migration-route (accessed Oct. 18, 2021); The New Humanitarian, *Risky journeys*, https://www.thenewhumanitarian.org/migration/risky-journeys (accessed Oct. 18, 2021).

Moreover, the program helps to contain, track, and regulate the migration flows from Central America to the United States.[70]

Another strength of the program is that it enhances family reunification between minors and their parents or guardians with lawful immigration status in the United States,[71] pursuing the best interest of the child in compliance with art. 3 of the United Nations Convention on the Rights of the Child.[72]

As concluded by Lisa Frydman—KIND's Vice President for International Programs—when interviewed by the author, overall, the CAM program had the merit of offering much-needed protection to minors:

> There is definitely a need for refugee protection for Central American children and to the extent that they have got a lawful way to come to the United States and avoid having to take the journey through Mexico, avoid having to go to smugglers, that is a really good thing. This program could have been a lot better [...] but the main thing that was good was this possibility to give children a lawful way to come to the United States and achieve safety here, rather than have to go through the migration route. [...] It also created an avenue for children to reunify with parents from which they have been separated for years, because the majority of parents who petitioned for children were TPS holders and had no way to petition lawfully to bring their children to the United States.[73]

4 Recommendations and Conclusions

The international nature of the refugee problem would require international solutions. Looking for solutions that involve the international community leads to evaluations related to matters of national sovereignty

[70] *See* The White House, *Executive Order on Creating a Comprehensive Regional Framework to Address the Causes of Migration, to Manage Migration Throughout North and Central America, and to Provide Safe and Orderly Processing of Asylum Seekers at the United States Border* (Feb. 2, 2021).

[71] Faye Hipsman and Doris Meissner, *In-Country Processing in Central America: A Piece of the Puzzle*, 1 Migration Policy Institute (Aug. 2015); Telephonic interview with Lisa Frydman, supra n. 58.

[72] "In all actions concerning children, whether undertaken by public or private social welfare institutions, courts of law, administrative authorities or legislative bodies, the best interests of the child shall be a primary consideration." UNGA, *Convention on the Rights of the Child*, 20 November 1989, United Nations, Treaty Series, vol. 1577, p. 3 art. 3.1.

[73] Telephonic interview with Lisa Frydman, supra n. 58.

and relationships between States,[74] making it difficult to respond quickly and uniformly to the current situation of emergency.

In the opinion of the author, the global adoption of in-country refugee processing programs following the model of the CAM program in the United States would constitute a beneficial first step in the international effort of protecting migrants. States should carry out this burden-sharing form of international cooperation and prioritize the promotion of international human rights law over their political objectives. However, it would be demanded to each national State to tailor the criteria for eligibility and the process itself in the most effective manner to manage the most pressing humanitarian issues involving migration flows to their territories. The involvement of subjects of international law such as the International Organization on Migration and the United Nations High Commissioner for Refugees, already part of the CAM program, would contribute to the success of in-country refugee processing programs.

The experience of the CAM program in the United States shows that in-country refugee processing programs can be a successful tool to fill the gap of protection for victims of human rights violations who remain in situations of danger in their country because their governments are unable or unwilling to protect them.

The global adoption by national States of in-country refugee processing programs tailored on the model of CAM would have the following advantages:

- it would provide effective protection for victims of human rights violations, who would not be forced to undertake a dangerous journey to be eligible for international protection. This aspect is particularly important to fulfill the international human rights obligation that national States assumed to give appropriate protection to the members of vulnerable groups, like minors, elderlies, and disabled people, who generally have limited possibilities to travel;
- it would enhance family reunification—or reunification with a legal guardian—for members of vulnerable groups who would have no other legal avenue to obtain immigration status through a petition from their parent—or guardian—in the country where they reside;

[74] Faye Hipsman and Doris Meissner, *In-Country Processing in Central America: A Piece of the Puzzle*, 1 Migration Policy Institute (Aug. 2015).

- States would have the opportunity to promote lawful, controlled, and orderly migration flows. As a consequence, the profits of organized criminal organizations who control the migration routes and take advantage of refugees would decrease;
- with the current COVID-19 pandemic, processing refugees from their own country would be safer because it would avoid unnecessary travel and reduce the spread of the disease.

Index

A

Abimbola Osarugue Obaseki-Adejumo, 302
Accessionism, 84
Acemoglu, Daron, 190
Achumba, 16
Adaka Boro, 32
Addis Ababa, 129, 132
Adedeji Adekunle, 48
Aderemi, 310, 318
Administration of Criminal Justice Act, 34, 35
Advance fee fraud, 28
Advisory opinion, 148, 149
Africa, 2, 14, 115–118, 121, 122, 125–127, 129, 137, 160, 187, 189, 313
African Charter on Human and Peoples' Rights, 123, 284
African Court of Justice and Human and Peoples' Rights, 117, 122, 124–131, 133, 135–138
African Union, 117, 123–125, 127, 129–131, 133, 135, 137, 138, 169
Aggression, 82, 87, 88, 95, 96, 116, 118, 120, 126, 135
Ahmad Gummi, 14
Akpor-Robaro, 16
All Progressives Congress, 32
Alma Ata Declaration, 168, 169
American Arbitration Association, 222
American Bar Association, 197, 198, 351
Amnesty, 322
Amotekun, 26
Anglican Church, 253, 257, 260, 261
Anglo-Iranian Oil Company, 149
Annan, Kofi, 70, 325
Annexation, 80, 82, 84, 93–97
Anzilloti, 148
Arbitration, 144, 216–230, 240, 298, 380–391
Argentina, 37, 121
Armenia, 80, 84, 85, 87, 91, 97
Armenians, 68, 81, 84, 85

E. Duruigbo et al. (eds.), *International Law and Development in the Global South*, https://doi.org/10.1007/978-3-031-13741-9

Artificial reproductive technology, 252
Asia, 160, 223, 253
Assets Declaration, 49
Australian Centre for International Commercial Arbitration, 223
Austria, 148
Austro-German, 148
Avakian, Shahen, 91
Azerbaijan, 80, 84, 85, 87, 97

B

Badinter Commission, 157, 171
Baltic States, 81, 168
Bandits, 14, 18, 24, 322, 334
Bangladesh, 5–7, 9–11, 242
Bangladesh National Women Lawyers' Association, 5
Banjul, 123
Barr, William, 346, 347, 349, 350
Bashir, Omar, 133
Bedjaoui, Mohammed, 162
Belarus, 81, 82, 91
Berlin, 89
Bernanke, Ben, 244
Biafra, 22, 32, 333
Biden-Harris, 404
Binding over, 47
Bloomberg, Michael, 344
Bloomenthal, Andrew, 244
Boers, 190
Boko Haram, 14, 24–26, 31, 322, 328, 332, 333
Borders, 17, 18, 23, 24, 31, 70, 74, 80–82, 90, 93, 95–97, 127, 171, 183, 238, 239, 310, 328, 402, 405
Bosnia-Herzegovina, 27
Botswana, 187–190
Brierly, J.L., 143
Budapest, 82, 96
Buddhism, 2, 253, 257, 270
Buhari, Muhammadu, 22, 23, 32, 333, 334
Bull, Hedley, 147
Burkina Faso, 123
Bush, George W., 339
Bynkershoek, Cornelius van, 142

C

California, 3, 103, 355–360, 363, 364, 366, 371
California Global Corporate Accountability Project, 178
Cameroon, 170, 171
Canada, 37, 52, 253
Catholic Church, 57, 253, 257, 258, 260
Caucasus, 80, 81, 83, 97, 98
Cavanagh, Tom, 38
Central African Republic, 14, 120
Central American Minors Program, 3
Charter of the United Nations, xii, xiii, 61, 97, 120, 165, 167
Chief Justice of Nigeria, 199, 202, 204, 208, 213, 308, 311
China, 36, 121, 239, 343
China International Economic and Trade Arbitration Commission, 224
Christianity, 2, 253, 257, 327
Cicero, 59
Civil litigation, 102
Civil Rights, 198, 349, 351
Clean-slate doctrine, 160, 175
Climate change, xii, 6, 181, 328
Coalition for Epidemic Preparedness Innovations, the, xi
Code of Conduct, 198–203, 207, 211, 214, 303, 306, 309, 310, 312, 313, 315, 317, 318
Comity, 102, 112, 114
Common law, 50, 289, 313, 316

Commonwealth of Independent States, 171, 174
Communist, 83
Community Service Centres, 43, 54
Community service order, 42, 43
Community trusts, 179, 180, 191–196
Comparative advantage, 242, 255
Compensation, 39–41, 45, 46, 53, 195, 294, 296
Competition, 26, 237–239, 241–243, 247, 324, 327
Comptroller General, 34, 48
Confiscation, 48, 49
Congo, the Democratic Republic of the, 14, 120
Constitution, 6, 7, 17, 22, 94, 156, 171, 198–201, 204, 214, 275–277, 282–284, 291, 293, 296, 303–306, 308, 310, 312, 313, 315–317, 319, 320, 338, 340, 374, 376, 377, 379, 382, 388
Consumer protection, 237, 238
Contractarian, 356, 361, 362, 364, 369, 371
Contracts, 10, 16, 101, 156, 205, 262, 266, 268, 334, 361, 362, 365, 367, 368
Cooke, Timothy, 225
Corona virus, 36
Corporal punishment, 46
Corporate governance, 3, 338, 357
Corporations, 128, 129, 180, 182–184, 186, 195, 355, 357–362, 364–371
Correctional Centres, 34, 37, 52
Corruption, 17–20, 26, 28–32, 48, 126, 129, 135, 179, 193, 195, 200, 207, 208, 285, 287, 293, 298, 304, 308, 318
Côte D'Ivoire, 120
Court of Justice of the European Union, 110
COVAX, xi, xii
Covered Persons, 133, 135
COVID-19, xi, xii, 2, 6, 33, 35–37, 44, 54, 181, 215–218, 220, 221, 223, 224, 228–230, 233–239, 241, 245–248, 347, 395, 398, 408
Crimes against humanity, 73, 116, 118, 119, 126, 130
Criminal justice, 34, 38, 42, 52, 53, 131, 138, 349
Cuba, 91, 343
Customary international law, xii, 63, 133, 135, 136, 172
Cyber-fraud, 228
Cybersecurity, 103
Czech and Slovak Federative Republic, 174
Czechoslovakia, 81, 147

D

Dadem, Yusuf, 198, 199, 201, 208
Defendant, 40, 41, 44, 46, 47, 51–53, 100, 101, 107, 111, 136, 147, 206, 289, 290, 293, 310, 319, 360
De-globalization, 248
Democracy, 3, 18–20, 31, 197, 327, 338, 339, 343, 345
Department of Justice, 337, 340, 346–350, 352, 353
Deportation, 51
Dhaka, 5
Dicey, A.V., 319
Disclosure, 49, 100–103, 105–107, 109, 111, 113, 114, 206
Discovery process, 100–103
Disposition measures, 34, 35, 48, 53
Dispute resolution, 2, 216, 218, 222, 229, 373

Dispute settlements, 236, 240, 391
Domestic obligations, xiv
Domestic workers, 6–11
Donbas, 93, 97
Donetsk People's Republic, the, 80, 84
Dumping, 127, 242, 243

E
Eastern Security Network, 27
Eboe-Osuji, Chile, 130
Economic and Financial Crimes Commission, 26, 28, 30, 49, 302, 304–307
Economic development, 3, 18, 180, 187
Economist Intelligence Unit, 333
Elections, 20, 21, 30, 161, 208, 341, 342, 344–347, 350, 358–360, 366
El Salvador, 3, 399, 401
Engle, Eric, 96
Environmental degradation, 273, 292, 293
Environmental pollution, 2, 183, 275, 277, 283, 293, 296
Environmental right, 282, 284, 286, 298
Environmental sanitation, 43, 47
Estonia, 81, 87, 171, 172
Ethiopia, 132, 253
Ethnic, 19, 22, 72, 73, 75, 79–81, 83–86, 89, 90, 172, 173, 188, 204, 325–327, 334
Euro-centric, 142, 143
European Commission, xi, 107
European Data Protection Board, 109
European Union, xii, xiii, 86, 88, 90, 92, 94, 99, 107, 237, 244
Eva Achjani Zulfa, 38

F
Failed states, 17, 24, 27, 28, 61
Fatou Bensouda, 122
Fawehinmi, 309
Fayemi, Kayode, 21
Federalism, 21, 31
Federalist Society, 352
Federalization, 93
Federal Rules of Civil Procedure, 102
Financial Crimes Act, 30
Fines, 41, 42, 54, 276, 344, 360
Finjan, Inc., 101, 103–105, 110, 111
Foreign direct investment, 3, 25, 26, 387
Forfeiture, 48, 49, 218
France, xi, 37, 82, 96, 147, 153
Fulanis, 17, 23
Functus officio, 145

G
Gas flaring, 273, 274, 277, 293, 295
Gavi, xi, xii
Gbajabiamila, Femi, 334, 335
Gender quota, 3, 355–357, 360, 362, 364–371
General Agreement on Tariffs and Trade, 234–236, 241–243
General Assembly, 7, 61, 63, 96, 134, 161–164
General Data Protection Regulation, 99–104, 107–111, 114
Genocide, 72, 73, 116, 118, 120, 126, 130
Georgia, 80, 85–88, 97, 118, 342–344
German Democratic Republic, 173
Germany, 26, 58, 82, 96, 147, 148, 244, 386
Gestational surrogacy, 254, 255, 268
Globalization, 70, 79, 234, 245–248
Global Peace Index, 14, 326, 332

Global Terror Index, 14
Global trade, 2, 240
Global warming, xii
Golinkin, David, 264
Gray, John Chipman, 141
Great Britain, 30, 147, 149
Greenhouse gas, xii
Grotius, Hugo, 75, 140, 142, 158, 159
Guatemala, 3, 399, 401
Gulf of Guinea, 322, 328

H

Haddi lashing, 46
Hague, 130
Herdsmen, 14, 18, 333
Herz, John, 151
Hinduism, 2, 253, 257, 269
Hitler, Adolf, 150
HIV-AIDS, 181
Hobbes, Thomas, 16, 58
Ho Chi Minh City, 382, 383
Hofeld, W.N., 319
Holocaust, 68
Honduras, 3, 399, 401
Hong Kong International Arbitration Center, 224
Host Community Development Trust, 193
Host Community Development Trust Fund, 193
Human Development Report, 324
Humanitarian, 55, 59, 65–67, 70, 71, 73, 76, 88, 399, 401, 404, 407
Human rights, 3, 7, 35, 47, 55, 56, 59, 60, 64–70, 72, 73, 75–77, 88, 123, 125, 126, 136, 137, 165, 173, 174, 177–182, 184, 186, 191, 196, 237, 238, 272, 275, 282–285, 324, 327, 331, 338, 339, 343, 351, 353, 394, 395, 398, 407
Human security, 3, 72, 321, 324–326, 335

I

Ibrahim Index, 332, 335
Ibrahim Magu, 28
Ighomereho, 16
Illiteracy, 286, 288
ILO Convention, the, 8
Imperialism, 118, 141
Imprisonment, 34, 35, 40, 41, 43, 46–52, 54, 276, 280–282
IMT Charter, 134
Independent Corrupt Practices & Other Related Offences Commission, 28–30, 49
India, 37, 224
Indian Council of Arbitration, 218
Intellectual property, 2, 338
International Centre for Settlement of Investment Disputes, 222
International Chamber of Commerce, 218, 221
International commercial arbitration, 2, 220, 225, 228
International Commission on Intervention and State Sovereignty, 70
International Court of Justice, 63, 145, 146, 149, 161, 162
International crimes, 2, 126, 127, 135, 137
International Criminal Court, 115–122, 129–132, 135–138, 181
International Criminal Tribunal for the former Yugoslavia, 69
Internationalists, 178–181, 184–186
International legal obligationsLegal obligations, xiv

International relations, xii, 2, 59, 60, 80, 90, 95–97, 113, 140, 141, 143, 165, 172
International trade, 233–239, 241–243, 245, 247, 248
Investor-state disputes, 3
In vitro fertilization, 254, 260
Iraq, xiii, 66, 121, 150, 152
Ishaku, Darius, 17
Islam, 2, 253, 257, 265–267, 327
Islamic State, 24, 322, 328, 333
Istanbul Arbitration Centre, 223

J
James, Lebron, 344
Janis, 59
Jesus Christ, 151
Johnson, Simon, 190
Jordan, Michael, 344
Judaism, 2, 253, 257, 262, 264
Judge, 20, 43, 52–54, 112, 118, 126, 136, 145, 146, 148, 197, 198, 203, 205–210, 212–214, 284, 303, 304, 306, 308–310, 312–316, 318, 320, 351, 352, 377–380, 388, 389
Judicial authority, 146, 209, 375
Judicial ethics, 2, 198, 199, 203, 211
Judicial independence, 3, 197, 198, 209, 376, 388
Judicial misconduct, 203, 212–214, 303, 309, 314, 317
Jurisdiction, 2, 52, 54, 66, 91, 103, 112, 114, 116–122, 125–130, 132, 134–140, 144, 145, 149, 187, 218, 219, 222, 224, 229, 235, 238, 241, 252, 293, 302, 303, 306, 308, 310, 312, 313, 315, 317, 319, 340, 358, 375, 376, 381–383, 386, 388, 393
Jus necessarium, 139
Justice Mahmud Mohammed, 208
Justice Nweze, 203–208, 319
Juvenile offender, 46, 47

K
Kaplan, Neil, 230
Karma, 270, 271
Kazakhstan, 82, 173
Kelsen, Hans, 61, 69
Kenya, 121, 130
Kenyatta, Uhuru, 133
Khadi, 202
Kleptocracy, 17, 19, 21, 31
Koranic, 210
Kosienkowski, Marcin, 92, 93
Kosovo, 70
Kremlin, 83
Kyiv, 94
Kyrgyzstan, 82

L
Lachs, 161
Lake Chad, 327
Lamy, Pascal, 236, 237
Latvia, 81, 87
Lauterpacht, Hersch, 144
League of Nations, 60, 144, 148
Legal obligations, xii, xiii, 2, 101, 145
Legal Practitioners' Disciplinary Committee, 315
Lesotho, 190
Liberia, 27
Libya, 14, 23, 120, 150
Licence, xiii
Liquefied natural gas, 195
Lithuania, 81
London, 225
London Court of International Arbitration, 218, 222, 225
Lord Denning, 146
Luhansk People's Republic, the, 80, 84, 91

Lynn, Kathleen, 230

M
Mackler, Aaron, 264
Magistrate, 41, 51, 53, 54
Malabo Protocol, 125–132, 135–138
Malaysia, 47
Mali, 14
Market economy, 237
McEwen, W.A., 42
Medieval, 56, 67
Merezhko, Oleksandr, 85, 95, 96
Microsoft, 101, 111
Middle Ages, 57, 58
Migrants, 6, 329, 394, 398, 404, 407
Mikula, Vadou, 162
Ministry of Justice, 388
Miyetti Allah Cattle Breeders Association of Nigeria, 26
Mohammed Lawal Garba, 305
Mohammed Umar Abba, 29
Moldova, 80, 81, 88–90, 93, 97
Money laundering, 126, 129, 307
Montenegro, 171
Montevideo Convention, 143
Moral obligations, xiii
Morgenthau, Hans, 144, 147, 150, 152
Most-favored-nation treatment, 236, 241
Movement for the Emancipation of the Niger Delta, 22, 27
Movement for the Survival of Ogoni People, the, 14, 22
Mozambique, 124
Mueller, Robert, 346
Multilateral agreements, 140, 234, 235, 237, 239
Multinational corporations, 177, 181
Muslim, 46, 343
Myanmar, 121, 343

N
Nagashima, Toru, 86
Nagorno-Karabakh Republic, 80, 84, 92
National Environmental Standards and Enforcement Agency Act, 276
Nationalists, 178–181, 185, 186
Nationality, 156, 162–164, 172, 173, 339, 393, 396, 397, 399, 400
National Judicial Council, 199–201, 203, 211, 212, 214, 302, 303, 305, 311, 314
National Judicial Policy, 213, 303
National Security, 3, 321–324, 326–335
National treatment, 241, 248
Natural resources, 2, 126, 129, 178, 186, 192, 244, 332
Nazi, 129
Neo-colonialism, 118
Netherlands, The, 240
New York Convention, 220, 383–385, 387, 388, 390
New Zealand, 224
Nganjiwa, 309, 320
Niger Delta, 14, 23, 273–275, 285, 286, 291, 292, 294–297, 321, 328
Niger Delta People's Volunteer Force, 22
Niger Delta Vigilante, 22
Nigeria, 3, 14–30, 32, 34–37, 40, 42, 46, 47, 52, 54, 118, 170, 171, 179, 187, 191, 193, 195, 196, 198–202, 204, 209–211, 214, 272–277, 279, 285, 287, 288, 291–298, 321–324, 326–329, 332–335
Nigerian Air Force, 18
Nigerian Correctional Services Act, 34
Nigerian Governors Forum, 21

Nigerian National Petroleum Company, 285
Nonintervention, 62–68, 77
Noriega, Manuel, 149
North Atlantic Treaty Organization, 66
North Korea, 343
Nuremberg, 68, 128, 133
Nwabueze, B.O., 313, 316
Nwagboso, 25

O

Obasanjo, Olusegun, 321
Odua People's Congress, 26
Offender, 34, 38–40, 42, 44–46, 49–54, 184, 276, 277, 288, 289
Ofili-Ajumogobia, 307
Oil and gas industry, 2, 274, 286
Oil pipelines, 274, 294
Oil spills, 273, 298
Okeke, Christian Nwachukwu, xi, 3
Okonkwo, 314
Olusanya, Gabriel, 272
Omotola, J.A., 148
Onifade Comfort, 18
Ontario's Employment Standards Act, 240
Onyegbula, 15
Oppenheim, Lawrence, 143, 152, 159
Option A4, 30
Organization for Economic Cooperation and Development, 238, 240, 241, 246
Organization for Security and Cooperation in Europe, 88, 90
Orton, Samuel, 17
Oshiomhole, Adam, 32

P

Pacta Sunt Servanda, xii–xiv, 165, 169
Padilla, Alex, 360
Pagan, 142
Pakistan, 47, 253
Panama, 149
Pandemic, xi, xii, 2, 6, 33, 34, 36, 181, 215–219, 221, 224, 228, 229, 233–236, 239, 241, 246, 347, 395, 398, 408
Parole, 39, 47, 48, 400–402
Pavement Dwellers Case, 238
Peaceful settlement of international disputes, the, xii
Penal systems, 2, 34, 41
Permanent Court of Arbitration, 145, 148
Permanent Court of International Justice, 144, 145, 148
Peru, 224
Petroleum Industry Act, 179, 191, 193, 195, 196
Pharand, Donat, 56, 60
Pharmaceutical company, xii
Pipeline gas, 195
Piracy, 126, 322, 328
Plea bargain, 39, 52, 53
Police, 17, 21, 22, 24, 52, 54, 90, 94, 180, 324, 333, 337, 338, 343, 350, 375
Pollution, 2, 183, 220, 273–281, 283, 285, 286, 288, 291–293, 295–297
Pope, 57, 145
Poverty, 6, 9, 18, 26, 178, 240, 242, 245, 286, 288, 292, 295, 296, 328, 333, 395
Pre-colonial, 188
Pre-Trial Chamber, 120, 136
Pre-trial detention, 53
Prison, 34–37, 39, 42, 44, 47, 48, 50, 54, 343, 348
Prison congestion, 35
Privacy, 6–8, 106, 228

Probation, 39, 41, 50, 51
Prosecution, 2, 6, 31, 48, 49, 53, 54, 116–118, 120, 130, 131, 133–135, 137, 138, 181, 276, 277, 286, 287, 293, 296, 305–308, 315, 316, 318, 320, 348
Prosecutor, 50, 52–54, 120, 131, 136, 276, 277, 288, 291, 293, 296, 347, 373–375
Protestant, 57

Q
Quasi-states, 92

R
Ratione Material, 156
Ratione Personae, 156
Rebus sic stantibus, xiii
Recognizance, 41, 50, 51
Refugee, 3, 25, 393–400, 402–408
Regional agreements, 234
Rehabilitation, 35, 40, 51, 52, 196
Reinhart, Carmen, 247
Reinsalu, Urmas, 87
Republic of Abkhazia, the, 80, 84, 92
Republic of Crimea, the, 80, 84, 94, 95
Republic of South Ossetia, the, 80, 84, 92
Republic of Transnistria, the, 80, 84
Responsibility to Protect, 2, 55, 56, 69–77
Restatement Third of Foreign Relations Law, 104
Restitution, 35, 39, 40, 42, 44, 45, 53
Restoration, 38, 39, 44, 45, 64, 334, 353
Restorative justice, 34, 35, 38, 39, 42, 52–54
Retributive justice, 35, 39
Robinson, James, 190
Romania, 68, 89
Rome Statute, 116, 118–121, 126, 128, 130–133, 135, 137
Roscoe Pound, 197, 198
Rose Revolution, 88
Ross, Alison, 225, 226, 228, 230
Rousseau, 59
Rule in *Smith v. Selwyn*, 310
Russia, 1, 81, 82, 87, 88, 91, 93, 94, 96, 97, 121, 153, 168, 171, 173, 274, 343
Rwanda, 27, 70

S
Saakashvili, Mikheil, 88
Sambo, Adesina, 151
Sarkozy, Nicolas, 88
Saudi Arabia, 343
Sebrenica, 70
Secessionism, 84, 90
Secure Web Gateway, 103
Security Council, 56, 62, 64, 66, 71–73, 77, 119–121
Self-defense, 65, 94
Separation of powers, 310, 315–317, 377
Separatism, 84, 90
Serbia, 171
Shareholders, 178, 285, 356, 357, 359–361, 363, 366–370
Sharia, 202, 210
Sharmin Islam, 268
Shen, Jianming, 67, 76
Shimazono, Susumu, 271
Sierra Leone, 27
Singapore, 47, 223
Singapore International Arbitration Centre, 223
Singh, N., 141

Sirleaf, Matiangai, 127, 128
Smith, Adam, 245
Socialist, 7, 11, 81
Soleimani, Qassem, 151, 152
Somalia, 14, 27
Somers, Chris, 244
South Africa, 37, 253
South Sudan, 14
Sovereign equality, xii, 61, 90, 95, 165
Sovereign immunity, 58, 386, 387
Sovereignty, 16, 55–60, 63, 67–70, 73–77, 82, 87, 96, 139, 141, 142, 153, 157, 168, 172, 406
Soviet Union, 80, 81, 83, 84, 88, 89, 91, 93, 96, 168, 169, 172
Stare decisis, 140, 146, 309
State continuity, 156
States, xii–xiv, 2, 21, 23, 34, 42, 54–56, 58–70, 72–74, 76, 77, 80–85, 89, 91, 92, 95–97, 116, 119–126, 128, 131, 132, 139, 141, 143, 145, 157, 162–165, 167, 170–175, 181, 186, 216, 220, 233, 342, 343, 397, 398, 407, 408
State succession, 2, 156–162, 169, 170, 172–175
Status quo ante criminem, 45
Statute of the International Court of Justice, xii
Stewart, Richard, 185
Stiglitz, Joseph, 244
Stockholm Chamber of Commerce, 223
Strict liability, 277, 278, 288–291, 293–297
Sudan, 14, 28, 120
Supreme Court, 52, 101, 103, 107, 114, 200, 206, 220, 226, 238, 240, 307–309, 312, 313, 315–317, 340, 341, 344, 351
Supreme People's Court, 376
Sureties, 41, 47, 50
Surrogacy, 2, 251–258, 260, 262–272
Suspended sentence, 39, 49, 50
Sutton, Agneta, 261
Sweden, 223
Swiss Parliament, 222
Switzerland, 222, 386
Sydney, 225
Sylvester Ngwuta, 307
Syria, 121, 153, 343

T

Taipei, 225
Tajikistan, 82
Tanzania, 224, 225
Tanzania Arbitration Centre, 225
Territorial integrity, 58, 64, 80, 82, 85, 87, 90, 94–97, 165, 169
Terrorist, 14, 24, 31, 127, 333
Tiba, F.K., 127, 128
Tibet, 343
Tivs, 17
Torah, 263
Traditional surrogacy, 253, 255
Traditional worship, 327
Transparency International, 18, 19
Trial Chamber, 136
Trump, Donald, 151, 345–351, 402
Trust funds, 191–194
Turkey, 223
Turkmenistan, 82

U

Uber, 240
Uganda, 120
Ukraine, 1, 80–82, 86, 87, 89, 92–97
Uncivilized peoples, 142
Unexplained Wealth Orders, 28–30
United Kingdom, xiii, 30, 104

United Nations, 56, 64, 68, 73, 77, 97, 149, 150, 157, 325, 326, 398, 406
United Nations Development Programme, 324
United Nations Framework Convention on Climate Change, the, xii
United States, 3, 82, 90, 99, 101, 102, 104, 107, 112, 113, 144, 149, 150, 152, 153, 183, 242, 246, 254, 277, 338, 339, 343, 345, 348, 352, 358, 393, 394, 399–407
United States Country Report of Human Rights, 24
Universal Declaration of Human Rights, 7, 69
Unknown Gun Men, 14
UN Secretary-General, 70, 72
Upazillas, 11
USSR, 81–83, 86, 87, 90, 168, 171, 172, 174
Utaz Mohammed Yusuf, 24
Uti possidetis, 171
Uwaifo, 308, 315
Uzbekistan, 82

V

Vaccine Alliance, xi
Vallat, Francis, 161
Vattel, 60, 159
Versailles, 170
Vienna, 162
Vienna Convention on the Law of Treaties, xii, xiii, 166, 170, 174
Vietnam, 3, 373–376, 378, 380, 382–391
Virtual hearings, 216, 217, 221, 222, 224, 226–230

W

Waldock, Humphrey, 161
Walgrave, 38
War crimes, 73, 116, 118, 119, 126, 130
Weller, Marc, 96
Westlake, John, 143
Westphalia, 56, 59, 67, 74
Wheaton, H., 60, 142, 143, 159
Wolff, Alan WM, 236, 246
Workers, 6, 8–11, 274, 283, 294
World Bank, 285
World Health Organization, 36

Y

Yanukovych, Viktor, 94
Yargata Byenchit Nimpar, 306
Yugoslavia, 64, 66, 81, 157

Z

Zoellick, Robert B., 236
Zscaler, Inc., 101, 104–106, 109–111

Kolibri 360 GmbH
Ferdinand-Jühlke-Straße 7
99095 Erfurt, Deutschland
produktsicherheit@kolibri360.de